WITHDRAWN

WITHDRAWN

parents and schools

the 150-year struggle for control

in american education

WILLIAM W. CUTLER III

THE UNIVERSITY OF CHICAGO PRESS   CHICAGO AND LONDON

WILLIAM W. CUTLER III is associate professor of history and educational leadership at Temple University and coeditor of *The Divided Metropolis: Social and Spatial Dimensions of Philadelphia, 1800–1975* (1980).

The University of Chicago Press, Chicago 60637
The University of Chicago Press, Ltd., London
© 2000 by The University of Chicago
All rights reserved. Published 2000
Printed in the United States of America
09 08 07 06 05 04 03 02 01 00   1 2 3 4 5

ISBN: 0-226-13216-1 (cloth)

Library of Congress Cataloging-in-Publication Data

Cutler, William W.
    Parents and schools : the 150-year struggle for control in American education /
William W. Cutler III.
        p.   cm.
    Includes bibliographical references and index.
    ISBN 0-226-13216-1 (cloth : alk. paper)
    1. Home and school—United States—History—19th century.   2. Home and school—
United States—History—20th century.   3. Education—Parent participation—United
States—History—19th century.   4. Education—Parent participation—United States—
History—20th century.   5. Educational change—United States—History—19th century.
6. Educational change—United States—History—20th century.   I. Title.
LC225.3.c86   2000
371.19′2′0973—dc21
                                                                                    99-088447

For Julia, Rosemary, and Rachel

Contents

Illustrations

Acknowledgments

When I began work on the project that eventually became *Parents and Schools,* I thought I was going to write a book dealing with the history of child care and early childhood education. But the more I read about this topic, the more impressed I was by the attention devoted in the literature to the relationship between the parents and teachers of young children. I began to wonder if the same could be said for the parents and teachers of older students. What did they think about one another in the nineteenth century? What did they expect of their relationship, and how did it change over time? These questions had not received much attention from social historians, but they struck me as both significant and timely, especially in view of the contemporary belief in the importance of the home to the school in American education. It seemed to me that they deserved a thorough historical investigation.

As I began to explore the history of parent-teacher relations, three colleagues gave me the encouragement that every researcher needs to hear at the beginning of any long-term project. Close to home, Temple's Morris Vogel and Mark Haller proved to be good listeners when I encountered obstacles of one kind or another. Steven Schlossman of Carnegie Mellon University showed enough interest in my work to come to Philadelphia more than once to discuss with me what I was doing. He also provided access to funding that allowed me to hire Rodney Hessinger, one of my doctoral students, as a research assistant in the summer of 1993. I am also grateful to Temple University for both a study leave in 1991 and a summer research grant in 1993. The freedom that these awards provided allowed me to build much needed momentum.

Several scholars have commented on part or all of the manuscript, giving me the benefit of their knowledge and criticism. Steve Scholssman and Martha de Acosta helped me refine the argument in Chapter One. Robert

Church, Herbert Ershkowitz, Margaret Marsh, Randall Miller, and Bill Pencak identified flaws in several drafts of the manuscript that appears here as Chapter Three. In 1996, it appeared in a somewhat different form in *Pennsylvania History,* and I would like to thank Bill Pencak, the editor of that journal, for permission to republish it here. I turned to Robert Taggart for reassurance that I had not made any mistakes in Chapter Four about the history of education in Delaware, and he saved me from some embarrassing gaffs. He also put his finger on some substantive and stylistic matters that I hope I have addressed successfully. Chapter Five is better for the suggestions that Anne Knupfer made after reading it in draft and John Rury offered in private conversations with me.

I owe a special debt of gratitude to Ronald Butchart, who read the manuscript when it was still unfinished and at a crucial stage. His frank and insightful criticism helped me to think through the structure of the book and the general argument that I was trying to make. John Tryneski, my editor at The University of Chicago Press, identified many ways to make this argument more explicit. Maris Vinovskis, who read the entire manuscript for The University of Chicago Press, gave useful suggestions that guided me as I put the finishing touches on a work that was by then in a well-developed state. I hope they will agree that I have made the most of what they had to say.

It is my special pleasure to acknowledge the many libraries and librarians, archives and archivists that made it possible for me to find the sources on which *Parents and Schools* is based. I would like to recognize the staff who helped me at the Boston Public Library, the Jenkintown (Pennsylvania) Library, the Philadelphia Jewish Archives Center at the Balch Institute for Ethnic Studies, the Delaware Historical Society, the Historical Society of Pennsylvania, the Schlesinger Library at Harvard University, the Special Collections Department of the Alexander Library of Rutgers University, the Pedagogical Library of the School District of Philadelphia, and the Interlibrary Loan Department in Temple's Samuel Paley Library. In particular, I would like to thank Kathy Tassini of the Haddonfield (New Jersey) Historical Society and Dr. Joseph Serico, principal of Haddonfield Memorial High School, who made it possible for me to obtain access to the records of the Haddonfield Board of Public Education. I am also indebted to Kenneth Rose, assistant to the director of the Laura Spelman Rockefeller Memorial Archives at the Rockefeller Archive Center in North Tarrytown, New York, and David Ment, director of special collections at the Milbank Memorial Library, Teachers College, Columbia University. Finally, I am grateful to the Schlesinger Library for giving me permission to quote from the Elizabeth Hewes Tilton Papers and *The American School Board Journal* for giving me permission to reproduce six cartoons that originally appeared as cover art in the 1910s and 1920s.

As every historian knows, some librarians and archivists deserve special recognition for going out of their way to help the eager but often fumbling researcher. In my case, this debt is owed to Gail E. Farr, who was a National Historical Publications and Records Commission Fellow at the Delaware Bureau of Archives and Records Management in 1991–92 and her supervisors, Joanne Mattern, Deputy State Archivist, and Howard P. Lowell, State Archivist and Records Administrator. They made it possible for me to find and use treasures that would otherwise have been out of my reach. If, as a researcher, I have a home base, it is the Urban Archives in the Samuel Paley Library at Temple University. Its director, Margaret Jerrido, and her staff—Brenda Galloway-Wright, Cheryl Johnson, and the recently retired George Brightbill—all supplied me with resources of every kind. I am very grateful to them.

When my labors on *Parents and Schools* were about half done, I became a school director in the community where I live. This experience has given an immediacy to my historical work, putting it into a different perspective. It was my wife, Penelope, who persuaded me to run for the school board. She has been a source of unfailing support in the preparation of this book. As both a teacher and a parent, she is an expert in her own right on home-school relations.

Introduction

Few Americans today doubt the importance of good relations between the home and the school. Educators and parents alike say that successful schools communicate well with the home. Caring parents, mothers in particular, cooperate with schools. Such views go unquestioned, if not unspoken. They inform discussions of educational policy and practice; they contribute to the process of decision-making. Equally important, they obscure a host of competing assumptions that deserve careful examination. For example, many Americans behave as if parents and teachers are at best distant relations.[1] Performing different functions that derive from the distinction between professional and moral authority, they must make a special effort just to establish contact, let alone work together to raise children. Faced with these disparate views, Americans are understandably confused. How should the home and the school interact? Their relationship has a long and complex history, which may provide some useful clues. Have these two institutions been at odds from the beginning? Have parents and teachers from different backgrounds been able to work together to achieve common goals? How has our thinking about their relationship changed over time, and in what ways has it affected public policy and private behavior regarding families and schools?

Parents and teachers have interacted since the inception of schooling in the United States, but their relationship has changed significantly over time. In the nineteenth century, the balance of power shifted from the home to the school. An all-purpose institution, the colonial family dominated the school, but between 1800 and 1850, when middle-class mothers began to concentrate on procreation and nurture and the urban poor seemed increasingly less able to care for their own, educators assumed more responsibility in the cognitive and even the moral domains. By century's end, this shift was well established and unmistakable to social scientists like Frank Tracy Carlton. "The scope of school work is being gradually extended," Carlton wrote in 1905, "as a direct result of the decrease in functions of the home and the changing status of women."[2] In turn, the social contract between the home and the school was also transformed. What once was informal and unstructured became self-conscious, legalistic, and bureaucratic — the object of studied attention and systematic organization. Institutional frontiers that were porous and indistinct grew more secure and well defined. The home and the school still share responsibility for the education of the young, but their relationship is far from spontaneous. Instead, it is contrived, being shaped and directed by men and women with different perspectives even when they possess the same expectations, values, and goals.

The functional and conceptual gap that separates the home from the school is not inconsequential. It affects how we think about the extent and nature of lay involvement at school. Parents may not be the teacher's natural enemy, but they are usually unwelcome in the classroom. Armed with professional certificates and advanced degrees, educators believe they have the authority to manage parental inquiries and even dismiss complaints about the judgments they make or the methods they use. Such autonomy carries a high price, justifying parental ignorance, apathy, and detachment. Even middle-class mothers and fathers may decide not to get too involved if the school is a world apart.[3] Seizing on this disequilibrium, reformers have argued that giving parents more control will improve education by breaking the monopoly of the school.

But parents and teachers are attracted to each other even as they push apart because they preside over common ground. Distinct and yet necessarily interdependent, parents and teachers have a symbiotic relationship. Were one to yield to the other, both would be transformed. This is not to say that parents and teachers have always accepted their reciprocity. In fact, the two generalizations that have emerged from this historical study point toward a more complex conclusion. First, the relationship between the home and the school in America has been political for a long time. Since at least the 1840s, parents and teachers have often vied with each other for influence and authority, and both have made alliances, sometimes with one another against a common foe and sometimes with other parties interested in controlling the schools. Second, this relationship has often served as a conduit for educational and social reform. Like kin in an extended family, parents and teachers have seldom been willing to leave well enough alone.

The political nature of the home-school relationship owes its vitality at least in part to the expansion of schooling in the nineteenth century. As the home lost ground to the school, parents found themselves jockeying for position with teachers in their children's lives. Commuters in social space, children learned to deal with two sets of masters. Over time, this balancing act became more and more problematic because parents and teachers enhanced their respective claims to different terrain in the landscape of childhood. Facing each other across an increasingly clear-cut boundary, adults maneuvered for advantage, often casting the relationship between the home and the school as a struggle for the hearts and the minds of the next generation.

School bureaucratization helped educators take control of their relationship with the home in the second half of the nineteenth century. Contrary to what many educational historians have maintained, bureaucracy did not drive parents and teachers completely apart.[4] Instead, the professional identity and occupational opportunity that it fostered gradually gave many teachers, principals, and superintendents the self-confidence to reconsider the home-school relationship. It did not have to be as antagonistic as the first public school officials frequently thought. Bureaucratic reform led educators to contemplate how parents could be transformed from vocal adversaries to loyal advocates by building them into the school's organizational framework. Properly sorted and arranged, mothers and fathers could be an integral and valuable part of the American educational system.

Of course, the efficacy of more and better schooling was not immediately self-evident. For many parents, the opportunity costs of an extended education seemed a high price to pay for the promise of later gain, and American educators failed to turn this attitude completely around in the nineteenth century. Teaching inspired limited loyalty even among its own practitioners, let alone much esteem in the lay community. The American tradition of local control placed teachers at the mercy of parents and taxpayers, especially in rural areas, and the defensive posture that resulted from this imbalance often stood in the way of cooperation between the home and the school. However, the bureaucratic reforms that went into effect between 1890 and 1930 did as much to break down such barriers as reinforce them. Compulsory school laws may have betrayed a lack of respect for parental judgment, but together with the growth of state aid, they strengthened the hand of local public schools. The introduction of standards for entry into teaching and the development of systematic methods for the assessment of pupils and the management of schools placed teachers and principals on what appeared to them to be more solid footing, giving them good reason to be more tolerant of parents and open to the community.

By the end of the nineteenth century, superintendents, principals, and even teachers were learning to cope with parents by organizing the school's relationship with the home. Individual parents or small groups of families were more difficult to manage than mothers' clubs or parent-teacher associations. Such organizations first appeared in rural America in the 1880s, spreading to many cities and suburbs soon thereafter, and school officials often collaborated with parents on their founding. These associations gave the home a recognizable but limited presence in school. They institutionalized the idea that parents had at least a small stake in educational policy-making, while acknowledging the home's role in cultivating student learning. These two activities were not necessarily complementary; organized interaction between parents and teachers to improve student learning often left school governance unaffected and sometimes devolved into a power struggle driven by disagreements about educational goals and methods. But at the beginning of the twentieth century, there was considerable optimism. Neither decision makers nor troublemakers, mothers and fathers were now to be the allies of the teacher and advocates for schools and schooling.

The bureaucratization of the home-school relationship did more than just prepare educators to deal confidently and systematically with the home. It forced parents to be more conscious of themselves as an interest group and provided some with an orderly and occasionally powerful means by which to interact with the school and other economic or political institutions. The mothers' club or home and school association focused parental attention and created a swift channel for the flow of parental energy. However, educators and most school board members preferred to think of the parent-teacher association as an extension of the educational establishment, "an auxiliary to the public school," as the Los Angeles County Board of Education put it in 1908.[5]

In the 1920s, school administrators, policy makers, and professors of education took the bureaucratization of the home-school relationship to another level. The rapid expansion of secondary schooling at the beginning of the twentieth century made the proficient management of schools increasingly important. With more and more Americans remaining in school past the eighth grade, budgets were soon stretched to the limit.

During and immediately after World War I, educators also had to contend
with spiraling costs brought on by inflation. Justifying burgeoning budgets
was no easy task, and those in charge decided that they could ill afford to
neglect their image. Not surprisingly, they focused on their relationship
with the home. Parents might be willing allies, but their support was not
guaranteed. The school's carefully cultivated professional image worked
to its disadvantage, encouraging parental disengagement and indifference. Consequently, the men and women of what historians David Tyack
and Elizabeth Hansot have called the "educational trust" turned the
school's interaction with the home into an exercise in public relations.[6]
When the Great Depression threatened to bankrupt many school systems,
the nation's educators became even more convinced that parental loyalty
and approval had to be manipulated for the school's ends. But they had to
contend with many families facing economic crises of their own.

In the new politics of the home and the school, there was one important constant. Social class continued to shape parental attitudes and behavior about child development and schooling, but even here, there were
subtle changes after 1900. While middle-class mothers and fathers continued to think of their children as moral and emotional dependents, they
also began to regard them as distinct personalities in the making. Com-
mencing in the 1920s, they looked to the school for help with their children's psychological health and socialization. Most working-class parents,
on the other hand, did not have the time to worry about their children's
mental hygiene. For them, the relationship among the home, the school,
and the workplace had changed, becoming more, not less problematic.
By 1910, a new generation of more effective compulsory school and child
labor laws had placed the state squarely between them and their children.
The public school now took primary responsibility for preparing working-
class children to be wage earners and citizens. It was the source of common learning, the basic skills and values that everyone needed to know. No
longer in control, working-class parents had to be content with lobbying
for their children in school or on the job. Across this functional and conceptual divide, parents and teachers continued to meet. The power relationship between them had changed, but many among them realized that
they could not afford to be enemies or even strangers. Theirs was a marriage between distinct but reciprocal institutions.

Since the introduction of public education in the 1830s, social issues
and economic interests have increasingly affected the association between
the home and the school. Constituencies like management and labor,

immigrants and natives, taxpayers and naysayers have pressed their views on schools. Shifting coalitions and ideological positions have confounded educators and policy makers by defying predictability.[7] Parents and teachers have interacted within this unstable environment. They have often worked together toward a mutual goal, but sometimes as accidental allies, collaborating despite differences about their reasons for moving in the same direction. For example, their common support for local control has usually not been motivated by the same set of hopes and concerns. Courted by others, both parents and teachers have also leveraged influence by cooperating with those beyond the inner orbit of the school. Teachers made common cause with physicians and social workers against the home conditions of their pupils. After joining with organized labor to oppose budget cuts in urban public schools, they became a part of the labor movement themselves, a decision that cost them the trust and support of many parents. Divided by socioeconomic and ethnic loyalties, parents have sometimes sided with businessmen and reformers in support of improvements like comprehensive high schools and vocational education or fought against them over such innovations as the medical inspection of schoolchildren and the teaching of foreign languages in the public schools.[8]

Shaped by the politics of interest, the relationship between the home and the school has entailed considerable ambiguity and possessed a sizable potential for conflict born not so much of fundamental differences as misunderstanding. Both parents and teachers have often misinterpreted what the other expected them to do. Not always deserving of parental respect, most teachers, for example, have expected it nonetheless. As early as the 1850s, they insisted that, no matter what, mothers refrain from criticizing them in front of children. The status of parents turns out to have been even more enigmatic, for once bureaucratization occurred, they qualified as both insiders and outsiders at school. Because it was a son or daughter they entrusted to the teacher's care, parents have always had a legitimate claim to influence—more so perhaps than anyone else—but after 1900, their personal stake in their child's classroom performance carried less and less weight with the professionals who were now in charge of America's schools. Classifying parents as outsiders, educators invited mothers and fathers to get involved with homework or special events without giving them any authority or even making serious work for them to do.

Gender, ethnicity, and social class enhanced the ambiguity of the relationship between the home and the school. In charge at home, middle-class women were also very important at school, far outnumbering the men in parent-teacher organizations at the beginning of the twentieth century. As mothers, women spoke for the home at school, bargaining with the men who served on boards of education and engaging those in positions of administrative responsibility. As teachers, they modeled the knowledge and objectivity of the educational establishment, but it was their gender that really qualified them to work with other people's children, especially the very young. Gender bias, on the other hand, diminished their credibility as representatives of the scientific and bureaucratic school.

Beginning in the 1870s and accelerating rapidly after 1900, some women competed for places on urban and suburban boards of education. Their moral authority carried considerable weight outside the home, but until after World War II, they often met with resistance when they tried to assert themselves in local school management or reform. Meanwhile, many women and men had to contend with racial, ethnic, and social class as well as gender bias at school. In the nineteenth century, school officials often oversimplified the relationship between parents and teachers by treating the home as if it was as monolithic as the school. But they gradually began to discover that families in the United States were not all the same. Fortified by their new-found professionalism, teachers, principals, and superintendents now questioned the competence of immigrant and blue-collar parents, paving the way for physicians, nurses, and social workers to enter the schoolhouse after 1910 without absolving the low-income family of responsibility for the welfare of its children. Even after being redefined as a partnership between two different but complementary institutions, the relationship between the home and the school never completely lost its adversarial dimension. Complicated by gender, ethnicity, and social class, the ambiguities of the relationship made it increasingly difficult for Americans to think through an acceptable division of labor between the home and school, let alone establish it. Deciding which one was in charge or when the two should share child-rearing and educational obligations became more and more problematic, leading to role conflict and confusion.

Parents, reformers, and educators now pursued an alluring but ambitious goal that contributed to uncertainty and invited conflict about institutional roles and responsibilities. They behaved as if cooperation between the home and the school could facilitate educational and social reform. At first, any such cooperation between parents and teachers was neither the expectation nor the norm. In the nineteenth century, most teachers, principals, and superintendents were too preoccupied with their own domain to worry much about changing the home. Parents took a more active interest in school reform. As early as the 1840s, some parents, especially mothers, acted on their own to express dissatisfaction with their children's public schools. They badgered school authorities, filing petitions about attendance, discipline, facilities, and curriculum.[9] By the end of the nineteenth century, the ideology of maternalism was magnifying their voice, projecting the virtues of motherhood across a wide social agenda.[10] But in the politics of American education, mothers seldom escaped the limits imposed by their gender role. Animated by specific problems at the local level, they exercised modest influence with male school directors and educational professionals in suburban settings.

But the natural connection between parents and teachers attracted the attention of educational and social reformers looking for a way to transform schools. Although bureaucracy and professionalism insulated educators against unwanted intervention, parent-teacher contact allowed outsiders at least some access to the inner workings of the school. Reformers like Jane Addams and Sophonisba Breckinridge could at least get the attention of educational decision makers when they spoke on behalf of mothers and teachers in the name of school reform. On the other hand, the school-home relationship now began to serve as a wide channel for educators and reformers to move in the opposite direction, recommending modifications in the behavior of families and the reorganization of community priorities, practices, and institutions. After World War I, for example, schools began to offer pediatric examinations, parent education, vocational guidance, and the teaching of "worthy home membership," one of the National Education Association's Seven Cardinal Principles of Secondary Education.

Many school directors and superintendents made a conscious choice to welcome the right kind of parental involvement in the politics of schools. After all, mothers and fathers could be persuasive advocates for the interests of public education. Their votes could mean the difference between victory and defeat in school board elections or bond referendums. Educators counted on them when confronted with diminished resources, especially during the Great Depression. Of course, parents were unpredictable and often fickle, turning suddenly on teachers or losing interest once their children left school. Even parent-teacher associations were inconsistent advocates for public education not only because there was constant turnover in their membership but also because educational policy was not necessarily their main concern. But parents and their organizations had a

vested interest in adequate accommodations and sufficient, even generous, educational appropriations. Pointed in the right direction, they could
be enlisted to support many structural, legal, and methodological innovations, such as kindergartens, building codes, and vocational education.
The school often persuaded parents that they should work together toward common ends.

Twentieth-century educators and reformers were not the first to hope
that the relationship between the home and the school could be a conduit for social as well as educational reform. In large cities like Boston
and New York, truant officers and home visitors appeared as early as the
1820s, making outreach to families a small part of their original mission.[11]
After 1900, a rising tide of cultural diversity and social dysfunction called
for a more comprehensive approach. Encouraged by middle-class reformers and private benevolent organizations, public schools in many cities became social welfare institutions. Between 1905 and 1930, visiting teachers,
vocational counselors, and school nurses joined the professional team. It
was up to them to save the American family by dispelling maternal ignorance about the nature of childhood and the principles of homemaking. It
was their job to keep dependent and neglected children off the streets,
preparing them for useful employment, while preventing idleness, delinquency, and the social burdens created by unwanted children. Combining
scientific knowledge with traditional values and beliefs, these outreach
workers spoke for the school in the home.

Educators often claimed that by adding social welfare functions to the
work of the school, they strengthened the teacher's hand. Knowledge of
the home informed and improved instruction. However, the addition of
such new and demanding tasks sometimes brought the school into conflict
with the home. Parents did not always welcome advice on how to raise
their children. At the very least, it complicated and confused the mission
of public education and increased the risk that educators might be held
accountable for what went on at home. The rewards for such ambition
might be great, but there were many uncertainties. Of course, anointing
the public school a social service station and an all-purpose panacea was
not just up to educators; it required no less than the tacit approval of the
general public, including many parents, who did not know where else to
turn. Americans have long resisted government involvement in family
life.[12] Off-limits to the makers of most public policy, the family has been
accessible to the school nonetheless. By 1925, most middle-class Americans at the very least accepted the school as a partner with the home. They
even allowed it to reach into the home, but by accepting this additional

obligation, educators exposed themselves to new kinds of conflict and criticism.

In reaching out to the home, professionals in education had to deal with important differences among themselves—some teachers, after all, were first-generation Americans—and especially with their clientele. Many teachers and school social workers disdained the people they professed to be helping, failing to distinguish between the real and imagined deficiencies of African-American, immigrant, and working-class parents and children.[13] Day care workers, school nurses, and visiting teachers found it difficult to understand why poor families often neglected their children's health or gave in so easily to the school-leaving temptation. Before World War I, they concentrated on reducing the incidence of such behavior, but soon raised their sights as they became more familiar with the American home. With help from the Commonwealth Fund in the 1920s, they turned from managing the school-to-work transition toward counseling the maladjusted child, regardless of his or her social class, and in the following decade broadened their scope still further, focusing on the relationship between academic success and mental hygiene. However, school nurses and visiting teachers were usually among the first to be laid off during the Depression. When faced with this unpleasant prospect, they appealed to their colleagues' sense of professional pride by reminding them that public schools should provide comprehensive services for poor families with school-age children.[14] But their argument did not stand up well against the widespread assumption that the home and the school were distinct, albeit reciprocal institutions.

School-based leadership in social reform was not confined to teachers, social workers, and other professionals in education. From its inception as the National Congress of Mothers in 1897, the National Congress of Parents and Teachers (NCPT) relied on its members to advance the cause of social reform. While urging all women to become better informed about household economics and the raising of children, NCPT Presidents Hannah Kent Schoff and Margaretta Willis Reeve steered their organization into the open waters of economic and social change in the 1920s, asking state and federal policy makers to reorganize the American juvenile justice system, regulate the practice of child labor, and improve the delivery of educational, recreational, and health services to children. They understood the relationship between the school and the home to entail a national agenda based not on conflict between parents and teachers but on cooperation.

Compared to some of their peers like those in charge of the United States Children's Bureau or the National Women's Party, the leaders of the NCPT held conservative views, especially about the status of women.[15] But for those middle-class, white women who comprised the vast majority of its rank and file, membership in the NCPT, one of its state affiliates, or even a local parent-teacher association (PTA) exposed them to a world of new ideas, problems, and concerns. It required them to measure their personal priorities against the more cosmopolitan and, in some respects, elitist standards of their regional and national leaders. It induced some to enter into an uneasy alliance with other women, educators and reformers alike, on behalf of social change. It provoked a few to confront and even reconsider the parochialism of their middle-class, white American homes. But parenthood, while a common bond, was not necessarily an antidote to the divisive effects of gender, culture, class, or race. White, middle-class mothers could be insensitive to cultures other than their own and undemocratic in their relations with black, immigrant, and working-class women. Along with the NCPT, state and local PTAs were almost always segregated during the first half of the twentieth century, and white, middle-class mothers often assumed a condescending attitude toward women from backgrounds other than their own. The National Congress of Colored Parents and Teachers offered black women the chance to lead themselves. But in its institutionalized form, the relationship between the home and the school often reinforced the inequality and injustice it was meant to overcome.

Cooperation between the home and the school has always been weaker at the secondary than the elementary level. Perhaps it is a question of age; more independent than their younger siblings, adolescents can be indifferent, even hostile, to parental involvement at school. Elders back away in part because they do not know how to help their children solve the academic and social problems posed by high school. Educators since the 1920s have been tempted to deal directly with adolescents, especially when it comes to personal behavior and matters of social hygiene. By expanding the right to privacy and due process for those under twenty-one, legislators and jurists in the last thirty years have given the professionals in public education greater freedom to cut parents out of the home-school equation. But not all parents have been willing to accept irrelevance. A desire to retain control may explain why some have always chosen to send their children to independent or parochial schools. By dealing unilaterally with teenagers on birth control or drug abuse, the public school has not reduced its exposure to role confusion and has increased the possibility that disillusionment will result from elevated but unfulfilled expectations.

Compared even with the 1960s, the relationship between the home and the school generates heated debate in the United States today. The presumption of reciprocity and trust between parents and teachers that characterized educational thought and practice after World War II gradually gave way as Red-baiting, white flight, and teacher strikes changed the climate of opinion and the balance of power between the home and the school. Convinced that their voice was muted or silent, many parents, both low-income and middle-class, began to insist they had rights at school. Once again, the home became the adversary of the school, but modern parents, unlike their nineteenth-century counterparts, had to overcome bureaucratic precedents against their having any influence. Rejecting the claim that parent education was a prerequisite for parents' rights, they argued instead that their right to be involved derived from who they were, not what they knew.

There is still no consensus about what steps to take or what benefits to expect from getting parents more involved in the education of their children. Improved student achievement is the most desired outcome, but advocates of school-based management or parent advisory councils often disagree with those who favor more radical forms of parent participation, such as vouchers or charter schools. Home schooling appeals to those whose first priority is not academic achievement but the protection of their children from intellectual or moral contamination. It was in the 1960s that reformers began to favor greater parental and community involvement in school decision-making, but political decentralization has never completely bridged the gap between the home and the school. The history of local control in New York and Chicago reveals how persistent the differences can be between those with personal and professional stakes in schools. Nor has such decentralization been any match for the economic and emotional problems that many children bring with them from home. Once prepared to assign the burden of proof for learning almost entirely to schools, social scientist James Coleman subsequently argued for the significance of the family and ultimately for the necessity of "social capital." Effective education, he said in 1987, depends on a functional network of intergenerational institutions, including the church, the family, and the school. Variations on this vision have come from parent educators like Dorothy Rich and such well-known scholars as James Comer and Joyce Epstein.[16]

In the past thirty years, not all reformers have responded to the crisis in education by focusing on the parents' and community's role in improving public schools. In the 1970s, Ronald Edmonds, Stewart Purkey, and Marshall Smith, among others, argued that educators should be held accountable for creating a school climate conducive to teaching all children self-respect and basic skills.[17] With the publication of *A Nation at Risk* in 1983, it became fashionable to stress academic rigor enforced by national standards. Such proposals returned the focus to the classroom and the curriculum but failed to relieve educators of a burden that is at least in part of their own making—the widespread feeling that the responsibility for educational failure in America lies chiefly with them. Eager to improve student performance or at least share the blame, many have embraced the idea that the school should be a more accessible institution. However, the perception that parents are outsiders at school has not been easy to overcome.[18] Changes in the structure and function of the American family have complicated the problem. Two-income families, single-parent households, and declining fertility rates have transformed the relationship among teachers, parents, and children. It is no longer clear who is in charge at home, let alone how to reach them. Households comprised of older adults, including those who never had children, are gradually but ineluctably becoming a larger proportion of the population. They are less inclined to favor increased levels of state and federal aid for education.[19] Nevertheless, many educators, reformers, and parents now believe that the interdependence between home and school must be reaffirmed if there is to be a future for education as we know it in America.

The challenge facing parents and teachers may be different today, but it is not unprecedented. It rests on a long history of functional divergence that has featured both conflictive and cooperative relations between the home and the school. Although eliminating mistrust and turning intermittent contact into regular collaboration will not be easy, they cannot be achieved by ignoring the past. The relationship between the home and the school has changed dramatically over time. Activated by school reorganization, parents and teachers switched places in the polity of American education during the second half of the nineteenth century. But instead of closing the door between them, bureaucratization cleared the way for educators to take charge of their collaboration, a state of affairs that remained largely unquestioned until the 1960s. Americans have also treated the bond between the home and the school as a nexus for educational and social reform. In the twentieth century, social services directed at immigrant and low-income families became an accepted part of public educa-

tion. As a result, educators have found themselves to be in conflict with
some parents much more than others but also vulnerable to criticism
prompted by elevated but unfulfilled expectations. These historical developments have important contemporary ramifications. Parents and teachers still have a lot to learn about helping one another and must now become more realistic about what can be reasonably expected from their
cooperation. Their relationship over time warrants careful scrutiny and
thoughtful contemplation. It is the purpose of this book to undertake this
mission.

CHAPTER ONE

From Adversaries to Advocates

How can he, a stranger in blood, not invited into your families, not tolerated in your society, on whom you do not call, in whose employment you scarce seem at all interested, be expected to, nay how can he feel and exercise the absorbing interest in the welfare of your children which his station demands — Anonymous, *The Massachusetts Teacher*

In the spring of 1840, the eminent American educator Emma Hart Willard became the superintendent of common schools in Kensington, Connecticut. The appointment was a tribute to her work as the founder and first director of the Troy Female Seminary. In a field dominated by men, women rarely rose to positions of leadership, but Willard was an uncommon woman and a great believer in the ability of all women to contribute to the cause of public education. Under her guidance, the Troy Female Seminary trained hundreds of teachers. In Kensington, she proposed to build a bridge between teachers and mothers, the two most important women in children's lives. Boys and girls need their mothers' attention at school just as much as at home, Willard thought. "But where is the mother? Where is she whose watchful eye and yearning bosom would be the surest pledge of their growing intelligence and virtue?" Mothers never visited the school or took an interest in its activities. "It is for want of this supervision," Willard said, "that the common schools are in the forlorn condition in which many of them, throughout the country, are now found."[1]

Encouraged by Willard, the women of Kensington organized a Female Common School Association in 1841. It met once a month, assembling at the school to hear student recitations and do good works. Its members made clothing for destitute families so their children could attend school. They oversaw the refurbishment of the schoolhouse and the purchase of books for a school library. They even concerned themselves with getting extra pay for teachers. It was worthwhile work, Willard thought. These women discovered "conveniences to be provided, . . . discomforts and dangers to health and physical constitution to be guarded against which, but for their personal attention, they would never have dreamed of."[2] Such benefits notwithstanding, the teachers in Kensington may not have wanted mothers in school. After all, most of their students spent little enough time away from home. However, the school could not afford to ignore the family. For good or ill, parents affected the education of their children. "The child is a faithful representative of his home sentiments," said one contributor to *The Massachusetts Teacher* in 1851. For the teacher to think otherwise "is a fatal mistake; nothing can be right, nothing can be safe, unless all is right and safe at home."[3]

But how should parents and teachers interact? Who should initiate contact? Was the home or the school primarily in charge of the education of the young? In mid-nineteenth-century America, social and economic developments were transforming the relationship between parents and teachers. Urbanization and industrialization meant less time for parents with their children. Once predominant, the family's role in the education of the young was in decline, while the school's was in ascendance. To explain and justify such an important change, educators spoke and wrote at length about the relationship between parents and teachers. They tied their image of themselves as incipient professionals to a new division of labor between the school and the home.

The Home and the School in America: A Historical Perspective

In colonial America, the school was one of several educational institutions. Children received instruction at home and in church as well as in school. The expansion of schooling in the nineteenth century transformed this situation, but the family certainly did not lose its educational function altogether. It maintained primary responsibility for the moral education of children and retained considerable influence over their cognitive development as well. A competitive relationship existed between the home and the school, characterized by blurred boundaries and shared functions. Both parents and teachers were expected to keep children from harm's way, protecting them from physical and moral danger while instilling a balanced respect for freedom and order.[4]

Beginning in the 1840s, the bureaucratization of formal education in America drove a wedge between the home and the school that would widen as the nineteenth century progressed. Increasingly, parents and teachers faced each other across a gap that featured systematic procedures and standardized expectations. Report cards replaced more personal forms of communication. Graded schools became the norm in lieu of less differentiated approaches to the management of instruction. The development of teachers' institutes and normal schools gave rise to the belief that esoteric knowledge made teachers uniquely qualified to oversee the education of the young. However, the reorganization of American education brought at least one innovation that helped build a bridge between parents and teachers. When elementary schools began to employ many young women as teachers, the similarity between home and school was reinforced. As mothers or teachers, women were the mentors of the young.[5]

Gender was but one of many factors that influenced the dynamic relationship between the home and school. Region and ethnicity also made distinctive contributions to their interaction. In rural America, parents retained considerable control over educational policy and practice. Throughout the nineteenth century, they asserted themselves on such matters as the curriculum and the school calendar. They often resisted expenditures to improve schoolhouses or standardize textbooks. Rural teachers grew accustomed to parental involvement, learning quickly that mothers and fathers expected a respectful hearing at school. Their counterparts in cities were able to offer some resistance. Concentrated in large and complex systems, they sidestepped accountability by deferring to the authority of principals, superintendents, or members of boards of education.[6]

Cultural differences were a source of friction between the home and the school. Some parents complained about the exclusive use of English as the language of instruction or religious bias in the curriculum. In San Francisco and Chicago, German families wanted their language spoken or at least taught in the classroom. Irish Catholics contested the use of the Protestant Bible in Philadelphia and New York and condemned textbooks that questioned the integrity of their church.[7] Parents did not always defer to teachers or school directors in matters of attendance or discipline. Official complaints about truancy, for example, often went unheeded in both rural and urban homes. Some parents objected to corporal punishment or the teacher's ethical expectations, defending their prerogative to be the final authority in matters of values, behavior, and discipline.[8] Schools often had to fight the perception that they taught children to disrespect their families and neglect their parents' needs in favor of their own.

It would be difficult to overstate the importance of social class to the link between home and school. Even in the nineteenth century, middle-class families were much more likely to enroll their children and keep them in school. They brought different social skills and higher educational aspirations to the parent-teacher relationship. Compared to their working-class counterparts, middle-class parents felt less self-conscious about talking to teachers or principals. The opportunity costs associated with schooling stood much more firmly in the way of working- than middle-class enrollment and attendance.[9] But social class was just one of several factors that affected parents' decisions about keeping their children in school. The location of the schoolhouse, the nature of the curriculum, and the status of the local economy could be consequential considerations. Class hostility did not necessarily motivate working-class parents to oppose the introduction of public high schools or withhold their children from school altogether. Equally important was the degree to which the home, regardless of its social class, believed that its opinions would carry weight with those who exercised control.[10]

Ethnicity also was significant in determining who went to school and for how long. At least until the 1920s, immigrants from southern Italy, Poland, Slovenia, and Serbia were much more likely to insist that their children exchange school for work than were their Eastern European, Jewish counterparts. High school principal Leonard Covello encountered such attitudes among the residents of Italian Harlem as late as the 1930s.[11] But no matter who they were or what choices they made, parents were seldom indifferent to the question of attendance at school. Influenced by a rising tide of expert opinion that counseled against the overstimulation of the very young, many parents in the towns and cities of Massachusetts decided in the 1840s to discontinue sending their children to infant school. In early Chicago, on the other hand, Irish and German parents may have based their decisions about attendance on the availability of a parish school. Families in Providence, Rhode Island, often took academic achievement into account when considering whether or not to enroll a child in high school or keep him there.[12]

In New England and New York, the first generation of school reformers and officials acknowledged the great impact of the home on the school. Teachers' institutes sometimes included evening meetings with parents to remind them of their responsibility for the character training of the young, for as Jacob Abbott explained to the American Institute of Instruction in 1834, children behave better in school when disciplined at home. Henry Barnard strongly agreed. Mothers "stand at the very fountain of influ-

ence," he said in 1840. They should visit schools and become involved in
the reform of public education.[13] Not every educator was as anxious as
Barnard to bring parents into school. More than a few, including Jacob
Abbott, regarded them as adversaries, as obstacles to the proper training
of children. But others were willing to concede that the home and the
school were not necessarily enemies; parents and teachers could collaborate successfully on the education of the young. They believed that parents
should help the teacher, performing mundane chores at school while deferring to her educational expertise. By the 1890s, some educators and reformers began to argue that the home and school could be partners, each
contributing significantly to the education of America's children. This
message was directed especially at teachers because, knowing less about
the home than many parents did about the school, they needed to be convinced that parents deserved their respect.

In the nineteenth century, the bureaucratization of public education
"facilitated and legitimated the divorce of school from community and the
subordination of parents to professionals," as Michael B. Katz, among
others, has pointed out.[14] However, it also opened the door to a wider
range of cooperation between the home and the school by the century's
end. Until after the Civil War, teaching was a temporary line of work in the
United States, and most Americans did not hold educators, especially
women teachers, in high esteem. But as schooling became more centralized and systematized, school boards and superintendents often expected
teachers to have more education. Many states and school districts introduced training and certification requirements, and more than a few teachers, including some women, made careers in the professional culture and
hierarchical structure of their changing occupation.[15] By increasing autonomy and longevity, the work culture of the bureaucratic school improved the chances that teachers would experience job satisfaction.

Both the family and the school were institutions in transition in the
nineteenth century. As family life became more insular and parenting
more specialized, at least among the white middle class, precedent had less
and less to offer those looking for guidance in the home-school relationship. More than a calling, teaching lost its affinity with parenthood, and its
practitioners went in search of a new occupational identity. When they
lacked the self-respect that would later come from training, experience,
and organization, teachers and even school administrators found the temptation to denigrate parents irresistible. But as they became better educated
and more organized in the second half of the nineteenth century, they could
take a different approach. Many educators now admitted that parents had

an important role to play in their children's education both at home and in
the school. At the same time, teachers, administrators, and reformers
came to believe that the relationship between the home and the school
should not be left to chance. Like schooling itself, it needed to be rationalized, and more than a few parents agreed. Isolated at home, many
middle-class mothers concluded that a more orderly and structured relationship would enhance their influence at school. Beginning in the 1880s,
parents and teachers organized, forming associations to facilitate interaction and even cooperation. The original impetus came from inside the
school, and rural America led the way. The recommendations of Emma
Willard would now be put to the test.

The Parent in the Eyes of the School, 1850–1915

In 1853, Charles Northend published *The Teacher and the Parent; A Treatise upon Common-School Education Containing Practical Suggestions to
Teachers and Parents.* Northend, the superintendent of schools in Dan-
vers, Massachusetts, wrote the book for teachers more than parents. He
believed that schools needed the help of families. "The full, cheerful, and
prompt cooperation of parents is as essential to the prosperity of a
school," Northend said, "as are the dew, the rain, and the sunshine to the
growth of the vegetable kingdom."[16] But parents often showed little interest in the cause of education. Ultimately, teachers were responsible for
their own success. They should see to it that the school had a good relationship with the home.

To win the respect and support of parents, teachers had to be both
qualified and caring. Command of pedagogy and the curriculum was not
enough; teachers had to behave like parents or at least like friends. They
had to possess common sense and a knowledge of human nature; they had
to be kind and courteous to everyone and enthusiastic about their work.[17]
"While it is urged that teachers should feel an *esprit de corps,*" Northend
said, "it is also recommended that they should feel ready, with cheerful
earnestness, to cooperate with others, in every suitable manner, and on
every proper occasion."[18] It was as if the personal and the professional
were indistinguishable. To be in control, a teacher had to be emotionally
involved and yet detached, humble as well as proud, deferential but also
independent.

That men like Northend advised teachers to wear a Janus face should
come as no surprise in view of the marginal status of teaching as an occu-

pation. To be accepted, after all, teachers had to be all things to all people. However, those with any experience knew that parents were not all the same. Some lived for their children, but many others ignored them and their education. "How few parents exhibit an interest [in school] equal to that manifested in . . . other concerns," Northend complained. His contemporary David Page, author of the widely read *Theory and Practice of Teaching,* concurred. The parents of schoolchildren, he observed, "*do not always feel interested as they should.*"[19] But other parents were intrusive and meddlesome. They interfered with discipline and questioned academic standards. Many parents, Northend warned, "can find nothing to their liking" at school. They were almost as troublesome as those "who are perfectly willing to throw all responsibility on the teacher, with little or no interest in the result."[20]

Close observers of middle-class family life like Lydia Sigourney and William Alcott believed that the home was preferable to the school as a setting for moral education, especially for the youngest children. Their natural innocence was more likely to remain intact under their parents' watchful eyes. However, many educators had a very different perception. Too often, they thought, schools had to contend with ignorance and immorality brought from home or acquired in the community. Family and friends taught children bad habits or gave them misinformation that had to be unlearned. Determined teachers could overcome such obstacles, Northend thought; but they had to be patient and persevere in their work with the home.[21] Parents could even be transformed from adversaries into allies if the school inspired them with a love of learning and involved them in the education of their children. "The teacher should consider it a part of his duty," David Page wrote, "to excite a deeper interest . . . among the patrons of the school than they ever before felt." Holding meetings for parents at school gave the teacher an opportunity to enlist their assistance. But there was no substitute for knowing the home. Both Page and Northend recommended visiting families, a suggestion that must have seemed ironic to those rural teachers who were forced to board around. That such teachers might not command the respect of their students only served to enhance the importance of building a strong bond between the home and the school. After all, it was "impossible to obtain a right feeling on the part of the pupils," Northend said, "without securing a corresponding feeling on the part of the parents."[22]

Many educators shared the concerns of Northend and Page. In 1844, the masters of one Boston school defended themselves when Horace Mann questioned their competence by blaming parents for failures in school. Barnas Sears, Mann's successor as Massachusetts secretary of education, thought that many parents did not take enough responsibility for their children's moral education, and both he and Seth Beers, his counterpart in Connecticut, believed that too many parents showed far too little interest in the education of their children.[23] The new professional journals for teachers frequently discussed the role of parents in education. "It is yours to establish your own authority over your child," said *The Massachusetts Teacher* in 1850, but parents often relinquished it or exercised it unwisely. "It is my candid opinion," said J. J. Reimensnyder, the superintendent of schools in Northumberland County, Pennsylvania, "that parents are much to blame for neglect of duty. . . . They do not, in a spirit of love and kindness, stimulate the minds and hearts of their children to enter the path of learning."[24] Many parents set a bad example for their children, compromising their authority by their own lack of discipline. Some expected more from their offspring than they did from themselves. Parents should not be surprised when their children disobey, said A. H. Trask to a group of teachers assembled in Clinton County, Pennsylvania, in November 1858. "They never practice themselves, those principles which they would teach them to observe."[25]

In the 1850s, teachers were reluctant to condemn parents too harshly. Unsure of their own status as educators, they sometimes gave mothers and fathers the benefit of the doubt. The irresponsible behavior of parents, said *The Massachusetts Teacher* in 1849, "arises oftener from neglect and procrastination than from absolute indifference."[26] But finding fault with parents had much to recommend it. Blaming them could be reassuring, making teachers less accountable for their work at school. Children failed not because of what the teacher did or did not do, but because their parents neglected to make them study. Some teachers denounced parents because they expected the impossible. "If his efforts are seconded properly," said A. M. Gow to a gathering of educators in Monongahela City, Pennsylvania, in 1854, the teacher "can do much, but there are some things he cannot do." He cannot "create talents where the Great Creator never intended they should exist."[27]

When confronted by uncooperative parents, teachers considered taking the initiative, but the standard remedy of inviting them to visit the school had its limitations. After all, most mothers and fathers were "ignorant of the business of teaching." Their presence in the classroom could even be disruptive. Instead, it was up to the teacher to act in loco parentis. The relationship between teacher and pupil, said *The Massachusetts Teacher,* "calls for the exercise of love." For the many "orphans" in America whose parents really were not dead, the school had to replace the family; "in such cases parental responsibility rests upon the teacher."[28] The idea that the school should be a surrogate family even became institutionalized. Appearing in the mid-nineteenth century, the family academy reunited teaching and parenting. At the West Newton English and Classical School, pupils who did not live in the neighborhood resided in the headmaster's home. Its founder, Nathaniel Allen, stressed the importance of cooperation and agreement between the home and the school. But he never left any doubt in the minds of his clients that their children, when in school, should honor him like a father.[29]

Among educators, the image of parents as adversaries persisted throughout the nineteenth century. In 1896, the *Pennsylvania School Journal* complained about mothers who demanded more from teachers than they did from themselves. "They believe that the teacher is appointed to relieve them of their parental and natural task of instructing their offspring," the editors maintained.[30] Such parents were never satisfied, and their constant criticism was especially unwelcome because it could undermine the teacher's credibility. Well-educated parents were a danger, too, because their opinions carried greater weight in the community. Even a doting mother presented a problem because she could be indulgent in her approach to discipline. Many "parents trust vaguely in some talk they have heard about the divine instincts of childhood," one sage observed in 1880, "not knowing that the really divine impulses they ignore and neglect," while elevating "to that high rank, very common desires and naughtiness."[31]

Despite persistent and widespread acceptance of the view that parents and teachers were adversaries, another vision of the home-school relationship developed in the United States. In the first half of the nineteenth century, Americans increasingly invested moral authority in wives and mothers, encouraging educators to reconsider the idea of parental involvement in school life and the need for parent-teacher cooperation. European theorists and practitioners in early childhood education attested to the importance of a close association between the home and the school. They made it an axiom of the kindergarten movement that attracted so much attention in the United States after the Civil War.[32] But even before kindergartens crossed the Atlantic, educational administrators and teachers in America were asking parents to help them. In 1856, the Superintendent of Common Schools in Connecticut, John D. Philbrick, urged parents to support teachers by making certain that their children were punctual, diligent, and obedient. Some of his contemporaries also thought this way. Addressing the patrons of his rural school, A. P. Frick asked parents to assist him by teaching their children to obey the rules of the school and do their homework regularly. In return, he promised to treat their children with kindness and respect. The governance of his school, he said, would "be of a parental nature—mild, yet firm, determined and unvarying."[33] The complete separation of the home and the school defied God's intent, said *The Massachusetts Teacher* in 1850. Each should avoid interfering with the other's "more appropriate functions," but "they are so far united as to have some sympathies in common, and to make possible a common destiny." Cooperation between them was natural. After all, "the family was the first school, and the very idea of a school grew out of the family." Who then had "a right to be so much interested in the school, as a parent? Or who should so exalt the mission of the father and the mother, as the teacher?"[34]

Teachers found it easier to regard parents as their helpers as they became more confident about their own professionalism. Brought to Harvard by Charles W. Eliot in 1891, Paul H. Hanus remained long enough to instill self-respect in a generation of teachers and administrators. Hanus firmly believed in the primacy of the school, but he also understood that home could add to or detract from a child's education. "The education which the community is constantly giving our children," he wrote in 1904, "will either strengthen or weaken the influence of the school. I ask the parents, which shall it be?" In the same year, the professional journal *Education* published a series of five editorials with the same perspective. Parents could facilitate the work of the school, the editors said, by imbuing their children with self-esteem, self-reliance, and respect for authority. Pupils from such families would "make teaching almost a pastime."[35]

Of course, educators did not want people to think that the home and the school were the same, but sometimes they chose to describe their relationship with parents in even more reciprocal terms. The editors of *Education* experimented with this idea by publishing an article in 1899 that envisioned parents and teachers as partners in the education of the young. "It was never intended," M. A. Cassidy wrote, "that the school should supplant the home in child training. . . . Nor is it desirable that the teacher should supplant the parents"; instead, "they should be co-workers."[36] This attitude reflected the growing preoccupation of middle-class, suburban America with neighborhood and family. Kindergarteners like Elizabeth Harrison and Alice Putnam easily embraced such thinking, arguing that immigrant mothers and childless teachers had much to learn from one another. Some public school administrators also fixed on this idea. The superintendent of schools in Brookline, Massachusetts, Samuel Train Dutton, demonstrated as much in an address delivered at the thirty-sixth annual meeting of the National Education Association (NEA). Should we be content, he asked, "with the relation of armed neutrality which so often exists? The importance of the issue at stake demands mutual sympathy and co-operation." By maintaining constant and complete communication, parents and teachers could "supplement the efforts of each other." [37] They could reintegrate the institutions of childhood, making growing up in America more like the seamless experience it once had been.

Partnership meant bringing the home and the school closer together on at least two fronts, moral and cognitive education. Educators who thought this way expected parents to instill respect for teachers. In return, children would "become more obedient sons and daughters" by virtue of their attendance at school. Meanwhile, the curriculum needed the active support of the home. The discoveries of developmental psychologists like G. Stanley Hall suggested that education could not be compartmentalized. Parents had to provide practical opportunities for nature study, reading, and arithmetic. In fact, they had to be teachers in their own right. Learning to think could not be accomplished part-time. Reinforced in one place but stifled in another, inquisitive minds would not grow.[38]

It was not a long step from belief in a partnership between the home and the school to the idea that parents should be advocates for schooling and cheerleaders for educational reform. Made to feel welcome at school, mothers and fathers would be inclined to elect conscientious school directors, who, in turn, would hire first-rate teachers and build excellent facilities. Popular with school administrators, this was a civic mission for the home with which many parents could agree, too. Formed in 1897, the National Congress of Mothers (NCM) adopted education as a field for reform to be achieved through better communication and more cooperation between the school and the home. The NCM first approached teachers in 1904, launching a campaign for parent-teacher associations to secure more influence for mothers, but its leaders agreed with school officials who saw much to be gained from collaboration. "Principals find the parent-teacher circle an excellent means of reaching all parents effectively when some general condition needs changing," said Mary Harmon Weeks, a vice president of the NCM, "when public sentiment in the district needs rousing, or when they wish to make certain courses effective which do not seem to take hold."[39]

Such an alliance was also thought to be capable of advancing the cause of political and social reform. Beverly Bland Mumford, a member of the

Richmond Education Association, believed that, as partners, the home and the school would improve citizenship by feminizing education. However, children would be the primary beneficiaries of parent-teacher cooperation. One contributor to *The School Review* urged parents and teachers to "undertake a systematic study of all the influences surrounding the child in the hope of increasing his welfare."[40] Inspired by such teamwork, community spirit would surely grow. After attending a meeting at school, explained one member of a Philadelphia parents' group, the Home and School League, in 1909, we were "conscious of a *neighborhood* interest new to us. Not only the teachers of the school, but the men and women with whom we have been 'touching elbows' through the evening have a problem in common with us."[41]

It was a sentiment with which reformers and progressive educators could readily agree. In 1899, John Dewey complained about the separation of the school from the rest of American society. Only artificial barriers stood between them. Parents and teachers should collaborate on social reform, Dewey said, making a point already expressed by one forward-looking superintendent. "The mission of the public school is closely related to all forms of social work," Samuel Dutton wrote in 1897. "Teachers must become conscious of the commanding importance of the school as a social factor, influencing every form of human endeavor, . . . and, in turn, drawing inspiration and help from every department of the world's activity."[42]

John Dewey laid the blame for the isolation of the school at the feet of educators. Their devotion to traditional subjects and methods made schooling irrelevant by detaching it from the experience of the young. Dewey received acclaim for such insights, but his was not an isolated lament. Although many educators and reformers thought that more bureaucracy was the answer, one speaker at the annual meeting of the NEA in 1897 captured the spirit of Dewey's complaint. "From year to year," said Ida Bender, the teacher "has allowed himself to be removed further from the life of the common people, until he has become part of a great machine." Teachers, principals, and superintendents had become too impressed with their own importance. Instead of welcoming citizen and parent participation, they deemed "any criticism of their work or expression of desire to share in it an unwarrantable intrusion."[43]

To bring the home and the school closer together again, parents and teachers at the very least had to share more information. Both Dutton and Hanus stressed the importance of openness and good communication. The teacher "needs information concerning the child's home life," Dutton said. "The parent, on the other hand, should have the frankest statement from the teacher concerning the child's interests, as displayed in the classroom." Well-informed mothers and fathers would understand "the viewpoint of the school." They would grasp what it "expects of the child, and why." The president of the Massachusetts Agricultural College may have put it best. Regular meetings between parents and teachers, said Kenyon L. Butterfield, "dispel fogs of misunderstanding. They inspire closer co-operation. They create mutual sympathy."[44]

Of course, there were those who believed that the work of the school was ultimately beyond parental comprehension, and it is probably no accident that they were inclined to make an analogy between education and medicine. There is much confusion about the teacher's role, said Arthur Perry in his book, *The Status of the Teacher*, and limits to her powers and obligations. Like a surgeon, she cannot explain to the layman the meaning of her every act. Parents had to have faith in her training and professionalism. According to the superintendent of the California School of Mechanic Arts, the teacher's relationship to the home ought to resemble that of the family doctor. "The teacher should have expert knowledge of the pupil," George A. Merrill said. But "even possessed of such knowledge, it would be more or less futile without a thorough understanding between the school and the home."[45] Teachers might have the last word, but they had to respect the importance of the contribution that parents made to the education of children.

The teacher's need to know her pupils did not end with their families. Getting the proper perspective required a larger context of social and economic understanding. To prepare students for employment, for example, teachers had to know what skills were in demand. "The school can scarcely be of great social service unless the teachers study the life of the community," said one sociologist. They also had to mediate between the home and the workplace, making certain to match the two, and in this regard, social class was an important consideration. To make the right decisions, teachers had to "learn something of the conditions under which school children are reared and something of the training they require for the life they will have to lead."[46] Clearly, the school could not be expected to exceed the home's limitations.

By 1900, there was almost a crisis mentality among those who believed that schools had lost touch with their social and economic surroundings. Scientific advances in educational theory and practice had not greatly improved the performance of schools or transformed American society. The bureaucratic structures educators had built to increase efficiency also protected them from criticism. But the bureaucratization of American education turned out to be a double-edged sword. Not only did it give teachers and principals at least partial immunity against outside interference, but also it empowered them to concentrate on the importance of the home-school relationship. The "interdependence between the school and the home . . . is *the* important influence" in education, said one observer. What the child "lives in the school determines what he will do at home," added another.[47] Kenyon Butterfield did not think that the growing chasm between the home and the school was irreversible. Based on his personal knowledge of rural America, he attributed it to correctable, albeit common, human failings. The distance between the home and school was "due more to carelessness, to the pressure of time, or to indolence than to more serious delinquencies," Butterfield argued, but just because it could be reversed, no one should discount its importance. Those familiar with the city were more inclined to rely on structural explanations for what they perceived to be the increasing distance between the home and school, but they were no less troubled by the trend. They cited the increasing complexity of modern life, the preoccupation of parents with the difficulties of making a living, and the increasingly esoteric and technical nature of school instruction.[48] Regardless of its origins, however, many parents and educators were convinced that they had to find a solution to the problem.

No less a figure than the social critic and reformer Abraham Flexner recommended more parental participation in schools. Modern parents, he advised, had to get involved in all aspects of their children's education. But to reconcile the home with the school, parents and teachers had to resolve a conundrum. Assertive parents ran the risk of being labeled meddlesome, while those who hung back could be called indifferent. "It was not uncommon," said Martin Brumbaugh, the Philadelphia superintendent of schools, "to regard the coming of a parent . . . as an interference with the work of the school," and, he added, "no doubt in some cases this was true, because parents came only to criticize and not to cooperate."[49] If Brumbaugh could see only one side of the problem, Paul Hanus kept the two faces of parental involvement in mind. Parents, he thought, were "often careless or indifferent" when it came to the education of their children. But they could be intrusive, too, insisting that the school adhere to ideas about curriculum and teaching methods that were "crude and out of date." Hanus and Flexner also recognized that when the home and the school failed to cooperate, teachers as well as parents were losers. "If parents are indifferent, the schools suffer from loss of contact," Flexner pointed out. If they are "meddlesome, the schools lose authority and continuity." What was the solution to this problem? "Is there no way out of these apparent inconsistencies?" Flexner asked.[50]

The schools could invite parental involvement. Because more and more educators and reformers believed that parents and teachers should be partners, such diplomacy possessed considerable appeal. To be sure, some parents were "over-zealous and even meddlesome," Edward Goodwin told the Harvard Teachers' Association in March 1908. "But this excess of zeal is much more wholesome than the indifference and neglect that characterize many communities which in consequence have poor schools."[51] In 1912, the Boston School Committee directed its annual report to the parents of the children in the city. It asked them to talk with their sons and daughters about their schools and get acquainted with the "principals and teachers who have charge of your children." They would be "glad to receive any suggestions or criticisms that you may desire to offer," the school committee said, "and to give them careful and thoughtful consideration." Such parental involvement, a professor at the University of Chicago said, would be certain to enhance teacher morale.[52]

But the prospect of one mother after another coming to inquire or complain did not necessarily uplift the spirits of teachers and administrators. The solution to the problem was organization. As Goodwin explained to his Harvard audience, the voluntary home and school association was "the most effective and permanent means of promoting close relationship and sympathy between the school and home." Such associations "could assume an unwarranted and meddlesome control over the organization and work of the school," Goodwin conceded. But "this is hardly to be feared" because "co-operation is their avowed purpose" and public opinion will not tolerate "direct and radical interference with the established procedure of a public school."[53] The founder and first president of the Philadelphia Home and School League would not have disagreed. According to Mary Van Meter Grice, every town and city in America should form a central committee to facilitate "cooperation between the home and the school." It should coordinate the efforts of parent-teacher associations in individual schools. But it should not be overbearing in its leadership, leaving the parents and teachers in each school free to work out the terms of their relationship as much as possible on their own.[54]

By 1910, opinions about the relationship between the home and the school had changed since the days of Charles Northend and David Page, when most educators viewed mothers and fathers as nothing more than adversaries. Parents could help them, collaborate with them, and even be persuasive advocates for the school. But a reciprocal relationship between distinct institutions required careful planning, organization, and management. Many educators were convinced that this was so, and by 1910, more than a few parents had reached the same conclusion. However, there were unanswered questions about politics and procedure. Who should take the initiative? Who should provide the leadership? In what ways should parents and teachers work together to reach common goals? These were important questions, and the answers to them became matters of not only theoretical debate but also practical reality in the search for a balance between parental authority and teacher control.

Organizing the Relationship between the Home and School, 1885–1915

During the second half of the nineteenth century, many Americans joined together to monitor the public schools. Businessmen, mechanics, politicians, and reformers counted education among their most important interests. Before 1860, they focused on the formation of common schools. In large cities like New York and Philadelphia, members of the local elite took primary responsibility for the schooling of the poor. But once public education became an established fact, the relationship between the school and its constituents changed. Professionals assumed control of management, while laymen turned their attention to monitoring the school's policies and performance. Trade associations, labor unions, political parties, ethnic brotherhoods, and civic organizations all included public education on their agendas.[55] More and more, mothers and fathers chose to do the same.

Prior to the Civil War, the interaction between parents and schools seldom was systematic. The Sunday school was one exception perhaps because this surrogate for the common school was often run by a church congregation. Beginning in the 1870s, this informality began to disappear, as parents whose only connection with one another was through their children organized for the first time. Mothers' clubs appeared among those who chose to patronize a new educational institution in the United States, the kindergarten. Gradually, parents' associations developed for families with children at all levels of elementary and secondary education.[56]

Farmers and educators in a remote part of Michigan conducted one of the first successful experiments in organized parent-teacher cooperation. Started in the winter of 1885–86, the "Hesperia movement" took its name from the small town north and west of Grand Rapids where it began.

Unable to participate in the meetings of the Oceana County teachers' association, the women working in the Hesperia school responded to their feelings of intellectual and social isolation by founding their own organization for professional development. They decided that their group would be stronger if they asked the local farmers to join. In doing so, they drew upon not one but two popular traditions in rural America, the teachers' institute and the Chautauqua meeting.[57] Each brought many adults together for the purpose of edification. But it was not just precedent that justified a policy of broad participation. Better organized themselves, the teachers could afford to reach out to those around them.

Convening on Saturdays, the Hesperia Teachers' and Patrons' Association devoted its meetings to both educational and agricultural subjects. The local farmers and their families responded enthusiastically, turning out in large numbers. In addition to being a welcome occasion for socializing, these gatherings gave parents and teachers an opportunity to express their commitment to public education. Rural parents made many demands in the 1880s, insisting that teachers be frugal managers and model citizens, while holding them to high standards for their children's behavior and achievement.[58] They saw both student learning and school policy-making as legitimate parental concerns. Self-directed teachers were better able to respond to such expectations. In Hesperia, they met with parents on Saturday mornings to exchange pleasantries and maneuver for influence and control.

In 1893, the commissioner of schools in Oceana County, D. E. McClure, persuaded the people of Oceana and Newaygo counties to found a Joint Grangers' and Teachers' Association. He believed that such organizations had an important role to play, and by taking the initiative, he determined what would be the order of the day. In Hesperia, he convinced the Teachers' and Patrons' Association to endorse a reading list for rural pupils that he prepared and to adopt a plan to put libraries in the town's schools. He wanted the Joint Grangers' and Teachers' Association to be a force for "better rural-school education." Its objective, he said, ought to be the elimination of "surroundings which destroy character," by which he meant "unkept school-yards, foul nasty outhouses, [and] poor, unfit teachers."[59] It was an agenda that most parents and teachers could love.

The "Hesperia movement" spread across rural Michigan in the 1890s. By the turn of the century, there were parent-teacher organizations in ten counties in the state. The Kent County association attracted an average of 500 participants to its weekend meetings. Rural educators in other states promoted the idea of organized parent involvement. Mothers and fathers

were invited to join teachers' institutes in Ohio and Pennsylvania. County
superintendents in Kansas formed associations for teachers, parents, and
school board members to bring policy makers together with those whom
their decisions affected "for the purpose of bettering school conditions."[60]

In Delaware, the state commissioner of education made a similar case
for structure and order in home and school relations. Speaking, no doubt,
for many of his colleagues, Charles A. Wagner praised parent-teacher organizations, attributing their achievements to careful planning and organization. Only through "conscious effort," he said, "the getting together
and being like minded," could great things be accomplished.[61] Left unsaid
was the fear that parents could become a disorderly and disruptive force.
Personally invested in their children's learning, they could easily overstep
their bounds, trespassing in the domain of educational policy-making. It
was important not to let them or their associations become loose cannons.

Leadership by educators in the development of parent-teacher organizations was not confined to rural areas. School superintendents in cities
and suburbs saw many advantages to marshaling parental participation
and support. Formed in an exclusive Boston suburb in 1895, the Brookline
Education Society took only two years to reach a membership of more
than 500. Superintendent Dutton hoped the society would reverse the perception that private schools were superior to their public counterparts. Its
most successful meetings brought "cultured women" together with their
less-favored counterparts in an atmosphere of mutual respect and self-
help. There was still "plenty of conservatism to overcome" in a community as affluent as Brookline, Dutton observed, but "parents have come to
see, perhaps for the first time, that the education of their children is a
deeper concern than houses and lands or the stock market." They were
even gaining an appreciation for "the newer phases of education, especially art, manual training, and physical culture."[62] In Lansdowne, Pennsylvania, the supervising principal of the public schools thought that the
home and school league in his community contributed to the development
of a "spirit of cooperation" between parents and teachers. "Teachers now
realize that the parents' point of view is to be considered and respected,"
Walter L. Philips said in 1916. Likewise, parents have learned that "the
teacher has rights and privileges, that she is a professional person worthy
of respect."[63]

While a growing number of parents and teachers agreed that the home
and the school ought to work together, they did not necessarily share one
opinion about how the process of cooperation should begin. Educators
like Philips believed that the school should take the initiative. "The desire

for a home and school league should originate with the school adminis-tration," he said. When parents realize that teachers and principals want to support the home, there will be "little or no difficulty in forming an organization for mutual support." Philadelphia's Mary Grice saw it differ-ently. "There must be a mutual coming together with the impulse largely from the home," she argued. "Otherwise, it becomes but another of the school activities and loses its local coloring."[64] There were those who thought that, once established, home and school associations could be democratic, representing teachers and parents alike, no matter who took the first step. But the circumstances of their founding had important po-litical ramifications. The side that set the process in motion could set the agenda for these organizations. This much was clear to Kenyon Butter-field, even though he chose to express himself obliquely. Of the Hesperia movement, Butterfield said, "[T]eacher and farmer must be equally rec-ognized in all particulars," but "the initiative must be taken by the educa-tors," not the lay community.[65]

Like Butterfield, most superintendents and professors of education be-lieved that the school should be the senior partner because only the pro-fessionals were at the cutting edge. Many parents, on the other hand, were not even well-informed. From its inception, the NCM stressed the im-portance of educating parents. Renamed the National Congress of Moth-ers and Parent-Teacher Associations in 1908, it advocated child study, do-mestic science, and health education. A survey of American educators on the eve of World War I revealed that many superintendents and college presidents thought parent-teacher organizations should be seminars in modern education. They improved "the educational sentiment in the community" by keeping it abreast of "present-day movements" in schools. Participation in such groups also made for more responsible citizen-ship, Mary Grice maintained. Guided by "the school and its faculty of trained leaders," mothers and fathers gained practical experience in self-government and social reform. Education gave parents the right to be more involved in both the community and the school, but the traditional perception of parents as adversaries remained strong enough to blunt such progressivism in many schools. For example, principals in California insisted on directing the activities of parent organizations to keep them "out of mischief" even though the California Congress of Mothers and Child Study Circles expressly condemned parental interference in school administration.[66]

Educators who felt this way might have had second thoughts after lis-tening to their colleague William B. Owen. "Failures in school," he said,

"are not due to technical difficulties in subjects studied, nor often to stu-
pidity in children." Instead, he told the NEA in 1911, "they are due to an
unregulated life which it is in the power of the humblest parent to restore
to order." Many families could not provide a stable and wholesome environment on their own. "The school is the consulting specialist for the
home," Owen said. "It is the business of the school to put itself at the service of the home and . . . to insist on the kind of co-operation that will
make individual and social success possible."[67] It was a question of not
only who should be in charge but also what the role of parents should be.
Hoping for parity at least, those outside the professional establishment
turned for leadership to home and school associations. Too many mothers
and fathers, said Mary Grice, know nothing about the laws of child development. Parent education should be a "primary object of the 'getting together' of the home and the school." In tandem, they could "train men and
women in the greatest of all professions."[68]

By 1900, it was almost conventional to believe that the relationship between the home and school should be cooperative and organized. No matter who took the initiative or what their respective roles should be, many
parents and teachers thought that both stood to benefit from contact that
was regular, orderly, and well defined. Between 1900 and 1915, the home
and school association became an established institution in American
education. Its origins were rural, but it was in cities and suburbs that such
organizations proliferated. Perhaps this should not be surprising. In
rural America, there was still a desire to maintain at least the illusion of
consensus and homogeneity. Urban educators, faced with growing diversity, were predisposed to support the centralization and standardization of
schools and, therefore, to think of the home as a separate, albeit related,
institution. Middle-class parents, living increasingly fragmented lives,
could be expected to agree. But it is surely ironic that bureaucratic organization—one of the reforms responsible for driving parents and teachers
apart—was now enlisted to reunite them.

The Growth of Home and School Associations, 1900–1920

By the end of the nineteenth century, the first wave of bureaucratic reforms had crested in American education, and a new generation of school
administrators was working to build on the foundation laid by others. Between 1890 and 1920, rural reformers made considerable headway in their
campaign to consolidate country schools. In the city, boards of education

were reduced in size and centralized. The curriculum was enlarged to include subjects like manual training, home economics, and physical education. Educators tried to bring greater uniformity to the classification of pupils and the measurement of their performance.[69] Symbolic and supportive of these changes, the schoolhouse became less plain and yet more predictable. High schools now contained an unprecedented amount of differentiated space.

No rooms in the schoolhouse represented these reforms better than the kindergarten and the auditorium. Widespread in America by 1900, kindergartens were supposed to help young children make the transition from the private embrace of the home to the public routine of the school and the self-discipline of citizenship. Such work required a specialized facility. It had to be big enough to accommodate at least thirty children but small enough to possess "a homelike atmosphere." A fireplace, window curtains, and suitable wall decorations conveyed a sense of intimacy, mitigating the impersonal effects of collective activity. Believing that "environment is the strongest of all factors in education," school authorities in Denver tried to make all twenty-one of its kindergartens feel like home in 1902.[70]

School managers also knew the importance of an auditorium. Its daytime use was specialized, confined to large-group testing or instruction, musical or dramatic presentations, and ceremonial functions. But it was also a room that the community could use. Reformers like Jacob Riis, Clarence Arthur Perry, and Edward J. Ward believed that the public school should function as a social center. For them, the auditorium was an invaluable asset. It "belongs to the community," said Aaron Gove, the man in charge of public schools in Denver, Colorado. "Any respectable, peaceable group of people wishing, in the evenings or even during the day, to assemble for the purpose of instruction or rational entertainment is welcome" there.[71] One such group might well be the home and school association. In the auditorium, parents and teachers could assemble to learn from one another or simply socialize. Here the relationship between the home and the school could be formalized.

Before 1900, associations for parents and teachers took root slowly and unevenly in the United States. In 1897, the superintendent of schools in Binghamton, New York, complained that not enough parents were interested in organizations of this kind in his state. His peers in Maine believed in the power of statewide organization to bring about change. Hoping to make parents more supportive of teachers and school reform, they formed the Maine School Improvement League in 1898. It brought together local home and school associations and encouraged them to purchase books and renovate schoolhouses.[72] Parents and teachers coalesced more readily in the city, forming many home and school associations in both private and public schools. But as a comparison of their work in Chicago, Detroit, Boston, New York, and Philadelphia reveals, they did not always take part with the same goals in mind. Differences surfaced about the role of parent-teacher organizations in educational policy-making.

At the demonstration school created by the faculty at the University of Chicago, parents organized themselves almost as soon as the school was born. The first president of the Parents' Association of the University Elementary School explained its function. It should give mothers and fathers, Mrs. Floyd Frazier said, "a thorough understanding of the aims and problems of the school, it should lead to a practical co-operation between teacher and parent, and it should result in a closer companionship between child and parent." Dedicated and determined, its members thought they should extend their work. "Our responsibility," said the head of the association's Home Committee, is "to the cause of education everywhere." If we do our job well, she wrote in 1904, we shall "blaze the way for the introduction of similar aims and ambitions in our public schools and make it possible for them more fully to serve the end of their being."[73] By then, her expectation was already beginning to be met. There were parents' clubs in twenty-five public and private schools in Chicago. One club could count more than three hundred members, including parents of sixteen nationalities. But the movement did not spread equally among all schools; it was strongest at the elementary level where the natural bond between parent and child reinforced the manufactured link between school and home.[74]

In the Boston public schools, a home and school association appeared for the first time in April 1905. Mothers' clubs, formed to share the wisdom derived from personal experience, were nothing new among Boston's elite at that time, the first having been established in nearby Cambridge nearly thirty years before. But by the beginning of the twentieth century, many educated women were open to collaboration with school professionals. At the Sherwin-Hyde Elementary School in what was then the middle-class district of Roxbury, parents and teachers organized "to bring the home and the school together; to instruct . . . parents concerning the care of their children; and to promote the social interests of the neighborhood." By the end of 1907, there were similar associations in a dozen public schools in the city, and led by Mrs. Quincy Adams Shaw, parents, educators, and reformers organized the Boston Home and School Associ-

ation. It worked for the modernization of the school district, the dissemination of information about education, and the formation of parents' associations in schools where none existed.[75] There was precedent in the city
for a reform-oriented parents' organization. In December 1901, some
civic-minded citizens founded a Fathers and Mothers Club "to improve
the condition of children in [the] home, school, and general environment."
It specialized in helping the poor, sponsoring summer outings for under-
privileged children, calling for nurses in the city's public schools, and even
running a maternity service that gave supplies to destitute mothers of infants.[76] But growth waited on the realization that parent-teacher cooperation could benefit more affluent Bostonians.

At the behest of the Fathers and Mothers Club and the Boston Home
and School Association, parents and teachers came together in many
schools throughout the city. By 1913, home and school associations could
be found in forty-seven elementary and three high schools, but such rapid
growth was not easy to sustain. Four years later the number of elementary
schools with such associations had dipped to thirty-eight. At the secondary level, only Girls' Latin and the High School of Practical Arts had parents' associations. Perhaps the patronizing attitude of school authorities
contributed to the decline. Franklin B. Dyer, the superintendent, ranked
parent education ahead of parent involvement in kindergartens. His assistant, Jeremiah Burke, thought the intense interest that he witnessed at
home and school meetings empowered not just parents, but also school
authorities by giving them the opportunity "to exercise tremendous influence in the creation of wholesome public sentiment."[77]

The need for parent education also sparked interest in organizing the
relationship between the home and the school in New York. Beginning in
1896, the progressive Public Education Association (PEA) sponsored lectures for mothers on such topics as curriculum, pedagogy, parent-teacher
cooperation, and child development. Wanting to prevent the home from
working at cross-purposes with the school, the PEA arranged talks that
were suited to those with a limited understanding. It expected the informal atmosphere of these meetings to remove "the little points of variance"
that came between them. But New York's principals do not appear to have
supported the PEA's efforts, and only a few reported having parent-
teacher associations in their schools before the onset of World War I.[78]

In Philadelphia, middle-class reformers had better success at building
parent-teacher organizations, perhaps because public officials gave them
more support. To get started, they established an auxiliary of the NCM in
May 1897. At the Heston School in the city's western suburbs, a mothers'

club soon appeared. It was followed by so many others that, encouraged by Superintendent Brumbaugh, reformers and educators joined to form a Home and School League in October 1907. Like its counterpart in Boston, the Philadelphia league represented those committed to real change. Its founders drew inspiration from the national movement to open public schools after hours to the community.[79] At the suggestion of Dr. Jesse Burks, the director of municipal research, the league reorganized in 1913, creating a central coordinating committee for the fifty-seven different branches that it maintained.[80] Coming together at the neighborhood level, parents and teachers might not need outside assistance, but modernizing a school district required elite leadership and citywide organization.

Both the fashionable women of the New Century Club in Philadelphia and the activists who led the Pennsylvania Congress of Mothers encouraged the league, and it soon claimed more than five thousand members in fifty-five neighborhood-based home and school associations. The work of these local organizations alternated between educational and civic. Monthly meetings often sought to teach mothers and fathers about "the relation of home and school, the qualities of good citizenship, the physical well-being of the children, [and] the influence of community environment." The authority conveyed by expert knowledge inhered in the school, but middle-class parents could feel in control when they worked together for neighborhood improvement. They built playgrounds, served lunches, and taught cooking and sewing to immigrant families.[81]

Under the leadership of Mary Grice, the Home and School League developed a more cosmopolitan orientation. Following up on the work of its affiliates at the local level, it bought books to help the schools educate working-class and foreign-born mothers about family health and hygiene. In 1915, the superintendent of schools, John Garber, threw his weight behind this effort. Endorsing the work of the league, he proposed to organize and extend it. Without proper food and sanitation, Philadelphia's immigrant and working-class children were falling further behind their more affluent peers every day. To secure what he called the "intelligent cooperation of the home" in forming proper habits of personal hygiene, he asked principals to arrange parental meetings at which "competent speakers" would "enlighten parents as to the health needs of their children."[82]

Mary Grice also believed in parent education, but she ranked parents ahead of teachers in the development of mutual understanding and cooperation. Overburdened by the demands of their jobs, teachers often were indifferent to the circumstances of neighborhood and family life.[83] By contrast, parents had a personal stake in the work of the school. What

Grice had in mind, of course, were middle-class parents of white, native-born stock. They were preferable to the upwardly mobile men and women from immigrant and working-class backgrounds who were establishing a beachhead in the teaching profession. However, the kinship ties that focused parental attention were not an unmixed blessing, for parents could become sidetracked by personal considerations.

The Fathers' Association of the new Frankford High School in northeast Philadelphia exemplifies the point. The school and its neighborhood were largely native-born and middle-class on the eve of World War I. Formed at the behest of the school's principal in January 1912, the Fathers' Association served the school by attracting a large and loyal community following. Membership grew rapidly, surpassing nine hundred by February 1916 and reaching two thousand by the early 1920s. The association helped plan a modern school building, persuading the board of education to install a swimming pool that local residents could use. It raised money for scholarships, athletic equipment, musical instruments, and books, but school improvement was never its members' first concern. Their lives were increasingly differentiated by occupational and familial obligations, and they wanted an organization that would satisfy their need for fellowship, "bringing them together to know each other and be friends." At each meeting, they devoted considerable time to entertainment. Between 1918 and 1928, the mayor of Philadelphia, the president of Haverford College, and the coach of the Princeton football team addressed them; but their most frequent guest was the Reverend "Jack" Hart, who was invited many times because he was an inspirational speaker.[84] The association gave fathers a prominent place in the life of Frankford High School but in ways that reformers like Mary Grice must have found less than satisfying.

Fathers' clubs were not at all uncommon in the early history of home and school associations. Sometimes they took the form of male auxiliaries within larger organizations dominated by women. In such circumstances, men reported being made to feel like outsiders, expected to assume responsibilities and perform tasks that were targeted for them. Perhaps being restricted to athletics, school finance, or business education was as comfortable for the men as it was for most women. But even the occasional election of a man to a position of leadership did not change the fact that women did most of the work in parent-teacher associations.[85] No doubt, educators preferred working with associations run by women because it was thought they would be less likely to demand a voice in policy discussions and decision making. As mothers or teachers, women were supposed to focus on child nurture and learning. However, the perception

that the school was not a place for men could also serve the political interests of volunteer women.

Toward a New Perspective on the Home and School Relationship

By 1910, organized cooperation between the home and the school was a
well-established pattern in both urban and rural America. Recognizing
the importance of regular communication, parents, educators, and reformers took steps to facilitate and formalize contact between the home
and the school. What most had in mind was a cooperative relationship
between two distinct but reciprocal institutions. However, there were still
many unanswered questions about this relationship and the organizations that were formed to enhance it. Were home and school associations
meant to be entertainment for parents or a means to improve education
and family life? Were they supposed to strengthen the hand of the family
or the school? At the beginning of the twentieth century, the nature and
future of the home-school relationship were far from resolved. Parents
and educators would continue to ask themselves whether they should be
equal partners in the education of children or participants in a relationship marked by limited influence and final authority. One thing was certain: parents found their position to be different from what their grand-
parents had known. Because it was no longer easy to manipulate or bully
teachers, they could not patronize them as readily as before. The public
school had become a formidable institution that parents could not redirect
on their own.

As parent-teacher associations became more and more commonplace,
educators also realized that the home-school relationship had changed.
But had it changed for the better? Although this question was not
new, some school officials began to think about it in a more focused way.
Building on the idea that parents were their best advocates, they defined
it as just a problem in public relations. As one educator said in 1905,
parent-teacher organizations should enlighten "public opinion on all educational matters." Interviewed by *The School Review,* a high school principal from Illinois told his colleagues three years later that "these associations both mold and reflect public opinion," but "their most important
function should be the education of the community regarding its own
schools."[86]

It would not be until the 1930s that educators fully committed themselves to the idea that the relationship between the home and the school

should be an exercise in public relations. Since the formative years of public education in the United States, parents and teachers had jockeyed for position. Their interaction became more structured over time but no less political. After World War I, many educators decided to reassert themselves. As private life once again captured the attention of most Americans, many principals, superintendents, and professors of education concluded that it would be best if they conceptualized and controlled the relationship between home and school. How would mothers and fathers react? Would they resist, withdraw, or acquiesce? Would they insist on speaking with an independent voice or defer to the professionals? Parents and teachers no longer needed to get reacquainted, but their relationship was not static. Between 1920 and 1940, it would be reexamined and rethought even as its reciprocity was reaffirmed.

CHAPTER TWO

Home Rule or Ruled at Home?

Standing side by side and back to back
Against the evil of dark attack,
Holding high together bowls of light
To guide the steps of future men aright;
This is our duty—more our pride—
Though forces of modernity deride.
Some by blood stand guard; while others face
Their tasks as "childless mothers of the race."
— Willard K. Bassett, *California Parent and Teacher*

Parents and teachers in New York City once knew the name Angelo Patri. Between 1913 and 1944, he was principal of Junior High School 45 in the Bronx. Such a lengthy tenure in one school was remarkable in and of itself, but his reputation in New York rested on more than that. Born in Italy, Patri came to the United States with his family in the 1880s. His father, Nicholas, could barely read; his mother, Carmella, hoped her son would become a priest. After graduating from City College in 1896, Patri began his career in education as a classroom teacher, ruffling his superiors almost immediately by his youthful enthusiasm for the progressive methods of John Dewey. In 1908, Patri joined the ranks of his critics as principal of Public School 4. But he was never content to be just a loyal soldier in the New York school bureaucracy. As a radio personality and newspaper columnist, he became a well-known expert on the subject of child rearing. When he died in 1965, he was hailed as a leading educator, a "pioneer in liberal education," said *The New York Times,* and a strong advocate for reciprocity between the home and the school.[1]

In the Bronx, Patri often worked with families who were unfamiliar with the routines and regulations of an urban public school. Parents could not be forced to get involved in the school's work, he thought. But educators could induce them to participate by taking advantage of their natural interest in their children. "Our object is to help children," Patri wrote, "though in helping them we bring pressure to bear upon the parents to help their own." At Junior High School 45 Patri encouraged the formation of a parents' association. It would supply practical knowledge to hard-working mothers and fathers and sponsor reform in the community. Parents could turn to it for the latest information about the health and development of children; they could marshal its resources to combat child abuse, neglect, or delinquency. But even if such a group might sometimes exert influence at school, it could never be relied on to function independently. "There is always a group [of parents] coming in and going out," Patri wrote. "They are always making mistakes, the natural mistakes of beginners. Their work is a constant challenge to the intelligence and patience of the school." Educators had to demonstrate leadership and exercise care in dealing with such a "dynamic factor, one that puts power and soul into the hands of the teacher because it puts power and soul into the people." [2]

Patri put his finger on a dilemma faced by every educator. For most parents, the relationship between the home and the school was personal and transitory, but for all teachers, it was a permanent feature of their professional lives. Their stake in the work of schools was certainly different from and perhaps greater than that of the home. Despite this imbalance, Patri believed that parents and teachers did not have to be adversaries. Cooperation was in their mutual interest, but unlike most parental activists, he thought that educators had to take the initiative for any positive relationship to have life (see figure 2.1).

The Peripheral Parent: Making the Most of Marginality

In the 1920s, there was widespread support in the United States for the idea that parents and teachers should work together. However, Americans were still uncertain about the nature and extent of this cooperation. It remained unclear to what degree parents should join in the education of their children. As the movement to connect home and school became more widespread and better organized, new questions appeared, while old ones took on new meaning or assumed greater urgency. Were the home and school separate, albeit interdependent spheres? Should educators interact with parents more or less systematically? What was the proper role of the parent-teacher association (PTA)? Should it act as the advocate for the establishment or keep its distance, laying claim to its own vision and priorities?

FIGURE 2.1. *A Regulated but Reciprocal Relationship.* Cover illustration, *The American School Board Journal* 70 (May 1925). A mother must help her child's teacher. Reprinted with permission from *The American School Board Journal.* Copyright 1925, National School Board Association. All rights reserved.

Educators and parents approached these questions from different directions. Inspired by a compelling image of themselves as rising professionals, many principals, superintendents, and professors of education came to regard parents as just another element in the school's constituency. Self-confidence gradually turned to arrogance among these instructional leaders, transforming the idea of an equal partnership between the home and the school into the bureaucratic concept of a professionally managed relationship. Like teachers, taxpayers, or even lawmakers, parents had to be co-opted, taught to appreciate the importance of the school and to accept the limits of their own influence and authority. Some laywomen, on the other hand, devoted themselves to the task of organizing parents and teachers nationwide. In the 1920s, they sought to build a network of parent-teacher associations across America, even as they tried to delineate the mission of these organizations and sort out the dimensions of their work at the local, state, and national levels.

When the National Congress of Mothers became the National Congress of Mothers and Parent-Teacher Associations in 1908, the movement to link the home and the school became more expansive and explicit. While it had always advocated parent-teacher cooperation, the National Congress of Mothers had also sought to promote "the kindergarten movement; . . . legislation for neglected and dependent children, and the education of young people for parenthood." The renamed organization hardly abandoned such general policy objectives, but it now symbolized the idea that parents and teachers belonged together as coworkers in a quest for both student learning and educational reform. In 1924, the organization modified its name once again, becoming simply the National Congress of Parents and Teachers (NCPT). "Many powerful agencies are working for the schools," said the president of the NCPT, Margaretta Willis Reeve, and her colleague Ellen C. Lombard, "but the parent-teacher association alone operates in and through them and enlists the active interest of all parents" and all those who are "concerned for the well-being of the community which the boys and girls will soon control."[3]

The leaders of the NCPT wanted to build a national system of home and school associations, grounded at the local level but tied together by lines of loyalty, authority, and responsibility nationwide. By the mid-1920s, there were strong state PTAs in every region of the country—New York, New Jersey, and Pennsylvania having led the way, followed closely by Illinois, Iowa, and California. Only Nevada remained without a state affiliate in 1924, and total membership exceeded 651,000.[4] But the movement was far from lockstep. Many local parent-teacher organizations insisted on being independent. The Philadelphia League of Home and School Associations withdrew from the Pennsylvania Congress of Mothers in 1909. "The League has grown too large, its interests too manifold, to do other than stand on its own feet," said its officers in their annual report. In states like Maine, South Carolina, and Virginia, school improvement associations that could trace their origins to the nineteenth century refused to join the NCPT.[5]

Home and school associations were not all the same. In the 1920s, they served parents and teachers at all educational levels from preschool to high school. Mothers' and fathers' clubs were still common as well, but the linchpin of the PTA movement was the elementary school. After all, many children left their mothers for the first time when they entered first grade. At this point, said one champion of PTAs, "the home and the school must cooperate to a very large extent if the child is to be adequately educated."[6] But even at the elementary level, most parent-teacher associations did not command a large or loyal following. A study of such organizations, conducted in 1925, revealed that fewer than 50 people belonged to a home and school association in towns of less than 2,500; in larger communities, the median membership was 86. In addition, most PTAs were incipient organizations. Their median age in rural America was 3.7 years; in cities, it was less than 6.[7] Such numbers might be explained by the relative youth of the parent-teacher movement in general. More likely, they reflect the white, middle-class bias of the parent-teacher movement and its loss of cachet after an initial burst of enthusiasm and approval. The turn away from reform after World War I may have been a factor as well. Whatever the reason, PTAs were commonplace but far from universal in the 1920s, and many did not have a firm grip on life. They came and went with remarkable regularity.

That parents graduated from school along with their children certainly contributed to the impermanence of many PTAs. Mothers often outnumbered teachers in these organizations by at least eight to one, and they were usually more interested in their children's future than educational policy.[8] Because most of their members and officers moved on, PTAs also suffered from a lack of focus and continuity. It was not always clear what they wanted or were meant to be. In 1923, the National Congress of Mothers and Parent-Teacher Associations adopted a five-point platform to define its own agenda and that of its member organizations. PTAs, it said, should educate their members in "the duties and privileges of the organization"; disseminate the principle that parenthood is a year-round job; lighten the load on the schools by restoring to the home some of the duties of child rearing; promote public education; and contribute to the practice of good citizenship.[9] Just what these goals meant on the ground was open to interpretation. By the 1920s, the family in America was anything but a generic institution, and at the grassroots level, parents and teachers often had their own ideas about what to make of their local home and school association.

When educators commented on the work of PTAs, they often complained that such organizations performed three functions, two of which met with their disapproval. Most PTAs were a forum for fellowship and entertainment, "a peg or handle on which to hang a lot of social activities." Some tried to be a second board of education. They sought "to dominate the school and its policies, instead of leaving them to the school officials." Finally, PTAs were community service organizations, committed to the idea that the home and the school were distinct but reciprocal institutions. "The ideal Parent-Teacher Association has as its ultimate goal the bringing about of a closer understanding between the home and the school," said James Newell Emery, the principal of the Potter School in Pawtucket, Rhode Island.[10] Parents found themselves attracted to all three activities, but setting priorities was no easy task. It meant making difficult choices that could lead to conflict among neighbors and friends. In the generation after 1920, a consensus about objectives remained elusive, as PTAs undertook several different and sometimes incongruous functions, including member entertainment, parent and teacher education, school and community service, political activity, and organizational maintenance.

Sometimes educators and school board members tried to discourage PTAs from becoming political by pointing them toward activities that might well be described as recreational. When home and school associations came into existence, those in authority often advised them to combine something useful like fund-raising with the pleasure of getting to know one another. According to Mrs. B. F. Longworthy, a vice president of the NCPT in 1932, educators were "afraid of the onslaught of interested parents, mostly mothers, and cast about to find activities that should keep them busy and out of the mischief of trying to run the schools." Some parents were just as eager to avoid conflict or embarrassment, and they restricted themselves. In 1925, a large sample of PTAs characterized the majority of their events as entertainment.[11] In both public and private schools, such ritual occasions as public assemblies, athletic contests, and graduation ceremonies afforded mothers and fathers many opportunities to socialize. In one suburban school system, the social committee of the PTA was "responsible for 'all-school' parties" that not only explained the school to its patrons but also enabled "parents to know teachers, teachers to know parents, and parents to know each other."[12]

While meeting your neighbors or your child's teacher might have been a good reason to join the PTA, such organizations usually looked for other ways to justify their existence. One popular rationale was parent education. In the 1920s, it was widely believed that Americans did not know how to bring up their children. This problem was not confined to black, immigrant, and working-class homes. Led by Lawrence Frank of the Laura Spelman Rockefeller Memorial Foundation, educators, social workers, psychologists, and social scientists devoted themselves to discovering the scientific principles of child rearing and teaching them to parents. Work in this field had already begun at places like the Iowa Child Welfare Research Station and the Merrill-Palmer School for Motherhood and Homemaking in Detroit. Frank persuaded Teachers College of Columbia University to house the Institute for Child Welfare Research and served as a catalyst for the founding of *Parents' Magazine,* which debuted in October 1926.[13]

Parent education united the educational establishment with parent activists around a common cause. Under the leadership of Margaretta Reeve, the NCPT actively promoted it. Established in 1929, its Department of Parent Education included a Home Education Committee, which developed and distributed materials for reading courses and study groups. Such training programs were supposed to transform parents, sparking their "interest in the school and the conditions there which each child must be equipped to meet." It was the job of the NCPT, said Mrs. Reeve, to convince Americans that parents should be "as well trained for the all-important task of child-rearing as are the teachers" for the demands of classroom instruction.[14] They could both contribute to children's learning, but what Mrs. Reeve and her colleagues did not realize or refused to acknowledge was that such thinking encouraged educators to believe that parents did not deserve to be involved in school policy-making.

In the 1920s, parent education found its way into many public and private schools. Cleveland and Des Moines sponsored it, as did the exclusive Tower Hill School in Wilmington, Delaware. The National Society for the Study of Education (NSSE) devoted its entire yearbook to the topic in 1929. As individuals, parents could not be relied on to educate themselves, the NSSE said. The school was the natural setting for such training. It already had most parents' attention; they naturally turned to it "for guidance in regard to problems relating to their children."[15] Why not make the most of this situation?

Both educators and activists believed that the PTA was the ideal host for parent education. "It is a great School for Parents—and for Teachers," said Margaretta Reeve, capable of creating a "single standard in home, school and community." It might even be a valuable weapon in America's struggle against the cultural deterioration that could result from too much ethnic heterogeneity. In the high school, the PTA could be a source of useful information about social life and the curriculum. At lower levels, it conveyed to mothers and fathers a better understanding of educational methods or the importance of proper habit formation. The parents of preschool children were not to be overlooked; they had to take responsibility for introducing their children to such values as "truthfulness, cleanliness, [and] respect for the rights of others."[16] It was up to the PTA to teach them how to give their children lessons in morality.

A responsible PTA made certain that parents and teachers knew their respective roles. At the North Shore Country Day School in Winnetka, Illinois, the chief function of the home and school association was "to educate the parents to a better understanding of their position in the scheme of education in their children's lives." The NCPT's Margaretta Reeve believed that mothers and fathers were indispensable but often ignorant or misinformed; they could be insensitive to the work of the teacher or blind to their children's flaws. They needed to learn about the school's aims and the principle behind each of the its rules and regulations. Teachers, on the other hand, could not be effective unless they understood the educational ideals of the home and the facts about each child's environment and heredity. It was up to the PTA to be the forum for the exchange of such information, building a community of understanding and a harmony of expectations between the home and the school.[17]

In the 1920s, educators and even leaders in the parent-teacher movement remained hesitant about the degree to which the home and the school could be equal partners. It was parent education, not teacher education, after all, that was sorely lacking. However, both educators and parent activists did not hesitate to say that the home should be an active and aggressive advocate for the public school. Led by a new generation of university-trained administrators, researchers, and instructional experts, public education was expanding rapidly in size and scope after World War I. Senior high schools began to attract more and more enrollment. The junior high school, ability grouping, special education, and mental testing debuted or proliferated.[18] Parents' votes could mean the difference between success or failure for such reforms. They could make a majority in favor of the requisite local taxation or persuade state legislators to enact a bill or authorize a vital appropriation. But could they be relied on to consistently back the schools? It was the job of the PTA to marshal parental support. "The primary reason for such an association," said *The American School Board Journal* in 1919, is "to create intelligent school sentiment and to give that sentiment organized form."[19]

As advocates for public education, parents found themselves in an alliance with the educational establishment that called for considerable diplomacy. While expected to make their views known, they had to avoid challenging or upstaging school authorities. Parents should "begin work from the outside," said Angelo Patri in 1925, and gradually make their way in. Discussion of such esoteric topics as the curriculum should not serve to introduce strangers. "Practice on the building . . . and the equipment first," Patri recommended, and whether or not it was because of him, this advice took form in the behavior of many home and school associations. Responding to a survey conducted in 1932, more than 150 PTAs in rural Pennsylvania mainly reported purchasing supplies and fixtures for their school library, playground, and music department. Local PTAs in California concentrated on improving buildings and grounds.[20] In the 1920s, the Delaware Congress of Parents and Teachers focused public attention on the state's pressing need for new schoolhouses. Following the Delaware example, the NCPT conducted an organizing campaign in North Dakota, hoping more resources soon would flow toward its public schools.[21]

It was an open question whether organizations dominated by women could be relied on to achieve political goals. After all, school boards and administrative offices were still largely the province of men. There were more than a few who strongly believed that for just this reason PTAs needed male volunteers; fathers had to be recruited to lobby for public education. In Denver, they joined the fray when hard times threatened the city's schools. Responding to an attack by "selfish interests," they organized themselves into councils that generated sentiment in favor of the schools and the good work they were doing.[22] However, Denver's fathers were exceptional because men were often made to feel unwelcome in parent-teacher associations. In 1933, the United Parents Associations (UPA) of New York conducted a survey that revealed the city's women to be at best ambivalent about the place of men in PTAs. Some said frankly that men did not belong, while others "thought fathers should be satisfied to perform those particular tasks which seem most fitting for men." But troubled times required new thinking, and the UPA urged PTAs to focus on issues like vocational guidance to inspire "a sense of mutuality" between men and women.[23]

Gender was not an impediment when parent-teacher associations considered whether or not to address social issues. With or without male members, most state and local PTAs joined with educators, social workers, and other helping professionals to improve children's health and welfare. Their work assumed a supporting role for government within the larger realm of female voluntarism. Begun by the NCPT in 1925, the "summer round-up" of schoolchildren to identify and correct such common problems as swollen adenoids and poor vision soon became a popular program at the grassroots level.[24] State, regional, and local organizations endorsed child labor legislation in Alabama; supported juvenile court reform in Iowa and California; sponsored dental clinics and vaccination programs in New York, New Jersey, and Washington; and fought for mothers' pensions and against immoral films and literature in a host of states. In Iowa, Florida, Missouri, Oklahoma, and Texas, PTAs distributed food and clothing to children made destitute by the Depression. It was even said that rural PTAs could counteract the exodus of the young from the countryside. By bringing children together with responsible adults at school, they could bind the young to their home surroundings, causing them "to question the city's call to novel pleasures and companionships."[25]

To be sure, some parents, educators, and reformers questioned the wisdom of PTAs involving themselves in school and community service or child welfare reform. Trouble was just around the corner if they became a forum for local disputes or an instrument of personal ambition. PTAs also had to guard against spreading themselves too thin. A study of the activities of home and school associations in the 1930s revealed that the presidents of 100 local PTAs ranked parent education far ahead of community service as an important function of their organizations. But for women like Margaretta Reeve, the relationship between the home and the school had profound implications for reform in America. They thought of themselves as their neighbors' conscience. Working together as mothers and teachers, middle-class women could be a force for enlightened public opinion.[26]

Home and school associations reached no consensus in their struggle for self-definition in the 1920s. Fellowship, enlightenment, advocacy, and community service all claimed a prominent place on their agenda. Although such functions were not necessarily complementary, each drew on a facet of the ideology of domesticity. PTAs gave women the opportunity to be both leaders and followers in defense of middle-class values and Protestant Americanism. The conflict between the home and the school that attracted attention as early as the 1840s had not disappeared. Writing nearly a century later, sociologist Willard Waller concluded that this conflict was inevitable. "Parents and teachers are natural enemies," he intoned, "predestined each for the discomfiture of the other." They came at the child from opposite poles, the former representing the interests of the school and the latter the family and community. Pupils might actually benefit from the contrast, Waller said.[27] However, many educators and parent activists rejected this assessment. In the 1920s, they aired opinions, discussed options, and sometimes formed alliances in pursuit of a common goal. They shared a vision of the home and the school as distinct but reciprocal institutions. But they also struggled with some basic and persistent questions. Should mothers and fathers speak in their own voice or only in harmony with the professionals? Should educators treat parents as equals, giving them the respect and power to which a partner is entitled, or only as subordinates, carefully managing all aspects of their relationship? As prosperity turned to depression, this dilemma became more, not less, important. The responses of educators and parents were not always conciliatory or predictable.

From Mutuality to Manipulation: Home and School between the Wars

In 1928, Carleton Washburne told the readers of *Child Study* magazine something they already knew. Principals and teachers could be aloof, holding parents at arm's length. Parents, on the other hand, could be opinionated, insisting that educators implement their recommendations. Having taught at the San Francisco Normal School before becoming school superintendent in Winnetka, Illinois, Washburne surely must have known people who behaved this way. The parental stereotype appealed especially to principals and superintendents because it simplified matters. Those who joined home and school associations could be dismissed as politicians or social climbers. My experience with PTAs, said one school administrator in 1935, has "convinced me that more often than not a few of the more aggressive parents will take charge of the organization." Treating it like an end in itself, they turned the PTA into a political fiefdom. Educators had to shed such biased expectations, Washburne thought. Schools needed both the confidence and the criticism of parents, and neither could be had unless the professionals respected the parents' right to make requests and express opinions.[28]

Washburne was not alone in believing that parents should speak with an independent voice. The idea received considerable play in the years after World War I because it called attention to an important point of ambiguity. If the home and the school were distinct but reciprocal institutions, just what did that mean? Some thought that parents deserved the teacher's ear because they were masters of a significant though separate sphere; they controlled the home environment whose relevance to the school's work was undeniable, if indirect. But parents were also every child's first teachers. Learning began at home, entitling mothers and fathers to the school's attention and respect. Clearly, teachers had to take them into account, but was it because they performed a distinct, albeit complementary function or because parents' and teachers' work was largely the same? Were parents specialists in a related field or direct competitors?

The final report of the White House Conference on Child Health and Protection maintained that the home and the school were separate institutions in an interdependent but differentiated system of education. Published in 1932, the report stressed the importance of the home as a source of strength and character. Parents who loved and respected their children taught them discipline and self-reliance; they built a solid foundation for emotional health.[29] Many mothers and fathers felt the same way. "The objective of the home is to care for and develop the emotional life of the child," researchers reported one mother as saying; "the objective of the school," on the other hand, "is to promote education, that is, . . . intellectual life and scholarship." Many educators, social workers, and child-rearing experts did not accept this division of labor. They took the position that there was a close relationship between the cognitive and affective domains. Of course, the professionals were not all of one mind; some authorities thought that schools should focus on their accustomed tasks because by the time most children entered first grade, the psychological die had been cast. "It seems safe to say," wrote Gerald Pearson of the Philadelphia Child Guidance Clinic, "that the personality and behavior of an individual are molded during his preschool years by the [emotional] interplay . . . between his parents and himself."[30] However, in the 1930s, many schools in the United States assumed responsibility for the promotion of good mental hygiene.

Parents could not hide from such internecine disagreements. They were forced to consider whether they should accept advice from the school on the affective and ethical aspects of child rearing. When it came to values, the NCPT believed that the family's sovereignty was supreme as long as ethnic, racial, and social class differences did not complicate matters. Margaretta Reeve cautioned teachers against relieving mothers and fathers of their obligation to provide moral and religious training. "You must throw back on the parents the duties which belong to them," she said, compelling them "to become what they were of old: the molders of the characters of their children." The functional difference between families and schools also impressed Helen Bott. "I believe that a much finer sense of justice and social obligation can be developed in an enlightened family group," she told the readers of *Parents' Magazine* in 1933, "than in any institution which rests on a basis of strict individual accounting."[31]

When it came to academic matters, teachers expected parents to respect their professional authority. The "bugbear" called homework revealed just how distinct some educators thought the cognitive work of the school should be. According to Angelo Patri, teachers should not assign homework to children under ten years of age. Boys and girls needed time for play and relaxation as well as work. For older pupils, Patri said, homework should do no more than "tie up the loose ends of the child's knowledge," giving him or her "the feeling of a finished, well-rounded day."[32] In the 1920s, many educators condemned homework, arguing that it threatened children's mental and emotional health without contributing much to their education. Teachers were the experts in conveying the subject matter taught at school, and mothers risked disaster if they tried to intervene. "The success of the school is not dependent on homework but upon the teacher herself," said one experienced educator, writing for *Child Welfare,* the national PTA magazine.[33]

Homework was counterproductive in another way. By making "the home subservient to the school," it alienated both parents and pupils and encouraged early school leaving, said Albert E. Winship, the editor of the *Journal of Education*. Educators in Newark, New Jersey, eliminated it altogether for being unfair to pupils whose homes were without many books and whose parents had little or no education. Most of Winship's peers were not prepared to go quite that far. According to the White House Conference on Child Health and Protection, total dispensation should be granted only to those in elementary school, but even at the high school level, homework had to be assigned in moderation. Such a policy, argued the chair of its Conference Committee on Home and School, would permit the very young to take advantage of the "real educational opportunities in the home," those arising from informal contact with adults. Adolescents should not have too much homework because they needed time to themselves.[34]

In the nineteenth century, teachers assigned homework to instill discipline in students and overcome parental indifference to the school. Educators thought of it as serving another purpose by the 1920s. The disintegration of family and community that seemed to be epidemic made it perhaps the only link between generations. But educators also said that homework was an external presence in the home.[35] Lobbying for exclusive control over academics, they advised parents to treat it like work, isolated in time and space. Approached in this way, it would be more likely to help them teach discipline and self-control. "A child's job is his school life," said Fred Arthur Nims, the school superintendent in Haddonfield, New Jersey, "and nothing should be allowed to distract from that." Lessons done at home were the equivalent of work adults brought home from the office, and parents should provide a sanctuary for their students "away from all distractions."[36] By the same token, teachers and children should not expect parents to assist with homework; "they have had their school days," said the president of the Montana State Normal School, and "do not wish to spend too many evenings teaching lessons to their children." Such sentiments, no doubt, often prevailed at home. "I am not prepared to teach arithmetic, grammar, reading, and spelling," one father complained; "those are the things my boy brings home as homework." The PTA could help parents understand their role. It could teach them not to confuse their children by questioning the school's methods. It could help them realize that homework and home life were not the same.[37]

In 1936, the readers of *Parents' Magazine* expressed their opinions about homework. While some favored it, most were opposed. It burdened them and their children unnecessarily, detracting too much from the simple pleasures of the family. The home should be off-limits to the outside world, including the school. As one man from Wisconsin put it, "Let the home, church, and just living have some leeway during these impressionable years."[38] Americans had grown accustomed to the fragmentation of their lives. The quality of life at home and the freedom of families from outside interference depended on the maintenance of substantial separation. Parents and teachers had much in common, but they also presided over different domains.

Their views about homework notwithstanding, most Americans were unwilling to hand the school an academic monopoly. The idea that parents had a cognitive contribution to make derived from the venerable belief that the family was every child's first and primary educator. "The home influence is the greatest of all," said *The Massachusetts Teacher* in 1850, "and, if this be defective, no other can repair the injury."[39] The family—especially the middle-class family—had lost its intellectual edge by the beginning of the twentieth century, but even the most dedicated educators still had to admit that they could never replace the home. So much "unconscious teaching" goes on there, said Martha Mason, the editor of *Child Welfare Magazine,* that a woman "cannot be a good mother unless she is a good teacher." The headmaster of an elite boarding school acknowledged the significance of the family. Among those institutions that educate the child, said Alfred E. Stearns of the Phillips Andover Academy, "none plays a more important part than does the home."[40]

But by the 1920s, it was widely recognized that the family was no longer authoritative in education or child rearing. Experts routinely questioned the behavior of parents, challenging their judgment and wisdom. Social agencies often displaced them in the lives of children. Paradoxically, the family's loss also may have been its gain. As the home has become less autonomous, wrote Benjamin and Sidonie Gruenberg, themselves well known for their views on child rearing, it has become more important than ever in the child's life. It was an integrating force, putting everything else in perspective. It, and it alone, could be "a continuous guiding influence," a constant source of affection, protection, and counsel. The leadership of the NCPT could hardly disagree. "The home as a molder of personality, as a controller of the social destiny of children, is still the leading educational institution for both parents and children," wrote Ada Hart Arlitt, the chair of its Committee on Parent Education. Professionals outside the home conceded that parents remained indispensable. No social agency can truly stand in loco parentis, said George Hastings of the White House Conference on Child Health and Protection. M. E. Moore, the school superintendent in Beaumont, Texas, put it bluntly: "Nothing can be invented," he said in 1923, "to take the place of the home in the education of the child."[41]

Before parents could make the most of their influence, they needed to become aware of its significance. They had to realize just how important they could be. Some educators believed that mothers and fathers would never learn to speak for themselves; they would always be inhibited by the fear of official resistance or hostility. Others complained that the PTA was a self-indulgent organization. Dominated by a handful of power-hungry parents, it usually became an end in itself. Parents turned this argument around, arguing that by working together they learned to believe in themselves. They realized just how much the relationship between parents and teachers was characterized by interdependence and reciprocity. The PTA is "neutral ground," said Margaretta Reeve, on which parents and teachers meet as equals "to discuss their common interest, the child, who is also the pupil." Educators, even those predisposed to agree, remained unconvinced. Without "the constant enthusiasm and encouragement" of the principal or headmaster, said Isabel Damman of the North Shore Country Day School, no parents' association such as ours would exist.[42]

It is worth asking whether educators really wanted free-thinking parents. They would be a constant problem that might force the school to adjust to the home rather than the other way around. Not unlike their predecessors, many school administrators in the 1920s took a proactive approach. Unlike most teachers and school directors, principals and superintendents believed that they should manage parents, using their esoteric knowledge and administrative experience to bring the home and the school into proper alignment. Working with parents and the PTA was not for the uninitiated; it required professional training in the science and art of public relations.

A Question of Trust

Between 1920 and 1940, there was a crisis of confidence in the United States. Change was ubiquitous. At first, Americans faced a world transformed by war; no longer could they assume that events in Europe and Asia would spare them. At home, the nation coped with Prohibition, women's suffrage, and rapid economic growth. The automobile was rearranging the utilization of space, altering the pattern of urban and suburban life. The Depression brought a different kind of uncertainty, as unemployment disrupted millions of lives. Capitalism itself seemed to be in jeopardy, and there were no simple solutions in sight. It was not even clear where to look for help.

Families and schools felt the stress associated with such change. In whom should Americans invest their trust? Were schools deserving of the power they exercised? Could parents be expected to live up to their responsibilities? These questions were met with no shortage of opinion. Educators, social workers, and psychologists wrote at length about families and schools. More often than not, they told parents and teachers what they wanted to hear. Trust yourself, the experts said, because your judgment or instincts are right. But compared to the family, the school inspired greater confidence among those trained to dispense advice. More and more, pundits proclaimed, educators must take command. They should persuade families to have faith in schools.

Parents struggling to retain some control over their children's schooling could turn to the pages of *Parents' Magazine* for help. Mothers and fathers could make a difference, its contributors often said, by making certain to find the right school for their child, if nothing else. They could insist that meetings with teachers occur not just on school grounds. "To establish the most thorough understanding all around," said Alice Fox Pitts in 1929, "you should invite your children's teachers to visit your home."[43] The president of the Progressive Education Association urged parents to take more responsibility for the quality of their children's schools. "The modern mother," said Stanwood Cobb, "is distinctly interested in the education of her child, and is not willing to delegate this important matter to others." She must acquaint herself with the newest methods in education; she must study her child's school, analyzing it for its strengths and weaknesses. "She must become qualified to choose the right school for her child."[44]

In sharing responsibility for the education of the child, said Benjamin and Sidonie Gruenberg, parents should not be the only ones to make concessions. "They will want to accommodate themselves to the requirements of the school," they wrote. "But it is fair for parents to ask: Must all the adjustments be made by the home, must all the adjustments be made *to* the school?" Cooperation was difficult to establish, let alone maintain, especially in immigrant and working-class neighborhoods. Most schools functioned more or less smoothly without any input from parents, and the resulting alienation was self-sustaining. "Schools don't use parents because they are unreliable," complained Martha Ray Reynolds in 1935, "and parents see no point in being reliable as long as schools don't need them."[45]

Between 1920 and 1940, the burden of adjustment fell more and more heavily on parents. Emboldened by a blizzard of research on child development and learning, educators and experts on family life urged mothers and fathers to cooperate with school authorities. Parents should reinforce the lessons learned in school; they should defer to the greater wisdom of those who had been professionally trained. In a series of articles published by *Parents' Magazine* in 1927 and 1928, Elizabeth Cleveland of the Merrill-Palmer School spoke to mothers and fathers from the vantage point of the classroom. Parents, she said, must not dominate their children. Family life, after all, was not an end in itself but "a means to worthy adjustment to the larger life of the community." Autocratic parents worked at cross-purposes with teachers and society. If parents would only listen to their children, giving them a "voice and choice," then the home experience could be made "to function in co-operation with, and not against [the] school."[46] Julian Butterworth went one step further, putting into words what many educators must have thought. A professor of rural education at Cornell University and the author of a popular book on PTAs, he advised school officials not to get too excited about parental suggestions or complaints. Such input might be "very beneficial," Butterworth said, but parents had to be made to understand that they were in no position to rule on the merit of their own ideas. Making decisions about educational policy and practice was "a technical job that should be left to the teachers and supervisors under the general direction of the board of education."[47]

Angelo Patri lent his considerable weight to the idea that parents should bend with the school. He urged them to make sacrifices, taxing themselves unselfishly and making time to learn about its work and monitor its performance. However, Patri did not expect mothers and fathers to alter the direction of education. Thinking perhaps of the immigrant families who patronized his junior high school in New York City, he advised parents to trust teachers. "Leave the child with the teacher and go away cheerfully," he said to those whose children were just beginning school. She "knows exactly what the first day's work should be" and "how it should be done. . . . Show her that you have faith in her." Teach your child to respect teachers. Above all, do not be afraid to confide in them. "All sorts of mistakes and misunderstandings occur," Patri wrote, "because mothers have not been frank with the teachers."[48]

Patri's belief in teachers never wavered, and he counseled parents to always have confidence in them. Even when the school's policies or methods confounded them, parents should not lose faith in the teacher's judgment or good intentions. Intelligence tests were a case in point. Developed for the United States Army during World War I, they became an integral part of the school's arsenal in the 1920s. Educators treated IQ scores as esoteric information not to be shared with parents, who might misinterpret them. But according to Patri, good teachers measured their pupils' moral as well as mental dimensions. "The teacher's judgment is to be given consideration equal to that of any test," he said. Living with the child, "she knows his purpose and his will power. No test has been devised to measure these." Like most educators, Patri applied a double standard: teachers might be more qualified than parents to evaluate and educate children, but if pupils fell short in school, no one was more to blame than the pupils themselves. Teachers could not be expected to do for them what they were unwilling to do for themselves. Parents had to teach their children to take responsibility for their own education.[49]

Such advice notwithstanding, most parents and taxpayers held schools accountable for the education of children, but assessing them was no easy task. What was the best indicator of their success or failure? In the minds of many laymen, the absence of grade repetition indicated all was well. It was a sign of trouble, on the other hand, when many students were held back, a problem that was sure to damage any school's reputation. By the late 1930s, some urban superintendents favored promoting students regardless of their academic performance. New York, Philadelphia, and Minneapolis implemented a policy of social promotion. Along with increased class size and homogeneous ability grouping, this practice closed the gap between income and expenses. But the school's image as a public trust was also important, and by the late 1920s, many educators concluded that to maintain their standing in the community they had to do more than just increase efficiency. They had to make a systematic and comprehensive effort to shape public opinion.[50]

As had been the case with scientific management and bureaucratic administration, American business supplied the model for educators to follow. Railroad companies like Illinois Central, Burlington, and Union Pacific were among the first to exploit the power of the press, and in the 1880s, both electric and telephone utilities also began to acknowledge the importance of good public relations. At the Westinghouse Electric Company and American Telephone and Telegraph (AT&T) management decided that the future should not be left to chance. Public acceptance of new products and regulated competition required company intervention, including a well-orchestrated campaign of popular education. Through paid advertisements, ghostwritten articles, press releases, and even films,

Westinghouse and AT&T sought to spread their message.[51] Not overlooking future customers, the telephone company distributed movies to schools, while the National Electric Light Association (NELA) made a concerted effort to influence curriculum. It published books for use in schools and tried to affect the content of textbooks written for the mass market. By 1921, more than eight hundred high schools in Illinois were receiving pamphlets from the NELA.[52]

The gains to be made from such efforts impressed more than a few managers and decision makers in American education. College presidents like Charles R. Van Hise at the University of Wisconsin and William Rainey Harper at the University of Chicago saw a parallel between their work and that done by public utilities because the state empowered universities to provide the public service that was higher education. Even more to the point, growth required self-promotion; to recruit students and attract donations, colleges and universities had to build their image. Along with Chicago and Wisconsin, such prestigious schools as Harvard, Yale, the University of Pennsylvania, and the University of Michigan devoted resources to public relations. In 1908, Harvard and the Massachusetts Institute of Technology hired the same consultant to massage their reputations, a move that anticipated the founding of the American Association of College News Bureaus by nearly a decade. In the same year that the noted public relations theoretician Edward Bernays published *Crystallizing Public Opinion,* he began a second career in higher education, accepting a teaching position at New York University.[53]

Elementary and secondary educators were also quick to recognize the advantages of systematic image-making. As early as 1920, prominent periodicals like *School and Society* and *The American School Board Journal* published articles touting the benefits of advertising. At Teachers College, students could take a course called Educational Publicity, and prominent members of the educational establishment such as Ellwood P. Cubberley of Stanford University and Arthur B. Moehlman, a professor of educational administration and supervision at the University of Michigan, taught prospective colleagues not to take the school's good name for granted. In addition, they advised those already in the field to develop a comprehensive strategy for public school relations.[54] There were many different ways to shape public opinion, and schools should take advantage of them all. But for men like Cubberley and Moehlman, one stood out from all the rest. Cultivating the relationship between the home and the school was the best way to develop a good reputation. Institutional reciprocity meant concentrating and building on the idea of parents as advocates for schools and schooling.

Arthur Moehlman specialized in the field of public school relations. Published in 1927, his first book on the subject set the standard for its time. Education has become so complex, he wrote, that "the average man is bewildered." Because he will not make the effort to inform himself, educators had to take the initiative. They had to organize a *"factual information service for the purpose of keeping the public informed of its educational program."* [55] Moehlman advised superintendents to leverage their social contacts. Teachers as well as administrators should call on churches, fraternal orders, and businessmen's clubs. They should make certain that the local newspaper was their ally, disseminating information about the school and creating a favorable impression. The voice of the press could be amplified—or, if need be, muffled—by such in-house publications as newsletters, annual reports, and the student newspaper. The school plant made an important contribution to good public relations. Beautiful school buildings and well-manicured grounds promoted civic pride and inspired confidence in the school.[56]

According to Moehlman, regular contact with parents was the most important element of any school's public relations campaign. Mothers and fathers, after all, had a vested interest that could be made into persuasive advertising. "The schools will progress," he said, "as the parents understand thoroughly their work, and insist upon the best of modern practice for their offspring." Communication with the home was the place to begin, and it had to proceed on many fronts. School officials could address parents' groups like the PTA; plays, concerts, exhibitions, and athletic contests were sure to attract parental attention. The California Congress of Parents and Teachers swiftly accepted the new mantra to good public relations. After studying educational trends for a decade, its Education Committee stated that its new purpose was to interpret the schools to the public and "create a strong body of support for education." But not all parent organizations were so cooperative, and educators always had to keep the nature of their audience clearly in mind. "Varying degrees of intelligence and comprehension," Moehlman said, made the effect of reports written for the home unpredictable at best. Open to misreading and misunderstanding, they might do more harm than good.[57]

In the 1930s, public relations in education became more important than ever. Straining budgets at every level of government, the Depression forced educators to rethink the way in which they laid claim to public resources. The president of the National Education Association (NEA) urged parents to insist on adequate funding for public education. "Parents," he said, "your defense of schools is the only hope in this period of taking stock and reconstruction."[58] School boards and superintendents

had to lead the way, polishing the public school's image even more carefully than before. Through the efforts of the Joint Commission on the
Emergency in Education, appointed by the NEA in 1932, and the Educational Policies Commission, which appeared three years later, educators
trumpeted the idea that the public school was the cornerstone of local government and the foundation of American democracy.[59] But to survive the
crisis without massive cuts, schools could neither rest on such ideological
laurels nor rely on the existing reservoir of good will toward education
that was based on experience and tradition. As Arthur Moehlman observed in 1938, educators had to adopt a more aggressive and functional
strategy of "social interpretation." They had "to maintain and improve
these attitudes by . . . educating the adult population to current institutional conditions and needs." They also had to stress "the importance of
good institutional practice and efficiency" and capitalize on "the fundamental value of confidence growing out of personal contacts." [60] In other
words, teachers and principals had to take advantage of every opportunity
to sell themselves and their work to the American people, enlisting parents to the cause by drawing on their intrinsic need to believe in the high
quality of their children's schooling. The reciprocal relationship between
the home and the school had to be exploited in hard times.

   Although it was by no means clear how to go about educational image-
making, most educators believed that knowledge was essential to good
public relations. Somehow parents and taxpayers had to learn more about
teachers and schools. In the 1930s, many school directors and superintendents concluded that they were not making the most of those occasions
when outsiders came to school of their own volition. Athletic events certainly fell into this category, but their outcome could never be guaranteed,
and educators decided that they were overlooking one of the most important opportunities for conveying accurate and up-to-date information
about the status and prospects of public education. Paralyzed by tradition,
they had failed to recognize the potential for better public relations represented by every graduate's last day in school. Commencement should be
not a meaningless exercise in academic formalism but an occasion for parent and community education.

   As early as 1927, Arthur Moehlman urged school executives to make
the most of the high school commencement. If they "would properly organize this event in the interests of the parents," he said, "much good
might be accomplished." It was a perfect opportunity to explain the school
program and strengthen the home's commitment to the school. The NEA
touted what it called "vitalized commencements," suggesting that edu-

cators use graduation day to teach the public about the Seven Cardinal Principles of Secondary Education. It recommended, for example, that commencements in 1930 focus on worthy home membership. "Let the activities of the commencement season interpret to the patrons the specific contributions of the school to the homes of the community, such as the teaching of better habits, wiser use of leisure time, [or] increased vocational effectiveness."[61]

For graduating seniors, such programs could not possibly improve their secondary education. Their high school days were over, but they could make a lasting contribution to the future of their alma mater by participating as speakers, not just listeners, at commencement. "The commencement program offers an unexcelled opportunity for the right kind of school publicity," said Robert Shaw, the deputy superintendent of public instruction in Pennsylvania. It gives the superintendent the chance to prove that the taxpayers' money has been wisely spent and call attention to the educational needs of the community. "The schools of the nation are passing through a trying and critical period," said the NEA's assistant director of publications, Lyle W. Ashby. They need to take advantage of "every opportunity to interpret their work to the public. The high school graduation is undeniably an opportunity for effective interpretation. . . . Why not use it as an instrument for informing the public about the schools —their needs, aims, and achievements?"[62]

In the 1930s, school authorities made the vitalized commencement commonplace. Families and friends of graduating seniors became a captive audience for educational salesmanship. Seated in high school stadiums, gymnasiums, or auditoriums to honor the graduates, they witnessed demonstrations of the curriculum, pageants about the history of education, and even discussions of school tax rates and building programs. In Amelia, Virginia, the 1934 high school commencement asked those assembled to reflect on the current status of education in their community. One student pointed out that tax rates on real property in the state were among the lowest in the nation, while another "discussed the retrenchment program carried on in the school system and made clear that the county board of education . . . had cut terms and reduced salaries so far as could be done."[63]

Vitalized commencements often adopted historical motifs. Both the importance of tradition and the prevalence of progress were themes that led graduation ceremonies to feature venerable alumni, commemorate school foundings, or examine the evolution of public education over time. Between 1933 and 1937, the senior high school in Lansdale, Pennsylvania,

devoted its commencements to such topics as the opening of the first public high school in the state, the virtues of the current curriculum, and the
fiftieth anniversary of the town's first high school graduation. In Madison,
Nebraska, the class of 1934 marched into the high school auditorium between a formation of alumni representing every class that had ever graduated from the school. Selected seniors then delivered speeches on the
value of a modern high school education. Exercises like these were re-
peated countless times across the United States during the Depression.[64]

Cultivating the school's reputation at home and in the community required more than just the careful orchestration of graduation day. School
boards and superintendents had to redouble their efforts to enlist the
PTA in their image-making campaign. "The parent-teacher association,"
Arthur Moehlman said, is "the best organized single agency around which
a public relations program may be developed."[65] Many teacher educators
and school administrators agreed. No other organization could explain
public education as effectively, promoting "cooperation and mutual understanding between the schools and the community." According to the
editor of *Child Welfare Magazine,* superintendents in fifty-six cities, including Philadelphia, Boston, New York, and Chicago, endorsed the PTA
as the best means of representing their schools to clients and constituents. After all, a well-run PTA itself reflected credit on any educational
system. More to the point, it could convince the community to accept curricular reform, maintain the system's operating budget, or finance school
plant expansion. Demonstrations of schoolwork became standard fare at
PTA meetings during the Depression, forming the basis for nearly three-
quarters of all home and school association programs in Philadelphia by
the mid-1930s. Instead of raising money to buy books or basketballs, Ellwood Cubberley said, the PTA should direct its efforts "toward the formation of public opinion in favor of higher taxes that the school may be
provided with all the needed equipment." The superintendent who approached his community about a bond issue without the help of the PTA
was imprudent indeed.[66]

Incorporating the PTA into a public relations program required a special kind of educational leadership. School authorities had to make their
influence felt without appearing to be interfering. Parent councils offered
an alternative to the PTA that seemed better suited to the special needs of
the 1930s. Attached to each grade or homeroom, councils improved communication, bringing "more intimate contact and knowledge" than was
possible in "the larger, more generalized parent-teacher association."
They also gave educators the advantage of more "complete control which
is not so easily possible in the parent-teacher organization." But, said

Moehlman, "this condition is its own greatest weakness since the desirability of complete institutional control of any parental cooperating group is questionable."[67] Dependence dampened parents' enthusiasm and ultimately made their endorsement politically less valuable by casting into doubt the depth of their conviction.

Published in 1939, *Home-School-Community Relations* by William Yeager further examined this dilemma. Simply extolling the schools to the public was no longer adequate, Yeager said. School boards and superintendents had to choose between interpreting them in a way that invited passive parental participation and actively involving the home and community through "mutual interaction."[68] Some educators preferred PTAs to classroom councils because they nurtured feelings of parental autonomy without sacrificing too much administrative control. A principal could join it, Cubberley said, but "remain somewhat in the background." As an ex officio member of its executive committee, she could "help direct the organization without seeming to do so or being too prominent in the meetings."[69] Maintaining the illusion of parental independence was no easy task. Superintendents had to rely on the subtle influence they exercised by being the primary source of information for PTAs. Serving as program coordinator, a chief school officer could help shape PTA policy, while avoiding the limelight. One superintendent had a standing place on the agenda of all eight home and school associations in his district, carefully preparing presentations for every meeting because he believed that parental support depended on such regular contact. But educators had to be careful not to insult the intelligence of laymen. Even the most cooperative parents would rebel if "undiluted propaganda [was] thrown at them without thought or study." Educators should always credit community leaders, Moehlman further advised, for "personal publicity" could quickly turn from good to bad and should never outrank leadership or integrity.[70]

Of course, the PTA could be an independent voice in the politics of education, and even experts occasionally argued that outspoken parents were an asset to the school and community. They could prevent school officials from falling "under the influence of a few powerful taxpayers," Julian Butterworth said, and be a potent force for constructive change. "Every school system," said the editor of the national PTA magazine, "needs back of it an organized, interested body of citizens, free from the control of any individual or group, free to express progressive opinions and to inspire clear thinking on the part of school officials."[71] Such advice notwithstanding, most mothers and fathers hesitated to question the policies and practices of their children's schools. It was, of course, a question of trust, and during the Depression, fear often undermined trust. But the

school was a symbol of continuity in a world threatened by change, and belief in a reciprocal relationship between the home and the school remained in place, even though many educators became more defensive,
convinced now more than ever that they had to exploit the family's natural
interest in and commitment to schools.

One small corner of American education resisted the temptation to
manipulate the home. Not all progressive schools were parent centered,
but in the 1930s, those teachers and administrators who considered themselves to be at the cutting edge did not give up on the idea, introduced at
the beginning of the twentieth century, that parents and teachers should
be equal partners, engaged in open cooperation. But the relationship between the home and the school was difficult to negotiate even in progressive circles, creating its own special dilemmas.

Parents and Teachers in Progressive Schools

Far from disappearing after World War I, child-centered education maintained a strong hold, especially among affluent parents who patronized
exclusive schools. In the Northeast and Midwest, many independent and
suburban public schools practiced the educational theories and tech-
niques of reformers like Francis Parker, Caroline Pratt, and John Dewey.[72]
Just as these schools wanted to make children more responsible for their
own education, they welcomed parent participation. At the North Shore
Country Day in Winnetka, Illinois, and the Shady Hill School in Cambridge, Massachusetts, parent associations tried to make mothers and
fathers appreciate the importance of their contribution to the educational
scheme.[73] However, parents presented a special problem for progressive
schools. Although most were well educated, they were often unfamiliar
with the newest ideas and methods in elementary and secondary education. Some even had doubts about progressive schools, and it was feared
that they might not reenroll their children if they did not learn to understand and respect what was happening in these schools' classrooms.

Being both mentor and partner created a problem for progressive educators that, while easy to recognize, was not so easy to solve. How could
they shift from one role to the other without breakdowns? Working with
families from all socioeconomic levels, teachers at a public school in Washington, D.C., tried to deal with this dilemma. In the fall of 1932, the W. B.
Powell Elementary School organized study groups for mothers and
fathers who had children in the first grade, hoping that through the "intelligent understanding gained from a first-hand acquaintance with the ideals

and products of a progressive school, the child's highest development would result." But the effort was handicapped from the beginning because the superintendent, Frank W. Ballou, who modernized the district's administrative practices, was never enthusiastic about child-centered instruction.[74] Even parents who chose a progressive school were not always prepared for what they encountered. Discipline was not maintained in the traditional way, and teachers did not appear to stress the mastery of basic skills. "Unfortunately," said one contributor to *Progressive Education* in 1934, "when experimental education broke through the thin assumption that teachers in themselves do the teaching of children, it brought with it a new need for them to retain the attitude of instructors of parents in methods of dealing with children."[75]

Progressive schools needed to educate parents, even as they relied on them for help, thereby testing the limits of reciprocity between home and school. At Shady Hill, for example, the Parents' Council took responsibility for parent education, helping new families adjust to the school's routines, methods, and expectations. Not only did progressive schools welcome parental support; they counted on it as well. Committed parents helped "gain general acceptance for innovations," it was thought. They also learned lessons about democratic living that could be applied in the world at large. Only through the participation of the "parent in the child's activities, of the teacher in home activities, of all in worthwhile social activities," said Ernest G. Osborne of the Child Development Institute at Teachers College, "can we hope to develop an education that matters, that changes people significantly, that can in any way direct social changes."[76]

Enthusiastic reformers like Osborne believed that parents should take "responsibility of a major sort." They should be offered and accept significant assignments at school such as library work, adjunct teaching, or service on finance and admissions committees. Taking collaboration to the extreme, Winifred Bain recommended that teachers confer with parents about the important matter of discipline.[77] If they gave parents access to this part of their professional domain, the home would identify more readily with the school. Artificial barriers would disintegrate, and parents and teachers would cooperate successfully.[78]

In the 1930s, progressive educators stressed the importance of educating the whole child. It was not a new idea, of course; reformers had spoken of it since the beginning of the twentieth century. But during the Depression, when many schools took responsibility for the child's mental hygiene, such language was used to link parents and teachers. "Progressive education today is concerned with all factors that influence the total personality or character of the child," said Lois Hayden Meek of Teachers

College in 1932, "and it can only succeed by bringing together the home and school in a united[,] consistent program for child development."[79] Her colleague, Winifred Bain, went one step further, claiming for progressive schools a special familiarity with the family. The procedure of such schools, she said, "looks very much like that of a well-regulated home where children live through the problems of daily life. . . . Progressive schools work actively with parents and seek by every means to coordinate the two educational agencies—the home and the school."[80]

But even Bain did not believe that parents and teachers were one in the same. While mothers and fathers might enrich their children's education at home, the school could not expect them to be familiar with all its methods or be objective about them. IQ test scores unnerved worldly as well as artless parents. Having had psychological training, teachers knew that not all children were alike. They recognized when pupils was ready to master basic skills or begin the study of major subjects. They should take primary responsibility for arithmetic and reading. Parents could supplement this work "by keeping supplies of good books in the home or by encouraging the habit of using the library." Parents and teachers were anything but natural enemies; between them, there was always room for broad-based collaboration. But the professionals should be in charge in school. In fact, parents should settle for nothing less, even—or perhaps especially—in progressive education.[81]

From Talk to Action

After World War I, the relationship between the home and the school became the subject of increased interest and activity in the United States. As Americans focused on family life and child rearing in the domesticated 1920s, the interaction between parents and professionals in education attracted more and more attention. The parent-teacher organization became more commonplace, even as it struggled to define itself by sorting out its mission. The Depression forced the nation to reexamine the purpose and prospects of schools and reaffirm the significance that Americans attached to the relationship between the home and the school.

What should be the nature of this relationship? Parents were not the equal of teachers even though they were responsible for a separate sphere that taught children much of what they learned. But mothers and fathers played an important role, setting the tone for their child's work in school. After 1920, many educators acknowledged their debt to parents in a self-serving way, treating the home-school relationship as an exercise in public relations. There were social and political factors like race and gender that shaped the way in which parents and teachers interacted, and an important factor in this regard was how parents related to boards of education. Would parents be satisfied to exercise influence with school boards, or did they want to have some authority over educational policymaking? To understand the relationship between the home and the school in the United States between 1900 and 1950, it is necessary to address this question.

CHAPTER THREE

In Search of Influence or Authority?

This letter "P" is, as you see,
The first one in this group of three.
It stands for the Mothers and Fathers, too,
Who try to do what's best for you.

This letter "T" that's next, is mine,
And represents our Teachers fine,
Who, with the Parents everywhere,
Are bound together in Child Welfare.

My letter "A" comes last of all,
But not the least—no not at all.
It stands for the link between Home and School
Where we go to learn the Golden Rule.

So when you see this P.T.A.
Remember what it means today;
That Mother and Father and Teacher, too
Are working together the whole year through.
— Mary Mitchell Reno, *Child Welfare Magazine*[1]

In a small town turned suburb, Emma Middleton made her mark. Born
in 1853, she moved to Haddonfield, New Jersey, as a child and lived
there for all but three of her ninety-three years. Religion, politics, and education were her foundation, providing the satisfaction that other women
found in marriage and children. She taught Bible classes at the First Bap-
tist Church for thirty-seven years. She belonged to the Daughters of the
American Revolution and served on the governing board of the Haddonfield Civic Association. A lifelong Republican, she was the party's
first committeewoman in Camden County. She clerked for New Jersey
Senator Joseph F. Wallworth and after the adoption of the Nineteenth

Amendment became one of the first women from Haddonfield to sit on a grand jury.[2]

The church and the party were not the source of Miss Middleton's livelihood. A career woman, she taught for forty-five years, almost all of which were spent in the elementary schools of Haddonfield. By itself, such longevity is not remarkable. But unlike many of her peers, she remained in education, even though she never abandoned the classroom for school administration. After retiring in 1917, Middleton served for sixteen years on the Haddonfield Board of Education. It was a post for which she was eminently qualified. A respected community servant, she knew the schools well not only as an experienced teacher but as a charter member and officer of the Haddonfield Mothers' and Teachers' Club as well. Initially, those in charge of these organizations stereotyped her, assigning her to work on such activities as parent education or member entertainment.[3] But the benefits of participation outweighed the liabilities. Patient and persistent, Emma Middleton exercised both influence and authority in Haddonfield, and there, or anywhere, few could say that they did so in as many ways as she.

The life of Emma Middleton calls attention to the importance of gender in the politics of American education. Women made their presence felt as mothers, teachers, and reformers. Men shaped the schools as teachers, too, but more often than not as policy makers or in administration. Middleton knew these alternatives, working for both the home and the school during the course of her long life. As a professional and a volunteer, she encountered firsthand the complexities and conflicting demands of being an active woman in the bisexual yet gender-divided world of American education.

Politics, Gender, and Public Education: The Nature and Nurture of Influence

Educators have long held a decided advantage over parents in the politics of American education. In the second half of the nineteenth century, the assiduous and unrelenting bureaucratization of public education gave teachers, principals, and especially superintendents increased control over the mission and management of schools. However, parents always have had a big stake in schools, and at the beginning of the twentieth century, they were eager to be heard. Because technological changes in the workplace helped make child labor and compulsory school laws more effective, even working-class children were staying in school longer than ever, while the rising tide of schooling convinced many middle-class parents to be increasingly committed to excellence at school. Teachers, administrators, and school board members could not ignore them, but parents did not necessarily wield much political clout. Most wanted to exercise influence over school policy and practice without having to become decision makers themselves. They were willing to accept a reciprocal, but distinct role in their relationship with the school. A few wanted to have a more direct and powerful impact. They aspired to elective office with all the authority and accountability that this entailed. But even to make their influence felt, parents could not afford to be passive. They had to organize and cooperate not only with each other but also with school officials. Board members, after all, were still public servants despite the trend toward smaller, more centralized boards of education, and their constituents could sway them.[4]

But to what extent could parents in such organizations affect the policy and practice of schools? Composed mostly of white, Protestant, middle-class women, parent-teacher associations (PTAs) often insisted on increased spending for local schools and the adoption of curricular and administrative innovations. To achieve these objectives, they drew on the moral authority of the Protestant, middle-class home, a strategy that sometimes blinded them to the needs of those unlike themselves. But was the integrity of the Protestant, middle-class home enough to move urban or suburban educational systems managed by professionals and governed by attorneys, physicians, and businessmen? Whether the political relationship between the home and the school was one-sided is a thesis that can be tested by examining the interaction between parent-teacher associations and boards of education. Elected volunteers were more exposed to political pressure than were appointed professionals, but parents were just one interest group among many that demanded satisfaction from boards of education. Framed by expectations imposed by social class, both gender and community context shaped the political relationship between parents and school boards and contributed significantly to its nature and outcome.

The politics of voluntarism forced parents, especially mothers, to ask pointed questions and make painful choices. Should they restrict themselves to subtle pressure tactics such as discrete lobbying or be more partisan, endorsing reforms and campaigning for candidates? Should they even run for office themselves, hoping to acquire real authority? Within parent-teacher organizations, leaders and followers often disagreed about the scope and direction of their work. Held to different expectations, national, state, and local PTAs had to choose between social reform and school improvement as their organizational mission. The National Congress of Parents and Teachers (NCPT) opposed child labor and advocated international understanding, while its affiliates focused on more mundane issues like lunchrooms, libraries, and health clinics in neighborhood schools.[5]

Between 1905 and 1930, political behavior by local parent-teacher associations increasingly became a subject of popular discussion and a source of official concern. As advocates for public education, PTAs might be useful allies, but when they pressured school boards or tampered with the work of principals and teachers, their actions ceased to be perceived as helpful or even appropriate. Addressing the National Education Association's (NEA's) Department of School Administration in 1919, the president of the Milwaukee Board of School Directors, William Pieplow, urged his colleagues to resist all outside interference from "various societies, clubs and associations." The "constant pulling of strings on fully empowered public representatives is a serious impediment to efficient public business," Pieplow said, "whether the pullers are club ladies of either sex or old-fashioned liquor men." Running schools was a technical business beyond the knowledge and understanding of most laypersons. School boards needed moral support from PTAs, which tread on foreign ground when they tried to tell trained practitioners how to do their jobs or board members how to make sound policy decisions.[6]

Such complaints were not lost on the men and women who joined PTAs. According to a survey of NCPT affiliates in the 1920s, less than 3 percent were willing to admit that lobbying the school board or staff was one of their activities. But almost from the beginning, some home and school associations tried to exercise influence by backing selected reforms. In 1896 the Mothers' Club of Cambridge established a vacation school that counted more than two hundred participants by the end of its second year, and the city's school committee soon assumed responsibility for it. In Milwaukee and Kansas City, home and school associations advocated the community use of the school plant.[7] Some adopted the political style of the temperance reformers and suffragists. In New Jersey, Delaware, and Pennsylvania PTAs at every level—state, regional, and local—

sang marching songs to their membership. At a Philadelphia rally in April 1909, four thousand women raised their voices "For Home and School," singing:

> To get the best for all of us each must do his best;
> And give the highest service for the good of all the rest.
> So the Home must give its mothers, and the School its Teachers send,
> With the children ready all the time their loving help to lend.[8]

National leaders acknowledged the importance of such collective consciousness raising. The director of the Publications Bureau of the NCPT claimed that "the associations which sing the best do the ablest work. The movement," said Joy Elmer Morgan in 1930, "has hardly begun to realize the possibilities of singing as a means of maintaining its spiritual vigor."[9]

But PTAs differed in their political tactics. Some adopted a cautious approach, avoiding open conflict with school authorities. Others were more direct, ignoring the expectation that parents and especially mothers should not be confrontational. The choice of strategy depended on many variables. What seemed inappropriate to some in an urban setting found even less favor in the suburbs. Gender and class contributed greatly to the mix; in the city, gender was not necessarily an inhibiting factor, while in Protestant, middle-class suburbs, the ratio of male to female leaders in a home and school association or PTA could change its political demeanor. In both settings, white, Protestant, middle-class parents did not bring immigrants or blacks into the political equation. Consider, for example, the experience of parents in Philadelphia and two of its middle-class suburbs, Abington Township, north of the city in Pennsylvania, and Haddonfield, to the east in New Jersey. Between 1905 and 1935, when most Americans were first learning about PTAs, organized parents tried to change the schools in all three communities, and they proved that both cooperation and confrontation with school officials could lead to reform. Conflict between them was not endemic, but those who decided that influence was no substitute for authority were more inclined to be confrontational, and in each case, gender, mediated by race and class, shaped the political dynamics of their relationship.

The Philadelphia Home and School League never shied away from taking a public stand. Founded in 1907, it quickly fashioned a loose affiliation with a well-established civic organization, the Public Education Association (PEA). The first president of the league, Mary Van Meter Grice, brought about this alliance from her seat on the PEA board. Both independently and together, the two organizations campaigned for school reform. The PEA took special aim at the Philadelphia Board of Education, which it perceived to be composed of corrupt and senile men. Old-fashioned and hidebound, they resisted "an impartial and independent survey of the schools." In 1917, 1919, and 1921, the PEA backed legislation to reduce the size of the board from fifteen to seven and make it elective.[10] Although unsuccessful, this reform was hardly original or idealistic. Enacted in 1905, the Public School Reorganization Act had already halved the size of Philadelphia's central school board, while stripping its ward-based counterparts of considerable power. Elsewhere, urban school reformers chased the same goal. In Detroit and Chicago, they achieved complete success, convincing voters and legislators to trust their public schools to small, consolidated boards in 1916 and 1917, respectively.[11]

The Philadelphia Home and School League was more inclined than either the PEA or the board of education to view the schools from a local perspective. In 1912, its fifty-five member organizations were concentrated in the city's middle-class neighborhoods north and west of the downtown. They focused on such parochial matters as the school building in their vicinity, classroom apparatus, and playgrounds. The league did not make immigrant or black parents feel very welcome: its local affiliates included only two from the Italian and Eastern European district of South Philadelphia. Parents in three of the city's twelve schools for blacks were associated with the league, but these black locals were not the same as the two that had belonged in 1909, suggesting perhaps that African-American parents found membership in the league to be something less than they expected.[12]

In keeping with the priorities of urban educators and middle-class reformers elsewhere, the league joined the PEA in support of such citywide improvements as new school construction, district high schools, and the transformation of public schools into community centers. It encouraged the Philadelphia board to hire home and school visitors and serve penny lunches, a practice for which the school authorities assumed full responsibility in 1915. It helped convince the superintendent that public schools could wield "community influence" by reaching parents through their children, a lesson that had special appeal during the xenophobic days of World War I. Working with the PEA, the league shaped the agenda of the Philadelphia public schools, encouraging the expansion of their mission.[13]

As the leader of the Home and School League, Mary Grice thought of herself as an advocate for all teachers, parents, and children. Eager to be consulted by the superintendent and board of education, she believed the league should be a laboratory for educational reform, experimenting with improvements that might become the basis for institutional change.[14] But Grice was not predisposed to compromise and never one to walk away from a possible confrontation. In 1919, she led the Episcopal Church-woman's Association in an effort to persuade the Finance Committee of City Council to authorize more funds for the abatement of unsanitary living conditions in Philadelphia. Conflict with the board of education arose over the community use of school buildings and the rate of pay for teachers. In January 1919, Grice publicly condemned the board for its failure to open the schools at night during World War I. Taking special aim at board member Simon Gratz, she characterized him and his colleagues as "tight fisted," insisting that "we can retrench on some things but never on education."[15]

As early as 1911, Grice convinced the PEA to endorse a salary hike for the city's elementary school teachers, most of whom were women. Such complaints were hardly one of a kind; suburban parents also challenged school boards to increase teacher compensation. In Abington Township, for example, parents made it clear in 1916 that they disapproved of their frugal school board's salary schedule. It made the Abington district uncompetitive with its neighbors, preventing the township from hiring the best-qualified teachers.[16] Inflation during World War I exacerbated the problem, and in its aftermath, teachers' wages lagged far behind the soaring cost of living. In 1918, Harlan Updegraff, a professor at the University of Pennsylvania, estimated that the cost of such essentials as food, clothing, and utilities had nearly doubled in four years, and he counseled school boards to increase teachers' salaries immediately by 45 percent. The Pennsylvania State Teachers Association put the problem in terms that its members could easily understand. It reckoned that the inflationary effects of the war had caused commodity prices to advance three times more rapidly than teachers' salaries. Of course, some blamed the teachers themselves, citing high turnover and low standards as reasons for their meager compensation. Others blamed reformers for this state of affairs. The high school building program that they favored in Philadelphia drained the budget, burdening taxpayers to such an extent that they could not meet the teachers' demands for increases.[17]

Educators and reformers agreed that something had to be done. In 1915, the governor of Pennsylvania, Martin Brumbaugh, campaigned for better teacher compensation. Addressing a crowd of school directors assembled for the annual meeting of the Pennsylvania State Educational Association, the former superintendent of schools in Philadelphia complimented those among them who had the courage to raise taxes and pay teachers what they deserved. By January 1919, the issue was being discussed widely in Philadelphia. Both the school board and the Civic Club urged the legislature to increase the mill rate in the city to benefit the teachers.[18] The leaders of the Home and School League certainly favored such legislation. The question was not whether the teachers were entitled to a raise but how much it should be. Some like Mary Grice insisted that their pay be doubled. Such an advance seemed outrageous to Simon Gratz, and he began to question the sincerity of the leaders of the league. In fact, the board felt so threatened by the behavior of these men and women that it temporarily locked them out of the public schools. While this tactic probably did not intimidate Mrs. Grice, it distressed her colleagues, who soon adopted a less confrontational posture, diminishing their pressure on the board. As league President S. D. Benoliel explained, many members are teachers and principals who feel that they cannot attend meetings if criticism is directed against "the Board of Education, who are their superiors." Moreover, "the league often meets in schoolhouses and aims to be a part of the school system itself."[19]

Mary Grice had a different idea. She refused to think of herself as an appendage of the board. If anything, she acted like its conscience, reminding it to mend its ways. The Home and School League had lost its nerve, Grice believed, and on the grounds that she could not exercise her right to free speech if she remained on its board, she resigned as a director in March 1919.[20] The remaining leaders of the league took Mrs. Grice's departure in stride. Some may even have been relieved, for Grice believed in testing the existing limits of cooperation between home and school. While many parents were satisfied to buy playground equipment or classroom decorations, she aspired to a position of authority as a full-fledged member of the Philadelphia Board of Education. It was not a post for which she lacked direct experience; living in Riverton, New Jersey, in the 1890s, she used her prominence as a founder of a local woman's club to run for the school board, to which she was elected on her second try. Could parents make a difference at school? Mary Grice believed not only that they could but also that mothers should serve on the body that made policy for public education.[21]

At the beginning of the twentieth century, women in politics attracted considerable attention on both sides of the gender line. Given the importance of the school to the home, suffrage for women in school elections seemed justifiable to some at least, and it was achieved in many states long before the Nineteenth Amendment. The Massachusetts legislature extended this right to women in 1879. New Jersey followed suit in the next decade, but its supreme court soon overturned the provision that allowed women to cast ballots for school directors. By 1891, twenty-eight states had experimented with such legislation. In some cities, women gained the right to vote in school elections. Toledo and Rochester added them to the school suffrage rolls in the 1890s. In Boston and Chicago, women not only voted but also won seats on the board of education.[22] Active in the New England Women's Club, Abigail May, along with three other Protestant women, won a seat on the Boston School Committee even before she could vote, but two years passed before the men on the committee allowed May and five other women, elected by the voters in 1875, to take their rightful places. In the 1880s, nativist women seized control of school politics in the city. Far from uplifting the process of electing school committee members, they reduced it to a contest between Protestants and Catholics. In fact, they engaged in such active and biased campaigning that in 1888 the Catholic clergy tried to defuse the tension by counseling Catholic women not to vote.[23]

In 1915 the Equal Franchise League of Philadelphia endorsed Mary Grice for a place on the city's board of education. To achieve this distinction, she would not have to stand for election. In Philadelphia, the court of common pleas appointed board members. Designed to shelter the public schools from partisanship, this procedure merely exposed them to politics of a different, less transparent kind. The PEA called for school board elections in which women could vote.[24] Grice stood with the reformers on this issue, but in seeking a place on the board, regardless of how it was chosen, she offended the more traditional elements in Philadelphia, including many women. Writing to express her support for the existing board, Mrs. William W. Birdsall reminded Simon Gratz that the woman "who recently so ostentatiously resigned from the Home and School League . . . has had for a long time an ambition to have a place on the school board and through her strident friends made an effort to be appointed and failed." Mrs. Grice's loss, Birdsall thought, was Philadelphia's gain. "I think I know a little about the Public Schools," she said, "and I say one only needs to look at the schools of Denver and Chicago to see what would be the situation here should some of the public women get their way."[25]

In many cities, women's clubs acted as an advocate for such "public women." By 1911, affiliates of the General Federation of Women's Clubs existed in every state, and they often tried to place women on boards of education. PTAs provided a ready supply of candidates, and in New Jersey, Pennsylvania, and Delaware, their members soon began to volunteer for service. In 1915, the mayor of New Brunswick, New Jersey, Austin

Scott, named the organizer of the city's PTA to the school board. That Mrs. Drury W. Cooper was married to Scott's predecessor at city hall certainly helped her candidacy. Nevertheless, she was the first woman to serve on the board in New Brunswick history. Two years later PTA women in rural Middletown, Delaware, decided to nominate one of their own for the school board, only to discover that their campaign got "started too late." Mothers in the Philadelphia suburb of Lower Merion were better organized. Working through the Neighborhood Civic Club, they endorsed Mary Stewart Gibbons for school director after the existing board discharged a popular principal. They carried their fight to the ballot box only after failing to get "any satisfaction out of an investigation of this act." The second woman to run for the board in Lower Merion, Mrs. Gibbons believed in the merit of her qualifications. "There are innumerable things in the work of the board," she explained, "on which mothers are more capable of passing judgment than are the men."[26]

Advocates for women on boards of education relied on several arguments to make their case. Echoing their sisters in the suffrage and peace movements, they maintained that women, especially mothers, brought special qualifications to educational decision-making. Women board members, said Edith Alvord, who was herself a school director in Highland Park, Michigan, can contribute an "intimate understanding" of children. "A woman member can make a mother's appeal to mothers," Alvord added, "and, if she is the right kind of woman, she can be a great help to teachers. She can see their problems as well as the children's from a woman's viewpoint." Even *The American School Board Journal,* a periodical dominated by the male establishment in education, advanced a similar opinion. Editorializing through the words of "a superintendent's wife," the *Journal* noted that school boards benefited from having access to the different talents of both men and women. The former knew more about such technical matters as budgets and taxation, but the latter had a better grasp of "the other half of the problem." Because of their knowledge of the home, they understood whether school expenditures produced "adequate results."[27]

Not every school administrator felt this way. According to William Estabrook Chancellor, the superintendent of schools in Washington, D.C., women made "undesirable board members." Their indifference to business was a big handicap, since it was "the only direct concern of the board," and their presence ruled out "the full discussion of several important topics." Reflecting on his experience with PTAs, another male administrator recalled "many wearisome minutes" when he was forced to sit through a "grave discussion as to what kind of salad should be served at a coming supper, or who should pop the corn, or what color the tickets should be." Such discussions threatened the self-image of male principals and superintendents. Striving to be accepted as scientific managers instead of moral exemplars, they could not take orders gracefully from politically active women.[28]

Women volunteers sensed the anxiety and hostility projected by such professional men. Some expressed fears about assuming the responsibilities of board membership, saying publicly at least that they knew "little" about education. Educational critic and reformer Harold Rugg recommended that superintendents and school boards cultivate and recruit parents. While teaching at the University of Chicago, he advised them to work with women's clubs and PTAs, treating them as places to identify and educate prospective board members.[29] Even Chancellor conceded that, as half of all parents, women deserved to sit on boards of education. However, no board should ever include more than one, and if elected, women—old or young, conservative or liberal—should defer to men (see figures 3.1, 3.2, and 3.3).

Adding women to boards of education was no easy task. According to economist Scott Nearing, who compiled data about school boards in 104 American cities, women accounted for only 7 percent of their members in 1916. By 1922, that proportion had risen to slightly more than 9 percent, with big cities leading the way. Of course, not just any woman could get appointed or elected.[30] In Detroit, Laura Osborn, a well-connected reformer, won a seat on the school board when the voters swept the old guard out of office in 1917. Two years later Adele Chase, whose husband was the president of the Gary Street Railway Company, became the first woman to serve on that Indiana city's board of education. School directors in Cedar Rapids, Iowa, and Dayton, Ohio, even elected a woman to lead them in the 1920s, but such distinctions for women were rare, and change was generally slow in coming and often halting.[31] "This writer recalls two cities which elected women to membership in their school boards for several years and later discontinued the practice," said the executive director of the Public Education Association in Philadelphia. "This apparently was not due to any deliberate change of policy," Bruce Watson went on to say, "and certainly not to dissatisfaction with women's service on the board."[32] There were those in Watson's own city, however, who were not convinced. According to one former member of a now advisory ward school board, the men on Philadelphia's central board were unwilling to accept women. "The Board of Education has only one principle that it adheres to," said Mrs. Mary Mumford, "that no woman shall be a member of the Board."[33]

FIGURE 3.1. *The Reformer.* Cover illustration, *The American School Board Journal* 55 (September 1917). A woman may be a school director, but the president of the board and his chief advisors are men.

FIGURE 3.2. *The Matron.* Cover illustration, *The American School Board Journal* 57 (August 1918). Distinguished, diligent, and determined, all board members shoulder a heavy public burden.

FIGURE 3.3. *The Young Mother.* Cover illustration, *The American School Board Journal* 57 (December 1918). Maternal virtue counts for something, but when difficult decisions have to made, there is no substitute for the wisdom of experienced men.

If there was such a principle, it fell in 1920, when Anna S. Lingelbach joined the Philadelphia school board. The wife of a geology professor at the University of Pennsylvania, Lingelbach was chosen ahead of three other prominent women, none of whom was Mary Grice. An academic in her own right, Lingelbach possessed a doctorate in history and high school teaching experience. The PEA counted her among its directors, but she also was the mother of three children, all of whom attended the Philadelphia public schools. She understood what her new colleagues expected of her. When interviewed by the press following her appointment, she declined to speak out on educational issues, saying that she wanted to confer with her husband first. "So the new member of the board is not an extreme feminist," *The Evening Bulletin* said, "disinclined to consult with men."[34]

Reorganized twice, the Home and School League struggled to stay alive in the 1920s. Perhaps its decline reflected a national trend. The political apathy of many white, middle-class women, especially compared to blacks, disappointed suffragists in the years immediately following the winning of the vote.[35] The league's prewar commitment to an expanded mission for the public school was less appealing in a more conservative time, and without Mary Grice to lead, its fortunes languished. A census conducted in 1925 revealed that only thirteen home and school associations still existed in the city, and two of them had not met for years. Of course, such dreadful returns may have been incomplete. In his annual report for 1928, the superintendent, Edwin C. Broome, reported finding a home and school association in about 85 of the city's 251 schools. No doubt, he wished for many more. "The schools have felt the need of selling themselves to the community," said Jean B. Hagerty, principal of the Robert Morris School. But they "have been rather hard put to find a medium dignified enough and yet sufficiently effective. I believe we have discovered in home and school associations the medium par excellence." Her counterpart at Germantown High School emphatically agreed. The Mothers' Association "has brought about a sympathetic understanding between parents and the school," said Leslie B. Seely, "which is extremely helpful."[36] In Philadelphia, school administrators believed that PTAs extended their reach into the community. The school and the home need not be in conflict so long as the former controlled the latter, not the other way around.

In the 1920s, teachers and administrators encouraged parents to form new home and school associations. And after the onset of the Great Depression, the professionals did not hesitate to take their own advice. Faced with declining resources and enrollments, they organized PTAs themselves, hoping to build political support. In 1935, half the PTAs in Philadelphia were less than six years old, and the principal had been the prime mover in the formation of more than 62 percent of these. Sensing that most parents focused on the needs of their own children, school officials promoted home and school associations as protectors of child welfare. According to a survey conducted during the winter of 1935, both parents and principals believed that PTAs improved cooperation and understanding between the home and the school, especially at the elementary level. But the professionals were far less likely than parents to think of PTAs as fostering solidarity at home or helping mothers and fathers monitor the performance of the school.[37] Such activities were not what school officials had in mind when they touted home and school associations as instruments of good public relations.

In retrospect, the outreach efforts of Philadelphia's principals seem only to have prevented precipitous decline. In 1935, the number of home and school associations in the city stood at sixty-one. They were still concentrated in white, middle-class neighborhoods, which now more than ever were at the fringe of the city. With just two associations inside its borders, South Philadelphia remained significantly underrepresented. However, nine of the city's twelve elementary schools with African-American personnel had active PTAs. The majority of Philadelphia's black children still attended integrated schools in the 1930s, but African-American principals and teachers could work only in all-black schools. Many faced dismissal when the Depression forced the district to impose cutbacks and consolidate. By organizing parents in Philadelphia's segregated schools, they strengthened their hand with the white school board in their fight against discrimination.[38] The common experience of being black erased any differences between African Americans who were either educators or parents.

The Depression posed a common threat to all parents with children in the Philadelphia public schools. In 1933, the district discontinued 19 junior high schools, 123 elementary schools, and 2 kindergartens, but even in the face of such a crisis, not all members of the Home and School League worked well together. Renamed the Philadelphia Home and School Council in 1935 when it broke relations with both the Pennsylvania Congress and NCPT in a dispute over dues, the league alienated more than a few of its locals. Many among the rank and file did not trust its leaders, as one school official explained, because the "women in charge seem somewhat out of touch with the parent's problem; and are engaged in this work to widen the scope of their own personal influence."[39]

Ambition was inappropriate for women in home and school associations. In keeping with the white, middle-class bias of the home and school movement, PTA mothers were expected to be modest and self-effacing, rejecting conflict in favor of harmony. In fact, reciprocity had a different meaning for middle-class men and women in the politics of home and school relations. Fathers could stand for election to positions of authority as long as they avoided being openly partisan. Mothers were supposed to be satisfied with exercising influence, especially through compromise and collaboration. Working with boards of education dominated by men, parents in many PTAs observed these unstated rules of middle-class gender relations. Between 1905 and 1930, some fathers became active and outspoken, using suburban home and school associations as a stepping stone to power. Where mothers remained completely in charge, they gently pressured school boards to affect policy. This pattern was readily apparent in two Philadelphia suburbs, Abington, Pennsylvania, and Haddonfield, New Jersey.

The Gendered Politics of Suburban School Reform: Two Case Studies

By 1910, much of middle-class Philadelphia had moved to the suburbs. The lure of nature and the appeal of open space were exceeded only by the ethnic and socioeconomic homogeneity promised there. Both inside the city and beyond its borders, many residential neighborhoods catered to the domestic needs of white-collar families. In the suburbs, schools stood atop the list of local civic institutions. After all, education spoke directly to the aspirations of the middle class. Not all suburbs were alike, of course. They differed by degrees of affluence and levels of commitment to educational innovation. By 1920, middle-class parents in many Philadelphia suburbs had begun to develop a distinctive domestic lifestyle, rejecting the urban trade-off between large families and well-educated children.[40] Such parents wanted excellent schools, and because they had both time and resources to invest in education, they formed home and school associations. These organizations also satisfied the urge, felt by many men and women, to be involved in the life of their residential communities.[41] But the political relationship between the home and the school was not the same in every suburban community.

Abington, Pennsylvania

In Abington Township, Pennsylvania, parents were not afraid to use organized pressure and confrontation. Eventually, some fathers even chose to trade influence for authority by running for the board of education. According to the superintendent, Edward S. Ling, the district's first home and school association formed to protest an unsanitary building after an "unsuccessful personal conference with an unprogressive school board." Based in a neighborhood called Weldon, the association reported in 1912 that it planned "to change the attitude of our school board to a more progressive one," and it quickly won two major victories, persuading the board to replace an ineffective janitor and hire Ling as the new superintendent.[42]

The presidents of the Weldon Home and School Association were invariably male. However, women comprised the bulk of its membership, and because "one able woman gave freely of her time and talent," interest in the association and its "standard of achievement" was kept high. Working together, fathers and mothers made this organization a constructive force in the community. They promised prospective members that they would be "agreeably surprised at the social time we have," but made it clear that their association's primary purpose was "to become better acquainted with the teachers and their methods as well as with the school directors and to suggest things of mutual benefit to all concerned." The association's reputation as a force for change was no doubt reinforced by its efforts to stay informed. In the spring of 1916, it heard Superintendent Ling speak about the Gary schools, a topic of hot debate among educators and school reformers at the time.[43]

As both the superintendent and the Abington parents were well aware, the Weldon Home and School Association had no official standing in the community. Legal authority for the schools resided in the board of education, and when its two most progressive members retired, conservatives replaced them. The attitude of the reconstituted board toward the home and school association "was either actively hostile, or contemptuous and indifferent." The association's most energetic members, said the new superintendent, "were regarded as meddlers and busybodies if their activities reached outward to any degree."[44] Ling found himself caught between the staid board to whom he reported and the reform-minded parents, with whom he was inclined to agree.

Parents soon organized two other home and school associations elsewhere in the township, and in the autumn of 1917, when a majority of seats on the board became vacant at the same time, the leaders of all three associations quietly forged a political alliance. Although careful not to associate their organizations with the election campaign, these fathers and mothers supported a reform ticket that included the former president of one home and school association and the current vice president of another. Composed of four men, this group easily won places on the board of education.[45]

The triumph of the reformers did not bring peace among parents in the Abington schools. A new faction formed, and soon it was vying for control of the Weldon Home and School Association. The need for reform did not divide the insiders and outsiders, since both favored more efficient management of the schools. The mission of the association was the issue, according to Ling, and the insurgents gained the upper hand by taking aim at the strong (but now anonymous) woman who had sparked the organization for five years. Once in charge, the new leaders took advantage of the expectation that parents and schools should be above politics, confining discussion of educational matters to the organization's executive committee. They delighted in "getting out large crowds," said Superintendent Ling, and sponsoring social occasions. This shift in focus deprived the school administration of a convenient forum for influencing public opinion, but the superintendent could not have been entirely displeased. After all, the insurgents' approach to decision-making kept any controversial discussions behind closed doors.

Opposition to the new leadership of the Weldon association had difficulty mobilizing. Connected to Philadelphia by railroad and street car, Abington Township was growing rapidly by 1920. New residents did not know one another or the community, and they quickly fell in with the controlling group. Far from condemning home and school associations, Ling believed they could be "a stimulus to teachers, superintendents, and school boards." Hired by the reformers, he thought of himself as evidence that parents made positive contributions. However, even he acknowledged that because home and school associations could generate conflict, they required close supervision. The triumph of the reformers in the board election of 1917 did not completely transform the parents' relationship to the educational establishment in Abington. Ling and the school board remained in control, for, as the superintendent pointed out, "election to a position on a school board tends to modify the attitude of a man toward home and school associations." [46] But by operating within the context of white, middle-class gender relations, Abington's parents had at least demonstrated that they could get the school board's attention.

Haddonfield, New Jersey

Compared to Abington Township, Haddonfield, New Jersey, was a more compact and well-established suburban community in 1910. Across the Delaware River from Philadelphia, it first attracted notice among upscale housing developers in the 1850s, but it did not turn from a country village into a suburb until the end of the nineteenth century. Convenient to both Camden and Philadelphia, it became a haven for the Protestant middle class, sheltering white-collar workers, professionals, business owners, and corporate executives.[47]

The people of Haddonfield embraced family and community life. As if to compensate for the diurnal separation made necessary by the male routine of commuting, they cultivated togetherness, forming several social and athletic organizations for men, women, and children. Two athletic clubs, a debating society, a literary society, and a natural science club provided the setting for many family activities. The women of Haddonfield also met on their own. Like respectable women everywhere, they assembled biweekly for meetings of the Fortnightly, a club that studied art, civics, and parenting. Founded in 1867, the Haddonfield Sewing Society gave them the opportunity to socialize while making clothes for others. Such charity may have no longer seemed compelling in 1903, when the organization disbanded. But the women of the new Haddonfield did not sit on their hands; instead, they put their energies to work for a cause closer to home. In 1905, they created a Mothers and Teachers Club (HMTC) "to establish an intelligent cooperation and sympathy between home and school."[48]

The HMTC derived support from mothers and teachers. Although they lived very different lives as married or single women, they joined hands to found this organization. The teachers took the initiative in April 1904, when they hosted a reception for the patrons of the school. One year later the president of the New Jersey Congress of Mothers told those assembled at the formative meeting of the HMTC that by coming together regularly mothers and teachers could avoid the unpleasantness that often occurred when the home and school communicated only about problems or difficulties. Of course, the mothers would have to defer to the pedagogical expertise of the teachers, but the intricacies of child care interested many club members. They wanted to know more about such matters as diet, nutrition, and friendships among the young. The hymn that they adopted in 1910 reminded them that children come "fresh from the kingdom of heaven" and have to be guided back to their "heavenly home." The HMTC maintained close ties with the Fortnightly and the local chapter of the Women's Christian Temperance Union (WCTU). Its first president, Mrs. Wellington Bechtel, belonged to both organizations as well as the Garden Club and the YWCA.[49]

Alice Bechtel moved in larger circles than just those surrounding Haddonfield. In 1914, she became president of the New Jersey Congress of Mothers. As early as 1906, she carried a resolution from the HMTC to the state women's club urging the legislature to prohibit the sale of cigarettes to minors. Keeping pressure on the politicians, the HMTC subsequently voted to form an alliance with the WCTU and many other women's organizations "to get the amendment to the present cigarette law passed," a campaign that achieved success in 1908.[50] But at home, the HMTC chose to be more reserved. Although the Haddonfield public schools might need to be improved, its members were not prepared to challenge the local board of education. When it came to such matters as athletics and property, they deferred to the men. Alice Bechtel accepted, even if she regretted, the constraints imposed by the situation. "Introducing physical training into the school, and better equipped school rooms, is beyond the province of the club, as it now stands," she reminded her members. "Such effort must come from the Fathers of the children, working hand in hand with the Board of Education," while mothers should concentrate on encouraging "sympathy" among parents, teachers, and children.[51]

What accounts for this apparent paradox? Why were Alice Bechtel and her peers willing to take on the political establishment in Trenton, but not the board of education in their hometown? Was cigarette reform so clearly a women's issue? The importance of social class and community spirit should not be underestimated here. In a small town turned middle-class suburb like Haddonfield, preoccupation with family life created a compelling context for cooperation between husbands and wives. Although men enjoyed more freedom to choose, each could enter, if only part way, into the others' lives.[52]

In 1912, the HMTC renamed itself the Haddonfield Parent-Teacher Association (HPTA), but it remained an organization for white, middle-class women. Unlike its counterparts in Abington and Philadelphia, it was led exclusively by women. The board of education, on the other hand, belonged to middle-class men. Between 1901 and 1917, all but one of its twenty-six incumbents were white men. In the 1920s, the ratio of men to women on the board was nearly twelve to one.[53] Challenging this male preserve in Haddonfield was stressful to say the least and could be daunting, as such behavior represented a greater threat to middle-class standards of domesticity and decorum than questioning the policies of faceless men, however powerful, in political arenas far from home.

Solid citizens served on the Haddonfield Board of Education. Its members reflected the white, middle-class character of the town, including many business owners, white-collar workers, civil servants, and attorneys (see table 3.1). The only woman on the board before 1918, Anna Eastburn Willits, came from a respected Quaker family. Between 1896 and 1909, she presided over the Fortnightly on three separate occasions, spending nine years in the top position. She had no personal interest in the welfare of the schools. She and her husband, a real estate and insurance executive, had no children. Elected once to a three-year term in 1908, during which she also was the board's vice president, Willits had a tenure that was brief by comparison to some others in her time. William J. Boning, who joined the school board in 1903, served as its secretary from 1907 to 1919. A civil engineer, he was twice elected president of the Haddonfield borough council and from 1895 to 1900 led the board of health. George B. Glover presided over the school board from 1903 until his death in 1917. He also served on the borough council and for ten years was president of the Haddonfield Republican Club.[54]

Two generations of Hodgson men anchored the board of education. President of the Phoenix Paint and Varnish Company in Philadelphia, William W. Hodgson served consecutive terms before World War I. His son, an attorney and a partner in his father's business, became school

TABLE 3.1   **Haddonfield Board of Education, 1900–1930**

Continuity on the Board	*1901–1915*	*1916–1930*
Mean length of service (years)	5.78	5.00
Median length of service (years)	4.62	4.00
Longest Terms of Service		
(number of board members)		
15 years	2	0
14 years	0	0
13 years	2	1
12 years	0	0
11 years	0	1
10 years	0	1
9 years	1	1

Occupations of Board Members	*1901–1915*	*1916–1930*
Attorney	3	3
Business owner	6	5
Civil servant	2	2
Dentist/doctor	1	0
Engineer	0	2
Housewife	1	1
Politician	0	1
Teacher (retired)	0	1
White-collar worker	9	10
Other	1	0
Unknown	0	5
	23	30

SOURCES: Minutes of the Haddonfield Board of Education, 1900–1930 Haddonfield School District, Haddonfield, N.J.; Twelfth Census of the United States, 1900, Manuscript Schedules, Haddonfield Borough, Camden County, N.J.; Thirteenth Census of the United States, 1910. Manuscript Schedules, Haddonfield Borough, Camden, N.J.; Fourteenth Census of the United States, 1920, Manuscript Schedules, Haddonfield Borough, Camden, N.J.; *Hoope's Haddonfield Directory Containing Names of Haddonfield and Vicinity* (Camden, N.J., 1901); *Directory of Haddonfield, Camden County, N.J. Including Batesville 1908* (Camden, N.J.: McGrath, 1908); *Derbyshire's Directory of Haddonfield, 1910–1911* (1911); *Directory of Haddonfield for 1914* (Kolb & Lehr, 1914); *1921 Haddonfield Directory Including Batesville* (1921); *Directory of Haddonfield Including Batesville, 1925* (Camden, N.J., 1925); *The Haddonfield Directory, 1929* (1929).

board president in 1923, his first year in office. Appropriately named W. Gentry Hodgson, the scion remained at the board's helm for a decade. He was a great booster of the Haddonfield public schools. After several rounds of pay raises for the district's teachers in the late 1920s, he called for "a full measure of cooperation between school and home," urging parents to regard money spent on education as an investment.[55]

Such eminent and stable leadership put the board in a formidable position. Of course, the officers of both the HMTC and the HPTA came from the same social background as their male counterparts on the board of education (see table 3.2), although by the 1920s, neither the HPTA nor the board was as exclusive as each once had been. Emma Middleton certainly deserved the recognition that came with her postretirement election to the school board in 1918, but she hardly was a member of the town's economic or social elite, and her colleagues never chose her to lead them. There were some kinship ties between the school board and the Mothers and Teachers Club. Between 1906 and 1908, Glover's wife, Rebecca, was both vice president and acting president of the HMTC. Attorney Henry S. Scovel, who served on the school board for no less than seventeen years, was married to an active member of the HMTC. Their daughter, Ethel, worked as the paid secretary of the board from 1919 to 1922.[56] Despite such overlap, it was not customary for leaders of the HMTC or the HPTA to get promoted to the school board. When Alice Bechtel ran in 1915, she received exactly one vote, probably her own. Another candidate in the same election, Harriet Dawson, did no better; she became president of the HPTA in 1920.[57]

Even though they were excluded from the board, the mothers of Haddonfield were not willing to be invisible or mute. The leaders of the HPTA understood that influence was at least in part a matter of numbers. They were never satisfied with the size of their organization, experimenting with different strategies to recruit and retain members. They awarded prizes to those classes in the district with the largest membership. They sponsored countless lectures and demonstrations on parenting and schooling. In 1919, they divided Haddonfield into twenty sections, assigning each to a resident mother, who was responsible for inviting her neighbors with children to join the association. They even tried decentralizing the association, holding separate meetings in three different parts of town. Such efforts were not without effect; HPTA membership more than doubled in eight years, reaching 476 in 1927.[58]

The HPTA wanted to make Haddonfield's teachers, especially the women, feel at home. It sponsored dinners for them and receptions that

TABLE 3.2   **Officers of the Haddonfield Parent-Teacher Association: Occupations of Husbands and Members**

HADDONFIELD MOTHERS AND TEACHERS CLUB, 1905–1910

Occupations of Husbands		*Occupations of Members*	
Business owner	3	Housewife	9
Civil servant	1	Teacher	4
Minister	1		13
White-collar worker	4		
	9		

HADDONFIELD PARENT-TEACHER ASSOCIATION, 1920–1928

Occupations of Husbands		*Occupations of Members*	
Business owner	3	Business owner	1
Dentist	1	Housewife	13
Politician	1	Teacher	2
White-collar worker	5		16
Unknown	4		
	14		

SOURCES: Minutes of the Haddonfield Mothers and Teachers Club, 1905–1910; Minutes of the Haddonfield Parent-Teacher Association, 1920–1928, both in the Haddonfield Historical Society, Haddonfield, N.J.; Twelfth Census of the United States, 1900, Manuscript Schedules, Haddonfield Borough, Camden County, N.J.; Thirteenth Census of the United States, 1910, Manuscript Schedules, Haddonfield Borough, Camden County, N.J.; Fourteenth Census of the United States, 1920, Manuscript Schedules, Haddonfield Borough, Camden County, N.J.; *Hoope's Haddonfield Directory Containing Names of Haddonfield and Vicinity* (Camden, N.J., 1901); *Directory of Haddonfield, Camden County, N.J., Including Batesville 1908* (Camden, N.J.: McGrath, 1908); *Derbyshire's Directory of Haddonfield, 1910–1911* (1911); *Directory of Haddonfield for 1914* (Kolb & Lehr, 1914); *1921 Haddonfield Directory Including Batesville* (1921); *Directory of Haddonfield Including Batesville, 1925* (Camden, N.J., 1925); *The Haddonfield Directory, 1929* (1929).

included the board of education. It made certain that the women among them who came from out of town found suitable apartments. It rejoiced in 1920 when every teacher became a member but despaired later on when they failed to attend afternoon meetings.[59] The relationship between mothers and teachers in the HPTA was not democratic. It was the home-maker's schedule that dictated when meetings would take place. Taking charge of hospitality, the mothers made the basis for their leadership perfectly clear. They derived their legitimacy from their status as married women at home. Teachers were entitled to respect in academic matters. When the HPTA decided to endow a scholarship at the New Jersey State Normal School for a graduating senior, this distinction came into play. The faculty would be "allowed to use any means they deem best to determine the most desirable pupil," the officers of the HPTA said. But "no one whose character is not of the best" would ever be considered.[60]

Status conflict between mothers and teachers was not confined to Haddonfield. Deferring to single women in the classroom must have struck many mothers as incompatible with the moral leadership commonly associated with motherhood and the Protestant home. That most teachers were young women only compounded the problem. Addressing the readers of *Good Housekeeping* in 1910, Elia Peattie urged parents to overcome age bias. Mothers, she said, should include "young teachers . . . in their social program" and lend them the weight of maternal authority.[61] No longer was it assumed that just because they were women, teachers carried the imprimatur of the home. Marriage and children conveyed social and moral legitimacy. Teaching, on the other hand, was for single women who wanted a career.

The mothers of Haddonfield wanted to make their influence felt at school. While unwilling to challenge the school board, they were not intimidated by it either. In fact, they often worked with the board. It granted their request for space in a schoolhouse to hold the first meeting of the HMTC, an indulgence that became precedent thereafter. The home and school association learned to initiate contact when it felt confident that the superintendent and board would listen. Only some educational issues fell within the province of the home; it was a mother's job, for example, to monitor the growth and behavior of children. "The school has a right to expect that the child be physically fit and happy," the new superintendent, Allen S. Martin, told the HPTA in 1923. The school board also believed that teachers would fail if they acted alone in matters of discipline. "There is need for definite cooperation from parents in this regard," it pointed out, "for all success of school work hinges upon sustaining the teachers' authority and influence with the child."[62]

Both the HMTC and the HPTA tried to sway the board on matters having to do with nutrition and recreation. Experts trained in physical education or home economics were taking charge of the playground and lunchroom at school, but mothers resisted losing control. They were accustomed to supervising their children's diet and play, and as white, middle-class women, they still commanded some respect in these domains. In 1910, the board permitted the HMTC to use a school yard during the summer as a playground, and at the bidding of the HPTA, it hired a playground director ten years later.[63] Food was a topic of special interest to the members of the home and school association. In 1908, the HMTC petitioned the board "to forbid the sale of all food stuffs, such as apples, candies, pretzels, hokey-pokey, etc. without a special license." It soon followed with a request to lengthen the lunch period from thirty minutes to one hour, presumably to allow the children enough time to eat at home. More than a few must have gone elsewhere, however, because in 1921 the HPTA complained about school leaving at the noon hour. Only those with written permission from their parents should be excused, it said, a policy that the board adopted at its next meeting.[64]

The board could have solved the lunch problem by serving hot meals at school. As early as 1920, it designated one of its two new female members, Mrs. Bertha Wilson, to confer with Harriet Dawson, the president of the HPTA, about the feasibility of catering soup at the Elizabeth Haddon School. When Wilson and Dawson decided that this was impractical, the noon hour issue remained unresolved. In 1925, the HPTA appointed a committee to look into it, but Superintendent Martin warned the mothers off, telling the HPTA that the board had been discussing "this matter . . . for some time, realizing the need for responsible persons to efficiently serve such luncheons in a period of time that would not necessitate lengthening the noon hour." [65] Even on matters that struck close to home, the board wanted the HPTA to know that it was well informed and would make the decisions.

By the early 1920s, the mothers of Haddonfield were becoming bolder. The HPTA now pressured both the school and the town to stop tobacco use by minors. The high school principal, Helen Woolston, refused to take the blame; "the amount of smoking could be reduced," she told the members of the HPTA, "if the parents would take this matter over and not leave it all to the school." [66] But the mothers of Haddonfield also knew that there still were strict limits on what they were supposed to do. Regarding school construction, the public issue that most concerned the town's parents and taxpayers alike in the 1920s, the HPTA kept its profile low.

Like many other urban and suburban school districts, Haddonfield faced a building crisis after World War I. Between 1911 and 1921, enrollment surged, increasing by 476 pupils to a total of 1,242. Expenses climbed right along with them, and in February 1920, the HPTA expressed support for the superintendent and his increasingly hefty budget. The district was now holding classes in several churches as well as outmoded schools. To rectify the situation, the board would have to face the voters, asking for permission to float bonds, buy land, and erect new schools. It had successfully traveled this road before, meeting with little or no opposition in 1903 and 1908 when the people of Haddonfield authorized the board to build a new elementary school and a new high school.[67] Larger and less self-contained, Haddonfield had changed by 1921, but there seemed to be no reason to doubt that the board would prevail again.

In June, the school board decided that the time had come to build a new high school, only to discover five months later that many residents did not agree. At a special meeting, the board's proposal was rejected overwhelmingly. Both the cost and the location of the project prompted widespread opposition that even a joint meeting of the board and the electorate could not dispel. Although many civic groups, including the HPTA, stepped forward to support the board, a second referendum, held the following May, suffered the same fate as the first. Haddonfield was not ready to invest $412,000 in a new high school, as the board proposed, and even when it countered with a much less costly plan to modify an existing facility, the voters disapproved.[68]

The community did not turn a deaf ear to all the school board's pleas. In May 1923, it authorized the board to spend $142,500 to build two new elementary schools, including one for the district's African Americans. These schools did not eliminate overcrowding, however, and the need for a new high school remained acute. "The unsatisfactory housing for the High School is obvious," Martin complained; replacing it would benefit the entire system, satisfying "the requirement of the elementary schools [for] several years because of the release of the classrooms now occupied by the high school." In the fall of 1924, the school board approached the voters again, but they had not yet changed their minds, twice rejecting plans to build a high school two blocks east of the business district. It took another year to bring them around, and it was not until October 1927 that the new facility finally opened.[69]

The building of new schools was not necessarily a gendered issue. Every parent of a young child had a stake in the condition of the town's public schools. Unorganized and not identified with any particular interest or group, the naysayers lacked political definition. Frustrated parents found themselves condemning their neighbors' want of civic spirit. No doubt echoing what he heard at home, one student blamed the failed referenda on "the opposition of a comparatively large group of people who are habitually against any measures for the benefit of the place." Another pupil complained of a chasm between the townspeople and the schools. "We don't want a new High School, as much as we want the help and interest of the people of the town," he said.[70] But persuading them to authorize new school construction was important to many families. What was the right strategy to get this job done?

The HPTA chose not to pressure the school board or challenge the voters of Haddonfield. It downplayed the problem of overcrowding and was not outspoken on the need for new schools. Instead, it followed the lead of the board, backing it when called on to do so. In September 1920, the executive committee of the HPTA asked its members to adopt a resolution informing the board of their support for the purchase of land on which to build a new high school. However, nearly twelve months elapsed before the committee followed through, agreeing by unanimous vote to send a letter to the members of the board "expressing our interest . . . and assuring them of our hearty co-operation and support when they deem it advisable to take action in the matter."[71]

The HPTA did not speak for all parents in Haddonfield. Although they were not represented on the HPTA or the board of education, the few African Americans in town refused to be ignored. In 1920, they comprised 6.5 percent of the borough's population, a slight increase over 1910, when they amounted to just under 5 percent. Mainly domestics, laborers, and other service workers, Haddonfield's African Americans possessed little or no political capital. Those working as housekeepers, gardeners, and chauffeurs often lived with their white employers. Most black families lived near one another on three segregated blocks and streets. Between 1910 and 1920, the number of blacks living in black families increased more rapidly than their scattered counterparts, accounting perhaps for an unprecedented show of interest by the black community in the condition of the schools. In December 1921, an independent committee of black residents presented a petition to the board urging it to include "better school facilities for the colored children of our Borough" in its construction plans. Four years later black parents asked for "a more competent teaching force" at their segregated school.[72] Such requests fell on deaf ears, but the black parents were nothing if not forthcoming.

Some white parents may have felt that the HPTA was too indirect in its approach to school politics. Married to an active member of the HPTA, Henry Pennypacker filled a seat on the board vacated by the resignation of an elected member in June 1922. When his colleagues made him president five months later, it must have come as a shock to those accustomed to more familiar leadership. Pennypacker believed in the need for new schools. He reached out to the HPTA in January 1923, informing its members about the board's building plans and receiving in return their promise "to do everything in their power to secure the adoption of the entire program." But Pennypacker soon found himself on the outside, looking in; he lost the next election, becoming the only officer of the board between 1900 and 1930 to serve as a member for less than three years.[73]

It is impossible to know for sure whether Pennypacker's stand on the school building issue cost him his seat on the school board. In the months following Pennypacker's defeat, Superintendent Martin acted as the board's liaison with the HPTA, calling for cooperation to solve the problem of overcrowding. It was not until October 1925 that another board member appeared before the HPTA to secure its support for the new high school. By then, the board was looking at the possibility of a third straight setback at the polls. But rather than meet with the women himself, Board President W. Gentry Hodgson sent his colleague Bertha Wilson to remind the mothers to vote. Meanwhile, the husband of the immediate past president of the HPTA quietly convinced one of the most influential organizations in town, the Civic Association, to endorse the new school.[74] Marshaling support without galvanizing the opposition was good politics. But in Haddonfield, parents exercised limited influence in the community, as many unsuccessful referenda demonstrated. The etiquette of white, middle-class gender relations affected the relationship between the home and the school. Not only were white mothers understated in their interaction with the school board, but the reverse was true as well. School authorities, volunteers and professionals alike, had to be decorous in relating to the public, especially mothers.

In Philadelphia and its suburbs, gender, race, and class intertwined to gird the relationship between the home and the school. The boundaries set by Anglo-American culture militated against the full participation of blacks and immigrants in PTAs. White, middle-class parents could exercise some influence at school if they organized, but their efficacy differed according to the context, urban or suburban. Expectations based on gender significantly affected parental involvement, encouraging middle-class men and women to set different goals for their participation in school politics and play different roles.

In Philadelphia, home and school associations made their presence felt primarily at the neighborhood level. Led by Mary Grice, the Home and School League got the attention of the school board by advocating the expansion of the public school's mission, but Grice had to deal with an entrenched educational establishment in the city. When the league struggled to stay alive in the 1920s, educators took control of the home and school relationship. In Abington and Haddonfield, PTAs got closer to the action, but the politics of gender shaped parental involvement there as well as in the city as male school boards and superintendents struggled to maintain control. White, middle-class men served on boards of education, while their wives belonged to PTAs. Of course, such restrictions were not absolute. Some fathers joined home and school associations, and when they did, they could aspire to positions of authority. Some women also became school board members, but they were expected to defer to their male colleagues on the board and cooperate with the men in school administration. Outspoken women like Mary Grice were unwelcome, and those who wanted to be influential learned to bite their tongues. Cooperation and collaboration gave white, middle-class women leverage at school. Working together in PTAs, they had a subtle but important effect on public education in their communities.

CHAPTER FOUR

Heard but Not Seen

Come let us live with our children,
Lives that are noble and true,
Letting the love of the Father,
Shine forth in all that we do,
Sent in His infinite wisdom,
That we may teach them aright
Ours for today, we must guide them,
Unto the heavenly light.
— Helen Grinnell Mears,[1] "Mothers' Hymn"

B etween 1902 and 1928, the National Congress of Mothers and Parent-Teacher Associations enjoyed a remarkable run of continuity in its leadership. Just three women served as president during these years. Born near Philadelphia in 1853, Hannah Kent Schoff held the top office from 1902 until 1920. Succeeding Katherine Chapin Higgins three years later, Margaretta Willis Reeve was at the helm when the National Congress changed its name, becoming simply the National Congress of Parents and Teachers (NCPT) in 1924.[2] It was a savvy gesture, befitting a woman who would be a national leader. Motherhood was still important in its own right, but equating parents and teachers acknowledged the changing nature of the home-school relationship and took better advantage of the educational establishment's increasing political clout.

Both Schoff and Reeve contributed significantly to the parent-teacher movement. While vice president of the National Congress of Mothers, Schoff founded its Pennsylvania affiliate, presiding over it for three years. During her administration, the National Congress established an endowment fund, opened headquarters in Washington, and began publishing a journal, *The National Congress of Mothers Magazine*. Reeve's apprenticeship in the parent-teacher movement was somewhat longer. Born Margaretta Willis Baldwin in 1871, she organized the first parent-teacher association (PTA) in Moorestown, New Jersey, at age twenty-eight before moving on to the presidency of the New Jersey Congress of Mothers. At the peak of her influence in 1927, she helped form the International Federation of Home and School, serving as its first president.[3]

In their personal and public lives, Schoff and Reeve were advocates for children. The juvenile court won Hannah Schoff's enthusiastic support. Appalled when she discovered that hundreds of delinquent and dependent children were in jail with adults in Philadelphia, she led the fight that persuaded Pennsylvania to establish a juvenile courts division in 1901. For the next eight years, she raised money to pay the salaries of probation officers employed by the Philadelphia juvenile court. In 1913, the commissioner of education appointed her director of the Home Education Division of the United States Bureau of Education. As a reformer, Schoff was no proponent of sweeping change. In the 1920s, she broke ranks with many of her colleagues and opposed the national child labor amendment, arguing that it was not in the best interest of those under eighteen years of age. It would deprive them of the "freedom to do what is legitimate and honorable," she said, that is, "earn their living by honest work."[4]

Reeve and Schoff shared a passion for social hygiene. Upholding the sanctity of the family, the two women opposed promiscuity and insisted on the primacy of marriage. Schoff denounced the Mormon Church because some of its members practiced polygamy. Divorced parents drew her fire for neglecting children and pushing them into lives of crime. Reeve recoiled from smut; in particular, she condemned the purveyors of degrading literature and immoral films. "The younger generation is much maligned because [it is] misguided by adults," she once wrote. "We find it easier to hand out a dollar and murmur weakly, 'don't stay out too late,' than to plan and carry out counter attractions to those we deplore." Under her leadership, the NCPT organized itself against books and movies that children should not be allowed to see.[5]

Reeve and Schoff also believed that PTAs should promote child welfare reform. "The mother's view of children's needs comes from experience and insight beyond any other," Schoff once wrote. Every mother should find a way to care for homeless and wayward children. "The average citizen may be aroused and his active cooperation secured," Reeve maintained, when the PTA becomes a forum for the free discussion of the problems that affect all the children of the community.[6] Such work required long-term planning and large-scale organization. It was not enough for parents and teachers to come together in times of crisis; nor could parents expect to be heard, let alone make a difference, if they confined themselves to the neighborhood school. In 1920, men did most of the talking at the regional or national level. As college presidents, school superintendents, and professors of education, they dominated such organizations as the American Council on Education and National Education Association (NEA).[7] Could women exercise widespread influence, too? Reeve and Schoff believed that mothers and teachers could work together over the long haul to achieve educational and social change. They could become a powerful interest group.

The Victorian image of women as natural experts on the subject of families and children gave mothers and teachers the right to claim a share in the development of public policy on education. But the assertiveness required to lead a political interest group stood in sharp contrast to the personal qualities associated with domesticity. In social work, professional women led the way to child welfare reform. Relying on their experience and training, they distinguished themselves from the mothers and children who were responsible for the problems that had to be solved. The leaders of the parent-teacher movement, on the other hand, were mainly volunteers, mothers who firmly believed that a woman's place was in the home. They spoke for reform at the state and national levels, but as mothers, they were disinclined to blame the family for society's ills. They wanted to strengthen it by teaching women the science of homemaking and protect it from the harm associated with such evils as factory work for mothers and children.[8]

As reformers, women like Reeve and Schoff focused on social and educational policy. However, they could not ignore the personal interests and private needs of homemakers who did not aspire to be state or national leaders. Their participation was essential if parents and teachers were to become a powerful interest group. Unfortunately, most parents had a short attention span on the subject of schools. As Hannah Schoff observed, the future of our work can be ensured only by a national body that year after year will "inspire incoming parents to continue it, as those whose children's schooldays are over pass out of the associations."[9] This was no small problem for an organization that wanted to have a nationwide impact on social and educational policy. Bridging the gap between local issues and the priorities of the NCPT was also a challenge that turned out to be more demanding than the founders imagined, and its leaders were not always able to win the support of the rank and file for their progressive agenda.

The NCPT and the Politics of Home and School Reform

When Alice Birney founded the National Congress of Mothers (NCM) in 1897, she could not have foreseen the extent to which her organization would grow and change over the next sixty years. Inspired by the work of kindergarten pioneer Friedrich Froebel and child study expert G. Stanley Hall, this widowed mother of three attracted widespread attention by touting the wisdom of maternity. As one speaker told some of the 2,000 delegates to the organization's first convention, the school should be a natural extension of the home. By the late 1920s, the NCM's successor, the NCPT, had grown exponentially not so much because it was still speaking up for mothers but because it was connecting them with educators and child development experts.[10] Only Nevada did not have a state congress affiliated with the national when membership reached 1.25 million in 1928. Slowed by the Depression, the pace of the organization's growth was still impressive as membership more than doubled over the next decade. But it was the postwar generation that carried the NCPT to unimaginable heights, bringing its ranks to more than 8.8 million.[11] By 1954, the PTA had become a staple in the lives of those who were giving birth to the baby boom.

From the beginning, mothers were more inclined to organize and affiliate in some states than others. Because support for women's rights around the country was also uneven, it should come as no surprise that Connecticut, New York, New Jersey, and Pennsylvania joined Illinois and Iowa in forming state branches of the National Congress of Mothers by 1900, and along with Ohio, California, and Texas, these affiliates remained among the largest or most prominent at mid-century. They probably benefited from the interest generated in the 1920s by university research centers on child welfare and development at Yale, Teachers College, the University of California at Berkeley, and the University of Iowa.[12] However, the leaders of what would become the NCPT were never content to let membership run its course. Alice Birney devoted herself to recruitment during her years as president of the NCM, taking advantage of the network already built by women's organizations like the General Federation of Women's Clubs. Dissatisfied especially with their standing in the South, her successors commissioned Katherine Chapin Higgins to recruit in 1916. A vice president of the National Congress at the time, she toured eight southern states, increasing total membership there from 60,000 to 122,000. But the focus on membership was not just regional. State congresses connected local affiliates to national leadership, and the organization maintained a Committee on PTAs in the Schools, whose charge was "to render every possible assistance to State Chairmen requesting information or aid in organizing Parent-Teacher Associations."[13]

The relationship between the national and its state and local branches could not have been more important to those women who rose to positions of significant responsibility in the NCPT. To be effective, they believed, the entire organization had to be run from the top down. With an eye for unity and coordination, the board of managers appointed a committee to study the constitutions of its state and local affiliates in 1923. It developed standards for PTAs and employed two field secretaries and a part-time field organizer to help state congresses form and grow. But this assignment proved to be too big for such a small staff. When an NCPT survey revealed that only a handful of locals adhered to the standards, it was decided that each state PTA would have to find a way to organize and manage itself, leaving the national free to concentrate on "educational activities."[14] In 1927, the NCPT took up "the matter of advertising and the standardization of the state bulletins." After all, a good image could not be left to chance. Margaretta Reeve did not want her members to be regarded as dilettantes. Dissociating the NCPT from the "club movement," she urged her colleagues to think of their work "not as one of many interests in busy lives, but as one which is for the time-being all important, a business in which success will have effects reaching far into the future, and in which failure, if it should come, will be due solely and entirely to our own inefficiency and indifference."[15]

The officers and managers of the NCPT were not alone in their belief that bureaucratic organization was the key to membership growth and influence in public policy-making. State congresses justified their existence by rationalizing their relationship with parents and educators. Formed in 1900, the Iowa Congress of Mothers became the child study department of the state teachers' association before developing an elaborate and highly differentiated governance structure of its own. By 1915, it had four vice presidents and fifteen committees working on everything from member recruitment to juvenile justice and sex education. In Connecticut, the state PTA organized county councils in the 1920s to facilitate communication and cooperation among suburban and rural PTAs. Located in West Hartford, the state's first association of urban PTAs appeared in 1925, reversing the California pattern, where the powerful state congress of mothers rested firmly on foundations laid by two separate federations of mothers' clubs, based in Los Angeles and San Francisco, respectively. In 1910, the California congress divided the state into eight districts, creating intermediate units that were to act as go-betweens, while in Iowa, the state congress made its organization conform to the five subdivisions carved out by the Iowa State Teachers' Association.[16] That parents from many communities should collaborate might have seemed self-evident, but getting them to work with one another, let alone with teachers, required more than good intentions.

Effective organization was important not just because the quality of education depended on it. The well-being of American society was at stake as well. Maternal love, said Alice Birney, was the keystone of social reform. A mother's work, Hannah Schoff explained, did not end with her own children. It could still go on, she said, "reaching out to better conditions for other children." Such work could take many forms, but to harness the power of motherhood required at least some planning and coordination. The National Congress of Mothers adopted an ambitious agenda in 1897. At its first meeting, it pledged to work for harmony at home, peace in the world, and reforms to improve the welfare of American families and children.[17] The NCPT and its state affiliates inherited and propagated this sense of direction. But the leaders of these organizations discovered that it was not easy to achieve consensus about what was wrong with America or convince parents that they should take responsibility for other people's children.

In their commissioned history of the NCPT, published in 1949, Harry and Bonaro Overstreet characterized the child as the most important source of community in the United States. Fragmented by economic self-interest and political partisanship, Americans found common ground only in the young, and, said the Overstreets, the NCPT deserved credit for "its discovery that the unifying force in our society is the child."[18] But if the NCPT served Americans well by calling attention to their collective, albeit tacit, concern for the child, it failed to show much faith in their ability to nurture children or improve society on their own. Its leaders were much more comfortable telling others what to do, say, and believe.

From the beginning the National Congress of Mothers advocated scientific motherhood and child welfare reform. Motherhood, said Alice Birney, meant "child study—that broad, deep theme, most worthy, in all its varying phases, of our . . . attention, because [it was] the fundamental one."[19] Defenseless and innocent, children also needed protection from the adult world. The NCM stood guard over the family, an institution whose integrity and independence it regarded as indispensable to the well-being of American society. It assumed responsibility for defending women and children against economic and social exploitation. It believed in active government, supporting legislation and policies that would strengthen its hand in the reform of education and the improvement of family life. But the NCM was not a democratic organization; its leaders believed in elite leadership and practiced centralized administration. They acted as the nation's conscience, pointing out to politicians and the general public the way America should go. The private woman had a public responsibility to the home and school. Representing her, the NCM articulated an ideology called maternalism and advanced a political agenda to go with it.[20]

Between 1900 and 1930, the National Congress backed such reforms as mothers' pensions, a national child labor law, and a constitutional amendment to standardize public policy on marriage and divorce in the United States. Formed in 1921, its Department of Racial Health sponsored one committee on monogamous marriage and another on social hygiene that championed the two-parent, one-income family and worked to educate parents and children about reproduction. This program extended the NCM's earlier emphasis on eugenics to include moral education. Likewise, the NCPT urged Congress to remain firm on the terms of the Volstead Act and consider legislation to restore the demographic distribution between northern and southern Europe that once prevailed in American immigration.[21] Reassuring to white, Protestant, middle-class Americans, these nativist positions were not inconsistent with the maternalist view that women belonged in the home, married and raising children. But they also implied that good homemaking entailed political activism and revealed a bias for national policy-making that prompted some blunt and unfair criticism. The long-standing chair of the organization's legislative committee, Elizabeth Tilton, resented being called a radical. "We are not Red because we favor nation-wide action for nation-wide evils," she said in 1927, "but Red, White, and Blue, that is, generous patriots wanting all States to share the good things of life equally."[22]

In child welfare, the NCM and its successor, the NCPT, endorsed a variety of progressive reforms. During the presidency of Hannah Schoff, the NCM took a special interest in the juvenile court. Schoff believed that the court's probation officers should receive special training and work closely with the schools because the care of "wayward children is an extension of the educational system, and must eventually be assumed by it." The NCM fought hard for laws requiring birth registration and better care for delinquent, dependent, and neglected children. In the 1920s, the NCPT never wavered in its support for a national child labor law even when it became apparent that such legislation could not withstand a court challenge.[23] Because such an agenda invited government to play a much larger role in private family life, it did not sit well with many parents and teachers nationwide. Perhaps this is why the NCPT's most successful venture in child welfare reform came by its own hand. Beginning in 1925, it initiated what would become a truly national campaign to evaluate the health of American schoolchildren.

The Summer Round-Up screened preschool children for common maladies that might get in the way of learning. Enlarged tonsils and adenoids, bad teeth, and poor eyesight were among its chief concerns. It was not the NCPT's first attempt to address the problem of disease in neglected children. In 1903, the NCM formed a committee to study the health needs of delinquent, dependent, and disabled children. It lobbied for legislation to eliminate tainted milk, urged every board of health to establish a child hygiene department and, in 1909, created one of its own that focused on infant mortality. State organizations concerned themselves with fitness, too. Thanks to Hannah Schoff, the Pennsylvania congress sponsored training in infant care, while mothers in other states worked to generate interest in health education. To publicize the need for parental vigilance, some embraced tactics that were sure to attract attention. Under the auspices of the Iowa Congress of Mothers and Parent-Teacher Associations, six women doctors took part in a baby health contest at the state fair in 1911. Farmers, they said, should devote at least as much attention to the wellness of their children as they did to their cows and pigs.[24]

The Summer Round-Up quickly received the endorsement of leaders in health, social work, and education. The American Medical Association (AMA) and the NEA, the United States Children's Bureau, and the Bureau of Education promptly backed it, and within two years, it was operating in forty-four states. In Michigan alone, 274 local PTAs registered their intention to conduct the NCPT health examinations. The program moved one of the chief lobbyists for mothers and children closer to the professional establishment in medicine as well as education, advancing a transformation in the NCPT that had been under way for some time.[25] Its decision in 1908 to call itself the National Congress of Mothers and Parent-Teacher Associations first acknowledged the importance it attached to expertise in education, and when the organization dropped all reference to mothers, becoming simply the National Congress of Parents and Teachers in 1924, it took another step in that direction.

The Summer Round-Up called on PTAs to offer parents the chance to have their sons and daughters professionally examined at community clinics. In Iowa, the state PTA made the Summer Round-Up a prominent feature of its program in parent education, and in many states, local PTAs sponsored preschool programs in health screening.[26] But the NCPT and its affiliates chose not to take on the health care establishment in the United States and its commitment to privatism. Careful to avoid any appearance of support for socialized medicine, they advised parents that if the examinations revealed any problems, the burden of obtaining remediation fell on them. Children free of health defects stood a better chance of doing well in school, but shaping educational and social policy was the national organization's most important job, not elevating the school achievement of individual children.

Aware that the AMA's opposition to the Sheppard-Towner Maternity and Infancy Protection Act had persuaded Congress to renege on its limited program of health education for expectant and postpartum mothers, Margaretta Reeve tried to reassure the medical profession that the Summer Round-Up represented no threat to its health care monopoly. "It should be clearly understood," she wrote in 1929, "that the Congress is *opposed to free medical or dental care* in carrying through the correction of defects (except in cases of financial inability)." But the AMA was not inclined to share responsibility for any medical evaluation or procedure. Taking aim at the NCPT's "so-called clinic plan," it insisted that all physical examinations be conducted by the family dentist or doctor. An Advisory Committee to the Summer Round-Up, composed largely of male physicians, recommended such a change in policy and eventually convinced the NCPT to discourage all group work, consigning even the diagnostic piece to the private realm of the individual doctor's office.[27]

The NCPT did not always follow the lead of the medical profession. After Congress failed to renew the Sheppard-Towner Act in 1929, the organization made its reinstatement a high priority. In doing so, it reached out to the leadership of the United States Children's Bureau, a politically shrewd and diplomatic step, especially because Grace Abbott, the bureau's director, had done nothing to improve cooperation between professional social workers and maternalist reformers by insisting that PTAs defer to the authority of the bureau in the management of services funded by Sheppard-Towner.[28] Meanwhile, the NCPT continued to sponsor the Summer Round-Up. In 1931, more than 75,000 children were examined nationwide, but the shift away from community clinics to private diagnosis cut into the program's numbers, and by the end of the Great Depression, it had ceased to be as important to the organization as it once had been. Nutrition became the NCPT's chief health concern; a school lunch project that it sponsored during World War II anticipated and perhaps even provided the model for a similar program sponsored by the federal government after the war was over. In the 1950s, the NCPT tried to revive the Summer Round-Up, expanding it to include children from birth through high school. The effort never got off the ground, but the organization remained true to the AMA's beliefs, holding fast to the idea that private practitioners should do the work because the social and educational effect was better when parents were in direct contact with physicians.[29]

Compared with its deference toward the medical establishment, the NCPT's attitude toward educators and child welfare professionals was more independent and self-assured. Like many other women's groups, the NCPT committed itself to parent education in the 1920s, but it did not concede the field to experts, rejecting the idea that only professionals should be in charge. By adopting child study as one of its original missions, the organization did admit that mothers had much to learn. G. Stanley Hall, whose name became synonymous with the scientific study of the child, spoke at the NCM's inaugural meeting. Led by Cora Bussey Hillis, the Iowa Congress of Mothers prevailed upon its state legislature to subsidize the study of normal child development by scientists assembled at what came to be known as the Child Welfare Research Station after it opened at the University of Iowa in 1917. An activist who first achieved prominence in 1900 when she convinced the NCM to hold its national meeting in Des Moines, Hillis would have preferred that the new Research Station focus its attention on abnormal or subnormal children. However, she was always a strong proponent of universal child study and comprehensive parent education.[30] Like her, other leaders of the NCM and later the NCPT believed that when dealing with educators and child welfare professionals, fathers and mothers should never be content to listen.

Parents had two contributions to make. First, they could draw on their wealth of experience to enlighten one another about child health and development. In addition, they should set and enforce moral standards for popular amusements and education. State congresses in Iowa and California preached these messages almost from their inception. Cora Hillis lent her support to the idea that women assembled in mothers' clubs could share practical knowledge about education and child nurture. She and many others also believed that parents were uniquely qualified to make policy about entertainment for children. Following the lead of its affiliate in Berkeley, the California Congress of Mothers formed an Amusement Committee that decided to focus on motion pictures in 1923. Four years later the NCPT paired up with the General Federation of Women's Clubs to found the National Board of Classification and Estimate, whose purpose was to rate Hollywood films. Drawing on their ethical acumen, middle-class mothers now warned parents about movies with content unsuitable for children.[31]

But for women like Hannah Schoff and Margaretta Reeve, there was something irresistible about putting experts in front of the untrained, and in the late 1920s, the NCPT launched a national campaign for parent education. At the organization's annual meeting in 1930, delegates adopted a resolution from the Worthy Home Membership Committee endorsing courses in parenthood and homemaking for every boy and girl enrolled in a high school curriculum.[32] Because it aimed to help present as well as future parents, teaching them to cooperate responsibly with the school, the National Congress had no trouble imagining a partnership between PTAs and higher education. With a grant from the Spelman Fund of New York through the National Council of Parent Education, it hired Ada Hart Arlitt, a professor at the University of Cincinnati, to stimulate and coordinate its state affiliates' educational work with parents and bring America's public colleges and universities into parent education.[33] Such work was hardly unprecedented. Due in part to the efforts of Lawrence K. Frank at the Laura Spelman Rockefeller Memorial Foundation, courses in child care and parenting were not uncommon in American higher education, especially at land grant schools and colleges for women. But the NCPT viewed parent education as its territory, a natural extension of its original claim. In 1932, Arlitt reported progress in eighteen states, including training conferences for "semi-professional leaders" and schools for parents to introduce them to modern methods of child rearing.[34] Respect for what mothers and fathers could learn from one another had not completely disappeared, but the NCPT behaved as if its leadership was required for states to raise effective programs in parent education.

The NCPT's Legislative Committee hewed to the organization's belief in national policy-making, consistently delivering enthusiastic support for centralized leadership and funding in American education. Chaired for a decade by temperance reformer and suffragist Elizabeth Hewes Tilton, the committee favored federal aid to public schools and throughout the 1920s called for the establishment of a cabinet-level department of education. In 1928, Tilton's colleague, Charl Williams, the chair of the NCPT's Committee on School Education, reported on her plans to educate the membership on the need for a secretary of education; she proposed to bring them around through articles placed in the bulletins of the NCPT's state affiliates. Tilton had no time for women who talked about change but did nothing to bring it about. She singled out Minnesota, California, Washington, and Wisconsin as states with PTAs deserving praise for political activism. Meanwhile, legislative committees in Iowa and Missouri pledged their allegiance to her reform platform. I "have used the National

Chairman's plan extensively in promotion work among local chairmen," reported Mrs. P. H. Crane of Kansas City.[35]

Generating interest in reform among the NCPT's rank and file had been a challenge for the organization's leadership from the beginning. Most women joined mothers' clubs out of concern for their own children; they could be convinced to adopt a more comprehensive agenda only after "talks on such subjects" as food, clothing, and health care had fostered a "feeling of intimate relation between home and school." Many resented the firm resolve of state and national leaders whose actions they perceived to be not only self-righteous but also self-serving. "Not self glory," said the vice president of the New Jersey Congress of Parents and Teachers to an audience in Middlesex County but "service to every child should be the aim of every P.T.A." Addressed to women in local and regional chapters, such talk undermined the rapport it was supposed to build by patronizing those women who thought of themselves as altruists, while doing nothing to reassure the many others who wanted to maintain the status quo. In Iowa, Cora Hillis quickly discovered how unpopular being "the agitator in school affairs" could be. Nellie Noble, an organizer for the California Congress of Mothers, often encountered what she labeled self-centered parochialism. "It was a real job for me as State Organizer to travel into every little town and wake up mothers to the idea that they had responsibilities to other people's children." No amount of pressure could persuade some to support programs for children whose mothers were dead or working.[36]

Even an optimist like Elizabeth Tilton had to concede that there were limits to national direction-setting. Plotting the course of every state legislative committee was counterproductive, and some initiatives of the national board could not expect to meet with universal approbation. The states "show an increase in interest in National Legislation," she wrote in 1927, "[but I must take what each gives me,] as I know if I criticize or press hard I might not be able keep our Legislative program going at all."[37] Despite such political awareness, it proved to be no easy task to dispel the notion that national leaders imposed their will on the whole organization, as one of Tilton's successors at the helm of the Legislative Committee revealed when she announced in 1942 that the NCPT had finally installed a more democratic procedure for adopting a reform agenda. "State congresses are no longer told," said Mary T. Bannerman, that "'this is the national program.'"[38]

The leadership of the NCPT found the urge to apply a firm hand difficult to resist because they perceived themselves to be different from the organization's rank and file. By the 1920s, women had made great strides as professionals in social work and education, and the officers of the NCPT desperately wanted to cast off the appearance of amateurism. But surveys confirmed that PTA "moms" conformed to the stereotype of the "average" middle-class woman. Conducted in California in the 1930s, two polls showed that most PTA members made the home "their main business in life." They had finished high school but not college, belonged to other community organizations, and lived with their husbands, devoting themselves to him and their children. Only one in eight worked outside the home in 1939. "She is not a 'glamour girl,'" said the NCPT, "but a wholesome, substantial sort of person that typifies the best American ideals and makes our country what it is today." It was an image that made for good public relations, but it did nothing to uphold the ambitious woman's aspirations. To be an effective advocate for the home, said Margaretta Reeve, the NCPT had to operate efficiently, convincing its volunteers to practice the same dedication to service and commitment to experienced leadership that were routinely demonstrated by women in the helping professions. That this might entail deferring to the superior knowledge and judgment of others was a small price to pay considering the exalted work of the whole organization.[39]

The leaders of large state affiliates like the California Congress of Mothers (CCM) had more in common with their national colleagues than with many of their counterparts closer to home. Formed in 1907, the CCM's Legislative Committee pressed PTA members and politicians alike to support kindergartens, birth registration, and child labor reform. It asked local chapters to settle for nothing less than full funding for public education in the 1930s but failed to achieve consensus on the wisdom of state support for child care centers during World War II. Even in California, where defense plants meant collective security and individual prosperity, it was widely believed that mothers should stay home, especially if their children were very young. Members of many California PTAs studied educational policy issues and advocated moral reform. Some wrote letters in favor of local restrictions like curfew laws and liquor licenses, while others endorsed bond issues for neighborhood playgrounds and school buildings. But only a few home and school groups like those in the state's major cities took something more than a parochial stand. For example, the first mothers' clubs in Los Angeles and San Francisco made an effort to help neglected and dependent children. Penny lunches served by the Los Angeles Federation of Parent-Teacher Associations eventually convinced the city's board of education to organize a milk service and provide breakfasts with food paid for by parent-teacher organizations. The school board also assumed joint responsibility for health screening, a program that was initiated by the federation before World War I and, by 1940, included twenty-two parent-teacher clinics, diagnosing children for sight, hearing, and dental problems.[40]

Local indifference to statewide issues like the development of the California School Code frustrated the CCM's leaders on many occasions. In the 1920s, the chair of its Legislative Committee, Rowayne C. Martin, urged all members to register and vote. The crux of the problem was the lack of local leadership. Women with the right mix of energy, tact, and self-assurance were thought to be very rare. Indifferent to or intimidated by the rigors of policy-making, many PTAs automatically deferred to the professionals in their schools such that by 1930 the women in charge of the state congress decided to take a more active role in setting the priorities of CCM affiliates and shaping their political agendas. They were careful not to back candidates for public office, but there were dangers inherent even in this nonpartisan approach. PTAs that learned to challenge principals, teachers, or school board members might also become more inclined to question the directives of their own organization. Perhaps this is why Martin also discouraged political independence, asking PTAs to refrain from endorsing measures not approved by the state board.[41]

The top-down leadership style of the NCPT and many of its state associations extended to their relationship with the National Congress of Colored Parents and Teachers (NCCPT) and its member organizations. A combination of white discrimination and black solidarity prompted African-American women to create their own benevolent and self-help organizations in the second half of the nineteenth century. Formed in May 1926, the NCCPT built on a strong foundation laid by the African Methodist Episcopal Church and the National Association of Colored Women, both of which encouraged black mothers to come together in conferences or clubs as early as 1900.[42] Georgia and Delaware contributed the most to the NCCPT's original complement of 300 PTAs and 3,000 individual members, but the movement was not confined to the South, Kansas and Oklahoma together accounting for 53 black parent-teacher associations. Those in charge of the NCPT quickly acknowledged the importance of their new competitor, assembling a national report on the "extension of work among colored people" in the same year the NCCPT was formed.[43]

Among women activists, African Americans took a less class-conscious approach than their white counterparts because all black women had to contend with racism.[44] However, in relating to the school, black and white mothers had much in common, setting similar goals at the state and local levels for their respective organizations and doing much the same work to improve the education of their own children. In Delaware, for example, black PTAs tried to upgrade the school plant, repairing buildings, purchasing equipment, and tending the yard. One black local, the Middletown Progressive Parent-Teacher Association, provided hot lunches and promoted health education. Nevertheless, the leaders of the NCPT were not about to propose that black and white mothers come together in one comprehensive association, even though they had seriously considered forming such an organization in 1908. Aware that such a recommendation would alienate many white members, especially in the South, they opted for segregation, instructing state branches to avoid soliciting or admitting those black women who could join the NCCPT. They offered to help African-American mothers build their own organization instead, giving advice on educational policy and sharing the benefit of the NCPT's experience on practical matters like membership, governance, and public relations. Not a little smug and condescending, they permitted their advisors to mediate disputes but drew the line when it came to settling disagreements within or between black PTAs.[45]

The leaders of the NCPT claimed to respect the dignity of black women and the autonomy of their national parent-teacher organization. The formation of the NCCPT, they said, expressed such "pride of race by colored citizens" that "[we hope and pray it will] arouse a corresponding nobleness of thought and life among their members." However, it was the pervasiveness of racism among whites in the United States and the almost universal acceptance of segregation before 1945 that stood in the way of full cooperation, let alone consolidation. The leaders of the NCPT revealed their racist feelings when they justified separatism by explaining that equality "will only come when the colored people train themselves and their children to be leaders among their own race, raising their standards of thought and living to correspond with those of the white race." There can be little doubt that the NCPT would have suffered the consequences had it taken a controversial stand. Reports from California, Colorado, Georgia, Oklahoma, and Pennsylvania expressed a preference for organizational segregation. Accordingly, the NCPT counseled its affiliates to press for the formation of a branch of the NCCPT in states with at least ten black locals and 300 members. However, the National Congress puzzled over the problem of chapters that already included both white and black women, encouraging them to adopt a membership policy geared to local attitudes and conditions. Communities with integrated schools, it said, should decide for themselves whether to insist on racially separate parent-teacher associations.[46] For once, the NCPT did not dictate policy to its local organizations.

Divided and confused about their relationship, black and white parents could not bring their collective weight to bear on educational policy in the United States. The big loser, as a result, was African-American education. Complain though they might about the degraded state of their schools, black parents discovered that in the absence of white support, most educators and politicians felt no compelling need to listen. Membership in the NCCPT suffered accordingly; in 1939, it could count only 1,586 locals and 26,000 members. Some of its state branches tried to generate interest by courting parents and attracting public attention. For example, the black congress in North Carolina ran workshops to train PTA leaders, while in Tennessee the NCCPT affiliate pressured the legislature to invest more money in black child welfare and education. These efforts achieved such modest success that in 1945 the United States Children's Bureau brought together twenty-seven members of the NCCPT's executive board to study the condition of the parent-teacher movement in black America. The conference called attention to the inferior status of black schools and the need for parent education among African Americans.[47]

Demonstrating the limitations of top-down leadership, white PTAs showed little interest in forging a new relationship with their black counterparts. In Mississippi, the state branch of the NCPT assumed a mentoring role, treating the NCCPT women like their interns or pupils, while in Georgia, the white congress continued the practice of reaching out only when asked, defending the principle of noninterference to justify inaction. The president of the white congress in Missouri understood that her members shared some of the blame for the scandal that was black education. She counseled them to jump-start reform by explaining to white parents that black schools were not inherently inferior, merely victims of economic and social discrimination. However, the best her organization could do was allow blacks to apply for one of its teacher training scholarships.[48]

At the state and national levels, the women of the NCPT struggled to find the right combination of leadership qualities capable of inspiring loyalty and prompting participation among the rank and file. Without formal training or credentials, they claimed the right to lead based on their good intentions. This was enough to give them legitimacy among their peers in voluntarism, but not enough for them to be taken seriously by most educators and politicians. In addition, there were many parents for whom an organization like the NCPT was no substitute for direct contact with school authorities. Consider, for example, the relationship between the home and school in Delaware. In this rural state, which often resisted change, parents had to contend with an unimaginative establishment in the schools and a powerful elite of corporate and professional people who sought to manage public involvement, while controlling the direction and pace of educational reform. To have any influence over educational practice, much less policy-making, Delaware's parents had to be persistent and employ a variety of political means.

Solo or Chorus in Rural America: A Case Study of Parents and Educational Reform in Delaware

In the nineteenth century, when most Americans still lived on farms, parents controlled rural schools. They decided where the one-room schoolhouse would stand and who would teach its pupils. They influenced the choice of textbooks, the style of discipline, and the length of the school session. The relationship between parents and teachers defined country schools. Its subjective and transitory nature troubled many educators, and beginning with Horace Mann, they pressed for the centralization and standardization of rural education as early as the 1840s. However, it was not until the end of the nineteenth century that the reformers began to see results in their effort to reorganize rural education. Many small, independent districts lost their autonomy to township school systems and county superintendents, reforms that were encouraged by the General Education Board and the NEA, whose Committee of Twelve called for rural school consolidation in 1897. The pace of such change picked up in the years just before and after World War I, when state boards and departments of education flexed newly acquired muscles and many rural school districts disappeared altogether in a flurry of educational reform.[49]

In Delaware, public education was decentralized before 1920. Local school districts in this largely rural state had what often amounted to a free hand. But reformers had a different plan, and, led by Pierre S. du Pont, they persuaded the General Assembly to strengthen the state board of education in 1919, giving it substantial authority over local school districts. Although the opponents of educational centralization counterattacked, du Pont and his allies held them off, and by the early 1920s, the state board had a real say in the finances and policies of public schools.[50] The Delaware Department of Public Instruction (DDPI), whose superintendent was a bureaucrat named Harry Vance Holloway, managed these schools for the board of education. Appointed in 1921, Holloway took his cues from corporate leaders like Pierre S. du Pont, who was himself vice president of the state board between 1919 and 1921. The superintendent was very comfortable and effective in his new role, maintaining cordial relations with school boards and administrators, while insisting that they adhere to the state board's regulations.

Such professionalism made Holloway popular with the reformers on the state board to whom he reported. He also shared their conservatism, especially concerning race. Pierre du Pont, for example, spent $5 million of his own money to build no less than 120 new school buildings in Delaware, but he never questioned school segregation. On the contrary, his investment in separate schoolhouses for blacks and whites undoubtedly reinforced it. In demand as a speaker, Holloway accepted invitations from both races to appear at school events. However, when the Dover Board of Education apparently paid some black teachers more than whites in 1928, Holloway threatened to recommend a commensurate reduction in the district's state allocation. "The State Board allotted $1750 last Fall to make it possible for you to pay your colored teachers on the same basis as . . . your white teachers," Holloway reminded the Dover school board, "not to make it possible for you to pay your colored teachers *more* than your white teachers of the same grade and experience."[51] The message for school officials was clear; they should not extemporize, particularly when it came to race.

But what did Holloway think about parents? If teachers, principals, and superintendents had to follow the state board's rules, what about mothers and fathers to whom such rules did not necessarily apply? By Holloway's time, the relationship between parents and schools was different from what it once had been. Parents still possessed considerable clout, for without their support educators still might find themselves out of a job. Dissatisfied parents could withdraw their children from public school or withhold their endorsement of school taxes, teachers, and trustees. But most did not have the means to send their children to schools that were not subject to increasing state regulation. If parents were to continue to exercise influence, they would have to change their ways. Their involvement might still be explicit, expressed as a private complaint. But it also might have to be secondhand, assembled and edited by a small group, such as a local parent-teacher association, or it might have to be truly vicarious, coming from a large organization such as a county or state PTA.

In dealing with parents, Holloway was no different from most of his peers in educational administration at the beginning of the twentieth cen-

tury. They modeled themselves after corporate leaders, seeking to mini-
mize the probability of political discord or outcomes they could not fore-
see and control. For them, collaboration, not confrontation, was the order
of the day. Parent organizations supplied a handle by which they could direct parental involvement. But controlling the PTA meant more than
managing conflict; it also meant shaping opinion because parents could
spell the difference between the success and failure of educational programs and policy. Of course, not all parents came neatly packaged, and
some even spoke for themselves. Holloway learned to isolate scattered
complaints and build public support by appealing to higher authority. In
this regard, he was not unlike his mentor, Pierre du Pont, who with his
cousins, Alfred and Coleman, set high standards for their chemical business and never settled for anything less than expert leadership. The superintendent relied on his knowledge of state law to disarm disaffected parents and maintained his political equilibrium by invoking the rationalized
policies and procedures school reformers put in place.

Compared to many of its counterparts elsewhere in the United States,
the DDPI was in very close contact with its constituency. Perhaps this
should come as no surprise, given the small size of the state and its domi-
nation by the du Pont family and its powerful corporation. But it was the
centralized system of school governance installed in the 1920s that actually made it possible for state officials to keep in contact with individual
districts. In his capacity as the superintendent of public instruction, Holloway regularly received detailed correspondence from board members,
teachers, and the parents of schoolchildren. They looked to him for advice
and assistance in solving local problems. Well organized and conscientious, he almost never failed to respond. His files registered Delaware's educational pulse during his long tenure in the DDPI, archiving the home's
concerns about the school and documenting his administrative style in
dealing with them.

The parents who chose to share their views with the superintendent focused on basic issues in rural education. They concerned themselves
mainly with teaching and learning; when they complained, it was usually
about the location of schoolhouses, the condition of these facilities, and
the teachers hired to staff them. The character and behavior of teachers
frequently attracted attention from home. Parents disagreed among themselves and with school trustees about who was qualified to instruct their
children. By law, the selection of teachers was a local responsibility, and
according to the superintendent's correspondents, personalities and patronage often determined who got hired and fired in Delaware's rural

schools.[52] Holloway avoided getting caught in the middle when communities fought about classroom personnel. But when confronted by a situation that required him to respond, he followed his bureaucratic instinct, counseling those involved to trust the system and be patient. Seldom, if ever, did he encourage people to seek redress through the electoral process or reform.

Perhaps the superintendent believed what many supervisors and teachers told him about the ignorance of parents and their apathy on public education. Attributing her dismissal to parental bias, one teacher, Ruth W. Lewis, told Holloway that the parents in her district needed "to be enlightened by being educated socially and morally." They never visited her school and made no effort to discover what she was all about.[53] According to Albert Early, a rural supervisor for the DDPI, most families in Farmington cared less about their sons and daughters than their chickens. Such an observation may not have been all that far off the mark. Many farmers in Delaware distrusted reformers and resisted change. Even after the Depression ended, they faced economic hardships that made it difficult for them to justify investing personal time or public money in school improvement. But in making this assessment, Early was responding to a complaint from a woman who wanted a better education for her children. According to Clara Dennis, they suffered from the poor condition of their schoolhouse, the incompetence of their teacher, and the lack of classroom discipline. She asked that they be transferred to another building.[54]

If the superintendent's files are any indication, Mrs. Dennis was not the only parent who was dissatisfied with the status quo. Holloway often heard from those who were concerned about unequal opportunity in Delaware's public schools. Parents living in the suburbs of Wilmington wanted their children to attend classes in the city. One family considered moving so that its children could enroll at Wilmington's du Pont High School, the most elaborate and well-equipped high school in the state.[55] Another planned to send a daughter to Howard High School in Wilmington if the girl could not prepare for college by attending an accredited twelfth grade program in the black school close to home. More than a few were willing to accept rural school consolidation if it meant that their children could have better access to secondary education.[56]

By the 1940s, many blacks could no longer contain their anger about the poor condition of their schools. Previously, they had confined themselves to complaining about being excluded from the patronage jobs dispensed through their schools, but now they questioned the educational quality of those schools. Compared with whites, black children were disadvantaged by ramshackle buildings, distracted instructors, and under-staffed schools. When three vocational teachers at the Louis Redding High School in Middletown slighted the needs of their pupils to moonlight in a defense plant, one resident expressed his conviction that Holloway would not allow "any white school" to be neglected like that. Predictably, the superintendent urged Redding's principal, Alfred G. Waters, to pro-tect his school's reputation by guarding against "any situation which would give credence" to such statements. But he did not know what to say to the black parents in Mt. Olive who refused to accept the blame for the disappointing performance of their children's elementary school, the only one in the county with one teacher for eight grades. "Because of the over-crowded conditions existing in our school," they said in a petition to Dover, "our children have not been properly taught and as a result have lost interest in School. This accounts for our not having a High School graduate in our community."[57]

Administrative arrogance could bring parents to life, prompting some to insist that they not be patronized or denied the chance to have a say. The parent of a junior at du Pont High School reacted angrily to the recal-citrance of local school officials in the face of his complaints. "How the school is managed is none of my business," Julian F. Smith had learned when he inquired about his son's compulsory class dues. After all, he was told, the school did not interfere in his affairs. Mounting a "last ditch de-fense" by writing Superintendent Holloway, Smith condemned the anal-ogy, calling it "muddy thinking" that was flawed in two ways. "First, a school executive is a public servant," he pointed out. "Second the school does not have its most precious possessions under the direct influence of my daily work, but I have a child enrolled in school."[58] As was his custom, Holloway chose to send this parent through proper channels. Professing his conviction that the problem could be solved, he referred him back to the source of the problem, the administration of du Pont High School.

Sometimes Holloway acted as the parents' champion with the state school board. When gasoline became scarce during World War II, he per-suaded the board to let rural districts set their own time schedule so that farm children would always be available for chores at home.[59] Of course, state governments could be demanding partners, hitching involvement to control. For example, some black communities across the South found their educational independence compromised after they asked outsiders for help with integration. But Holloway never felt threatened by local ini-tiative. Repeatedly, he urged parents to undertake special projects not be-cause he wanted to empower them, but because he thought they could contribute only by working with the professional establishment.[60] Like most of his contemporaries, Holloway believed that the home and the school were distinct but reciprocal institutions.

In 1924, Holloway urged Delaware's PTAs to get behind school reform, lending their support to changes that would ensure sufficient tax support, adequate facilities, and qualified teachers in the state's public schools. He had reason to believe that his plea would not go unheeded. Rural PTAs often took on a wide range of school improvement projects because there was usually a great need for fund-raising and social advocacy in farm communities.[61] In Delaware, businessmen and reformers settled on the PTA as the perfect instrument to modernize the state. Widespread and growing, such problems as illiteracy, poverty, and poor health predicted a bleak future unless something was done. The Service Citizens of Delaware promised to make a difference. Formed in July 1918 by Pierre du Pont and his friends among the state's elite, its stated objective was "to federate men and women of lofty ideals in a common enterprise for intellectual, moral, and spiritual betterment, to discover the paths of progress and give our citizens the incentive to follow them."[62] Unlike most local PTAs, the Service Citizens proposed to engage in policy-making, but the means by which to achieve its goals were not immediately at hand.

In Delaware, parent-teacher associations were slow to develop. Although some were established as early as 1911, such organizations were still uncommon before World War I, especially in rural areas. Some of the most prominent women in the state, including three du Ponts, formed a committee in 1914 to arouse indigenous interest in the work of the National Congress of Mothers and Parent-Teacher Associations.[63] But it was the decision by the Service Citizens to collaborate with the newly formed Delaware State Parent-Teacher Association (DSPTA) that energized the cause. Handpicked by the board of the Service Citizens, Etta Wilson became the DSPTA's executive director in 1921. Her background included staff work for a commission that developed a new state school code and three years as a member of the Bureau of Education, an information agency operated by the Service Citizens to promote school reform through centralization. The two organizations worked to multiply the number of parent-teacher associations, efforts that soon proved fruitful throughout the state. By June 1924, there were PTAs in 86 percent of its school districts, both black and white. Even farm parents responded; the 293 associations they formed meant that 81 percent of rural districts were organized by 1925, and men constituted half their members.[64]

Such accomplishments were not insignificant considering the suspicion of outsiders and the tradition of local control in many Delaware communities. Of course, the Service Citizens and the DSPTA appealed to parochial interests when they encouraged parents and teachers to organize at the district level. But to improve the quality of rural life, the Service Citizens insisted, community involvement in educational reform was indispensable. Parents had to transcend their personal concerns. In the 1920s, the DSPTA made the betterment of home conditions one of its primary objectives. In this endeavor, its work was in keeping with similar efforts mounted in the Deep South by northern philanthropies like the Jeanes Fund. Together the Service Citizens and the DSPTA also sought to promote the community use of the school.[65] But there was a certain irony in their professed commitment to citizen initiative and local control. After all, their ultimate goal was modernization. Delaware would remain an economic and social backwater unless the rural elements in the state abandoned their old-fashioned ways.

Perhaps the DSPTA's rapid growth also occurred because it did not rely for its leaders on the state's elite. There was not a du Pont among them in the 1920s. Instead, its officers represented the respectable middle class, men and women from every county who could be counted on to work hard for local school improvement and progressive policy-making. Mary Caulk Lewis, DSPTA president from 1924 to 1928, taught school as a youth, and after marrying Robert E. Lewis, the owner of the Dover Flour Mills and Flour Feed Exchange, she became a dedicated club women and reformer, serving as a director of both the Girls Industrial School and the Detention Home for Juveniles. Her recording secretary in 1925, Mary Cochran Pool, was active in the Delaware Federation of Women's Clubs. Clara McCleavy Harrington, the corresponding secretary, lived in the small town in Kent County that bore her husband's last name. Garrett S. Harrington was a member of the Service Citizens and president of the Harrington Chamber of Commerce. He surely must have known Frank C. Bancroft, DSPTA vice president from 1924 to 1930, who led the Delaware State Grange Mutual Fire Insurance Company and was vice president of both the First National Bank of Wyoming and the Wyoming Ice and Cold Storage Company. These progressive men and women tried to organize every school in the state, but they had reservations about reaching out to one important constituency. Black parents could form PTAs, but they could not lead the DSPTA. It had a separate group of black officers whose work accounted for 27 percent of all the PTAs in Delaware in 1926, a proportion that increased when the number of white associations declined during the Depression.[66]

In the 1920s, the DSPTA devoted itself to bringing parents up to speed. It developed materials for parents to use and sponsored programs in adult and parent education, taking a particular interest in the widespread problem of illiteracy. It generated grassroots support for progressive school reform and social welfare legislation. The Delaware General Assembly might have decided against investing in new school construction in 1927 had there been no pressure from both the Service Citizens and the DSPTA.[67] However, the tension between community control and statewide direction did not disappear with the enactment of this legislation. In describing its plans for the future in 1930, the DSPTA revealed itself to be still concerned about the possibility of such conflict. "The Delaware Parent-Teacher Association," it said, "will continue to place the development of leadership, the ability to work together on the part of the rank and file . . . , [and] the dissemination of knowledge concerning the findings of psychology in regard to child care, before the public as matters of paramount importance."[68] The leaders of the DSPTA were committed to their reform agenda, but what would induce parents to follow their lead? What kind of pressures faced local PTAs in deciding between the DSPTA's agenda and going their own way?

In theory, no organization is more closely tied to its community than a home and school association. It epitomizes the principle of local control. School boards are required to observe laws and regulations imposed by the federal government and the states. But parents have jealously guarded their authority over the family and their independent standing as a source of influence at school. The leaders of the NCPT faced this problem frequently. As child welfare reformers, they discovered that the private family was beyond the reach of most public policy makers. But could the same be said for mothers assembled in a community organization devoted to the home and school?

The history of the Middletown, Delaware, PTA in the 1920s illustrates the dilemma faced by home and school associations subject to entreaties by an active department of education and a well-organized state PTA. A prosperous farming community not far from Wilmington, Middletown was familiar to the leading educators and reformers in Delaware. When the town's parents formed the Middletown Parent-Teacher Association (MPTA) in January 1915, the state commissioner of education, Dr. Charles A. Wagner, attended their first meeting. One year later he returned not once but twice to enlist their support on behalf of a package of proposed school reforms. He called on them, for example, to support changes in the compulsory school laws about to come before the General Assembly. Above all, he wanted them to endorse a plan to enhance the power of the state board of education, "thereby centralizing school authority, unity of management being the only way to obtain good schools."[69] Wagner's refrain was a familiar one in Delaware at the time, but just as important as his message was the way he chose to disseminate it. He used local PTAs to trumpet his statewide agenda for school reform.

Almost as soon as he became superintendent of public instruction, Holloway approached the MPTA. In the fall of 1922, he wrote to the organization and attended a meeting, seeking support for additional changes in the school code and asking it to join Pierre du Pont and the Service Citizens in their new initiative, a school building program for the entire state.[70] Like many communities in Delaware, Middletown needed a new school. As early as 1920, the MPTA sought to arouse sentiment for such a project, but local taxpayers resisted, balking at the cost. For the next seven years, the MPTA faithfully carried the reformers' message to the parents of Middletown. It received enthusiastic assistance in this endeavor from the local school administration. After collaborating on a study of overcrowding in the lower grades, the MPTA pledged to work with the board of education to pass a bond referendum. In 1925, it backed a resolution sent to the General Assembly by the DSPTA endorsing the du Pont construction plan. It even publicized a letter from Assistant State Superintendent John Shilling, scolding Middletown for failing to build a new school.[71]

Notwithstanding their support for the du Pont plan, the mothers of Middletown did not want to remake the world. What mattered most to them was the education of their own children. The statewide agenda that seemed so important at first soon lost its appeal, and the MPTA turned its attention to teaching methods, their effect on pupils, and the need for amenities in the Middletown school. The most well attended meetings in the 1920s featured teacher demonstrations and student presentations. Buying equipment for the schoolhouse and playground always seemed like a good idea, but these stopgap measures fell far short of insisting that local taxpayers go into debt for a new building.[72] The MPTA's support for the program of the state school reformers rested on shaky parochial ground.

In January 1927, the MPTA appointed a committee to lobby the Delaware General Assembly for school building funds. By then, the reformers' agenda finally seemed to be having an impact in Dover. When the General

Assembly appropriated $2 million for new school construction in April, the MPTA responded immediately, endorsing this action at its next meeting and appointing a committee to work with the school board to take advantage of the situation. At the same time, it agreed to help raise money for the DSPTA, whose existence was threatened by the impending demise of its chief benefactor, the Service Citizens.[73]

With the help of state funds, Middletown built a new school, which opened in 1929. Meanwhile, the MPTA continued to field offers for help from reformers and advice from educators on parent-teacher cooperation. Successor to the Service Citizens, the Delaware Citizens Association (DCA) made the improvement of educational practice its first priority. According to the DCA, parental ignorance was the biggest obstacle to educational reform, a view that almost certainly reflected the thinking of its leader, H. Fletcher Brown, a successful businessman and prominent philanthropist who was also president of the state board of education. "Understanding on the part of parents of what their children are doing in school," Harry Vance Holloway wrote in the DCA *Bulletin,* is a prerequisite for "cooperation between the home and the school." Together the DCA and the DSPTA should educate them, thereby "bringing about that understanding" and "making possible a progressive program in the schools." In 1927, the executive committee of the MPTA agreed to implement a program of parent education prepared by the DCA but rejected the suggestion that even the entertainment at each meeting should incorporate the topic prescribed for discussion.[74] The price of outside assistance turned out to be mandates from on high and ultimately less parental control. In exchange for help in financing a new school, the parents of Middletown found themselves relinquishing some of their autonomy at home.

Educators and reformers believed that public schools needed private organizations like the DCA and DSPTA. An educational system is "like an army," Holloway told the DCA Board of Directors in 1932. It "can only hold its own when the people are working in back of the lines." By funding the DSPTA, the DCA gained access to an existing network of community leaders and grassroots associations. "The success of the two organizations is inseparable," said J. Edward Goslee, the president of the DCA. Together they constitute a sign of promise for "a thinking, well-informed public." Perhaps the people of Delaware could not be counted on to think for themselves. Certainly, Etta Wilson had her doubts. Meeting with the MPTA in 1934, she told the assembled parents that the mission of the DSPTA was to explain the school's problems to "as many as possible so that they will be ready as a unit to demand of the legislature next year what they need." Given the threat to government budgets posed by the Depression and the state's long history of educational neglect, Wilson may have had good reason not to want to leave anything to chance. After all, 110 PTAs had recently lapsed across the state. Reformers argued that private organizations like the DCA served as a counterweight to the public school establishment.[75] But Delaware's educators had always had much in common with its civic leaders, and those in charge of the DCA and the DSPTA had more than just citizen participation in mind when they justified their existence. They represented a particular point of view, a platform of child welfare and bureaucratic school reform, not to mention a top-down approach to achieving change.

Cosponsored by the state board of education and the DCA, the short-lived demonstration school in Georgetown tested the capacity of the reformers to impose their views on the whole state. Located in rural Sussex County, it was intended to uplift farm family life as well as bring modern educational theory and practice to the pedagogically unregenerate. The two aims were, in fact, interdependent: "the absence of living conditions sufficiently satisfactory to attract the most ambitious and successful teachers," said the directors of the DCA, "has been long accepted as one of the greatest handicaps of rural education." If Georgetown's parents and teachers could be brought up to speed, then the future of educational reform looked bright indeed, but as it turned out, the experiment failed, a casualty of both arrogance and ignorance.[76] The reformers failed to prepare the locals for the changes they tried to impose. Despite endorsement by the Georgetown school board and the state superintendent, the new "activity" curriculum and its informal methods of instruction were not embraced by many parents or the faculty already in place. The demonstration school's director, Alan Hulsizer, alienated far more parents than he won over with his patronizing ways. Visiting educators and reformers left disappointed because "the freedom of the new school that they saw degenerated into idleness, if not into sheer disorder," and the DCA withdrew its subvention after three years.[77] Partnership with the DSPTA did not give the DCA a license to remake traditional ways. Rural parents and teachers in Delaware could not be forced to become advocates for change.

Working less and less closely with the DSPTA, the DCA continued to speak for educational and social reform. As the Depression deepened, it agreed to evaluate the status of dependent children and even considered taking responsibility for coordinating a statewide welfare program.[78] However, the alliance between parents and reformers was breaking down

in Delaware. It had never been a match made in heaven, and when the
coming of World War II changed the climate of opinion, rural parents felt
less constrained about expressing their comfortable conservatism. Educators like Holloway never stopped courting them, but reformers became
discouraged, and the executive committee of the DCA voted to suspend
operations in 1942.[79] For the time being, the relationship between the
home and the school would not be recast.

From Top Down to Outside In: The Home, the School, and the Direction of Change

The history of the relationship between the home and the school in Delaware was reflective of larger trends. Like reformers in other states and at
the national level, Delaware's elite seized upon this relationship as an instrument of educational policy-making and social change. They accepted
the idea that the home and the school should collaborate, but they also developed an elaborate organizational structure to impose their own program on parents from the top down, and they often encountered resistance from the rank and file, who wanted at the very least to maintain their
independence if not sustain the social and political status quo. The leaders
of the DSPTA, like their colleagues in the NCPT, learned that parents and
teachers did not always welcome help from outsiders, let alone accept
someone else's agenda for change. So, too, did educators like Harry Vance
Holloway and the leaders of such reform organizations as the Service Citizens and the DCA. But while many parents preferred autonomy to reform, not all were equally free to have things their own way. Educators and
reformers often perceived the home, especially if it was black, poor, or foreign, to be incapable of making its own decisions. Between 1900 and 1940,
they made the school an instrument of social and economic outreach to
immigrant and working-class families. They assigned it the task of re-
forming some homes from the outside in.

CHAPTER FIVE

Twenty-Four Hours a Day

And once when I was sick in bed
You came to our old wrecky place
And set by me and stroked my head—
I know you well. I know your face.
— Knowles Witcher Teel

Even at the age of sixty-two, Anna Beach Pratt made a striking appearance. Tall and slender, she wore her white hair long, arranged in a bun; her oval face featured shining blue eyes, a delicate nose, and a firm yet graceful chin (figure 5.1). But Pratt was not just a beautiful woman; she enjoyed wide recognition in her profession and commanded great public respect. The second woman elected to Philadelphia's consolidated Board of Education, she won primarily because of her reputation as a distinguished leader in the field of school social work and a pioneer in applying the principles of mental hygiene to education. By the time she made the school board in 1929, she had also paid her dues as a volunteer, having spent four years as the president of the Philadelphia County Council of Home and School Associations.

Pratt's career began in Elmira, New York, her hometown, where she organized the first welfare federation and served as assistant secretary of public relief. National recognition did not come her way, however, until after 1916, when she became the executive director of the White-Williams Foundation, a philanthropic social agency based in Philadelphia that specialized in vocational guidance and school counseling. The way up had not been easy. Once chosen to be an overseer of the poor in New York, she did the work while her father carried the title because the state legislature refused to give the post to a woman. Her selection as a delegate to the second White House Conference on Children, convened by Herbert Hoover,

FIGURE 5.1. Anna Beach Pratt, executive director of the White-Williams Foundation, 1916–
32. *Philadelphia Bulletin* Photo Collection, Urban Archives, Samuel Paley Library, Temple
University, Philadelphia.

acknowledged conclusively the depth of her community and professional
standing.[1]

Pratt believed in the importance of close ties between the home and
school. Children were not like jigsaw puzzles, to be dismantled and re-
assembled at will; educators had to think of them in their entirety—at
home, on the job, and in the community as well as in school. But teachers
could not come to know the whole child by themselves. They needed

social workers to help them consider all the factors that enter into a child's life. Only in this way could they see the "interplay of intellectual, emotional, and social characteristics and realize how necessary it is to study their relative strength if they want to teach each child as an individual." Parents also figured prominently in any well-balanced educational equation. To reconcile the home and the school, social workers had to factor them in, relying in part on the parent-teacher association.[2]

As a champion for social work in education, Anna Pratt stood for more than better communication and cooperation between the home and the school. She, and others like her, proposed a new and expanded role for the school. Knowledge of the social and economic context of children's lives might improve prospects for success in teaching, but it also raised the possibility of a more efficient and effective method of social reform. What better institution than the school to represent the values of the middle class to immigrant and working-class families? What better way to bring the findings of modern science to bear on traditional parents ignorant of the basic principles of health care and child rearing, let alone the latest innovations? In the hands of school nurses and social workers, the relationship between the home and the school became a channel for social reform. However, as the school increased its involvement with the home, the nature of their interaction lost some of its clarity, while becoming controversial and even distressing. Parents and teachers were forced to ask some difficult and troubling questions: How much could or should the school contribute to the home? Were there any limits to the scope of its influence? Would expanding the role of the school disturb the balance of power in their relationship? Perhaps some parents had reason to be less concerned than others about the new social conscience at school. But ironically educators themselves discovered that more responsibility was not necessarily a boon or blessing. Expanding the mission of the school not only increased their burden but also enhanced the likelihood that they would be held accountable for their teaching. Incorporating the home as well as the school into their domain made it more difficult for educators to deflect criticism by saying that others should take the blame for children who failed to make the grade.

Social Service Station

At the beginning of the twentieth century, a crisis faced American education. As immigrants and blacks poured into the nation's towns and cities, the demand for educational and social services fell heavily on both public and parochial schools. Overcrowded classrooms and understaffed schools defied attempts at reform, while belying glib rhetoric about the importance of schooling. Instead of sounding an alarm, educators, settlement workers, and reformers rejoiced at the relentless expansion of the mission and scope of schooling. Beginning in the 1880s, they concentrated on the children absent from school—dropouts, truants, and the unenrolled. There were legislative remedies for nonattendance to which they could appeal, but until children became an anachronism in the American workplace, compulsory school and child labor laws seldom delivered the promised relief. Critics like Joseph Mayer Rice and Leonard Ayres cited the schools for incompetence and inefficiency; they were at fault when children failed to keep up with their peers or left to go to work. Many educators and social workers, on the other hand, pointed the finger at the family. When children did not start or finish school, the explanation could be found at home.

Reformers and researchers disagreed about what to look for in the home. Many focused on the behavior of parents, attributing truancy and early school leaving to their ignorance, indifference, or immorality. The school had no choice but to monitor the family and discipline the home. William Henry Maxwell, the first superintendent to manage the consolidated schools of New York City, considered himself an expert on parental deficiencies. Some parents, he said, overestimated their child's talent or ambition, inadvertently poisoning his or her attitude toward school. More often, truants and dropouts had mothers and fathers who failed to exercise strict control. The secretary of the Public Education Association in Philadelphia was even more judgmental: fatherless families and mothers who worked were responsible for absenteeism. "The picture of squalid, ignorant, vicious home surroundings," said James Hiatt, "can not but impress one as being the largest contributory cause" of irregular attendance. "The only wonder is that so large a proportion of children living in such so-called 'homes' do regularly find their way into the schoolroom."[3]

More sophisticated observers recognized that the relationship between parents and teachers was not necessarily adversarial. Resisting the temptation to condemn parents as a group, they appealed instead to the effects of culture and class on attendance and performance at school. Immigrants from southern or eastern Europe often feared and sometimes resented the teacher. Her language and values threatened to estrange their children from them. Leonard Covello, who was both an Italian American and the principal of a New York City high school, understood such feelings. His compatriots frequently tolerated, and many even encouraged, truancy and nonattendance not only because they expected their children to work but also because they distrusted the school. It was the most visible and direct agent of Americanization, undermining the teachings and authority of the home. The Anglo-Christian culture of the public school also alienated many parents of Russian Jewish heritage. Although they usually supported an extended education for at least some of their children, they seldom showed their face at school. The parent-teacher association was not a meaningful organization for them, and because they valued public education for economic reasons, they sometimes sent their first-born to work at an early age so that younger siblings could attend.[4]

By 1915, social scientists had begun to demonstrate an interest in the causes of early school leaving. More than a few called attention to the class standing of the home. Conducted at the Boston High School of Commerce between 1906 and 1914, one investigation of early school leaving identified paternal occupation as the most powerful predictor of what educators called "elimination." That the sons of unskilled laborers were the most likely to drop out might have been due to working-class disdain for school. But to the author of this study, family income seemed a far more satisfactory explanation. Published in 1919, the fifteenth yearbook of the National Society for the Study of Education reported the findings of an extensive inquiry into the relationship between home conditions and persistence in school. Above all, it concluded, "the advantages of the home, its educational, economic, and social stations," account for the years of schooling that different children receive.[5]

Relying on Chicago for their data, Edith Abbott and Sophonisba Breckinridge prepared an extensive and detailed report on truancy and nonattendance, perhaps the best of its time. Not surprisingly, they deplored the social and economic waste resulting from such shortsighted behavior as early school leaving, but true to their roots in the settlement movement, they were conflicted about just where to place the blame. Their contempt for those who denied their children an education can hardly be denied. "Ignorant and desperate parents need to be protected against themselves," Abbott and Breckinridge argued. "They gain nothing in the end by being allowed to take their children out of school and see them grow into worthless men and women." But did such parents have any choice? "No study of the causes of non-attendance in the immigrant sections of the city," Abbott and Breckinridge admitted, "can fail to emphasize the fact that poverty is only too frequently the real excuse." Too often, they added, "the pressure of poverty is so great" that the children, if allowed to work, would be classified as necessarily employed under the existing compulsory school laws.[6]

What could be done about such conditions? Although Abbott and Breckinridge acknowledged that economic necessity required many children to work, they refused to accept the consequences for the child and society of early school leaving. Solving the problem meant making some fundamental economic changes. "Only when wages have been raised to correspond to the rising standards of child-care," they said, "will the real weaknesses in the present system be wholly done away with." But not many reformers were prepared to defend such radical recommendations. Instead, they turned to the school for answers, arguing that it should expand the scope of its mission. As economist Frank Tracy Carlton explained, industrialization and urbanization left parents unable to perform many of the social and educational tasks that had once been exclusive to their domain. "Our educational and industrial life has become so complex," Carlton argued, "that few mothers are capable of assuming entire charge of the care and training of the child." Choosing "to be identified with interests which are not of the household," some women forced the school to take more responsibility for the upbringing of their children.[7]

Educators chose their words carefully when naming an institution to substitute for the working-class and immigrant home in caring for neglected and dependent children. Boston established the first "parental school" in 1896, and Illinois soon enacted a law requiring cities of more than 100,000 to establish boarding schools for truant or disruptive children. By 1910, there were at least thirteen such schools across the country serving cities large and small, including New York, Chicago, Kansas City, and Spokane. Whether organized by the congregate or cottage system, they claimed to provide the home life that was judged to be missing from the lives of the boys assigned to them. Some parental schools were open only to truants, while others accepted delinquents, too, but none proved capable of eliminating recidivism. The problem was so acute in Chicago that Abbott and Breckinridge recommended "supplementing the work of the school, which deals only with the child, by some agency for dealing with parents and the home or with the neighborhood to which the child is returned."[8]

Short of replacing parents, the school could do more to advise and train them. The relationship between home and school could become the means by which to enlighten, guide, and strengthen the family (figure 5.2). Such thinking did not originate in the 1890s; some educators in Horace Mann's time justified public education on the grounds that the lessons

IT IS THE DUTY OF THE PARENT
TO SEND A CHILD TO SCHOOL
IN A TEACHABLE CONDITION,—
CLEAN, HEALTHY AND
WELL MANNERED.

FIGURE 5.2. *The Good Parent and the Bad Parent.* Cover illustration, *The American School Board Journal* 73 (October 1926). Reprinted with permission from *The American School Board Journal.* Copyright 1926, National School Board Association. All rights reserved.

taught in primary school would have a salutary effect on the parents at home.[9] But many educators resisted this idea even at the end of the nineteenth century. They feared that by expanding its mission the school would soon become "overburdened" and not live up to expectations. Others defended the autonomy of the home and cautioned against social programs at school that might discourage parental initiative and independence. "The child belongs to the parent, and not to the school," said Aaron Gove, Denver's venerable superintendent. "The encroachments of the public school on the rights and duties of the family have tended so much to paternalism on the part of the government as to seriously threaten the usefulness and efficiency of the American home." [10]

Still, many educators recommended a larger scope for their work. "Unless the activities of the public school can be so extended as to control and direct the home and neighborhood," said Charles E. Holley, "slow progress and early elimination on the part of some" must be expected. In reaching this conclusion, Holley felt compelled by social and economic circumstances because in the best of all possible worlds such an ambitious role for the school was "beyond its proper sphere." However, there were many others who believed that schools should be more involved at home and in the community. New York School Superintendent William H. Maxwell and kindergartner Lucy Wheelock wanted them to enlarge their mission, becoming what Wheelock called "social-service stations." Of course, this policy was not without disadvantages. "It is infinitely easier to improve the schools than to improve the parents," Maxwell pointed out, "but every improvement in the schools means some improvement in the parents, existing or prospective." [11] Despite being tempered by such optimism, the challenge facing educators who hoped to uplift the home was even greater than this famous superintendent claimed. Limiting themselves to what went on in school reduced the number of variables educators had to manage. But by enlarging the work of the school, they invited unprecedented criticism and risked losing focus, both of which threatened to compromise their ability to maintain control.

Parent education held a special attraction for the many educators and reformers who wanted the school to change family life and the child-rearing practices of Americans. Teachers and parents were natural partners, said the National Society for the Study of Education. "The school already has the interest of the parents and is more likely to reach a larger percentage of them with the least effort than any other agency." Ignoring the home greatly increased the school's chances of failure because children spent far more time with their parents who could easily, if inadvertently, counteract the school's influence. In the name of prevention, many educators and reformers believed that training in parenthood should become an integral part of the high school curriculum. The Child Study Association of America, the American Association of University Women, and, of course, the National Congress of Parents and Teachers (NCPT) joined the American Home Economics Association in support of such preparental instruction. In 1918, the National Education Association's Commission on the Reorganization of Secondary Education made worthy home membership one of the Seven Cardinal Principles of secondary education.[12]

The threat to America posed by immigrant and working-class families encouraged many educators and reformers to take parent education beyond the confines of the school. At the urging of Mary Simons Gibson, a former schoolteacher, the California Commission on Immigration and Housing persuaded the state legislature to pass the Home Teacher Act in 1915. It endorsed Americanization classes in the home and workplace that with private funding soon brought teachers representing the Los Angeles public schools into contact with many immigrant women.

Pennsylvania introduced a similar program in 1925 to teach the English language and American customs, and by 1928, school districts throughout the state were sending such emissaries of assimilation into the home. When they sent subject matter specialists into the community, California and Pennsylvania broke new ground, but at the beginning of the twentieth century, direct outreach to parents was hardly an innovation. In fact, some urban school districts first dispatched "visitors" to their pupils' homes long before the Civil War.[13] They were expected to counteract the vicious influence of selfish parents who neglected their children's education. Inspired by the child study movement and the rise of professional social work, many educators and reformers decided that home visitors could do much more. They could change family conduct and school performance through parent education. According to the leading social scientists of the day like G. Stanley Hall, the child's mind and soul were interdependent domains, the joint responsibility of parents and teachers. Just to keep poor children coming to school, specialists, trained in nursing and social work, had to engage the home, reeducating immigrant parents and monitoring their children. That school outreach efforts might also improve scholarship and help educators appear to be agents of progress did far more than reconfirm the wisdom of such innovations.

Whether in health or behavior, school outreach rested on the premise that parents were the "real problem." The best way to reform them, said the National Society for the Study of Education, is not through launching a direct attack, but by bringing the home into a relationship with "other social institutions that will automatically reveal to the family its faulty practices."[14] If at the beginning of the twentieth century school outreach efforts still focused on the needs of the urban poor, by 1930 they had shifted to a more comprehensive concern with social and psychological maladjustment. However, in either case the expansion of the school's mission prompted and sustained role conflict and confusion. For the first time, educators had to decide whether the school was to be more than an educational institution. They were forced to ask if social welfare was complementary to or even compatible with the school's educational aims. Hidden beneath the surface of this question were some important ramifications for the relationship between the school and home. Not the least of these was whether the school would be held accountable for the contributions of the home, good or bad, to the socialization and education of children. Even more important was the implication of such outreach for the separate, albeit interdependent, work of parents and teachers. Expanding the school's mission could threaten or at least compromise the family's social and psychological space.

Role conflict and confusion affected both elementary and secondary education. But it was acute at the preschool level because the dividing line between the home and the school was most unclear for very young children. Until long after World War II, the vast majority of Americans expected the mothers of infants and toddlers to remain at home. Educators and reformers might choose to help them, but the kind of assistance they should offer was the subject of a major difference of opinion. Some favored forming schools to educate small children, while others recommended developing programs to compensate for ignorant parents and single mothers employed outside the home. Those in charge of kindergartens and day nurseries had to make a difficult choice between education and social welfare or try to combine these two functions in their work with young children. In so doing they also had to confront their feelings about the extent to which the home and the school should be cooperating or competing institutions.

Day Nursery or Nursery School: A Case Study of the Home, the School, and the Problem of Role Conflict and Confusion

During the nineteenth century, Americans experimented with special institutions for very young children. In the 1820s, educators and reformers like Robert Owen and William Russell introduced infant schools, importing them from England. German immigrants brought kindergartens to the United States just before the Civil War, and by 1900, kindergartens could be found in the school systems of most big cities. Day nurseries appeared in response to the working woman's need for child care, taking root in Boston, New York, and Philadelphia. Justifying each of these institutions seemed simple enough at the beginning. Infant schools appealed to those who wanted a head start for their very young children, but middle-class parents abandoned them in the late 1830s, after educators and physicians concluded that such schools led to premature social and intellectual stimulation. Kindergartens sprouted because educational reformers proposed to tap the creative potential of preschool children, while day nurseries came to life to satisfy a growing demand for neighborhood and family welfare services, including the moral elevation of working-class parents and children.[15]

Unlike infant schools, kindergartens and day nurseries survived in part because they adjusted and diversified. Associated with settlements like Chicago's Hull House, some kindergartens linked education with social outreach, teaching children through play, while conducting home visits and supplying adults with medical, housing, and parenting information. Faulted for discouraging self-reliance by sharing responsibility for child care, day nurseries responded by turning this criticism on its head. They took credit for making "the dependent mother independent by keeping her children safe" while she supported her home. At the same time, they gave working-class children and their parents a significant measure of health and moral education. Both kindergartens and day nurseries took credit for teaching immigrant children to be Americans.[16]

By adopting a multifaceted relationship with the home, day nurseries and kindergartens increased their public appeal but suffered as a consequence from having to reconcile competing and conflicting priorities. In Philadelphia, for example, the school board's failure to open enough public kindergartens forced some day nurseries to hire a kindergarten teacher. "There is no reason," the day nursery people complained, "why these nurseries should take on this public school function at the sacrifice of so much else that they need." That education and social welfare were not readily compatible troubled some kindergartners more than others. In the 1880s, Kate Douglas Wiggin reached out to some of San Francisco's poorest families from the Silver Street kindergarten. But by the beginning of the twentieth century, many kindergartners felt diminished by outreach work; according to Nina Vandewalker, who published a book about American kindergartens in 1908, it detracted from the importance of their contribution to education. The director of a public kindergarten in New York feared being involved in a zero sum game. Kindergartens might do both education and social welfare work, but time devoted to one was necessarily denied to the other.[17]

In the 1920s, educational researchers persuaded some middle-class

Americans to consider a new institution for young children, the nursery school, whose quick acceptance by many parents and reformers further complicated the identity crisis in early childhood education. Associated with universities and educational research centers like the Merrill-Palmer School in Detroit, nursery schools promised to advance basic knowledge in the fields of education and child development. In New York's Greenwich Village, Caroline Pratt's and Harriet Johnson's progressive nursery schools operated on the principle that parents were part of the problem, not the solution. Nevertheless, nursery schools attracted paying customers because of their strong emphasis on socialization and cognitive training. "The education of the little child," said Merrill-Palmer's director, Edna Noble White, is the nursery school's "primary function." Pupils started their schooling off on the right foot by learning to respect themselves and others. "It is a real school, with a real educational program," reported one contributor to *Parents' Magazine*.[18]

However, nursery schools could not completely walk away from the outreach function that adhered so closely to the other forms of early childhood education. They struggled to reconcile it with the idea that the home and the school were distinct, if reciprocal, institutions. Effective schools enjoyed the understanding and assistance of the home; on this point, most experts in education and child psychology agreed. But those experts, like Yale University's Arnold Gesell, also believed that responsibility for achieving continuity between the home and the school fell largely on the teachers' shoulders. Even upper- and middle-class parents could not be counted on to help raise their children properly. Cooperative nursery schools represented one solution by requiring parents to be directly involved in the school's delivery of care and instruction. Monitored and guided by educators, parents not only assisted the school but also learned how to prevent the family from becoming the failed institution that it so often turned out to be.[19] In the cooperative nursery, the line between the home and the school became much less distinct, and the reciprocity of their relationship lost some of its meaning.

Trained at places like Merrill-Palmer, nursery school teachers asserted themselves in early childhood education, replacing many day care workers and kindergartners in the 1920s. Led by educators like Abigail Eliot, who founded the Ruggles Street School in Boston, they condemned day nurseries as drab, lifeless, dispiriting places. Of course, institutional change was slow in coming; in 1930, the federal government reported finding only 262 nursery schools in the United States. Most were in private hands or associated with universities. But their preference for education as opposed to outreach recycled and intensified the debate about the relationship between the home and the school. As the value of custodial and welfare functions came under attack, parents and infants found themselves less and less welcome at day nurseries. Their deficiencies and needs became secondary to those of the preschool child.[20] Day nurseries in settlements experienced a special kind of anxiety. Long associated with social welfare, their leaders now found themselves debating the relative merits of education and outreach. This discussion may have obscured the importance of the home environment to learning, but it called attention to a dilemma for all American schools—how to maintain their focus and sidestep criticism as new expectations and added responsibilities blurred their relationship with the home.

These problems came to a head in Philadelphia, where working mothers had trouble finding a good day nursery in 1915. There were no such facilities in many neighborhoods, and those that did exist could not be counted on to provide satisfactory care.[21] Reformers were divided about how to deal with children abandoned by their parents during the day. Some urged mothers to remain at home regardless of the economic consequences. Others recommended the organization of more day nurseries, an institution that Philadelphians first embraced in 1863. By the beginning of the twentieth century, some immigrant and black groups were turning to day care as a form of self-help. Assisted by their German coreligionists, newly arrived Russian Jews, for example, had four Jewish nurseries to choose from. Established in 1893, the day nursery at the Young Women's Union, a settlement house in South Philadelphia, ranked as "one of the best in the country" in 1920. It understands what it means to promote community welfare, said the Bureau of Jewish Social Research. Unlike some of its counterparts, it "maintains intimate contact with the mothers, seeks to improve living standards, and assists in family rehabilitation."[22]

Before becoming the head of the Young Women's Union in 1917, C. Marion Kohn directed its day nursery. She advocated mothers' pensions as a permanent solution to the child care problem of widows and abandoned wives. Until more women qualified for them, however, Americans had to rely on alternatives like the settlement's nursery, which prevented families from breaking apart and paved the way for uplift and refinement of immigrant lives. Keeping parents and children together was "justification enough for its existence," Kohn said of her nursery in 1913, but she was just as interested in "the reconstruction of the whole family," and she felt no ambivalence about the two sides of her work. By trying to counter-act the bad influence of "sordid and abnormal homes," she acknowledged the educational needs of immigrant children, but she also placed their moral and cognitive training squarely within the larger goal of family wel-fare and preservation.[23]

In keeping with its dedication to its community as a whole, the Young Women's Union changed its name to the Neighborhood Centre in 1918. Consistent with this broader mission, the settlement's day nursery en-larged its scope, assuming some of the characteristics of a nursery school. The new aims were threefold—the education of the child, the education of parents in the methods of child care, and scientific research on the physi-cal and mental development of preschool children.[24] The move was not unprecedented or unilateral; both the Cleveland Day Nursery Association and the Franklin School Nursery of the Chicago public schools augmented their work by adding educational tasks to their custodial and welfare func-tions in the 1920s. The decision by the Federal Emergency Relief Admin-istration to promote nursery schools as one of its projects gave the move-ment momentum in 1933. Within a year, there were four day nurseries in Philadelphia, teaching needy children under the aegis of the board of education. But the nursery school of the Neighborhood Centre pioneered in preparing its charges for the transition from day care to elementary school.[25]

The reform of the day nursery at the Neighborhood Centre prompted no little trepidation among the staff. Kohn's successor as day nursery di-rector, Rae Lewis, was not sure the merger of functions would work. When she and her colleagues mixed education with social welfare, they came up with a set of objectives that was paradoxical at best. On the one hand, the school was supposed to teach "sound and useful habits," just what immigrant and working-class children would need if they were to blend with their surroundings. At the same time, it was expected to instill "a spirit of greater independence, not only on the part of the children themselves but also on the part of the parents. We believe," said Carrie Younker, the head of the day nursery in 1929, "that our achievements should not be measured by what we are doing for the children and their families but rather by what we are encouraging and making possible for them to do for themselves." This conflict between social welfare and educational thinking persisted for many years. Speaking to the nursery's parent-teacher association (PTA) in 1941, Dr. Nathan Schlezinger en-dorsed both conformity and independence, security and risk in child nurture, rehearsing the ideological line that prompted doubts about whether the experiment could succeed in the first place.[26]

That there was a PTA associated with the Neighborhood Centre's nursery school is unremarkable. Most day nurseries in Philadelphia sponsored a mothers' or parents' club because day nursery educators strongly believed in parent education. Teaching families to accept the school's standards and practices conflated its educational and social welfare missions. "Our larger purpose is the projection of Nursery ideals into the home," said the head of the Neighborhood Centre in 1929. "The lessons in hygiene, proper feeding, social habits and the like that are acquired in the nursery would be of little avail unless we emphasized through parent education a continuation of this program in the home."[27] Occasional visits to the home by the nursery school staff reinforced the effect of conferences with mothers at school and parental observation in the classroom. The last director of the nursery, Esther Siegel, often paid lip service to parental involvement, but she preferred to be in charge, threatening to deny recalcitrant parents access to the services provided by her school.[28] It was at the end of her administration that the Neighborhood Centre came to terms with its split personality by abandoning its attempt to be a nursery school.

Between 1938 and 1942, debate raged at the Neighborhood Centre about the complex mission of the settlement's nursery school. Was it to be a stand-in for working parents, providing the daytime care and socialization that they could or would not? Or should it also continue to be an "extension" of the home, empowering parents to take more responsibility for the education of their young? The clientele of the school had always been working-class. But as more and more mothers took defense jobs during World War II, they could not give their children as much attention as they had while operating a family business or taking care of the home. By 1942, Philadelphia's "latch key" children had become the object of citywide concern.[29] At the Neighborhood Centre, the nursery school staff still wanted to have it both ways. We have "the same standards as a nursery school," said one teacher, "plus adequate case work." But when a survey revealed that half the school's families had no choice but to rely on it for day care services, the settlement's board of directors decided that the time had come to make a change. Over the protests of parents who still saw a "need for early childhood care and training," the board voted to revamp the nursery school, returning exclusively to the provision of child care, which had been its only function at the beginning.[30]

At the Neighborhood Centre and elsewhere, the fault line between day care and early childhood education affected admissions policy as much as anything else. Since the early 1920s, child care professionals in the United States had asked themselves to what degree case work should be a part of day nursery admissions. If day care was just a baby-sitting service for working mothers, case work might not have any role to play; it seemed even less relevant if the day nursery was really a nursery school. But by arguing that they kept families together, day care workers opened the door to the idea that what they did was really a form of social work. Maladjustment became an accepted criterion for what many child care professionals now called "intake."[31] In 1925, Philadelphia's Jewish Welfare Society took administrative responsibility for investigating the background of all applicants to the Jewish day nurseries in the city. Not every family welcomed the change; it was embarrassing to be associated with the stigma attached to social work. At the Neighborhood Centre, Esther Siegel finally managed to persuade the Jewish Welfare Society to relinquish control over her nursery school's admissions process in 1939, arguing successfully that she took many children for educational reasons, but her triumph would be short-lived.[32]

As part of its decision to focus on child care once again, the day nursery at the Neighborhood Centre restricted its services to children whose parents could not give them "proper attention during the day-time." No longer aspiring to be in the business of education, the settlement's day nursery resumed its working relationship with the Jewish Welfare Society, turning to it once again for case work in admissions. Too much was expected of those who proposed to fold social work together with early childhood education. "If there is anything we have learned in the past 20 years," said one Philadelphia day care official, "it is that we cannot make people do things, nor can we make people over."[33] Spoken in 1943, such reservations reflected the experience of a generation in both social work and education. Between 1900 and 1940, the public school assumed more and more responsibility for what went on at home. Attention to pupils' hygiene and health evolved into a concern for their social, psychological, and emotional well-being. A better return on the educational dollar was not to be the only payoff of such outreach; educators hoped to transform family life itself. But remaking the American family proved to be a formidable task. It was not just day care providers who met with difficulty and disappointment combining education with social welfare reform. Those in public education found out as well that the consequences of such expansionism were not all good and there were indeed limits to the possibilities of schooling.

Health and the Politics of the Home-School Relationship

At the beginning of the of the twentieth century, the American city hardly qualified as a healthful place. Poor sanitation, tainted food, and over-crowded housing contributed to high morbidity, especially among immi-grants and working-class citizens. Reformers were especially distressed at the sight of frail or infirm children. The plight of diseased adults could per-haps be overlooked; after all, they were probably responsible for their bad physical condition. But the child afflicted by infected tonsils, bad eyesight, and rotten teeth or crippled by such debilitating conditions as rickets and tuberculosis deserved their immediate attention. Of course, such problems had to be detected before they could be corrected. The public schools offered ready access to many American children, and following the lead of progressive Europeans, educators in Boston, New York, Chi-cago, and Philadelphia began the practice of investigating and document-ing child health in the 1890s. The New York public schools, for example, appointed 134 medical inspectors in 1897.[34]

Helped along by legislation, the systematic evaluation of schoolchild-ren for physical defects and contagious diseases expanded rapidly be-tween 1900 and 1915. New Jersey and California authorized boards of education to provide for medical supervision; Connecticut and Vermont required public schools to examine children's eyes. In 1906, Massachusetts became the first state to mandate general medical inspection, a policy adopted by six other states soon thereafter. By 1911, there were 443 towns and cities in the United States that had organized programs of medical in-spection, and over 300 more were moving in this direction. But even though schools might be the most logical place to begin improving child and family health, could they really get the job done? Overworked and undertrained, most teachers were in no position to teach basic hygiene, let alone make an accurate assessment of their pupils' physical condition. The 354 cities that employed school physicians by 1911 discovered that while most doctors could spot existing problems, many were indifferent to the importance of health education.[35]

By introducing home economics into the curriculum, some educators and women's activists thought they had found the perfect solution to the nation's family health problems. Courses in domestic science promised to inform children and parents about personal hygiene and nutrition. Students of home economics also learned how to use scarce resources more efficiently, lessons that were expected to improve not just the home but also society as a whole. Founded in 1908, the American Home Economics Association brought such enthusiasm to its work that it almost seemed unpatriotic to imagine even the possibility of conflict between the home and the school. Rural educators took a special liking to domestic science, especially in the South, arguing that it offered unprecedented help to the neglected farm family. It became a staple in white outreach to southern blacks through the Jeanes teachers program and the Slater Fund's support for county training schools.[36] However, the school nurse remained first in the line of defense against child neglect in the city and a visible link between the home and the urban school. She is "the most important adjunct of medical inspection," said Luther Gulick and Leonard Ayres, two outspoken advocates for reform. "She is the teacher of the parents, the pupils, the teachers, and the family, in applied social hygiene. She is the most effective possible link between the school and the home."[37]

By lending Lina Rogers, one of the visiting nurses at the Henry Street settlement, to the city of New York in 1902, Lilian Wald set in motion changes that would lead to a significant expansion of health work in the public schools. New York's board of education soon appropriated $30,000 to hire twenty-seven school nurses, and within five years, many cities had them. The American Red Cross initiated a school nursing service in 1912, which raised the consciousness of rural Americans to the value of health education.[38] Reformers urged educators to accept their new colleagues because education and good health were interdependent (figure 5.3). Diseased and frail children often missed school and, when in attendance, could not be expected to learn as well as their more robust peers. According to Gulick and Ayres, one New York study confirmed the association between learning and health by demonstrating that dull children had many more physical defects than their bright or normal counterparts. The degree to which social class was responsible for the high correlation between health and achievement was at best imperfectly understood. Researchers and reformers had yet to grasp completely the importance of the relationship between poverty (or wealth) and education. However, almost no one doubted that schools had a great deal to lose by ignoring their pupils' health situation. "It was recognized," said Lina Rogers, that "large sums of money were being practically wasted in trying to educate children physically unfit to take advantage of their opportunities."[39]

FIGURE 5.3. *A Healthy Mind in a Health Body.* Cover illustration, *The American School Board Journal* 74 (March 1927). Reprinted with permission from *The American School Board Journal.* Copyright 1927, National School Board Association. All rights reserved.

Educators and reformers agreed that many parents could no more be trusted with their children's health than with their education. "It seems impossible any longer to fix responsibility for the child's health exclusively on the parents," said Isabel Stewart and Adelaide Nutting, coauthors of the lead article in the *Ninth Yearbook of the National Society for the Study of*

Education. "Because of ignorance, or poverty, or inefficiency in the home; because of the large proportion of the foreign element in our population, the employment of mothers in industry, the congestion in cities," Stewart and Nutting continued, "the school is compelled to take over many functions which formerly devolved on the home." The school nurse was responsible for the prevention of sickness more than its remediation. Teaching children the basics of hygiene was her most important job; changing the way their parents thought about health came in a close second. Diplomat, philosopher, and friend of the family, she was expected to strengthen the bond between parents and teachers, "interpreting the ideals and purposes of the school to the home," while "discovering the limitations and adverse conditions" that existed there. By virtue of her contact with immigrants, she was "a very potent force for Americanization." However, even Lina Rogers did not believe that the school should replace the family. Nurses might perform some parental duties, but, like teachers, theirs should be a partnership with those in charge at home.[40]

Perhaps more than any other issue, health focused attention on the relationship between the family and the state. Left untreated, epidemics did not respect the social boundaries that otherwise divided Americans. The New York Committee on the Physical Welfare of School Children discovered that social class was no guarantee for or against the neglect of children's health. "The existence of physical defects," said its secretary, William H. Allen, "throws little light on income at home, but conclusively shows lack of [parental] attention or understanding." Neglected and abused children threatened to become a burden on the state, but how far was the conscience of the community to reach? To what lengths should the government go to alter the way things were done at home? Parents did not always welcome the advice of public officials; in Los Angeles, for example, some resisted the implementation of medical inspection. Immigrants feared that the school nurse would undermine their parental authority. Educators hoped that by being sensitive to cultural differences the nurse could overcome suspicion and mistrust at home.[41] But they never anticipated that enlarging the school's mission might gainsay expectations of reciprocity, creating confusion and expanding exposure to criticism.

Many educators, social workers, and reformers believed that the government had at least a limited right to intervene in family life. They wanted children protected from harm inflicted by adults, especially the neglect of health. New Jersey threatened to prosecute parents for failing to remove defects that excluded children from school, while those too poor to pay for medical treatment in Indiana could obtain financial help from the state. However, parents received reports on their children's health in just ten states, a situation that Luther Gulick and Leonard Ayres could not understand. "It is difficult to find a logical basis for the argument that the state has not the right to inform the parents of defects present in the child," they said in 1917, "and to advise as to [the] remedial measures which should be taken to remove them." Linking poverty with education and health, Lina Rogers urged the state to take a more comprehensive and pro-active stand. The school nurse, she thought, should search for the "underlying causes" of disease, poverty, and unemployment so that a permanent remedy for them all could be found.[42]

Between 1910 and 1930, advocates for school nursing frequently revisited the question of the state's role in the home. As much as they desired to expand their influence, educators knew that there would be strong resistance to any policies or reforms that promised to invite dependency by substituting the school for the family. Instead of trying to take the place of parents, said the former secretary of the New York Committee on the Physical Welfare of School Children, teachers, principals, and physicians had to harness them to the school's health program. Even then, there were limitations on what educators could do. "We cannot alter the home environment or compel attention to any directions given," said Dr. S. W. Newmayer of Philadelphia. But school nurses could teach mothers to appreciate the importance of their contribution to family health and perhaps, in time, make them advocates for reform.[43] Parents who understood the impact of fitness on learning would not tolerate unsanitary conditions at school or the neglect of physical education. As Elizabeth Cleveland, an experienced teacher, wrote in 1927, they might even demand to be "systematically furnished with the latest authoritative information on all matters related to the health of children." However, Cleveland had little faith that most parents would behave in such a responsible way. A strong believer in the right of the state to protect children at home, her work at the Merrill-Palmer School in Detroit convinced her of the need for strict standards to judge the physical, mental, and emotional growth of children.[44]

The economic crisis of the 1930s revealed just how hesitant Americans were to absolve the family of responsibility for the health of children. Although more young people now went untreated for minor ailments, let alone serious disorders, nurses at school found themselves faced with expendability. In response, they argued that the school nurse was both a teacher and a healer, disseminating health information as well as an occasional spoonful of medicine. In the eyes of the nursing profession, she remained the most effective link between the home and the school, interpreting the child's family life to the teacher, while explaining the school to the home. When the increased participation of women in the paid labor force made such cooperation problematic during World War II, the emphasis shifted back to public health; the school nurse might substitute as a direct caregiver when parents, especially mothers, had a good excuse for not being home.[45] However, the peripatetic nature of school nursing did nothing to resolve the uncertainty surrounding the relationship between the school and the home. Americans proved willing to delegate responsibility to medical experts, especially when a child's life was at stake, but they remained conflicted about the degree to which the school should be a health and welfare institution.

The Visiting Teacher: Social Work and the Politics of the Home-School Relationship

When Julius John Oppenheimer published his doctoral dissertation in 1924, he acknowledged his mentors, George Strayer and Nicholas L. Engelhardt, two of the most distinguished professors at the most prestigious school of education in the United States: Teachers College, Columbia University. Under their direction, Oppenheimer had written about the visiting teacher, an outreach worker who had by then become a celebrated addition to the professional staff of several urban school systems. Introduced to America in 1906, visiting teachers brought together the related fields of education and social work, expanding the scope of schooling to address the private problems of impoverished and immigrant families with young children. In the development of school social work, "the more objective evidence of maladjustment naturally stood out . . . in poor neighborhoods and in foreign districts," Oppenheimer said, but visiting teachers soon extended their outreach to include "negroes [sic], the shiftless native population, and the better classes of foreign and native" Americans. Blacks were the least likely to receive attention in part because many white social workers preferred not to deal with African Americans. Those who did not let such feelings affect their work sometimes found their way blocked by black parents who wanted to protect their control over child-rearing practices for religious or cultural reasons. In a survey taken in 1920, visiting teachers across the country reported working with immigrants 67 percent of the time, while native whites and blacks accounted for 23 and 6 percent of their efforts, respectively.[46]

Like other functional additions to public education at the beginning of the twentieth century, visiting teachers originated in the private sector. In New York and Philadelphia, for example, settlement houses first sponsored them. Hartley House and Greenwich House collaborated in New York City, forming a committee in 1906 to oversee the labors of two social workers they assigned to three public schools. A settlement maintained by the Child Welfare Committee of the Friends' Quarterly Meeting brought visiting teachers to Philadelphia, who soon attracted the attention of other social welfare organizations. In 1909, the Juvenile Aid Society and the Juvenile Protective Association arranged for a home and school visitor to work out of the city's Bureau of Compulsory Education. One year later the Armstrong Association, an advocacy group for African Americans, placed a visiting teacher in the all-black Thomas Durham school.[47] The visiting teacher idea appealed to the reform-minded among white, middle-class American women. In 1916, the Chicago Women's Club committed itself to such outreach as an antidote to poverty. But its initiatives were belated compared to those mounted by its counterparts in Boston. Almost as soon as the concept took root in New York, the Boston Women's Education Association established a home and school visitor in the Winthrop Public School, and by 1909, this effort was being multiplied by neighborhood civic groups and the Boston Home and School Association. The latter put visiting teachers to work in two of the city's poorest districts, Roxbury and the North End, both of which were then becoming predominantly immigrant and working-class.[48] Middle-class women saw nothing wrong with expanding the school's mission as long as their homes were left alone.

Public school authorities were not always quick to accept the need for visiting teachers. Boston's school directors hesitated at first but soon joined with counterparts in New York, Chicago, Kansas City, and Minneapolis, where visiting teachers were brought on board between 1913 and 1919. Led by Rochester, New York, many smaller cities also made room for them, bringing the number of municipalities with visiting teachers to twenty-eight by 1921. The formation of the National Association of Visiting Teachers and Home and School Visitors two years before had given the field an established presence, but it was the New York Public Education Association's and the Commonwealth Fund's joint decision to create a Committee on Visiting Teachers that really spread home visitors across the educational map.[49] Reporting to the fund's Program for the Prevention of Delinquency, the committee organized a three-year demonstration project in 1924 that placed visiting teachers in thirty communities, large and small, including two major cities, Detroit and San Diego, as well as regional centers like Birmingham, Alabama, and Burlington, Vermont. In addition, the lack of social services in rural America persuaded the committee to reach out to places like Monmouth County, New Jersey; Huron County, Ohio; and Boone County, Missouri. When the demonstration project closed, twenty-four more school boards had assumed responsibility for visiting teacher work, but the national totals still remained very small. In 1927, there were only 211 visiting teachers in the United States.[50]

The Commonwealth Fund adopted the visiting teacher movement because of its interest in preventing juvenile delinquency. The fund initially took a remedial approach to such deviance but soon shifted to a strategy that focused on identifying and treating emotional and behavioral problems before they got out of hand. "Only very recently has there come to be some conception that early study of the individual who is out of adjustment, and scientific diagnosis of his social difficulty, may make possible a considerable degree of prevention," the fund reported to its friends and benefactors in 1922. The visiting teacher promised to help young children adjust to their environment by harmonizing the home and school. She was to act as an intermediary, breaking down barriers of misunderstanding that separated busy mothers from teachers who no longer lived in the neighborhood and whose large classes or extra duties made it impossible for them to visit their pupils' homes.[51]

First, and foremost, the visiting teacher spoke for the school. Her training and experience convinced her that teachers were usually not responsible for the maladjusted child; more often than not truancy, misbehavior, and poor scholarship began at home. Parental ignorance and neglect denied a proper upbringing to many immigrant and working-class children whose educational prospects were made even bleaker by low levels of parental involvement in the work of the school. Whether obligations at work, indifference to education, or feelings of alienation kept them away, too many poor and foreign-born parents failed "to realize the importance of their active participation in their children's progress and school experience."[52] They were not living up to their part of the reciprocity bargain. Faced with such irresponsible conduct, classroom teachers could not be expected to go it alone, especially considering the small proportion of the day that their pupils spent with them. "The visiting teacher is the arm of the school extended into the home," said the chair of the New York Public Education Association's Committee on Visiting Teachers, Nathalie H. Swan, in 1916. It is her job "to visit and establish friendly relations with the homes of those children who exhibit the first symptoms of falling below the school standard in scholarship and conduct."[53] Working with immigrant and blue-collar families, she had to explain the school's requirements and routines to parents, a task that frequently forced her to mediate between them and their children. No doubt, her presence in the home often looked like interference to those on the receiving end, but for many teachers and reformers, it was clear that the school was a partner, not an intruder, in the raising of forgotten children.

Like school nurses, visiting teachers encountered such a broad array of problems at home that they often looked to the community for help. Acting on the presumption that the school was the mother of all social agencies, visiting teachers referred troubled children and their parents to colleagues in law, medicine, and social work. Professionals in these related fields often found this conceit off-putting; some even worried that educators might harbor grander aspirations. Nevertheless, social work was not the school's chief concern; visiting teachers thought that by giving their counterparts in the grades a better understanding of the home environment, they could increase the chances that even "the most unpromising child" would remain in school and become a good citizen.[54]

Visiting teachers were expected to raise the school's standing with the middle class even as they relied on its well-established reputation for moral leadership to challenge the behavior of immigrants and others thought to be neglectful of their children. Middle-class parents were more likely to see themselves as partners with the school, but confusion about the school's new role and its impact on parental authority troubled at least some of them. Eager to maintain good relations with the middle-class home, school administrators expected visiting teachers to produce the same effect as a well-run PTA, better public relations. In fact, visiting teachers were supposed to help organize new PTAs, enhancing the school's credibility with the middle class by exercising leadership through the powerful medium of personal contact and informal relations.[55]

Of course, those parents most in need of the visiting teacher's help seldom attended PTA meetings. The bad attitudes and habits that caused immigrant and working-class children to fail in school had to be attacked on the street or in the home. But by the mid-1920s, most visiting teachers believed that success in school and in life required more than dutiful parents and observant educators; it depended on good mental hygiene. What began at the turn of the century as therapy for mental illness had become a regimen to prevent such illness by instilling self-control, self-reliance, and, most of all, self-esteem.[56] Children developed healthy personalities when the home worked with the school, an expectation that required even middle-class parents to broaden their vision and visiting teachers to monitor both the sentiments of their classroom colleagues and the emotional climate of the home. "Feelings and habits of behavior must be constantly nurtured or corrected, as the case may be, in the entire daily life of the child," said the chairman of the National Committee on Visiting Teachers in 1927, because "how children act, in school and out, and why they act as they do are . . . of the utmost importance to education." By reducing the tension between the home and the school, visiting teachers could help the child "participate more effectively in the social life around him."[57]

Educators who wanted parents to bond better with their children and their children's teachers were not willing to accept full responsibility if things went wrong. After all, most psychologists in the 1920s believed that children matured in a holistic way, carrying with them for life the indelible marks of their upbringing as well as their pedigree. As distinct, but interdependent, institutions, the home and the school should share both credit and blame. Teachers, of course, had selfish reasons for thinking that they should not be held more accountable for the child's achievement or conduct than the family. Constantly pressured to maintain standards at school, they were fair game for administrators when students came up short in their schoolwork or misbehaved.[58] Such outspoken advocates of the visiting teacher as Jane Culbert and Mary Sayles consistently placed responsibility for maladjustment at the feet of parents who failed to build their children's self-esteem. They found particular fault with those who expected too much or too little of their sons and daughters, setting them on the road to poor mental hygiene.[59] Spokesmen for immigrant groups turned this argument around, insisting that the family should assert itself, not just take the blame. Roman Catholic educators, for example, rejected any idea that the school should dictate to the home. "The time is ripe," said the Reverend James H. Ryan in 1925, "for a national campaign which shall center the attention of Catholic parents on the functions and duties of the home, which they have allowed to be transferred to the weak shoulders of the school." According to Father Ryan, visiting teachers were to convey this message, making the school responsible for teaching parents that it "cannot, even if it would, take the place in the process of education which properly belongs to the home."[60] The irony of this recommendation was apparently lost on him.

Many educators in the public domain did not trust immigrant and working-class parents to meet the social, psychological, and educational needs of their children. When it came to child rearing, traditional attitudes and practices resisted even the strongest pressures for change. Visiting teachers frequently turned for help to the juvenile court, the business community, or private welfare agencies. They urged their colleagues in the classroom to do the same, but as newcomers to the educational establishment, they lacked the credibility needed to bring about such basic change. The visiting teacher "can be effective in a school only as she can make the teachers realize that she understands their problems," said the Public Education Association's Harriet Johnson in 1916.[61] Schools could take more responsibility for the child's welfare, compensating for the bad effects of the home by coordinating referrals to social welfare agencies, while adjusting their own expectations and routines. But teachers and principals had to do this for themselves, for none but they controlled the students and the school day.

In the 1920s, visiting teachers were not inclined to ask their colleagues to alter established ways. Instead, they encouraged teachers to reexamine their feelings about difficult children, especially those from immigrant and working-class homes. "The attitudes and conditions existing in the school," said Jane Culbert, "are as potent . . . in effecting an adjustment [in children] as the attitudes and conditions in the home." She blamed many failures on teachers who failed to cooperate with parents but claimed that most would take a different approach once they identified the family as the source of their students' problems. Her Philadelphia colleague, Anna B. Pratt, held the same view. "In many instances," she wrote in 1923, "knowledge of home conditions has had the effect of completely changing the attitudes of the teacher toward the child," transforming the response of the school.[62] But too often, she believed, the teacher failed to adjust, especially to immigrant children. Faced with five or six nationalities, she dealt with her pupils and their parents without understanding their particular history and customs. The Philadelphia public schools isolated the most recalcitrant, assigning them to special classes or schools for backward or unruly children. Such a policy reinforced the ethnocentric bias that many teachers felt; only by being more open to the home could the public schools live up to Pratt's high expectations.[63]

By urging the schools to accept responsibility for the whole child, reformers went far beyond the original scope of public education. No longer was it considered sufficient to provide children with a basic education. The school now had to help children make decisions that had once been the family's exclusive domain. As the executive director of the White-Williams Foundation, Anna Pratt carried this message to the Philadelphia public schools. It was a prescription for change that probably had to originate outside the educational establishment. After all, the home and the school were separate, but reciprocal, institutions, and the costs, not to mention the consequences, of such reform were by no means insignificant. But in the expansive atmosphere of the 1920s, educators in America did not back away when private organizations like the White-Williams Foundation recommended that the public school take more responsibility for the children who passed through its portals every day. On the contrary, many embraced the idea that the school should be a social welfare agency.

From Vocational Guidance to School Counseling:
Philadelphia's White-Williams Foundation

For more than a century, the Magdalen Society of Philadelphia worked
with fallen women. Founded in 1802, it operated an asylum that promised
personal rehabilitation through a combination of physical isolation and
moral education. At the beginning of the twentieth century, the society's
directors concluded that solving the problems of illegitimacy and prostitution depended more on prevention than cure. In 1916, they closed
Fairview Farm, the society's home for unwed mothers, and hired Anna
Beach Pratt to help them rethink their mission. After doing fieldwork in
Boston, New York, and Chicago, Pratt persuaded her new employers to
look to the public schools for answers to the "girl question." She told those
assembled for the society's annual meeting in 1917 that the transition from
school to work was fraught with danger. Parents had once monopolized
this function, but in urban America, conditions had changed. "Thrown
unprepared and unguarded into the great sea of temptation," many working girls went astray, but they "might be saved if there were some organization to provide a friend to advise and guide them."[64] That organization
ought to be the Magdalen Society, Pratt contended, and in January of the
following year, it was reborn as the White-Williams Foundation (WWF).[65]

Vocational guidance was nothing new to American public education
in 1917; school directors had assumed at least some responsibility for this
placement function in Chicago, Boston, and New York by then. Of course,
educators everywhere felt a strong incentive to keep children enrolled in
school. In Chicago, the Department of Vocational Guidance and Employment Certificates employed five visiting teachers whose main job was
to convince black and working-class families that eighth graders should
think twice before entering the labor force. The Armstrong Association
introduced vocational guidance in Philadelphia, assigning the first industrial counselor to a black public school in 1910. But those in charge of Philadelphia's schools hoped for more, and at the urging of John C. Frazee,
associate superintendent for placement in the Bureau of Compulsory
Education, the directors of the WWF answered the call in the spring of
1917, agreeing to take up the work of vocational guidance for girls. However, it soon became apparent that most of those applying for employment
certificates needed more than help finding work. They had such "meager
education" that "little vocational guidance was possible"; yet most could
not be persuaded to postpone their premature departure from school.[66]

Even before committing themselves to vocational guidance, the directors of the WWF believed that they could best engage in preventive work by cooperating with the Philadelphia public schools. They considered running a referral service for institutions that dealt with troubled girls or doing follow-up work for the school system's placement bureau but chose vocational guidance instead because it allowed them to do both social and occupational counseling. In 1917, the strength of the city's war economy persuaded many girls to consider dropping out of school, if only to work at home. The WWF's counselor might not be able to turn them all around, but by being at the Bureau of Compulsory Education when they applied for work certificates, she could at least establish "friendly relations" with the family. The home visit that soon ensued kept alive the possibility of reenrollment, while providing "the social guidance, in addition to the vocational guidance, which nearly all of them needed." [67]

Between 1918 and 1925, the WWF gradually convinced Philadelphia's school authorities to accept responsibility for vocational guidance. Ironically, the federal government acted as the WWF's ally, creating a junior section of the United States Employment Service, which Anna Pratt kept alive after the war while she lobbied the superintendent and board of education. When Pratt offered to subsidize the work of the junior section, the school board agreed to manage the service, and it was not long before the supervisor of junior employment became a public employee. In 1924, she was overseeing ten counselors in the Social Service Department of the Compulsory Attendance Bureau and organizing five district offices for vocational guidance. The board soon decided to appoint regular teachers as employment counselors in each of the city's junior and senior high schools, further institutionalizing the transfer of the guidance function. In 1925, the directors of the WWF discontinued their employment division, secure in the knowledge that they had already expanded the mission and scope of public education. [68]

Educators in Philadelphia were content to wait until the last minute to prepare students for the transition from school to work. But Pratt and her colleagues at the WWF were not, arguing persistently that good vocational guidance required a more comprehensive approach that entailed early intervention and regular contact between the school and the home. By the time a young woman applied for a work certificate, said the WWF, she probably could not be persuaded to remain in school, and the consequences of her dropping out were almost certain to be far-reaching. Those with just a sixth grade education were prime candidates for prostitution. "In leaving school for industry," Pratt maintained, "the girl, as well as the boy, is probably making the greatest change of her life and it comes at that most difficult period of adolescence when she is awakening to her own womanhood and is impatient of home control." Educators who chose to intercede at home risked undermining parental authority by teaching "higher ideals" to immigrant and working-class children. However, Pratt never apologized for wanting the school to reform the family. As a social worker by training, she was less accustomed than teachers and parents to the idea of reciprocity between the two institutions. The child's behavior at school was "often an index to less conspicuous causes," not the least among them being ignorant, lazy, and foolish parents. The guidance provided by the WWF might "be called 'educational' in the broadest sense of the word," she said, addressing, as it did, "health, recreation, standards of living and other problems of social adjustment."[69]

As early as October 1917, the school district allowed the Foundation to place guidance counselors in two South Philadelphia elementary schools. Working with ninety girls in grades six, seven, and eight, they reported that they could not be effective just by interpreting the home and the school to one another. Awkward and overaged, their clients were mostly second-generation immigrants who felt out of place in school. They had "no one at home to help them with their studies or to give them the right kind of American ideals," the executive director observed. To keep such girls from dropping out, the counselors practically had to live with the family, slowly winning the parents' acceptance and trust. Cooperation with other social agencies was a must. The WWF workers at the McCall School collaborated with more than one hundred sister agencies in the first year alone. They also tracked the alumni of their program to determine how many were still enrolled in high school after an initial term. In 1917, the Foundation began to give small scholarships for books and other expenses to encourage persistence in high school. Actually granting the money, however, was "but a small part of the scholarship work," Pratt explained three years later. "In every case the advisor administering the fund has made it her business to know the child well, and to help him overcome home and school difficulties as he meets them."[70]

The WWF did not have sufficient resources to assign counselors to more than a few schools, but its board of directors agreed to cover a representative sample as a demonstration project. In 1919, there were WWF counselors in four elementaries, serving, respectively, Catholics, immigrants, African Americans, and pupils from "average" homes. The list also included two high schools (one for boys and a second for girls), a junior high, and the girls' trade school. At the city's special school for unruly boys, the WWF worker discovered that her students often did not have a "normal family life." Single-parent households were all too common as well as "homes in which both the father and mother were away all day working." Her counterpart at the Logan School reported that one of her most important duties was advising black parents, recently arrived from the South, about the physical condition of their children. The neighborhood needed a day nursery as well because "the mothers have to go to work, leaving their children without any supervision."[71]

When the WWF began to give scholarships to high school students, it worked closely with the American Red Cross, dispensing money to the sons and daughters of servicemen. After the war, the WWF recycled the program as a complement to its basic function of guidance counseling. Subject to intensive casework as a prerequisite for funding, the recipients of the WWF's awards spread the foundation's message across the city's educational system. They modeled the idea that the school should be a social welfare institution. Financial support came from private sources, as did the money for similar scholarships in three other cities: Chicago, Cincinnati, and New Orleans.[72] The directors of the WWF struggled with the idea that they were promoting dependency. "The aim was to keep boys and girls in school," they said, but unless students "really wanted to remain in school and the parents were also eager and willing to cooperate even to the point of making some sacrifice," the program would be self-defeating. Besides financial need, an applicant's personal ambition and school citizenship were important criteria for selection. To promote self-sufficiency, each beneficiary was counseled to reach "an understanding of the difficulties of his own situation."[73]

Between 1917 and 1937, the WWF distributed more than $271,000 to 1,161 scholarship recipients. High levels of unemployment during the Depression greatly increased the number of applicants, while shrinking the WWF's resources, but government relief programs like the National Youth Administration at least made its dollars go further.[74] Anna Pratt thought that the WWF scholarship program combined social democracy with mental hygiene. By making equal educational opportunity more than just a promise, it diminished the chance that adolescents would grow up to be maladjusted. Whether it alleviated emotional distress, the program certainly targeted those who could not help themselves. In 1926, 90 percent of its scholarships went to students who did not have an employed father living at home. First- or second-generation immigrants were the clear majority; after all, they comprised nearly half the children in the Philadelphia public school system. Blacks, on the other hand, were held to a higher standard of personal integrity and academic performance because, as the Scholarship Committee averred, the WWF could not afford to invest in someone who did not stand a chance of getting a good job after graduation.[75]

Anna Pratt and her staff sincerely believed that ethnic background and social class represented obstacles to success in school and teacher cooperation with the home. The results of a study conducted between 1919 and 1921 convinced Pratt that, among immigrant children even more than blacks, physical defects largely accounted for grade repetition or retardation. In correcting these deficiencies, many immigrant parents welcomed the help of the public school, but according to Pratt, "[B]arriers of language and custom, together with attitudes toward authority and lack of confidence in outsiders make the problem of school counseling in a foreign neighborhood a delicate and often baffling one." Social class affected the way some families thought about their children's education. In 1917, Hazel Ormsbee, a WWF counselor whose territory included working-class districts in Germantown and West Philadelphia, complained that some of her "American" clients had not responded well to the rapid growth of inflation after the United States entered World War I. Their first reaction had been to exchange school for work among their children.[76]

Pratt, Ormsbee, and their colleagues in school social work did not hesitate to blame educators for being insensitive to the complexity of the problem. As Mary B. Sayles pointed out, "[T]he teacher who is called upon to deal with a child in trouble needs to make very sure that her attitude is completely objective and unbiased, free from any emotional coloring due to prejudice or past experiences of her own."[77] But many teachers displayed an even more basic flaw: they did not know or care enough about what went on at home. Outreach to immigrant and working-class families had to start on the parents' own terms. "There must be a sympathetic understanding of the history, religion and attitude of the foreigner," Pratt said, "before we can meet on common ground." The WWF's work with Catholic schools underscored the importance of mutuality between the school and the home. Set in motion in 1921 under the auspices of the Philadelphia Committee on Protective Work for Girls, the Foundation's collaboration with one of the city's parochial schools convinced Pratt that parents were more receptive to counselors from a system that was their "chosen agent for the training of their children. A common faith facilitates [the] understanding of many problems."[78] Of course, Catholic educators thought that schools should respect the authority of the home, but if Pratt was aware of this, she did not let it deter her from pursuing her professional goals.

In the 1920s, Anna Pratt moved the WWF beyond the challenge presented by immigrant and working-class children. A study conducted in 1924 revealed that the average White-Williams client was an "American girl," twelve or thirteen years of age, whose dissatisfaction with school had less to do with "economic necessity" than with social and emotional maladjustment at home. The purpose of education was to prepare children for life, but the school was "missing its function" because it was not teaching the practical skills needed by homemakers, parents, and citizens.[79] Referring to its visiting teachers as "educational engineers," the WWF welcomed the chance to enlarge the scope of public education. Considering the changing composition of its board of managers, this is hardly surprising. Like the Magdalen Society before it, the WWF attracted many volunteers from the Philadelphia establishment, but in the 1920s, they were joined for the first time by high-ranking professionals in social work and education. In 1921, the WWF board included the head of the social economy department at Bryn Mawr College, the dean of education at the University of Pennsylvania, and the superintendent of the Protestant Episcopal City Mission. The board's president was Philip M. Rhinelander, the Episcopal Bishop of Pennsylvania, but he relinquished his office to a professor of sociology at Haverford College, Frank D. Watson, and the Commonwealth Fund promptly rewarded the WWF with a grant to teach the principles of casework to counselors in education.[80]

Between 1923 and 1925, the WWF trained a select group of five Philadelphia high school teachers to be counselors. The experience convinced one participant in the program, Charles Palmer of Northeast High School, that it was up to him and his colleagues to understand the home. It gave Anna Pratt confidence in her belief that counselors had to be specialists; one individual could not do an adequate job of educational, social, and vocational guidance alone. Vocational counselors had to be industrial experts, well versed in the complex requirements of work in modern times. School counselors, on the other hand, had to understand the social and emotional realities of family life.[81] Home and school associations might lend a hand, but by themselves, parents were no better able to deal with maladjustment than with any other serious medical disorder. However, the principle that the school had to take more responsibility for the home had not been totally won. In 1925, the Philadelphia Board of Education revealed itself to be only partially committed to professional counseling when it authorized the principal of each junior and senior high school to appoint a teacher to act as counselor with no increase in salary and minimal training. The decision forced the WWF to withdraw from the city's high schools, and only a grant from the Keith Fund allowed it to maintain a training program, preparing eight junior high teachers for work in school counseling.[82]

Collaboration between the WWF and the Philadelphia Home and School League represented an opportunity for both organizations in the 1920s. With its membership down and its reputation sullied by its recent battles with the board of education, the league was looking for new leadership, and it turned to Anna Pratt to arrest the decline. She turned down an offer to be the league's president at first but took the job in 1925 when the WWF board accepted her argument that the office would increase the WWF's influence and might also facilitate the growth of counseling in the city's elementary schools. The chance to involve parents in the renegotiation of the home-school relationship was too good to pass up. Working together, the WWF and the league could make the education of the "whole child" more nearly a reality by promoting "mutual understanding between parents and teachers." Since poor communication between the home and the school often led to conflict, PTAs even promised to augment the work of school counselors, who were usually too busy with maladjusted children to settle minor difficulties.[83] By 1929, Pratt was urging all social workers to rely on PTAs for help in understanding the school's community. Not surprisingly, her board voted to formalize its existing but still casual affiliation with what was by then known as the Philadelphia County Council of Home and School Associations.[84]

Anna Pratt used this partnership to stimulate both parent and teacher education. Encouraged by the WWF, local home and school associations organized study groups that often relied on principals and counselors to help them with their children's problems. Educated parents made the counselor's job easier, but teachers needed training, too. At the Conwell School of Practice, they learned to be "a little less 'standoffish' from the parents' point of view" and to join more freely in projects sponsored by home and school associations. "This is in accord with the new teaching of mental hygiene," Pratt explained, "namely, that children suffer if those who come in contact with them are pulling in opposite directions."[85] However, parents were not always willing or able partners. Some never followed through, while others were uncomfortable with the give-and-take of PTA meetings. Social class differences stifled communication and discouraged full participation, making it essential that schools have access to trained counselors and social workers to deal with complex situations.[86]

In the 1930s, the WWF continued to show a strong interest in the work of parent-teacher associations. The Depression elicited a generous response to families in distress from many local PTAs, but for the leaders of the WWF, the emergency presented an exceptional opportunity to dis-seminate "the principles of mental hygiene." A survey conducted by the WWF in 1931 revealed that even principals and teachers now thought that counselors should concentrate on the social and emotional health of school children. Out of step with those around them, obstinate, ob-streperous, and compulsive students suffered from genuine feelings of anxiety and loss that interfered with learning. Many adults also needed the school counselor's help because they, too, were experiencing the debilitat-ing effects of mental and emotional strain. Ina Eddingfield, a WWF coun-selor at the Blankenburg School, understood her role to be broadening the teacher's perspective and helping anxious pupils and parents cope with fears resulting from uncertainty. "The school has become a haven of secu-rity in the neighborhood," she wrote in 1933. It has benefited children both materially and spiritually and lifted the morale of the community.[87]

In the 1930s, the WWF shared the spotlight with others who called for better mental hygiene, but even Anna Pratt would have had to concede that there was no consensus about whether the school should take primary responsibility for children's mental health by instilling self-control and in-spiring self-esteem. William John Cooper, the United States commissioner of education, acknowledged that there was a place for mental hygiene in the schools, especially "in disciplining the child" and laying "the foun-dation of character education in the curriculum." But educators in cities were more willing to attack the problem of pupil maladjustment than were their rural counterparts.[88] Two of America's most prominent educational reformers took opposing positions on the school's role in promoting men-tal hygiene. Burton P. Fowler, the president of the Progressive Education Association, advised parents against expecting more of the schools than they did of themselves. On the other hand, Carleton P. Washburne, the su-perintendent who turned the Chicago suburb of Winnetka into a synonym for progressive school reform by enhancing the curriculum without short-changing basic skills, thought that schools should satisfy the child's every need for security, self-expression, and social living.[89]

The leaders of the WWF had less in common with Fowler than Wash-burne. But with counselors in just seven buildings, they served by their own estimate only about 5 percent of the Philadelphia school popula-tion. Nevertheless, Philadelphia was an acknowledged leader in the field of school counseling. Elsewhere in Pennsylvania, vocational guidance was still the model for those junior and senior high schools that provided any counseling at all. The Depression prompted many school districts in the United States to curtail or eliminate social services in order to maintain academic programs. One New York educator probably spoke for many of his colleagues when he said in 1944 that they could ill afford to ignore the one million maladjusted children enrolled in America's schools. But it would not be until after World War II that such services would reappear in schools to any great degree, now geared to the special needs of suburban children.[90]

The Philadelphia school board expanded its commitment to social outreach, if not counseling, during the Depression, assigning a home and school visitor to each of its thirty-six junior and senior high schools in 1934. Transferred from the Bureau of Compulsory Education, these former attendance officers were more like visiting teachers than school counselors, performing a wide range of administrative, diagnostic, and referral services. They consulted with parents, teachers, and principals on such matters as home conditions, personality disorders, testing, and placement. According to Edith Everett, Pratt's successor as executive director of the WWF, this experimental plan recognized the need for school counseling and was at least "a step toward the eventual development" of a full-fledged guidance department.[91] Eight years later the school board followed through, replacing the Division of Compulsory Education with one responsible for pupil personnel and counseling. The WWF agreed to help this new department by supplementing the counselors' salaries and helping the district with their training.[92]

The WWF scholarship program now was the centerpiece of its educational program, and it seemed to be working. When 83 percent of those who received scholarships between 1935 and 1940 answered a WWF questionnaire, the foundation learned that most held full- or part-time jobs in business or the professions. Everett interpreted these results to be a manifestation of the WWF's farsighted commitment to mental hygiene. "For these individuals," she said, "it seems safe to assume that skylines have been broadened, [and] that they have been helped to function in the world that has been created for them."[93] The relationship between the home and the school brought educators together with social workers in pursuit of a common end. Rethinking the idea that this relationship was reciprocal, they advanced the cause of social efficiency and emotional adjustment by expanding the mission of the school, but at what cost? As a social welfare institution, the public school was perhaps a better educator as well as a force for social justice. However, by consigning more social and economic responsibilities to schools, educators and reformers like those in charge of the WWF not only increased the school's chances for failure and its exposure to criticism but also justified the belief that Americans had done all that was required of them. As long as the school was in charge, the nation would not need to mount a more systematic and comprehensive assault on such endemic problems as poverty and discrimination.

Anticipating the Postwar Debate

Between 1910 and 1940, American educators, social workers, and reformers transformed the character of the home-school relationship, forging an alliance that made the school into an educator of parents as well as children. The urge to remake the working-class and immigrant family profoundly affected early childhood education and brought a new cadre of outreach workers into many elementary and secondary schools. Urban school districts gradually added school nurses, visiting teachers, and guidance counselors to their professional staffs. Educators accepted at least some responsibility for family health, youth employment, and by the 1930s, the psychological adjustment of even middle-class parents and children. Expanding the school's mission challenged the accepted meaning of the idea that the home and the school were separate, if interdependent, institutions, leading to role conflict and confusion. After all, parents in America retained considerable legal and moral authority, especially among the middle class, and as the functions of the school increased, it became less and less apparent where the obligations of teachers left off and those of parents kicked in. Working-class families found themselves more and more vulnerable to questions about their competence and even to outright criticism. After World War II, the introduction of life adjustment education in many public and Catholic high schools extended the school's outreach into more middle-class homes, but it was not extensive enough to bring about the kind of conflict with parents that would erupt when demands for desegregation, proposals for community control, and the condemnation of teacher unions struck schools. The accompanying clamor for parents' rights betokened a new militance in home-school relations.

Educators meant no harm when they proposed to expand the mission of schools, but they did not think through the consequences of their goodwill and ambition. Being all things to all people might mean kudos when things went well, but such hubris also invited doubt and dignified criticism.[94] Since 1945, American schools have paid a high price for not living up to expectations. Unable to deliver on all their promises, educators have become a convenient scapegoat for their own and the nation's lack of vision.

CHAPTER SIX

From Advocates to Adversaries

I hope that when you go to school
You won't disgrace your mother.
They will expect much more, you know,
From you—than from another.

You can't afford to push in line
Nor whisper. No, you can't, sir!
You'll always be expected to
Know every question's answer.

You'll have to have a brilliant mind,
The manners of a preacher—
Or else they'll say, "We might have known—
His mother was a TEACHER."
— Pauline S. Chadwell, "Stigma"

In September 1951, Mary Wellbrock was living in Peoria, Illinois, with her husband, Dick, a local businessman, and their three young sons. Herself the daughter of a school principal, she had always believed in public education, but now that she had small children of her own, two of whom were already attending the Peoria schools, there was more at stake than just her views. The teachers, she thought, deserved her support; after all, her sons were going to be spending countless hours with them for the next ten or twelve years. But what could she, a housewife, do to help them and the schools? She had already joined the parent-teacher association (PTA), only to discover that it was primarily a social organization that rarely dealt with educational issues. Feeling the need to do something more, she sought inspiration by visiting her children's classes.

Mary Wellbrock was not angry or disgruntled. She did not go looking for trouble when she first entered her children's school. In fact, she believed from the start that her sons' teachers deserved a raise. But she soon discovered that low salaries were not the only, or even the most, serious problem facing Peoria's teachers. They also had to contend with the high cost of textbooks, which made it difficult for some pupils to get them, and with burgeoning enrollments, a seemingly inevitable but clearly troublesome consequence of the ongoing baby boom. Her eldest son, Kent, had thirty-six classmates in his fourth grade room at the Washington School, while his younger brother Scott was one of fifty-six in the kindergarten. Disturbed by these numbers, Mrs. Wellbrock decided to attend a school board meeting. The board turned out to be a well-intentioned group with limited options. Just months before, the city's voters had defeated three bond referenda that would have allowed it to raise teacher salaries, renovate existing facilities, and build more schools. Budget woes even forced it to cut home economics and music from the junior high curriculum, eliminate high school counseling, and drop the adult education program.

After the meeting, Mrs. Wellbrock decided that she had learned an important lesson. Public schools were not off-limits—closed to outside input or intervention. On the contrary, they were community institutions that responded to political pressure. If parents wanted to make them better, they would have to help. A conference with the superintendent, Melvin G. Davis, reassured her that school authorities welcomed parental interest and involvement. "The board feels let down by the public," Dr. Davis said. Working together, educators, school directors, and parents could make improvements. Conferring with some of her teacher friends, Wellbrock learned that most did not feel underpaid. Instead, they were really bothered by public apathy; no one in town seemed to know or care about what they were doing. At the next PTA meeting, some parents attributed their indifference to "a lack of knowledge about the board and a lack of trust." But the forty parents, mostly mothers, who were in attendance conceded that this problem was at least in part their own fault, and they decided to devote more time and energy to the needs of the schools. Shortly thereafter the board responded by agreeing to lower textbook costs and study the salary question.[1]

In 1952, middle-class parents like Mary and Dick Wellbrock wanted to trust teachers and schools. They were learning from Benjamin Spock that belief in experts came from belief in themselves. But teachers deserved special respect because the future of democracy rested on American shoulders in a divided world and the job of educating good citizens belonged primarily to the public schools. Those women who returned home from the workforce after World War II now felt a new respect for their sisters in the teaching profession, identifying with them as never before.

Schools floated on a reservoir of goodwill, but many administrators, teach-ers, and even some parents believed that public support could easily evaporate if educators took their good standing for granted. Overcrowded buildings and understaffed schools would undermine public confidence sooner or later. Sensational allegations about subversives in the classroom and Communist control of teachers' unions demonstrated just how fragile the public's trust could be. Beginning in the mid-1940s, school officials determined to deepen and widen their channels of communication with the home.

In Concert

In 1944, the National Congress of Parents and Teachers (NCPT) pub-lished an official history, but, in actuality, the book did more to assess the present status of the parent-teacher movement and its flagship organi-zation. Among its many contributors, none was more emphatic than Vir-ginia Kletzer, the immediate past president, who argued that World War II had clarified the importance to democracy of both the home and the school. The failure of either "to do its part in the joint enterprise" of citi-zenship education "would mean that all the money, all the effort, and all the heartbreak" would be in vain. Charl Williams, director of field service for the National Education Association (NEA) and for many years the chair of the NCPT's Committee on School Education, took a more posi-tive approach, arguing that the example set by local PTAs taught children the attitudes and principles of "democratic cooperation." But even among the NCPT's most ardent supporters, there was still some disagreement about just what that should mean. Both Williams and Anna H. Hayes, chair of the organization's Committee on Publicity, thought that parent-teacher associations had the potential to uplift their communities, teach-ing the right values in the proper way. These associations offer a me-dium, Hayes explained, "through which the philosophy and program of learning of the most enlightened homes and . . . the most dependable schools may become available to all the people of the community." Edgar Dale, professor of education at Ohio State University and chair of the NCPT's Committee on Audiovisual Education, had a different opinion. In a nation composed of people from many different lands, he said, "the blending of all these elements into a truly American culture . . . is one of the PTA's most valuable contributions."[2]

In the late 1940s, most educators and many parents did not want that quintessential American institution, the PTA, to be the setting for dissent or conflict. The threat of Communism both at home and abroad, combined with the pressing need for more teachers and school buildings in almost every American community, required parents and teachers to show respect for one another and settle for nothing less than full cooperation. A good PTA, said Anna Hayes, finds facts, not fault. It does not try to run the schools but makes itself available to help the administration. Disagreements did not imply fundamental differences but, like lovers' quarrels, arose when there was a breakdown of common sense or communication.[3] Some school administrators did not hesitate to remind parents that they should be advocates for public education; a good PTA member, said Angelo Patri, is always "watchful, quiet, and encouraging." But teachers, principals, and superintendents also had to accept the lion's share of the burden for turning parents away from apathy or, even worse, criticism. "If our schools are to receive the full appreciation and support of parents," said Paul Misner, the superintendent of schools in Glencoe, Illinois, "we must seek to make them active and responsible members of the partnership." In an article published in *Educational Leadership,* a new journal in the field of educational administration, Misner and one of his teachers argued that parents would not always cooperate unless they were included in educational planning. Goodwill notwithstanding, reciprocity between the home and the school depended in the long run on mutual respect and common understandings.[4]

It was one thing to work together but quite another to conflate the separate responsibilities of parents and teachers. In the 1950s, many social scientists and educators urged their colleagues and clients alike to acknowledge that the home and the school, while interdependent, were separate and distinct institutions. In his landmark study, *Education as a Profession,* Myron Lieberman argued that teachers deserved to be recognized as professionals even though their work was neither as scientific as medicine nor as precise as law.[5] There ought to be a clear division of labor between the home and the school, Lieberman implied, and most child-rearing experts, whose advice the parents of the baby boom generation eagerly sought, could not have agreed more. As Mary and Lawrence Frank, Grace Langdon, and Sidonie Matsner Gruenberg often explained to their readers, parents were in charge of emotional development, while teachers had to make sure that children learned social skills. Langdon's reputation in the field rested on her leadership of the parent education program delivered by the Works Progress Administration in the 1930s. Gruenberg, who was self-taught, published the first of many articles and books on child rearing in 1911 and subsequently achieved national prominence as head of the Child Study Association of America, an organization devoted to parent education. She advised working mothers who were too busy to meet with teachers not to feel guilty but thought they should at least acknowledge the toll their jobs took on their homes. Because Lawrence Frank spent many years at the Rockefeller Foundation funding research and reform programs for parents and children, he and his wife commanded respect when they said that it was up to the family to stamp "patterns of warmth and intimacy." The school, on the other hand, had to instill respect for fair play so that children would learn to "get along with others in any working relationship."[6] Angelo Patri seconded these sentiments when he reminded doting parents that they needed the teacher's objectivity, but Sidonie Gruenberg put this thought better than he. "The teacher cannot take each child's problems too deeply to heart," she said, but "the parent cannot do otherwise."[7] Only by honoring their differences could parents and teachers strengthen the bond of trust between them.

However, achieving the proper balance was no easy task. Teachers had to know more than a little about each student's family life but should not be expected to compensate for serious problems at home. Children who came to school so confused about themselves and their families that they could not concentrate might not be able to learn how to read. Parents had to create a safe and supportive home environment that taught children to recognize their strengths and believe in themselves. They had to instill feelings of independence, confidence, and self-esteem. Building on the foundation laid by the mental hygiene movement in the 1930s, the Franks and Sidonie Gruenberg cautioned parents against making success in school a condition for love and approval. Good grades and promotions should not be mistaken for a child's inherent worth as a human being. Knowing that many young families were coping with the trauma of sending children off to school for the first time, the Franks urged parents not to make too much of this transition. Going to school should not seem like the end of life at home, nor should work brought home from school become the occasion for a stressful confrontation.[8] Although the home and the school were clearly not the same, the difference between them should be all but imperceptible to America's youngest children.

Good parents did more than just nurture their offspring. They made certain their children learned good manners and morals, not counting on teachers to assume primary responsibility for such a basic parental duty.

According to Martha Shull, president of the NEA, parents were educators, whether they knew it or not; they taught their children what to expect and how to behave in school. In the early 1950s, it was certainly nothing new to say that the home and the school were dependent on one another or that family life affected how well children did at school. Parents and teachers had been sorting out their respective, but reciprocal, roles since the beginning of the twentieth century, while the question of the home's impact on school performance was no longer revolutionary. Sociologists and psychologists had been researching this for many years. Shull spoke to the problem of achievement when she urged parents to cultivate a positive attitude toward education in their children, but she also counseled them to be reasonable in their expectations. Trust between parents and teachers depended on a mutual understanding that schools could not work miracles or get the job done alone.[9]

The importance of cooperation between parents and teachers argued against leaving anything to chance. Teachers were urged to take the initiative just as they had been in the 1920s, but the stakes were higher now because America had changed. Advances in child psychology, together with such accelerating social trends as working wives and suburbanization, meant that even middle-class parents needed help understanding children and recognizing the difference between good education and bad. James L. Hymes Jr. cautioned educators against patronizing parents when he wrote *Effective Home-School Relations,* a book that went through seven printings in six years, beginning in 1953. An assistant director of the Kaiser Corporation's Child Service Centers during World War II and the author of many pamphlets for parents, Hymes subscribed fully to the view that the home-school relationship was a two-way street. However, he challenged teachers to take charge of improving the school's standing with the family. It was up to them to bring out the parents' latent goodwill by showing respect for their practical knowledge. "Many parents today need reassurance much more than they need blame," Hymes wrote; "they need praise for what they have done well rather than advice on what they might do; they need awareness of their own good ideas rather than the other fellow's answers to their questions."[10] Like Benjamin Spock, Hymes believed that the home could not honor the school until teachers helped parents find the courage of their convictions.

James Hymes was not alone in his belief that educators should leverage the trust that they wanted parents to place in them. Alice Sowers, a vice president of the NCPT and a professor of family life education at the University of Oklahoma, blamed parental apathy on the school. Parents have heard and read so much about what is wrong with them, she explained, that they hesitate to come to PTA and other school meetings. Educators had to encourage them, pointing out that many families had the same problems and feelings. Grace Langdon counseled teachers to be more forthcoming with parents. The more information the school shared freely and willingly, the more parents would feel at ease. The home and the school could then engage in a "two-way conversation" that would build confidence in the school and allow "the things [that] both wonder about" to come out in the open.[11]

In the 1950s, parent participation became the sine qua non of good home-school relations. It was still fashionable for mothers and fathers to lend a helping hand, providing the volunteer services that had made them the teacher's most reliable assistant for a long time. Parents have a "work-right," said Eunice S. Allen, principal of the Chelsea Park Elementary School, near Seattle, Washington, whether that meant filing student papers, sewing denim book bags, or organizing an after-school hobby program. Some principals and teachers also welcomed parental collaboration. In Wilmington, Delaware, parents shared their knowledge of the real world with the high school faculty when the business education curriculum was being revised. In Exeter, Alabama, they helped conduct a community needs assessment that led to the establishment of a recreation center. Parent advisory councils began to attract favorable attention because they made it possible, according to the director of the Campus Laboratory School at Wisconsin State College, for "staff to obtain a broader perspective and to reflect the parents' objectives more distinctly in school planning." Any inconvenience, James Hymes claimed, was a small price to pay for the "atmosphere of trust and approval" created by such participation.[12]

Parents themselves wanted to be involved in the school's work, especially the curriculum. The rush to rebuild family life that followed World War II did not bypass the home-school relationship. Surveys conducted in the South and Midwest revealed that many Americans felt unprepared for the responsibilities of parenthood and some even sought the school's help with such private matters as sex education and interpersonal relations. "Parents are ready to give their opinion of what schools should emphasize," said Bess Goodykoontz from her lofty perch as associate commissioner in the U.S. Office of Education; they tell us that what they want is "a broad, life-centered curriculum." At the peak of its popularity in the early 1950s, the life adjustment movement ranked "education for family living" as the school's most important function.[13] But not all Americans felt this way. Many parents remained convinced that sex education did not belong in the schools forty years after the American Social Hygiene Association and educators like Ella Flagg Young began work on the subject. Reformer Maurice Bigelow's argument that sex education had a positive impact on marriage fell on deaf ears in many homes.[14] In Minneapolis, critics of such thinking organized a Parents Council to oppose the local school district's "common learnings" program, objecting because they believed that it neglected basic subjects and took control of moral education away from the family. But the immediate past president of the North Carolina Congress of Parents and Teachers believed that the home and the school, working together, could devise a program that would direct young people toward social and emotional maturity. According to the president of the Pasadena Council of Parents and Teachers, her district had already developed a modern curriculum that taught students and parents how to deal with the tensions resulting from problems at home and conflicts between the school and the home.[15] Together, parents and teachers could build on the desire for trust that existed between them.

Leaders in the field of Catholic education joined in the common praise for good home-school relations, but they added another dimension, putting the church as well as the family into the equation. In fact, they believed that the school was actually "subsidiary and complementary to the Church and the family" and should never oppose either one of them. Parents were the first and primary teachers; only they, said the editor of *The Catholic School Journal,* could "co-ordinate the forces of education." Strict attention to this basic principle built the confidence that Catholic schools enjoyed at home, but parent involvement could be a mixed blessing. Some of the faithful were ignorant about child development; others had unreasonable expectations for their children's education. In such situations, the church had "to teach parents cooperation with the school," helping them understand and accept the judgments its teachers made for them. Here, the clergy counted on the Home and School Council to act as the go-between.[16]

Catholic educators were no different from their secular counterparts in wanting to maintain regular contact with the home. After all, the trust parents felt for teachers might turn to suspicion if communication broke down. A misunderstanding about homework, for example, could lead to trouble, especially if parents tried to help their children with core subjects like reading and arithmetic. Grace Langdon and Irving Stout recommended that teachers think of homework as "a form of communication to the parents," keeping them informed about what was happening in school and inviting them to contribute to their child's education.[17] But teachers could never know just how well homework conveyed the intended message, and in the 1950s, a more direct method, the parent-teacher conference, attracted widespread attention. Face-to-face meetings between parents and teachers were nothing new, of course, but they took on a new importance for educators who did not want to risk losing the confidence parents placed in them.[18] James Hymes thought that the home should be the setting for such conferences. Teachers and principals resisted, citing inconvenience and inefficiency, but they hastened to add that meetings at school should be informal. Putting parents at ease would take much of the dread away, and the resulting rapport might even build respect for the school by preventing incipient problems from getting out of hand.[19]

The popularity of parent-teacher conferences rested on the belief that the home and the school could cooperate. Parents who felt comfortable at school would volunteer information about their personal lives. Teachers who knew children's families would realize just how much parents wanted to be involved and make allowances for their participation.[20] The threat posed by America's enemies during World War II called forth pledges to interdependence that justified a presumption of trust. But the respect that parents and teachers felt for one another was never rock solid, and it began to show signs of strain in the 1950s. The loyalty oaths many states adopted put the teaching profession on the defensive. Progressive education came under fire, first for undermining parental authority and then for weakening educational standards. When juvenile delinquency reached crisis proportions, high schools took part of the blame for tolerating a self-indulgent youth culture.[21] These well-publicized problems affected the way parents and teachers thought about each other, but reciprocity between the home and the school became increasingly problematic because it also rested on the false assumption that Americans were all the same. Blacks certainly understood that interdependence between the home and the school could not be achieved merely by saying that both institutions were on the same page. Calling attention to cultural bias and racial discrimination, they identified some of the major obstacles to parent-teacher trust and cooperation. During World War II, the need to believe in togetherness outweighed other considerations, justifying practices that seemed innocuous but actually put schools in conflict with more than a few Americans. The celebration of Christmas in the nation's public schools illustrates the point because what seemed unexceptional to many gave some people good reason to think that the home and the school could not enjoy perfect reciprocity.

In the 1940s, most Americans believed they lived in a Christian country. Educators could not ignore the Christmas season, but the secularization of this holiday, which was well under way by the 1920s, made it even more difficult for schools to ignore religion.[22] In December 1944, Zinnetta Hastings, the president of the National Congress of Parents and Teachers, urged all her readers to pray that "the vision of Christmas" would never fade but continue to work miracles in a divided world. Peace did not put an end to such thinking, as Hastings's successor, Mabel Hughes, made clear in her holiday message for 1947. She found the spirit of Christmas in every PTA, keeping the message of the season alive throughout the year.[23] Until the mid-1950s, it was not uncommon for parents and teachers to express such sentiments openly and un-self-consciously, but by then, some educators had begun to realize that they risked the goodwill of the home if they continued to behave as if the United States was a culturally homogeneous nation. Polled by the editors of *The Nation's Schools,* a national sample of superintendents agreed that while public schools should acknowledge the major Christian holidays, the tone and character of such observances should reflect the individual preferences of America's many different communities.[24]

Symbols of Christianity might still be acceptable in many school districts, but to be on the safe side, educational leaders recommended treating Christmas as a family holiday. It should be a celebration of the child, said Karla Parker, the president of the NCPT. A commission appointed by the American Association of School Administrators encouraged its members to exercise good judgment by recognizing "the differing rites and customs of families, cultures, and creeds."[25] Changes in the nature of holiday observances corresponded to a larger shift in the relationship between the home and the school that began in the 1950s and accelerated in the following decade. Teachers, principals, superintendents, and school directors gradually realized that they no longer enjoyed the unquestioned trust of parents or the community. In the 1970s, collective bargaining, civil rights, and a general crisis of confidence in American institutions changed the way schools were perceived. More than at any other time since the nineteenth century, there was an adversarial edge to the relationship between schools and their constituencies.

In Conflict

In the spring of 1968, Jonathan Kozol was a young writer on the rise. Basking in the glow of praise for *Death at an Early Age,* a vivid account of his ten months as a Boston public school teacher, Kozol turned his attention

to the teaching profession, blaming it for the poor state of community relations in America's urban schools. A misguided attitude of professional
detachment prevented teachers from working closely with parents, he
wrote, and in the absence of real collaboration, the home could not place
its trust in the school. Kozol's criticism probably sounded unfair to many
of his contemporaries, but most of them must have recognized the problem he identified as nothing new. Seven years earlier Ernest Osborne, a
professor at Teachers College, had characterized as unprecedented the
dissatisfaction parents felt with their children's schools. Apropos of the
Cold War, he blamed the situation on both parents and teachers, whose
failure to communicate fed their respective anxieties and insecurities.[26]

On the subject of home-school relations, Kozol and Osborne differed
from James Bryant Conant, the most respected educational critic of his
time. In *Slums and Suburbs,* Conant had blamed any disillusionment on
"Negro" parents who sent their children to school unprepared.[27] James
Coleman's important study of equal educational opportunity, published in
1966, implied a similar conclusion, but Kozol's perspective, which picked
up on negative feelings about schools dating from the 1950s, would win the
day. Bureaucracy, teacher strikes, institutional racism, and even the federal government's growing involvement in elementary and secondary education were increasingly perceived to be responsible for a widening gap
between the home and the school. "The urban school is isolated," Peter
Schrag complained in 1967. "It is distant both from the contemporary
world and from the people and community it presumes to serve, and it
spends a great deal of energy inventing devices to maintain that distance."
Suburban schools were rapidly becoming no different from their urban
counterparts, according to *The New York Times,* and even though many
teachers and principals remained accessible to parents and other outsiders, especially in rural areas, they mirrored the attitudes and expectations
of their communities less and less frequently.[28]

In the 1970s, parental respect for teachers experienced a steady decline. The Gallup organization discovered that fewer than half of all those
it polled in 1983 wanted a child of theirs to become a teacher, down from
three-quarters of those it asked fourteen years before. Over the same span
of time, more and more parents had come to express concern about the
school's commitment to excellence in education, while holding fast to the
belief, common in the 1960s, that teachers often failed to maintain classroom discipline.[29] Educational muckraking became a cottage industry, as
one author after another sought to capitalize on the popular idea that parents should not automatically think of principals and teachers as legiti-

mate authority figures, much less friends. The autobiographical *36 Children* attracted national attention for Herbert Kohl by condemning the cynical attitude of teachers in a Harlem public school. James Herndon, Richard De Lone, Kenneth Keniston, and James Comer, among others, addressed the erosion of trust and respect between the home and the school. Scholars like Keniston and De Lone, for example, questioned the sincerity of anyone who still maintained that the poor could expect fair treatment by schools. Comer recognized that race and class affected the parent-teacher relationship significantly because middle-class whites, worried about college, and low-income blacks, struggling against the odds, had every reason to be concerned about the performance of their children's schools.[30] In the mid-1960s, *The Journal of Negro Education* published both opinion and research criticizing the nation's teachers for not doing enough to improve student performance by welcoming parents at school. "There is a feeling," said Earle H. West, a member of the journal's editorial board, "that parents are at best to be grudgingly tolerated, and at worst an influence to be actively counteracted." Even *Phi Delta Kappan,* an influential periodical read by many school administrators, could not buck this trend. In 1977, it asked its readers to consider whether educators treated parents as the "natural enemy" of the school.[31]

In the face of such suspicion and mistrust, almost no one proposed turning for help to the existing network of parent-teacher organizations. In fact, critics described the PTA as a company union—part of the problem, not the solution. According to Peter Schrag, Boston's Home and School Association was "wedded to the rest of the system," acting as a front for the administration and the School Committee. Much more white than black, it could not speak for all parents equally during the city's desegregation crisis. Reformers in New York were even more negative, looking on PTAs as an obstacle to meaningful dialogue. They gave the illusion of parental influence, while discouraging the formation of community groups that might be more aggressive about the need for change.[32] The PTA's most ardent supporters had to admit there was a problem. In 1969, the president of the NCPT, Elizabeth S. Hendryson, acknowledged that many parents dismissed her organization as irrelevant. Preoccupied with superficial service tasks, PTAs seldom asked hard questions or challenged management, especially in the inner city, where they had historically failed to recruit minorities or represent them against the educational establishment. Even the bureaucrats at the United States Office of Education had to concede that PTAs needed to do a better job of "interpreting the community's wishes to the school," a view that by the late 1960s must have seemed conservative, at least to those responsible for the many new and vigorous demands then being made for more significant parent involvement.[33]

Some urban superintendents anticipated this trend, inventing ways to bring low-income parents into more frequent contact with public schools. But their strategies were anachronistic because they ignored the special needs of the wage-earning mother, who was becoming common, especially in the lower middle class, thinking instead in terms of her stay-at-home counterpart. In Baltimore, school officials organized an early childhood program to teach women about very young children; in Chicago, it was a series of get-acquainted workshops held in the spring. School-home coordinators in Philadelphia not only worked with low-income mothers who were enrolling their children for the first time but also sought to engage parents of students at the high school level. Mothers in St. Louis were encouraged to pledge their cooperation, committing time to help their small children do well in school. It was not that the experts thought inner-city parents were indifferent to education. They just lacked the requisite knowledge and skills to prepare their children for success in school.[34]

But by the mid-1960s, many reformers believed parent education was not the answer because it did not guarantee parents a meaningful role in school activities, much less power. Urban school boards and superintendents used it to control community input, while they monopolized authority. Beginning in 1964, the federal government endorsed parent involvement in educational policy-making, requiring parent advisory councils for Head Start Centers funded under the Economic Opportunity Act and for a related program to increase low-income student achievement known as Follow Through. In its original form, the Elementary and Secondary Education Act (ESEA) called only for cooperation between school boards and community groups, but in 1968, the United States Office of Education interpreted this to mean parent participation in school planning. As amended by Congress in the 1970s, Title I of ESEA required school districts to form parent advisory councils to assist in the design, development, and implementation of its programs for low-income children. Policy makers in California, South Carolina, and Florida seconded this effort, mandating multipurpose advisory committees in their public schools.[35]

The rediscovery of poverty in the inner city was a big incentive to such parent involvement because many bureaucrats and reformers believed that low-income and minority parents felt alienated from the public schools. However, parent advisory councils did not begin then and there.

They originated at least fifty years before when America's school superintendents were first learning to make communication with the home an exercise in good public relations. In December 1919, for example, the school board in Mitchell, South Dakota, decided to appoint a women's advisory council, which would provide guidance on such varied matters as school furniture, compulsory education, and the living conditions of its mostly female teaching staff. The PTA could have served as a sounding board in Mitchell, just as it did in many other communities, but according to the town's superintendent in the 1940s, Lloyd T. Ueker, the women's advisory council was preferable from a bureaucratic standpoint, being free to deal with topics "that could not be taken before so public a body as the parent-teacher association." [36]

During the Depression and World War II, many school districts formed citizen advisory councils to obtain guidance on the problems of the day. However, it was the civil rights movement and the reexamination of democracy in America resulting from it that justified a new commitment to involve parents. The legal assault on segregation called attention to the frustration felt by many blacks regarding the treatment of their children in the nation's public schools. Both the Rockefeller and the Charles Stewart Mott Foundations invested in school advisory councils to develop minority leadership and promote community development. As part of his efforts to integrate the Boston public schools, Judge W. Arthur Garrity directed principals to establish Racial-Ethnic Councils to be elected by and composed of parents, both black and white, an order that actually elevated racial tension in some schools. In addition, he required school officials to set up nine District Advisory Councils and a Citywide Parents' Advisory Council to thwart those who might stand in the way of integration at the neighborhood level. [37]

The effort to bring parent pressure to bear in New York City derived much of its energy from the deep mistrust that minority parents felt for the city's schools. By the mid-1960s the *Brown v. Board of Education* decision had not made much difference, despite years of protest and political action by the Reverend Milton A. Galamison, a Brooklyn pastor, who spearheaded a parent movement for desegregation. To force the issue, he proposed a citywide boycott of the schools in 1960, but even when such a strike by nearly 500,000 black and Hispanic children occurred four years later, it failed to produce an acceptable desegregation plan, prompting many minority parents to throw up their hands in frustration. Nor were they as prepared as they once might have been to accept blame for their children's failure at school. Community control, said psychologist

Kenneth B. Clark, should be understood as a demand for "accountability by parents to whom the schools have never accounted." It should be understood as "a demand that their children be respected as human beings with the potential all normal children have" and as an indictment of the "flagrant racism that afflicts so many of the institutions of American education." Ford Foundation official Mario Fantini could not have agreed more. The demonstration districts that put decentralization on trial in East Harlem, Brooklyn, and the lower East Side of Manhattan arose, he said, from the atmosphere of distrust that was created by the racist behavior of the city's teachers, administrators, and central board of education.[38]

Thanks to federal, state, and local programs, opportunities for more parent involvement in public education proliferated in the 1970s. With 900,000 participants, parent advisory councils under Title I were the largest group, but numbers alone can be deceiving, not necessarily adding up to meaningful participation whether that be defined as political influence or the authority to make decisions. In the Head Start program, parent involvement meant adult education more than clout. Reducing the cultural deficit at home would help low-income parents prepare their children for school.[39] Other reformers hoped that advisory councils would make it possible for parents to enhance their children's education. "Parent participation is not viewed as a mere privilege or as a legal right," said Preston Wilcox, one of the most outspoken advocates for community control in New York. "Rather it is perceived as natural right . . . in which the love and security offered by parents are consciously perceived as being a learning tool."[40] In Maine, Rhode Island, and California, some parents became very active, making certain that local officials did not misuse Title I money, but many advisory councils existed only on paper, and, for the most part, they never graduated from a supporting role. School administrators hesitated to give them any power without also sharing accountability. Principals must take the lead, said C. C. Carpenter, the superintendent of schools in Holyoke, Massachusetts. Parent advisory groups "need to know from the beginning just what they are supposed to do, as well as the limits of their participation." By the late 1970s, many parent councils, especially those created by government, found themselves co-opted, having become organizations tied by function and funding to the bureaucracy.[41]

Both race and class contributed to the ineffectiveness of parent advisory groups, making it difficult for them to bring about change in the policies and practices of schools. White reformers and black parents sometimes brought different expectations to the task of redefining the relationship between the school and its community. In the Adams-Morgan district of Washington, D.C., advisors from Antioch College were surprised to discover that many black parents objected to neighborhood interns teaching in the local elementary school. Race also complicated discussions among parents and teachers, either separately or together, about how to revise the school's curriculum or its methods of teaching. In big cities like Atlanta, Boston, and Los Angeles, poverty weakened the parents' collective voice, standing in the way of parental independence by encouraging parent advisory councils to accept the establishment's financial support. By the late 1970s, cooperation, not confrontation, had become the order of their day. In fact, school reform by itself was not compelling enough to sustain parent activism in declining neighborhoods in need of comprehensive redevelopment.[42]

Administrative and political reorganization also did not mandate meaningful involvement by handing parents real opportunities for influence or control. A Decentralization Task Force in Los Angeles went only so far as to include parents in councils that advised principals. Parental dissatisfaction with poor conditions in Detroit's segregated schools forced its board of education to subdivide the system, sharing authority with eight regional boards, but even though these boards had some power over curriculum and staff, they still had to operate within guidelines that applied to the district as a whole and honor its contract with the teachers' union. To make matters worse, the anxieties and conflicts that resulted from Detroit's half-hearted efforts to deal with school segregation made for a climate that was hostile to any significant realignment of power between the home and the school.[43] However, Detroit did not put the efficacy of decentralization for parent power to its sternest test. That honor belonged to New York City, where, according to the decentralization law of 1969, each community school board had to be in regular contact with the parents' association or PTA that was required of every school in its subdistrict. Those elected to these boards tended to be white men whose children attended nonpublic schools, and most resisted giving parents meaningful power, especially over such hot-button issues as the evaluation of teachers and budgeting. Some even dragged their feet about implementing the federal order for parent advisory councils in Title I programs. They preferred parents to be easygoing, available for input, and useful as window dressing but outside the loop when it came to actual decision-making.[44]

If racial discrimination gave some parents a compelling reason to formulate opinions and make their weight felt, the changing relationship between management and labor in American education constituted a powerful prompt for many more to pay attention and get involved. Teachers' unions were nothing new in the United States in 1960, especially in cities, but most Americans had yet to experience a strike that closed their child's school. Some, no doubt, could remember the flurry of walkouts that occurred right after World War II when teachers' salaries fell far behind the soaring cost of living. Money was still the problem in 1956 when strikes halted instruction in such dissimilar places as Minneapolis; Pawtucket, Rhode Island; and Avoca, Pennsylvania, where the entire faculty of twenty-three refused to work until they had received more than three months' back pay. By the mid-1960s, many states permitted teachers to bargain collectively, and the NEA represented nearly 400,000 school personnel in 1,179 districts across the country. Millions more remained unaffiliated, sparking a fierce competition between the NEA and the much smaller American Federation of Teachers (AFT). As more and more teachers organized, the number of strikes rapidly increased, especially in the Upper Midwest and Northeast. But militance was not confined to those regions with a strong labor tradition. Statewide walkouts occurred in Florida and Utah as well as Indiana, Pennsylvania, and Kentucky. Between 1967 and 1973, there were ten times as many teacher strikes in the United States as in the preceding seventeen years.[45]

Contrary to expectation, parents did not always condemn teachers who organized and engaged in collective bargaining. After all, better salaries and working conditions might translate into better schools. Elizabeth Hendryson believed that such demographic variables as race, class, and region affected parental attitudes about teacher unions. From her perch atop the NCPT, she had learned that small towns and rural communities associated organized labor with trouble. Some professional parents accepted teacher unions, especially if they could equate them with medical or bar associations. African Americans might support them if they included black members and appeared friendly to reforms that would improve inner-city schools. But parents rarely welcomed strikes because they disrupted family routine, created doubt about the reliability of adults, and, worst of all, interrupted the education of children (see figure 6.1).[46] In 1968, the NCPT issued a policy statement to guide its state and local units in matters having to do with labor relations. "Because work stoppages and negotiations . . . create dissension and low morale that are harmful to children, the PTA should do all it can to prevent such situations from developing." In the event of a strike, it should help parents and teachers reconcile, once a settlement had come.[47]

Collective bargaining by the NEA and AFT changed the nature of home-school relations, making teachers an independent force in the politics of American education. They did not have to defer to parents or serve as management's silent partner in decision-making. Elizabeth Hendryson

FIGURE 6.1. Parents picketing against striking Philadelphia teachers, October 18, 1973. Courtesy *Philadelphia Bulletin* Photo Collection, Urban Archives, Samuel Paley Library, Temple University, Philadelphia.

remained hopeful that PTAs could bridge the widening gap between parents and unionized teachers. According to her, they could play an important role in negotiations by providing a forum for discussion, but many parents and reformers found this argument unconvincing. Unions have made it possible for teachers "to give priority to their own welfare," disconnecting the two parties closest to the learner, said Mario Fantini. The result, almost inevitably, turns out to be "conflict and collision."[48] However, union solidarity was often the consequence, not the cause, of parent dissatisfaction. In the 1960s, many teachers joined a union because they felt unjustly blamed for the failings of public education. Some strikes resulted from discord between the home and the school over issues like student achievement, for which teachers could not escape at least some responsibility. But many teachers felt they had the right to defend themselves if they were held accountable for the breakdown of efforts to achieve such systemic reforms as school integration or confronted by what they considered to be intrusive attempts to invade their professional domain. Bitter strikes in New York, Newark, and Detroit resulted from struggles between black parents and organized teachers over accountability and community control of the schools.[49]

By the mid-1970s, collective bargaining was well on its way to becoming a fact of life in public education. Legislation gave teachers the right to negotiate in twenty-nine states, and the courts had begun to reject the idea that school strikes were prima facie illegal. In 1976, John Ryor, the president of the NEA, addressed the charge that teachers diminished themselves when they joined a union. Collective bargaining actually enhanced professionalism by giving teachers more control over their work, he said. Strikes were not just manifestations of self-interest; they showed that teachers cared enough about their students to insist on having sufficient resources. Parents, on the other hand, seldom noticed problems at school until teachers took drastic steps to bring them to the public's attention.[50] Such arguments did not convince many parents that school strikes deserved their support. Collective bargaining might be protected under the law, but the concomitant possibility of a work stoppage made for a less trusting, more adversarial relationship between the home and the school. This is not to say that parents no longer accepted the authority of teachers in the classroom. Their professional expertise still commanded respect, especially among white, working-class parents.[51] But the balance of power was changing, and at least some parents decided that they needed to take another approach if their interests were to be protected in the new politics of American education. They gravitated toward advocacy organizations that were for parents only, a shift that coincided with the more combative climate then at work in American home-school relations.

Parents' Rights

In the history of parent-teacher associations, parents have been more active than teachers almost from the beginning. In fact, school administrators often urged principals and teachers to play second fiddle because they thought the professionals could accomplish their objectives more effectively if they stayed in the background. But a low profile is not the same as no profile at all; educators always expected to have a formal presence in organizations devoted to improving parent-teacher relations. This expectation came under attack in the 1970s when unionized teachers reached for parity with management, and many parents decided that they needed to be more independent of the educational establishment. They had to form organizations whose membership would be limited to parents. Founded in 1972, the Parents Union for Public Schools (PUPS) claimed responsibility for this constituency in a time of crisis for Philadelphia's public schools. However, associations just for parents did not originate in the 1970s; they were pioneered in New York City fifty years before. The citywide federation known as the United Parents Associations (UPA), formed in 1921, quickly became a distinctive but generally conservative voice in New York school politics. Like the PUPS, it sponsored parent education and spoke for parents' rights, but even in the 1960s, when nothing in the United States was beyond reproach, the UPA did not cut the ties it had developed with the city's educational establishment. Assuming a more aggressive posture in unsettled times, it still worked closely with the school board and the professionals headquartered at 110 Livingston Street. As an advocacy organization, neither the UPA nor the PUPS could make change unilaterally. But each in its own way questioned the idea of reciprocity in the home-school relationship.

United Parents Associations

From the outset, the UPA took the position that only parents should belong. Not every affiliate observed this policy, especially in the 1920s, because the organization resulted from the merger of two parent federations, one of which was composed of PTAs that had come together to demand a salary increase for teachers working in New York City's public schools. For principals and even teachers to be no more than ex officio members represented a departure from the standard PTA, but it must not have seemed unreasonable to the UPA's first president, Robert E. Simon, whose previous experience with such groups had been with the Horace Mann School Parents Association. Under Simon's leadership, the UPA lived by the principle that autonomy was a prerequisite for success in parent organizations. Professional advice could then be taken for what it was worth, and local units could concentrate on whatever interested them. Since many of the UPA's original affiliates had once been mothers' clubs associated with public and private kindergartens, learning about the parent-child relationship appealed to many of its charter members. But this agenda did not attract many working-class and immigrant parents, most of whom had more pressing concerns, and it established the foundation for the UPA's reputation in later years as a middle-class organization.[52]

In 1925, the UPA represented just 3,400 people in thirty-seven local associations. These numbers increased steadily over the next decade before exploding after World War II. By the mid-1960s, the UPA's 450 units and 400,000 members commanded attention and respect at city hall as well as school headquarters. When it was new and small, the UPA cultivated the establishment by touting the merits of working within the system. In 1922, for example, it identified as its primary role helping parents know their children's schools so they could cooperate "intelligently" with teachers and the administration. It also sought "to formulate city-wide parent opinion" and "bring influence to bear on public officials" to improve not just public education but also health, welfare, and recreation. However, the UPA's first priority was parent education. Maria Lamdin Rogers, the UPA's executive secretary from 1925 to 1929, betrayed the middle-class bias of her organization when she complained that many parents were not interested in such education or intelligent enough to profit from it. Principals, on the other hand, were skeptical about the wisdom of it, let alone associations for parents only. But they had no right to expect "unquestioning acquiescence to their policies." Well-informed parents could be an asset, especially if they educated themselves, and by building parent knowledge, Rogers thought the UPA could look forward to a time when its members would be "regarded with respect" by those in charge of the schools in the system.[53]

The idea that parents might have rights began to form in New York City in the 1930s. Prompted by the introduction of junior highs, a policy change required principals to discuss pupil transfers with parents and gave parents the right to appeal if they disagreed with the decision. The superintendent acknowledged the legitimacy of parents' associations by deciding that they could meet free of charge in school buildings. Hard times made the board of education more receptive to the idea that parents had the potential to be powerful advocates for public education, but the accompanying fear that they might embarrass the establishment gave rise to a resolution, adopted in 1934, that parents' associations had to take responsibility for their actions. Educators in New York did not want to be held accountable for any loose cannons. In 1939, the UPA and the school board commissioned a joint report that spelled out the means by which to achieve good home-school relations. Parents would be welcome at school, but not without warning. There should be carefully planned programs, featuring student work and school activities, that would help parents exercise their rights by giving them the proper training.[54]

Complaints about domineering principals called attention to the need for a parents' bill of rights after World War II. In 1947, New York's acting commissioner of education, Dr. Lewis Wilson, ruled that a school board might take action against principals who did not cooperate with PTAs, but this directive did not stop some administrators in New York City from interfering in the affairs of parents' associations. Charges that they hand-picked officers and meddled in other ways prompted the president of the UPA, David Ashe, to call for a formal policy on parents' rights in the schools.[55] His organization already participated in a liaison committee with the school board president and a representative of the superintendent. But the teachers' union increased the stakes when it condemned the UPA for not rallying around those instructors who stood accused of being Communists, and the UPA soon recommitted itself to the principle that only parents should belong to its associations.[56]

In May 1950, Superintendent William Jansen issued a parents' bill of rights that he called "Parent Associations and the Schools." It required every school to have such an organization, while obliging principals to co-operate by allowing notices to be sent home with children and dues to be collected at school. Endorsing the by now familiar idea that parents should take full responsibility for their actions, Jansen linked parents' rights with parent education in an argument reminiscent of Thomas Jefferson's beliefs about citizenship in a republic. Under the guidance of principals, Jansen said, the home and the school can have a relationship based on "mutual understanding and trust" because parents will be "better informed . . . and more effective in reinforcing the efforts of the school." As a leading anti-Communist, Jansen may have been motivated by fears of subversion at home, but in 1951, Ruth Farbman, the new president of the UPA, threw her considerable weight behind the superintendent's thinking. Only as parents inform themselves about the schools "can they truly discharge their responsibilities," she said.[57] Clearly, there was agreement at the highest level that parents' rights were not inherent but derived from education.

The UPA's trust in the city's board of education and school administration that underpinned such understandings began to erode in the late 1950s. Budget adjustments that eliminated 900 teaching positions in 1959 trumped reductions in class size for which the UPA had fought throughout the decade and slashed funds for textbooks, supplies, and construction as well as some guidance and enrichment services. The UPA itself came under fire from some among its natural constituency, as parents, especially minority parents, took exception to its positions on desegregation and de-centralization. Although supportive of integration in principle, the UPA's white majority resisted implementation strategies like busing and school pairing, which threatened the homogeneity of the neighborhood school. Black and Hispanic parents also parted company with the UPA when it opposed the reinvigoration of local school boards. Mandated by the state legislature in 1961, the revitalization of these boards received the en-dorsement of the East Harlem Schools Committee, which wanted them to be the central board's surrogate in each community. But the UPA thought they might pose a problem for parents' associations, interfering with their access to teachers, principals, and especially the powerful decision makers at 110 Livingston Street.[58]

By the mid-1960s, the UPA had rethought its approach to minorities in the New York City public schools. Reaching out to blacks and Hispanics, it said that teachers should not be restrained and detached when interact-ing with the low-income home. In fact, UPA President Florence Flast ac-cused the professionals of being disingenuous: they complain about being "asked to compensate for social and family inadequacies . . . not of their own making," she said, but "they continue to exclude the family" from the public school. She urged teachers and principals not to bristle if minor-ity parents were impatient or rude. "When recognized as interest," Flast maintained, hostility "represents greater hope than the apathy which has previously prevailed."[59] In 1965, the UPA undertook what it called a Self-Help Program in Parent Education, which expanded from four schools to thirty-eight before its funding ran out after just two years. It trained low-income parents to run workshops on school board policies having to do with practical matters like homework, report cards, and promotion. Armed with such useful information, they would be better able to rein-force the school at home. The Self-Help Program drew on the UPA's long-standing assumption that parent education was a prerequisite for parent participation. But the organization was moving toward a less reciprocal, more adversarial position. By "making parents aware of what the school is expected to do," it said, the Self-Help Program taught them "to express themselves effectively without feeling intimidated in the presence of pro-fessionals." Perhaps parent education could serve the cause of parents' rights rather than be a justification.[60]

Even parents who had never felt comfortable questioning the policies of the school board or the professionalism of their children's teachers had second thoughts in the 1960s. The board's efforts to integrate a school system that was enrolling more and more blacks and Hispanics satisfied no one. Collective bargaining presented a new challenge to which the UPA tried to respond by making demands for systemic reforms that would become part of any labor agreement. However, negotiations often broke down, and three strikes within six years—the first in 1962 and the last a bitter struggle that continued on and off for nearly ten weeks—drove parents and teachers apart. In 1968, race and ethnicity were as important as economics to the politics of the situation. Reacting to controversial experiments with community control in three neighborhoods and proposals for more comprehensive decentralization, Jewish teachers and black parents faced off over the future of the New York public schools. They were set on a collision course by the Ocean Hill–Brownsville community school board's decision in May to designate for reassignment thirteen teachers, five assistant principals, and one principal. The United Federation of Teachers did not hesitate to defend what it regarded as its members' right to due process under the union contract.[61]

Most parents in New York were willing to accept the teachers and administrators assigned to their children's schools. But some minority parents wanted to have a say in the transfer of particular personnel, and a few even welcomed structural reform. The United Bronx Parents, for example, argued that there were well-defined neighborhoods in the city capable of making sound policy for their own schools.[62] Not surprisingly, the UPA condemned both the strikes and decentralization. When the United Federation of Teachers closed the schools, the UPA had no choice but to claim that the union was making war on parents and children. As a major player in the existing power scheme, it had a vested interest in maintaining the political status quo. But when forced to accept structural change in the aftermath of the 1968 strike, the UPA also found a way to champion the principle of parents' rights even as it questioned the practice of decentralization. If New York must have community school boards, the UPA said, parents should constitute the one and only electorate. Otherwise, special interests would intrude on the parents' natural right to control the education of their children.[63]

The New York legislature did not implement the UPA's electoral recommendation. The bill that it passed in 1969, authorizing community school districts in New York City, permitted all registered voters to participate in local school board elections. "When the decentralization law was formulated," UPA President Blanche Lewis quickly responded, we warned that enfranchising "a general electorate would undermine and dilute the special role of the parents." Public education may not be only our domain, she explained, but parents are "the most important part of this public," and today they "feel that their rights are being invaded and eroded." Community school board candidates included teachers, principals, and even clergy, leading to frustration and anger over what the UPA perceived to be politics as usual. What had been intended as a vehicle for parent participation had actually marginalized and demoralized the very people it was supposed to empower. But it was not easy for the UPA to make this argument without appearing to be self-serving. In defense of parents' rights, the organization found itself in the awkward position of attacking a reform designed to democratize educational decision-making.[64]

The UPA was not the only defender of parents' rights in the late 1960s, and given the climate of opinion in New York at the time, it is hardly surprising that the board of education soon chose to revisit Superintendent Jansen's 1950 policy statement. In 1967, Frank S. Samansky, a New York State Supreme Court justice, ruled that parents' associations could send their literature home through the schools. Applauded by the UPA, this decision resulted from two separate suits filed by parents who objected to what their children brought home, demonstrating that not all parents identified with New York's parents' associations.[65] The school board sided with the UPA, equating parents' rights with those of their associations, perhaps because the 1969 decentralization law required every school in the city to have such an organization. As revised in April 1971, "Parent Associations and the Schools" reinforced the idea that teachers and administrators had to treat parents with respect regardless of their background or training. In the 1950s, the UPA had refrained from referring to Jansen's policy statement as a parents' bill of rights because that term was deemed too militant. It called the new statement a "contract" that, like the board's agreement with its teachers, was supposed to protect inherent rights—in this case, those belonging to parents with children in the public school system. But the 1971 document was no more a "contract" than its predecessor because it did not guard parents against arbitrary behavior or unilateral decisions. It required only that they be informed, or at most consulted, before definitive actions were taken.[66]

In 1977, the board of education once again revised "Parent Associations and the Schools," strengthening its provisions for parent input into the selection of administrative and supervisory personnel. This small concession followed on the heels of the Parent Legal Education Assistance (PLEA) project, which involved the UPA in a privately funded, two-year effort to inform parents about their rights in the schools. Decentralization notwithstanding, many principals and district superintendents continued to be aloof, resisting parent participation in matters relating to budget, curriculum, and personnel. Even more disheartening, some community school boards "erected walls of secrecy," denying parents information to which they were entitled. Through a series of workshops, some conducted in Spanish, PLEA trained parents to know their rights and sometimes supplied pro bono counsel so that they could obtain what was "rightfully theirs."[67] For the UPA, the PLEA project must have seemed like a fulfilled prophecy. Instead of bringing the home and the school closer together, the structural reforms it opposed had driven them farther apart, making the UPA itself more an adversary than an advocate of the city's public schools. Slowly but surely, reciprocity between parents and teachers was becoming a thing of the past.

Parents Union for Public Schools

In 1974, the Family Educational Rights and Privacy Act became federal law. Authored by James L. Buckley, a conservative Republican from New York, the legislation discouraged school districts from denying parents access to their child's records or releasing such information to a third party without parental consent.[68] In trying to protect the autonomy of the American family, Buckley strengthened the hand of many parents and reformers with whom he would not otherwise have been in concert. The founders of Parents Union for Public Schools, for example, did not share Senator Buckley's political views, but they agreed with him about the need to redress the balance between parents and schools. In Philadelphia, teachers, administrators, and the school board no longer seemed to respect the people they were meant to serve. Parents had to stand up for their own interests because no one else would.

Not unlike parents elsewhere, many Philadelphians distinguished between the schools their children attended and the system as a whole. They were much more likely to find fault with the district than with their neighborhood school. Fear of the unknown accounts for this disparity, especially after 1967, when Philadelphia School Board President Richardson Dilworth hired Mark Shedd to run the Philadelphia public schools. Trained at Harvard, Shedd came to Philadelphia from Englewood, New Jersey, where he implemented a state-ordered desegregation plan. Together, Dilworth and Shedd challenged the status quo, introducing educational innovations like the Parkway Program, a high school without walls, and developing a citywide desegregation plan that relied heavily on busing. Among the white, working class, such reforms did not go down well; tampering with the familiar structure of schools was bad enough, but mixing the races was what they feared most. Black Philadelphians, on the other hand, did not know whether they could trust Dilworth and Shedd to bring about real change, a feeling that was exacerbated by the superintendent's abrupt resignation following Frank Rizzo's election as mayor in 1971.[69]

The strikes that plagued the School District of Philadelphia in the 1970s did nothing to diminish the anxiety mixed with anger that many parents already felt. Walkouts by teachers, custodians, and even city transit workers disrupted classes for thousands of students. Sixteen days of instruction were lost in September 1972, when the Philadelphia Federation of Teachers (PFT) struck the schools. Barely three months after returning to work, the teachers formed picket lines again in a continuing dispute over wages and working conditions that almost kept the schools closed until spring.[70] Frustration mounted as the strike persisted, leaving parents and children to make the best of a bad situation. The Home and School Council, a parent-teacher organization that could trace its lineage back to the militant Mary Van Meter Grice and the Philadelphia Home and School League, sought relief in common pleas court by asking for an injunction that would force the teachers back to work. But the union did not capitulate, and some parents concluded that their interests needed to be represented more forcefully. In response to a radio editorial calling for compromise, Happy Fernandez, the mother of three, pointed out that parents had "no voice in what was going on," and within days, the Parents Union for Public Schools (PUPS) was born (figure 6.2). It drew its strength initially from an existing network of parents who had previously formed the Powelton-Mantua Educational Fund, a nonprofit corporation providing child care services to low- and moderate-income families living in the integrated neighborhoods adjoining the University of Pennsylvania and Drexel Institute in West Philadelphia. But dissatisfaction could be found everywhere, and it did not take PUPS' founders long to decide that they should take their new organization citywide.[71]

According to its first mission statement, PUPS' primary purpose was "to get adequate funding for our school system and quality[,] humanizing education for our children" by pressuring public officials. It modeled itself after a labor union because it hoped to bargain from a *"position of power."* By pulling together and speaking with a singular voice, parents, like teachers, could make themselves felt in the city's public schools.[72] Similar organizations set an example elsewhere; in New York City, for example, the United Bronx Parents and the Harlem Parents Union (HPU) offered

FIGURE 6.2. Happy Fernandez, cofounder of the Parents Union for Public Schools, c. 1973. Courtesy *Philadelphia Bulletin* Photo Collection, Urban Archives, Samuel Paley Library, Temple University, Philadelphia.

more militant alternatives to the UPA. The Harlem parents came together, according to HPU founder E. Babette Edwards, to defend themselves against "a highly organized, self-regulating, heavily funded, and authoritarian school system" that blamed minorities for their children's poor achievement. Edwards wanted her organization not only to get parents more involved but also to make them a "formidable presence" in collective bargaining.[73]

There was no shortage of parents in Philadelphia who wanted to get more involved. In its first year, the PUPS recruited more than one thousand members, mainly middle-class white and low-income black women who thought the Home and School Council was too homogeneous and too close to the city's political and educational establishment. "I was just the token black in Home and School," said Helen Williams, one of PUPS' cofounders.[74] In an attempt to immunize the new organization against divisiveness, PUPS' by-laws required its executive committee to be cochaired by a member of the "majority" race and one of the "minority" race. Parenthood was to be the bond uniting blacks and whites against a common enemy. The PUPS also chose not to focus on forming locals in individual schools because it did not see itself competing with the Council. Wanting instead to influence educational policy in the city as a whole, its leaders began to attend school board meetings, where they refused to be silent. But their confrontational tactics alienated many influential people, including the officers of the Home and School Council, who complained to the new superintendent in 1974 about "problems" PUPS' behavior was causing in the schools.[75]

It would be a mistake to conclude that the PUPS always disagreed with the policies and practices of those running the schools. Its relationship with teachers is a case in point. As an organization, the PUPS often challenged the PFT, especially during the 1970s when the teachers seemed to be perpetually on strike. In 1975, the PUPS sued the board of education, claiming that its contract with the PFT was illegal because it unlawfully allowed teachers to participate in the making of financial and personnel decisions. Nor was the PFT afraid to condemn the PUPS, as it did, for example, when the PUPS sponsored educational activities for children idled by a strike.[76] However, some members of both organizations believed that their relationship did not necessarily have to be adversarial. A volunteer in her children's elementary school, PUPS cochair Kathe Zepernick sympathized with the striking teachers she knew. "The union was clearly necessary" to protect them from administrative harassment, and so when strikes came, she and her faculty friends agreed that each had their own job to do. Helen Williams was more philosophical. She believed that the PUPS could benefit teachers by demanding reforms in the bureaucracy. It dehumanizes teachers, she said, "turning them into non-thinking machines." Parents could help by supporting those teachers and administrators who wanted to remake the schools.[77]

However, the realities of urban education in the 1970s convinced many parents in Philadelphia that their relationship with teachers and principals could not always be reciprocal. If lengthy strikes did not make this clear, then parents learned it from school officials who treated them with indifference or even disrespect. Both the Home and School Council and the PUPS came to the conclusion that a parents' bill of rights was needed in the Philadelphia public schools. The idea first occurred to Happy Fernandez when an attorney from Community Legal Services pointed out that parents had a right to inspect their children's records at school. Marie Schobert, president of the Home and School Council, proposed a Parents' Bill of Rights and Responsibilities to the school board at its May 1974 meeting. Parents have the right to be kept informed, consulted, and treated with respect, she said. But they also have an obligation to know and accept the school's rules and work for the success of its programs. They should "suggest, not dictate," "plan, not administer," and strive to "prepare the child emotionally and socially so that he will be receptive to learning and discipline."[78]

Not to be outdone, the PUPS developed its own bill of rights, which it shared with the Home and School Council as a basis for joint discussions. Consistent with PUPS' more adversarial style, it made no mention of parental responsibilities, concentrating on what parents should expect from schools. They had a right to be treated courteously and with respect "regardless of race, creed, national origin, economic status, sex or age." They had a right to see their child's official records, participate in "meaningful" parent-teacher conferences, and be kept informed about "all policies, regulations, guidelines and administrative decisions." As if the omission of parental responsibilities was not combative enough, PUPS' draft called for parent involvement in the selection of principals, the evaluation of teachers, and the reassignment of pupils. New Yorkers would not have been shocked by any of these proposals, but in Philadelphia, neither the officers of the Home and School Council nor the superintendent and his staff, much less the teachers' union, could accept them, and when the school board approved a parents' bill of rights and responsibilities in May 1975, it made no allowance for parental influence on professional decisions.[79] That the board chose to endorse even the concept of parents' rights, however, demonstrates just how different thinking about the relationship between the home and the school had become.

The impact the new policy had on the daily operation of Philadelphia's public schools is anybody's guess. Meanwhile, the PUPS availed itself of other means to defend the rights of parents and children. Made law in 1975, the Education for All Handicapped Children Act (PL 94-142) advanced the cause of parents' rights by requiring educators to consult with parents and inform them in writing about plans for the education of their special needs children. It strengthened existing due process procedures by which parents could appeal official decisions having to do with the identification, evaluation, and placement of such children. Dissatisfaction with the way in which public schools dealt with special children brought out many parents, both black and white, in support of Public Law 94-142, but, once enacted, its implementation created many new problems.[80] A grant from the Pew Charitable Trusts allowed the PUPS to hire two full-time counselors whose job it was to help parents cope with the school district's special education policies and programs. Another grant from the United States Justice Department made it possible for the PUPS to extend this effort and develop a collateral strategy to assist the parents of all children who were suspended or transferred for disciplinary reasons. The goal was to help parents become self-reliant, but the PUPS always held in reserve the option of collective action. It deserved some of the credit when the district stopped suspending truants in 1984 and decided that for other kinds of misbehavior suspensions would be used only as a last resort.[81]

As an advocate for educational reform, the PUPS enjoyed more success when it worked with the establishment, but cooperation did not always come easily, especially with administrators for whom the PUPS had little or no respect, as the administration of Superintendent Michael Marcase demonstrates. Almost from the moment he was appointed, Marcase was the object of ridicule, as the PUPS held him up for public contempt. That he was perceived to be the choice of Mayor Frank Rizzo, PUPS' least favorite politician, did nothing to protect him against subsequent charges of impropriety and incompetence. Monthly meetings with Marcase and his staff failed to build feelings of trust; in fact, PUPS leaders refused to speak freely among themselves while waiting to meet with the superintendent because they believed that his conference room was bugged. The PUPS called on both the PFT and the school board to make concessions during the two strikes that occurred on Marcase's watch, and it might be argued that the PUPS shortened the one in 1978 by orchestrating vigils at board headquarters to dramatize the need for a settlement. During the 1980 strike, the PUPS staged a large demonstration outside city hall that tied up rush hour traffic, but its influence on contract negotiations was limited at best. On the other hand, its campaign to unseat the superintendent ultimately achieved success. In 1982, he resigned, together with four of his backers on the school board, because the PUPS and other community organizations kept up the pressure.[82]

By the early 1980s, the PUPS was no longer what it once had been. The grants that it received turned its attention toward serving clients more than advocating change. Not unlike its counterparts in Atlanta, Boston, and Los Angeles, the PUPS discovered that this shift placed a premium on professional leadership and good working relations with the school district. It moved to larger quarters, hired a CEO, and transformed volunteers into paid staff. It also made peace with the bureaucrats, forsaking confrontation even though the new superintendent, Constance Clayton, did not always treat the PUPS with much respect. Clayton assigned subor-

dinates to meet monthly with many groups, including the PUPS, and refused to cooperate with the Council for Educational Priorities, a coalition
founded by the PUPS, among others, which undertook management studies designed to make more efficient use of the district's scarce resources.
Clayton's reputation as a reformer helped justify working with her, but the
time had come for the PUPS to adopt a more conciliatory manner. "We
weren't going to be able to serve parents if we were shut out," Kathe Zepernick recalled. "I wouldn't call it appeasement; we just . . . tried to get
along."[83] Precedent for such an approach existed in the form of projects
like the Year of the Good Principal, which the PUPS sponsored before
the end of the Marcase administration. Between 1981 and 1984, it built on
this idea, bringing parents and teachers together to encourage children
to read.[84]

As organizations just for parents, the PUPS and the UPA added a new dimension to the politics of American education. By demanding that parents be acknowledged as a distinct interest group, they gave notice to the
reality that the home and the school sometimes disagreed. Of course, they
also demonstrated a commitment to the idea that the home-school relationship could continue to be reciprocal. Even during the 1960s, the UPA
preferred pressure to protest, and the PUPS discovered before very long
that it could not sustain itself forever by confrontational means. Neither
organization ever mounted a serious challenge to the authority of school
officials or the legitimacy of professionals. Both aspired to be influential,
not definitive, in school decision-making. However, their declaration and
defense of parents' rights confirmed a way of thinking that did not pre-
sume the presence of trust in the home-school relationship. The concomitant claim that parents possessed those rights by virtue of their status, not
their education, helped transform the balance of power in this relationship, and in the 1970s, state and federal legislation like Public Law 94-
142 codified what these parents' associations were saying. Expertise was
no longer a justification for arbitrary or paternalistic behavior. Schools
had to show respect for their clients no matter what their background or
qualifications. Legal rights for parents also meant that the home-school
relationship could easily turn more adversarial, and many Americans
thought that it would. By the mid-1970s, it had become clear that equal opportunity was even more difficult to achieve than school reformers had
once believed. The economic, social, and cultural gaps that stood between
some families and schools seemed wider than ever, inviting the conclusion that parents and teachers were natural enemies. But not all Ameri-

cans agreed. Reformers like David Seeley and social scientists like James Comer and James Coleman addressed this concern in the hope that they could explain the problem and show everyone how to work together more successfully.

Reconciliation?

It became conventional wisdom in the 1970s to portray conflict between the home and the school as part of a much larger problem. Friction between parents and teachers was taken as symptomatic of the family's alienation from its social and economic surroundings. Marginalized by modern life, the family was in no position to defend itself against bureaucratic and therapeutic institutions like the welfare department and the public school. But the family was not the only victim of sweeping cultural change. The school was forced to justify its intellectual and moral authority when any semblance of consensus about the meaning of citizenship disappeared.[85] Making sense of conflict between parents and teachers also required understanding the crisis of confidence in American education.

The disintegration of community explained social change to many scholars writing about American history and life at the time. This argument also surfaced in analyses of the home-school relationship, not only to elucidate dysfunction but also to guide reform. David Seeley, the executive director of New York's Public Education Association in the 1970s, witnessed for himself some of the most disheartening examples of political infighting in the recent history of American education, and he made sense of the problem by seeing it as a breakdown of institutional legitimacy. "The concept of public education as a professionalized, bureaucratized, governmental service-delivery system is doomed beyond recall," he said in 1981. No meaningful partnership between parents and teachers could exist now that schooling had become an undemocratic sorting machine. Rebuilding trust meant reclaiming community by reconciling individual freedom with social justice. Public schools would have to provide both "voice" and "choice" by giving parents the dignity that comes with respect and the satisfaction that results from exercising their natural rights with responsibility.[86]

Seeley drew upon others to confirm his beliefs. In particular, he admired James Comer for his work with parents and teachers in New York and New Haven, Connecticut. According to Comer, the cynicism Americans felt for their schools could be traced to the demise of the intimate social networks that used to bind the home to the school. To counteract the depersonalization of social relations, principals had to involve parents as stakeholders, bringing them together with teachers and administrators to plan the future of their children's schools. Working with low-income blacks and Hispanics in New Haven, Comer discovered that parents hesitated to assert themselves when they felt excluded either by defensive professionals or by their own feelings of inadequacy. But their anxieties could be assuaged if their relationship with the school featured more reciprocity. Parents did not need to be in charge; they merely wanted to be included in school governance without compromising the principal's authority or involved with activities that did not threaten the teachers' domain. What empowered parents was knowing that they were an integral part of the team. Making a community of the school was the key to improving student achievement and discipline.[87]

In the 1980s, it was James Coleman who made the most sophisticated and controversial case for community. Well known for his research on education and inequality, Coleman set out to discover why independent and Catholic high schools seemed to produce better results, even with low-income and minority students. Building on his previous work, which implied more than it asserted the importance of family, he argued that successful schools lived in functional communities. They participated in a network of social relations characterized by the presence of a dominant value system and regular contact between generations. The social capital existing in such communities reinforced the schools' message, making it easier for all students to achieve. According to Coleman, the nature of modern life prevents the formation of functional communities by separating work and family, but some institutions like the Roman Catholic Church are still able to create a reasonable facsimile. This explained for him the superior performance of parochial high schools, even when compared to more selective and expensive alternatives.[88]

According to this argument, the home-school relationship does not account for much per se; it is the social context within which that relationship exists that really saves the day. But as if to reempower an institution that he once dismissed as unable by itself to overcome inequality, Coleman now maintained that schools could increase the social capital of their communities by strengthening both parent-teacher and parent-parent relationships.[89] His faith in the efficacy of open and honest communication between the home and the school placed him on common ground with David Seeley and James Comer. All three believed that educators could do a lot to improve their relationship with parents and that by so doing they could remake American education for the better. These ideas have achieved widespread acceptance in the 1990s, affecting the debate about schools in countless ways. They turn up in the work of researchers like Comer who think the existing system can be saved and those reformers who believe that progress requires radical change. The latter disagree among themselves, differing about many things, including the importance of parent-teacher reciprocity. Proponents of vouchers, for example, argue that schools will improve only when parents can threaten educators with the loss of job security. Advocates for charter schools do not doubt the importance of competition as a force for constructive change, but many of them also hope to build educational communities that will ensure excellence by bringing together parents and teachers who are on the same page. Such disagreements notwithstanding, Americans in general remain committed to the same conceptual categories that emerged when serious consideration of the relationship between the home and the school began in the nineteenth century. They continue to believe that parents and teachers can be adversaries, allies, or advocates for each other and the cause of better education. The appeal of one category over another has changed from time to time, but the categories themselves have largely remained the same.

Epilogue: Recurring Themes

In October 1997, angry parents came together in New York's Green-wich Village to protest the dismissal of Lauren Zangara, a fourth grade teacher at Public School 41. To reverse the increase in class size that occurred when her students were reassigned to other fourth grades in the building, some parents did more than complain. They volunteered to help pay her salary, an offer that school officials rejected on the grounds that such an arrangement would violate the principle of equity in public education. After a week of intense negotiations, a compromise resulted that returned the laid-off teacher to her classroom, while eliminating any possibility that the parents might some day share responsibility for faculty remuneration.[1] The incident attracted national attention by calling accepted theory and practice into question. But it also invites reflection about the nature of the home-school relationship in the United States today.

Four broad generalizations come to mind. First, the relationship between the home and the school is still political and can quickly turn confrontational. Parents may be more welcome at school than ever before and are perhaps more influential, but they are not part of the educational establishment, which has always resisted when outsiders propose changes that threaten existing relationships. Of course, most teachers and administrators (not to mention school directors) prefer to avoid conflict with parents or other members of the community. They are well aware of the need for good public relations, as they have been since the 1920s, although they now refer to such image building as authentic "public engagement," an example of modern educational jargon that implies more parental participation than is usually delivered.[2] Third, most parents want to be a part of their children's education, but as suggested by the events in Greenwich Village, their class status can have an impact on the nature and extent of their involvement. Parents who possess more than a few social and economic resources are less likely to think that they cannot or should not make a difference.[3] Finally, the relationship between the home and the school attracts considerable attention in the United States because many Americans believe that the home affects student achievement. Whether parents merely encourage their children or participate actively in school governance, their involvement appears sensible and seems to make a difference. The existence of research and advocacy organizations like the Home and School Institute, the National Coalition for Parent Involvement in Education, and the Center on School, Family, and Community Partnerships explains in part why the national press seized on the story at Public School 41.[4]

Although few would argue with the claim that the home and the school are interdependent, the nature of their relationship is just as unsettled for us as it was for Americans in the days of Horace Mann. Many educators and reformers perceive it to be distant, if not unfriendly. For example, the 1998 report of the Philadelphia Education Summit concluded that schools must take primary responsibility for increasing parental involvement because far too many parents will not get involved on their own. But when California enacted legislation in 1990 to improve communication from the school to the home, one critic dismissed it as just another attempt to impose the authority of the school on the home.[5] Whether the home and the school are engaged in a power struggle in which parents are the underdog remains an open question. But this interpretation, which is essentially adversarial, may work to the disadvantage of those committed to improving public education by strengthening the appeal of vouchers, which appear to give parents more leverage in the schooling of their children.[6]

Although proponents of school choice do not necessarily think of the home-school relationship as adversarial, their criticism of public education can leave that impression. For much of the 1990s, the Christian Coalition condemned outcomes-based education, claiming that it interferes with the parents' right to teach values. Some conservative legislators in Pennsylvania have given form to their constituents' misgivings about public schools by introducing legislation that would give parents the opportunity to review instructional materials, consent to any physical examinations, and withhold their children from surveys about family life. Not surprisingly, mistrust like this often prompts an equal and opposite reaction. Many teachers and administrators are loathe to work with parents they perceive to be unreasonable or meddlesome. They hardly need to be reminded that controversial issues like bilingual education, school prayer, and sex education can motivate some parents to intervene without regard for the rights of others or that a few want to have veto power over every aspect of their child's education.[7]

Such adversarial thinking notwithstanding, the idea that parents and teachers are allies is as widely accepted today as it was a century ago. But it is also understood that to collaborate successfully the home and the school must negotiate their way around obstacles unknown to those whose children attended one-room schoolhouses. Teachers' unions, for example, have made parental involvement a priority in places like Dade County, Florida, and New York City. By keeping parents informed, union leaders believe they can turn suspicion into trust, restoring faith in the notion that parents and teachers are on the same side.[8] The National Congress of Parents and Teachers (NCPT), now known simply as the National PTA (NPTA), remains committed to this point of view. Responding to the nationwide call for more parental participation, which made "school-based management" a familiar phrase by the late 1980s, the organization published a self-help book that advised parents not to be intimidated or misled by educators who seem to prefer complete control. Parents can work with the bureaucracy, its author, Melitta Cutright, advised: "if you are patient, persistent, and diplomatic, you will probably find that in time your school staff will become more open to your participation." By monitoring their children's progress; informing themselves about school policies, procedures, and routines; and showing interest in education, parents can contribute to their children's learning even after they start school.[9]

In 1997, the NPTA adopted a set of standards for parent involvement at school. Building on the work of Joyce L. Epstein, director of the Center on School, Family, and Community Partnerships at The Johns Hopkins University, these standards stressed the importance of regular communication between the school and the home. At the same time, they made it clear that teachers and administrators must take the lead, providing support for parent education and encouragement for the right kind of parent participation. According to the NPTA, parents should accept invitations to give their time, assist with student learning, and join in school planning and decision-making.[10] But it has left to local interpretation just when such behavior ceases to helpful and becomes instead interfering.

Epstein has written at length about how to restore respect and trust between the home and the school by involving parents in meaningful activities that affect learning without compromising the teacher's hegemony over his or her domain. The conscientious parent helps with homework, volunteers at school, and is active in the PTA or other ancillary organizations. The professionals are ultimately responsible for the success or failure of the school, but teachers and administrators who respect the family will be rewarded with parents who make sure that students meet their obligations. Higher levels of educational and life achievement usually follow from positive and constructive home-school relations.[11] Of course, Joyce Epstein is not the only one who still believes that the family is the school's most important ally. Both James Comer and Dorothy Rich have given the NPTA reason to take this position, but they have done so without being as committed as Epstein to the idea that the school stands first among equals in the partnership of educational institutions.

After nearly three decades of distinguished work in the field of home-school relations, Comer ranks as its elder statesman. His firm conviction that parents and teachers must collaborate rests on the idea that "child development" should be the objective, not just formal education. Social, emotional, and intellectual growth cannot be achieved in the absence of a caring community of adults, drawn from the home, the school, and the community. Comer comes by this belief naturally. By providing continuity and structure at home, while insisting that his teachers do the same, his own parents taught him to believe in himself and take responsibility for his dreams. It never occurred to his mother that she would not play an important role in her son's education, but, according to Comer, cooperation between the home and the school now requires a different kind of leadership, a more systematic integration of effort, especially for low-income, minority children. He has assigned this task primarily to the school, in keeping with the respect for expertise that he was taught as a medical student. But he concedes that educators will have to organize more effectively and be more responsive to their students' social, cultural, and economic circumstances before they can weave the "seamless web" of school and community resources that parents need to feel in control and children need to achieve.[12]

Like James Comer and Joyce Epstein, Dorothy Rich has never disputed the primacy of school. But for more than thirty years, she has maintained that it cannot be the panacea envisioned by Americans a generation or two ago. To dispel the disappointment and mistrust that many parents feel because schools have not lived up to their unrealistic expectations, parents must learn to work differently with teachers, dividing accountability between them in a "separate but complementary" way. Of course, teachers can help parents help themselves, but, according to Rich, parents must agree to accept more responsibility for their children's education. "I look to the day," she has said, "when the blaming between parents and teachers stops, when more parents turn to themselves and to other parents for help, when parents stop looking to the school to solve their problems."[13]

In 1964, Rich founded the Home and School Institute (HSI) to show parents how to instill "the basic motivation, skills, and attitudes [that] children need to do well in school." It focused on improving self-discipline, teaching good study habits, and building self-esteem. Working with the National Education Association, HSI cosponsored the Parent-Teacher Partnership, which developed educational activities for families to do at home. However, the American family had changed by 1985, when this partnership was formed; now there were many more two-income and single-parent families than twenty years before. As some researchers argued, the influence of the home-school relationship on student achievement may well be mediated by the family's structure, culture, and socioeconomic status. Rich conceded that family structure affects parental involvement, but she held fast to her belief in parents as partners with teachers, citing studies showing that many single and working mothers still made time at home to help their children with work brought from school. In fact, such women could only be involved this way because they could not attend meetings during the day or volunteer time at school.[14]

Whether employed or not, all parents, according to Rich, can and should teach what she has called "MegaSkills." The qualities she has in mind are the personal attributes like motivation, perseverance, initiative, and effort that help children think positively and respect themselves. By turning everyday activities and situations into scripted lessons, modern parents can deliver on their responsibility to be the classroom teacher's most trusted ally.[15] But even though Rich has always been careful to acknowledge the independent contributions of the home, she has also circumscribed the parental role, restricting it mainly to the affective domain. Conscious of professional status and pedagogical training, she has tried to make an asset from the reality that the home and school, while overlapping spheres as Joyce Epstein has pointed out, are not the same.

Taking Dorothy Rich's faith in parents as educators to the next level, the home schooling movement also reflects the twin themes of conflict and cooperation between the home and the school that run through the long history of their relationship. What began in the 1970s as a biting challenge to the subject-centered pedagogical methods of the educational establishment has evolved into an amicable disagreement between public educators and those parents who believe that they can do a better job of teaching cognitive and especially moral lessons at home. The movement had extended the discussion of parents' rights by arguing that the authority of the state to make schooling compulsory does not constitute a license to violate the individual's right to privacy or religious freedom. Its relationship with the establishment has become less adversarial in recent years as dissatisfaction with public education has mounted, tolerance for the unconventional has increased, and litigation has forced school boards to accept home schooling as the price for legal peace. Many school districts now provide some curricular and methodological help to home schoolers, but such accommodation has not been cost-free because, without a common enemy, parent educators have discovered that ideological differences often divide them.[16]

The acceptance of home schooling notwithstanding, advocacy continues to be a compelling role for parents in the traditional home-school relationship. Identified and embraced by educators at the beginning of the twentieth century, it retains much of its original meaning. Many school officials and reformers still believe that parents can and should be the premier advocates for public education. For them, what justifies the home's involvement in school decision-making is the parental loyalty it inspires and the support it cultivates for new policies or programs. In Carpentersville, Illinois, for example, parents working with teachers, administrators, and community members on school improvement teams achieved acceptance for innovations like multiage classrooms and block scheduling that otherwise might have been the subject of controversy. Parents for Public Schools, an organization founded in Jackson, Mississippi, spread to twenty-five states in ten years by urging parents to uphold public education in tandem with teachers, superintendents, school directors, and other civic leaders.[17] However, there is an adversarial dimension to parental advocacy in the United States today. As Myron Lieberman has pointed out, organized teachers have usually put parents on the sidelines in labor negotiations and on the defensive in policy debates. Co-opted by the National Education Association and the American Federation of Teachers, the NPTA has not encouraged its affiliates to challenge the positions taken by teachers' unions or to intervene when they strike.[18] But more than a few Americans now believe that parents should speak and act for themselves when they relate to schools, making decisions that are based on their own priorities and needs. In other words, parental choice lends some credence to the claim that the center of gravity is beginning to shift in the politics of the home-school relationship.

Because some families have always exercised control over the enrollment decision, parental choice is nothing new in the history of American education. The Roman Catholic school systems that appeared in urban America at the end of the nineteenth century still attest to the validity of this claim. But since the 1960s, magnet schools, alternative schools, and open enrollment plans have democratized the power once possessed mostly by those whose race or social class gave them the freedom to decide where they would live or whether their children would go to private schools. In Minnesota, Iowa, and Nebraska, for example, parents now have the right to decide which public school their children will attend. Both private school vouchers and a public school choice program have redistributed many minority students in Milwaukee and its suburbs.[19] Those who favor the voucher system believe that real choice will come only if all parents behave like consumers when making the enrollment decision and that such freedom is the key to progress in education. For example, John Chubb and Terry Moe contend that parents cannot be effective advocates for their children, much less excellence in education, if they cannot select among numerous options for schooling.[20]

Other reformers have argued that political power offers parents the means by which to advocate for both their families and change in American education. Rejected by Chubb and Moe, who think that bureaucratic gridlock is inevitable when politics rather than markets drives the schools, the idea, nevertheless, commands a considerable following, accounting perhaps for the impressive growth in recent years of measures to increase local control in public education.[21] The Chicago School Reform Act, more than any other single piece of legislation, exemplifies this trend. Made law in 1988 after a disruptive teachers' strike, the act drew on nearly twenty years of experience with parental involvement to maximize community control of the city's schools. The local school councils that it mandated gave not just parents but also all citizens a significant role in school finance, educational planning, and personnel evaluation. According to historian Michael B. Katz, it demonstrated the viability of democratic governance and the fallacy behind "the assumption that highly centralized bureaucracies are inescapable" in urban education.[22]

But the Chicago School Reform Act was not a step forward for those committed to maximizing parental power. They have found a cause in charter school reform, which has steadily gathered political momentum as a viable alternative to vouchers in American education. Between 1991 and 1999, thirty-five states plus the District of Columbia and Puerto Rico enacted charter school legislation, and while these laws vary widely, all are said to empower parents by making it possible for them to decide where their children will go to school and by giving them more control over the schools their children attend. In keeping with the generalization that advocacy in education is now more adversarial, accountability ranks as perhaps the most common justification for charter schools. After all, their survival depends on meeting parents' and in many cases public officials' expectations. Some charter school reformers have argued that their main objective is educational innovation. They predict that the competition engendered by charters will lead to progress through experimentation. Still others believe that by giving parents and teachers the chance "to commit to a common mission," the collaborative process of developing a charter can build the social capital needed for success in elementary and secondary education.[23] More and better student learning may be the reformers' ultimate concern, but it is by no means clear that when parents opt out of the local public school, their only or even their primary goal is enhanced achievement. Some may be moved by personal circumstances or nonacademic considerations; others may be making a political statement.[24]

In the last thirty years, Americans have turned the relationship between the home and the school into a litmus test for excellence in education. But the conflicting aims of school reform are testing the resilience of this relationship by pulling it in opposite directions. On the one hand, parents are promised increased freedom and control. On the other, they are led to believe that the moment has arrived when a community of interests can be fashioned that will be unprecedented in American education. Going forward, there can be no partnership between the home and the school that does not take into account the legacy of conflict from a generation ago. Protected by rights codified in law, parents are more inclined to challenge school policy and practice, and their disrespect for teachers and principals is often quick to show. This state of affairs embodies a historical irony as well. Many parents say that they have the will but not the time to be involved at school. Their grandmothers had more time, especially if they were white and middle-class, but most accepted marginal status. They expected teachers, administrators, and school directors to make all the important decisions.

Today it would be unusual for parents to believe that they should not be active at their children's school. Educators, reformers, and even politicians have made such an issue of parental involvement that many well-meaning mothers and fathers probably feel guilty about not being more active than they already are. Of course, the educational establishment still deserves much of the blame for schools that remain its exclusive domain, but single parents and two-income families often cannot be more than a fleeting presence at school. Just making a living can be all-consuming, while super-moms have trouble finding enough hours in the day to accomplish all they want to do. No matter whether their alienation is self-inflicted or imposed, many parents have an adversarial relationship with their children's schools. Some have chosen to respond by taking more control, while others seem content to complain. But can satisfaction ever be guaranteed, or is accountability an illusion, almost certain to reinforce the widespread perception that schools can never succeed?

A cycle of failure will repeat if the home and the school continue to follow their historical paths. What began as an adversarial relationship has come full circle; too often parents and teachers are ready to believe the worst about each other today. Breaking the cycle begins with the knowledge that families and schools are farther apart than ever before. Home life is more private and family structure more diverse, making it difficult for educators to understand what families want or need. Likewise, the modern school puzzles many people because of its complexity but does not do enough to reveal itself to parents and the community. Conflict between them will continue or indifference will intercede unless parents and teachers learn to meet halfway. The school cannot replace the home any more than the home can stand alone. Each has a separate, but related, task to perform that can be accomplished only in collaboration. Communication is the key to reaffirming their interdependence. Without it, there cannot be the reciprocity that once seemed to describe the relationship between the home and the school in the politics of American education.

Notes

Introduction

1. Sarah Lawrence Lightfoot, *Worlds Apart: Relationships between Families and Schools* (New York: Basic Books, 1978).

2. Frank T. Carlton, "The Home and the School," *Education* 26 (September 1905): 214. See also Maris A. Vinovskis, *Education, Society, and Economic Opportunity: A Historical Perspective on Persistent Issues* (New Haven, Conn.: Yale University Press, 1995), esp. chap. 3.

3. Kathleen V. Hoover-Dempsey and Howard M. Sandler, "Why Do Parents Become Involved in Their Children's Education?" *Review of Educational Research* 67 (Spring 1997): 33.

4. David B. Tyack, *The One Best System: A History of American Urban Education* (Cambridge: Harvard University Press, 1974), 96–97, 104–9, 129–47; Michael B. Katz, *Class, Bureaucracy, and Schools: The Illusion of Educational Change in America* (New York: Praeger, 1971), 28–48, 103–4; Dwight Roper, "Parents as the Natural Enemy of the School System," 59 *Phi Delta Kappan* (December 1977): 239–42. For more recent manifestations of the same argument, see David B. Tyack, "School Governance in the United States: Historical Puzzles and Anomalies," in *Decentralization and School Improvement: Can We Fulfill the Promise,* ed. Jane Hannaway and Martin Carnoy (San Francisco: Jossey-Bass, 1993), 12–17; Michael B. Katz, *Improving Poor People: The Welfare State, the "Underclass," and Urban Schools as History* (Princeton, N.J.: Princeton University Press, 1995), 120–21; idem, *Reconstructing American Education* (Cambridge: Harvard University Press, 1987).

5. Margaret Strong, ed., *History of the California Congress of Parents and Teachers, 1900–1944* (Los Angeles: California Congress of Parents and Teachers, 1945), 31.

6. David Tyack and Elizabeth Hansot, *Managers of Virtue: Public School Leadership in America, 1820–1980* (New York: Basic Books, 1982), 113–14.

7. Paul E. Peterson, *The Politics of School Reform, 1870–1940* (Chicago: Uni-

versity of Chicago Press, 1985); Ira Katznelson and Margaret Weir, *Schooling for All: Class, Race, and the Decline of the Democratic Ideal* (New York: Basic Books, 1985), 84–85, 148–49.

8. Katznelson and Weir, *Schooling for All,* 136–49; Julia Rosenberg Raftery, *Land of Fair Promise: Politics and Reform in Los Angeles Schools, 1885–1941* (Stanford, Calif.: Stanford University Press, 1992), 21–46; Steven L. Schlossman, "Is There an American Tradition of Bilingual Education? German in the Public Elementary Schools, 1840–1919," *American Journal of Education* 91 (February 1983): 165–77.

9. For evidence of parental involvement and protest drawn from New England in the nineteenth century, see Carl Kaestle, "Social Change, Discipline, and the Common School in Early Nineteenth-Century America," *Journal of Interdisciplinary History* 9 (Summer 1978): 8, 12; Carl F. Kaestle and Maris Vinovskis, *Education and Social Change in Nineteenth-Century Massachusetts* (New York: Cambridge University Press, 1980), 157–58; from Virginia in the second half of the nineteenth century, see William A. Link, *A Hard Country and a Lonely Place: Schooling, Society and Reform in Rural Virginia, 1870–1920* (Chapel Hill: University of North Carolina Press, 1986), 27–46; and from California at the beginning of the twentieth century, see Raftery, *Land of Fair Promise,* 21–32.

10. On maternalism, see Theda Skocpol, *Protecting Mothers and Soldiers: The Political Origins of Social Policy in the United States* (Cambridge: Harvard University Press, 1992), 317–20, 336–37, 354; Seth Koven and Sonya Michel, eds., *Mothers of a New World: Maternalist Politics and the Origins of Welfare States* (New York: Routledge, 1993).

11. Stanley K. Schultz, *The Culture Factory: Boston Public Schools, 1789–1860* (New York: Oxford University Press, 1973), 292.

12. W. Norton Grubb and Marvin Lazerson, *Broken Promises: How Americans Fail Their Children* (New York: Basic Books, 1982), 11–35.

13. Lightfoot, *Worlds Apart,* 28–34; Grubb and Lazerson, *Broken Promises,* 144–49, 225–28; Michael W. Sedlak, "Attitudes, Choices, and Behavior: School Delivery of Health and Social Services," in *Learning from the Past,* ed. Diane Ravitch and Maris A. Vinovskis (Baltimore: Johns Hopkins University Press, 1995), 61–62.

14. Anna B. Pratt, "Training for Educational and Vocational Counselors from the Standpoint of the Field Worker," *Vocational Guidance Magazine* 5 (April 1927): 320–22; Sedlak, "Attitudes, Choices, and Behavior," 67–79.

15. Molly Ladd-Taylor, *Mother-Work: Women, Child Welfare, and the State, 1890–1930* (Urbana: University of Illinois Press, 1994). Referring to those women who led the NCPT as "sentimental maternalists," Ladd-Taylor argues that they idealized motherhood even as they engaged in the politics of reform. See pp. 45 ff.

16. James S. Coleman, "Families and Schools," *Educational Researcher* 16 (August–September 1987): 36. See, for example, James P. Comer, *Maggie's American Dream: The Life and Times of a Black Family* (New York: New American Library, 1988).

17. Ronald Edmonds, "Effective Schools for the Urban Poor," *Educational Leadership* 37 (October 1979): 15–23; Stewart C. Purkey and Marshall S. Smith, "Effective Schools: A Review," *Elementary School Journal* 83 (1983): 426–52.

18. See, for example, Jane Roland Martin, *The Schoolhome: Rethinking Schools for Changing Families* (Cambridge: Harvard University Press, 1992), which argues that the school must be more like the home if America is to avoid cultural fragmentation and moral disarray.

19. Vinovskis, *Education, Society, and Economic Opportunity*, 198–211.

Chapter One

1. Alma Lutz, *Emma Willard: Pioneer Educator of American Women* (Boston: Beacon Press, 1964), 104; "Female Common School Association of the East District of Kensington, Conn.," *American Journal of Education* 15 (December 1865): 613.

2. Lutz, *Emma Willard*, 106; "Female Common School Association," 615–16; Margaret R. Meyer, "Parent-Teacher Relationships in the Early Nineteenth Century," *Journal of Educational Research* 56 (September 1962): 48–49. Traveling and corresponding widely in the 1840s, Willard encouraged many women to form community associations for the support of common schools. Not only would such activism benefit the schools, but also it would help women to help themselves. Anne Firor Scott, "What, Then, Is the American: This New Woman?" *Journal of American History* 65 (December 1978): 698–700.

3. "Parental Training," *Massachusetts Teacher* 4 (July 1851): 197–98; see also "Some Defects in Education," ibid. 3 (March 1850): 65–77.

4. Geraldine Jonçich Clifford, "Home and School in 19th Century America: Some Personal History Reports from the United States," *History of Education Quarterly* 18 (Spring 1978): 15–18, 23–26; Lawrence A. Cremin, "Family-Community Linkages in American Education: Some Comments on the Recent Historiography," *Teachers College Record* 79 (May 1978): 689–95; Maris A. Vinovskis, "Family and Schooling in Colonial and Nineteenth-Century America," *Journal of Family History* 12, nos. 1–3 (1987): 26.

5. David B. Tyack, *The One Best System: A History of American Urban Education* (Cambridge: Harvard University Press, 1974); Barbara Finkelstein, "In Fear of Childhood: Relationships between Parents and Teachers in Popular Primary Schools in the Nineteenth Century," *History of Childhood Quarterly* 3 (Winter 1976): 321–25, 328–30; David L. Angus, Jeffrey E. Mirel, and Maris A. Vinovskis, "Historical Development of Age Stratification in Schooling," *Teachers College Record* 90 (Winter 1988): 217–18; Vinovskis, "Family and Schooling," 26; David B. Tyack and Elizabeth Hansot, *Learning Together: A History of Coeducation in American Schools* (New Haven, Conn.: Yale University Press, 1990), 287–88; Thomas Bender, *Community and Social Change in America* (New Brunswick, N.J.: Rutgers University Press, 1978), 138–41.

6. Carl Kaestle, *Pillars of the Republic: Common Schools and American Society, 1780–1860* (New York: Hill & Wang, 1983), 22, 39; Carl F. Kaestle and Maris A. Vinovskis, *Education and Social Change in Nineteenth-Century Massachusetts* (New York: Cambridge University Press, 1980), 151–53; William A. Link, *A Hard Country and a Lonely Place: Schooling, Society and Reform in Rural Virginia, 1870–1920* (Chapel Hill: University of North Carolina Press, 1986), 30–31, 37–39; Stanley K. Schultz, *The Culture Factory: Boston Public Schools, 1789–1860* (New York: Oxford University Press, 1973), 119–25.

7. Paul E. Peterson, *The Politics of School Reform, 1870–1940* (Chicago: University of Chicago Press, 1985), 53–59; David W. Galenson, "Ethnic Differences in Neighborhood Effects on the School Attendance of Boys in Early Chicago," *History of Education Quarterly* 38 (Spring 1998): 31; Michael Feldberg, *The Philadelphia Riots of 1844: A Study of Ethnic Conflict* (Westport, Conn.: Greenwood Press, 1975), 89–96. Many immigrants to the United States in the twentieth century also insisted that the school respect their religion and native language. John Bodnar, "Materialism and Morality: Slavic-American Immigrants and Education, 1890–1940," *Journal of Ethnic Studies* 3, no. 4 (Winter 1976): 3.

8. Carl F. Kaestle, "Social Change, Discipline, and the Common School in Early Nineteenth-Century America," *Journal of Interdisciplinary History* 9 (Summer 1978): 8–9, 12–13); Link, *A Hard Country and a Lonely Place,* 35. According to one historian, the attack on corporal punishment in schools was not so much a reflection of parental desire to maintain control over children as it was one result of a larger movement in antebellum America to curtail brutality and promote self-discipline in society as a whole. Myrna C. Glenn, "School Discipline in Antebellum America," *Journal of the Early Republic* 1 (Winter 1981): 397–401.

9. N. Ray Hiner, "Look into Families: The New History of Children and the Family and Its Implications for Educational Research," in *Education and the American Family: A Research Synthesis,* ed. William J. Weston (New York: New York University Press, 1989), 17–20; Kaestle and Vinovskis, *Education and Social Change,* 36–37, 62–63, 66; David L. Angus and Jeffrey E. Mirel, "From Spellers to Spindles: Work-Force Entry by the Children of Textile Workers, 1888–1890," *Social Science History* 9 (Spring 1985): 139.

10. Maris A. Vinovskis, *The Origins of Public High Schools: A Reexamination of the Beverly High School Controversy* (Madison: University of Wisconsin Press, 1985), 89–106; William J. Reese, *The Origins of the American High School* (New Haven, Conn.: Yale University Press, 1995), 99.

11. Thomas Kessner, *The Golden Door: Italian and Jewish Immigrant Mobility in New York City, 1880–1915* (New York: Oxford University Press, 1977), 95–99; Bodnar, "Materialism and Morality," 5; John Bodnar, "Immigration and Modernization: The Case of Slavic Peasants in Industrial America," *Journal of Social History* 10 (Fall 1976): 57; Stephen A. Lassonde, "Should I Go, or Should I Stay?: Adolescence, School Attainment, and Parent-Child Relations in Italian Immigrant Families of New Haven, 1900–1940," *History of Education Quarterly* 38 (Spring 1998): 42–50.

12. Galenson, "Ethnic Differences in Neighborhood Effects," 26–33; Joel Perlmann, "Who Stayed in School? Social Structure and Academic Achievement in the Determination of Enrollment Patterns, Providence, Rhode Island, 1880–1925," *Journal of American History* 72 (December 1985): 588–614.

13. Meyer, "Parent-Teacher Relationships in the Early Nineteenth Century," 49; "Female Common School Association," 612; Edith Nye Macmullen, *In the Cause of True Education: Henry Barnard and Nineteenth-Century School Reform* (New Haven, Conn.: Yale University Press, 1991), 88; Vinovskis, "Family and Schooling," 29–30.

14. Michael B. Katz, "Chicago School Reform as History," *Teachers College Record* 94 (Fall 1992): 59; David Tyack and Elizabeth Hansot, "Conflict and Consensus in American Public Education," *Daedalus* 110 (Summer 1981): 9–11; Marjorie Murphy, *Blackboard Unions: The AFT and the NEA, 1900–1980* (Ithaca, N.Y.: Cornell University Press, 1990), 5–6, 34–36, 45. Murphy argues that teachers allied with parents against reformers at the turn of the century despite their incipient professionalism rather than because of it. But her argument fails to explain the rise of formal cooperation between the home and the school in the 1890s. Bureaucratization may have changed the way parents and teachers interacted, but it did not drive them completely apart. Ibid., 10–15, 20.

15. Nancy Hoffman, *Woman's "True" Profession: Voices from the History of Teaching* (Old Westbury, N.Y.: Feminist Press, 1981), xvii, xxii; Murphy, *Blackboard Unions,* 11.

16. Charles Northend, *The Teacher and the Parent; A Treatise upon Common-School Education Containing Practical Suggestions to Teachers and Parents,* 5th ed. (New York: A. S. Barnes, 1853), 253.

17. Ibid., 29–47, 69–77.

18. Ibid., 77. "Almost every man," Northend said, "thinks he knows all about teaching." Faced with such constituents, the teacher must be "truly intelligent, wisely independent, and courteously decided; ever open to conviction, and yet willing to have others entertain an honest difference of opinion." Ibid., 74–75.

19. Ibid., 283; David P. Page, *Theory and Practice of Teaching: or, The Motives and Methods of Good School-Keeping* (New York: A. S. Barnes, 1851), 254–55 (italics his).

20. Northend, *The Teacher and the Parent,* 311; Kaestle, *Pillars of the Republic,* 159–60.

21. Barbara Beatty, *Preschool Education in America: The Culture of Young Children from the Colonial Era to the Present* (New Haven, Conn.: Yale University Press, 1995), 31–34; Northend, *The Teacher and the Parent,* 29, 47.

22. Page, *Theory and Practice of Teaching,* 249–50; Northend, *The Teacher and the Parent,* 47, 125–29, 296–97.

23. Schultz, *The Culture Factory,* 59–60; Dwight Roper, "Parents as the Natural Enemy of the School System," *Phi Delta Kappan* 59 (December 1977): 239–40.

24. "Home Influences," *Massachusetts Teacher* 3 (July 1850): 202; "Some Hints

to Parents," ibid. 3 (May 1850): 138–40; J. J. Reimensnyder, "To Parents," *Pennsylvania School Journal* 7 (February 1859): 235.

25. "Influence of Home upon the School," *Massachusetts Teacher* 1 (July 1848): 222, 228; "Leaves from the Diary of a Teacher," *Pennsylvania School Journal* 11 (January 1863): 208–9; A. H. Trask, "Responsibility of Parents," ibid. 7 (January 1859): 214. See also A. M. Gow, "The Parent and Teacher," ibid. 2 (June 1854): 389–90.

26. "Out of Door Influence of Teachers," *Massachusetts Teacher* 2 (October 1849): 317–20. Consistent with the need for teachers to be diplomatic when speaking about parents, the author of this article was unwilling to condemn completely even the most irresponsible mothers and fathers. "The evils of which I speak," he wrote, "arise oftener from neglect and procrastination than from absolute indifference." Ibid., 319.

27. "Sympathy between Parents and Teachers Essential to the Highest Good of the Pupils at School," *Massachusetts Teacher* 4 (June 1851): 172; Gow, "Parent and Teacher," 390.

28. "Hints to Parents," *Massachusetts Teacher* 2 (April 1849): 107; D. W. Elder, "Parental Co-operation," *Pennsylvania School Journal* 12 (June 1864): 374; "Schoolmaster and Pupil," *Massachusetts Teacher* 2 (September 1849): 259–60; "Relation between Teacher and Pupil," ibid. 2 (February 1849): 52; "Outline of Subjects and Exercises," ibid. 4 (December 1851): 368.

29. Sharlene V. Cochrane, "Private Lives and Public Learning: Family Academy for the New Middle Class. The West Newton English and Classical School, 1850–1910" (Ph.D. diss., Boston College, 1985), 90–94, 99–100, 125–26, 174–75. Family life became the model for living and learning arrangements at other educational institutions in this era. Women's colleges like Smith, Wellesley, and Vassar as well as some early reform schools took this approach. Helen Lefkowitz Horowitz, *Alma Mater: Design and Experience in the Women's Colleges from Their Nineteenth Century Beginnings to the 1930s* (New York: Knopf, 1984), 75, 79–80, 87–90, 92–93; Joseph M. Hawes, *Children in Urban Society: Juvenile Delinquency in 19th-Century America* (New York: Oxford University Press, 1971), 84–85.

30. "Parents and Directors," *Pennsylvania School Journal* 44 (January 1896): 323. See also "How to Spoil a School and Disgrace a Teacher, " ibid. 18 (February 1870): 231.

31. Alice Hamilton Rich, "Duty of Parents to Teachers," *Education* 12 (February 1892): 351–52; Mary W. Hinman, "Home Life in Some of Its Relations to Schools," *Journal of Social Science* 12 (December 1890): 50–51, 55–56; Kaestle, *Pillars of the Republic*, 159.

32. Beatty, *Preschool Education in America*, 52–57.

33. "Common or Public Schools in the United States," *American Journal of Education* 2 (September 1856): 262; A. P. Frick, "Address to the Patrons of the Southern School in Lancaster Twp., Lancaster Co.," *Pennsylvania School Journal* 4 (June 1856): 379–80.

34. "The Family, the School, and the Church," *Massachusetts Teacher* 3 (July 1850): 219–20, 222.

35. Paul H. Hanus, *A Modern School* (New York: Macmillan, 1904), 138–41, 146–51; Paul H. Hanus, *Adventuring in Education* (Cambridge: Harvard University Press, 1937); "Home Life That Is Helpful in School Education: Editorial," *Education* 24 (March 1904): 439–42; ibid. 24 (April 1904): 504–6; ibid. 24 (May 1904): 567–68; ibid. 24 (June 1904): 633–34; ibid. 25 (September 1904): 56–57. See also Northend, *The Teacher and the Parent*, 290–304.

36. M. A. Cassidy, "Home and School," *Education* 19 (April 1899): 535–36.

37. Margaret Marsh, *Suburban Lives* (New Brunswick, N.J.: Rutgers University Press, 1990), 83–89, 92–103; Beatty, *Preschool Education in America*, 88–89; Fannie Fern Andrews, "Parents' Associations and the Public Schools," *Charities and the Commons* 17 (1906–7): 336–37; S. T. Dutton, "The Correlation of Educational Forces in the Community," in *Journal of Proceedings and Addresses of the Thirty-Sixth Annual Meeting* [of the National Education Association], vol. 36 (Chicago: University of Chicago Press, 1897), 241. Philadelphia Superintendent of Schools Martin Brumbaugh made a similar comment in 1912. There should be a division of labor, he said, among the home, church, and school. Working together, "these three great agencies" can give us "the finest type of citizenship" imaginable. *Ninety-Fourth Annual Report of the Board of Public Education, School District of Philadelphia, Pennsylvania* (Philadelphia, 1912), 31.

38. William M. Thayer, "How the Home and School Help or Hinder Each Other," *Education* 14 (October 1893): 59–73; ibid. 14 (November 1893): 143–45; Frank H. Palmer, "How the Home May Help the School," ibid. 21 (January 1901): 293–96; Cora Hamilton, "The Relation of the Home to the School," *Elementary School Teacher* 7 (November 1906): 136–39; Cassidy, "Home and School," 539–40.

39. Cassidy, "Home and School," 541–42; National Congress of Parents and Teachers, *The Parent-Teacher Organization: Its Origins and Development* (Chicago: National Congress of Parents and Teachers, 1944), 147–49; Mary Harmon Weeks, ed., *Parents and Their Problems: Child Welfare in Home, School, Church, and State* (Washington, D.C.: National Congress of Mothers and Parent-Teacher Associations, 1914), 106.

40. Link, *A Hard Country and a Lonely Place*, 76–80; Henry W. Holmes, "Educational Progress in 1908," *School Review* 17 (May 1909): 300–301.

41. Mary Van Meter Grice, *Home and School: United in Widening Circles of Inspiration and Service* (Philadelphia: Christopher Sower Co., 1909), 75 (italics hers).

42. John Dewey, *The Child and the Curriculum, The School and Society* (1915; rev. ed., with an introduction by Leonard Carmichael, Chicago: University of Chicago Press, 1956), 17, 28–29, 75, 79–80; Dutton, "The Correlation of Educational Forces," 247.

43. Ida C. Bender, "Relations of Citizens and Teachers," in *Journal of Proceedings and Addresses of the Thirty-Sixth Annual Meeting* [of the National Education Association], vol. 36 (Chicago: University of Chicago Press, 1897), 250–52.

44. Hanus, *A Modern School,* 128; Dutton, "The Correlation of Educational Forces," 241; Stanton Olinger, "The School's Co-operative Agencies," in *The Modern High School: Its Administration and Extension,* ed. Charles H. Johnston (New York: Charles H. Scribner's Sons, 1914), 333–34; Kenyon L. Butterfield, *Chapters in Rural Progress* (Chicago: University of Chicago Press, 1907), 130. See also Andrews, "Parents' Associations and the Public Schools," 338. Unlike their predecessors, parents' associations today live by "the principle of joint responsibility in the development of the child," said Henry W. Holmes in 1908. It used to be the purpose of such organizations "to get the parents to help the teacher in her efforts to develop the child and to assist the parents in caring for their children outside of school." But now, Holmes said, they help parent and teacher enter into "an organized plan for sharing the responsibility for the child outside of school." To make his point, Holmes cited the Public Education Association of New York City, an organization that included reformers as well as parents and advocated the use of progressive theory to transform the city's schools. In this regard, it transcended the scope of most parent-teacher associations. Holmes, "Educational Progress in 1908," 300–301. For a history of the Public Education Association, see Sol Cohen, *Progressives and Urban School Reform: The Public Education Association of New York City, 1895–1954* (New York: Teachers College, Columbia University, 1963).

45. Arthur C. Perry, *The Status of the Teacher* (Boston: Houghton Mifflin, 1912), xii, 21–22; Elia W. Peattie, "Friends of the Family; The Teacher," *Good Housekeeping* 50 (February 1910): 184.

46. Edward J. Goodwin, "The School and the Home," *School Review* 16 (March 1908): 320–25; Irving King, *Social Aspects of Education: A Book of Sources and Original Discussions with Annotated Bibliographies* (New York: Macmillan, 1916), 54–55.

47. Louisa May McCrady, "The Background of the School," *Outlook* 89 (August 1908): 749 (italics hers); William B. Owen, "Co-operation between Home and School," in *Journal of Proceedings and Addresses of the Forty-Ninth Annual Meeting* [of the National Education Association], vol. 49 (Chicago: University of Chicago Press, 1911), 1107. For a discussion of the growing independence of urban teachers in the early twentieth century, see James W. Fraser, "Agents of Democracy: Urban Elementary-School Teachers and the Conditions of Teaching," in *American Teachers: Histories of a Profession at Work,* ed. Donald Warren (New York: Macmillan, 1989), 139–42.

48. Kenyon L. Butterfield, "Neighborhood Cooperation in School Life,—The 'Hesperia Movement,'" *American Monthly Review of Reviews* 23 (April 1901): 443; Olinger, "The School's Co-operative Agencies," 330.

49. Abraham Flexner, "Parents and Schools," *Atlantic Monthly* 118 (July 1916): 25–27; Grice, *Home and School,* xx–xxi.

50. Hanus, *A Modern School,* 116–17; Flexner, "Parents and Schools," 25–27. See also Hamilton, "The Relation of the Home to the School," 133.

51. Goodwin, "The School and the Home," 326.

52. Boston School Committee, "School Document No. 10," in *Annual Report of the School Committee of the City of Boston, 1912* (Boston, 1912), 9–10; Nathaniel Butler, "Parents' Associations," *School Review: A Journal of Secondary Education* 16 (February 1908): 80.

53. Goodwin, "The School and the Home," 327–29.

54. Grice, *Home and School,* 43–48.

55. Peterson, *Politics of School Reform,* 3–25; Ira Katznelson and Margaret Weir, *Schooling for All: Class, Race and the Decline of the Democratic Ideal* (New York: Basic Books, 1985), 68–85; William J. Reese, *Power and the Promise of School Reform: Grassroots Movements during the Progressive Era* (Boston: Routledge & Kegan Paul, 1986), xxii–xxiv.

56. Anne M. Boylan, *Sunday School: The Formation of an American Institution, 1790–1880* (New Haven, Conn.: Yale University Press, 1999), 160–64; Andrews, "Parents' Associations and the Public Schools," 336.

57. Butterfield, "Neighborhood Cooperation in School Life," 443–44. See also Butterfield, *Chapters in Rural Progress,* 104–7.

58. Butterfield, "Neighborhood Cooperation in School Life," 444; Wayne Fuller, "The Teacher in the Country School," in Warren, ed., *American Teachers,* 104–7.

59. Butterfield, "Neighborhood Cooperation in School Life," 444–45.

60. Ibid., 445; Butterfield, *Chapters in Rural Progress,* 117–18.

61. Minutes of the Middletown [Delaware] Parent-Teacher Association, January 29, 1915, Middletown [Delaware] PTA Minute Books, 1915–34, 2 vols., Papers of the Delaware Department of Public Instruction, Box 2962, Delaware State Archives, Dover.

62. Samuel T. Dutton, *Social Phases of Education in the School and Home* (New York: Macmillan, 1899), 246; Dutton, "The Correlation of Educational Forces," 243–46.

63. Walter L. Philips, "An Urban Home and School League," in *The Annals of the American Academy of Political and Social Science,* vol. 67 (Philadelphia: American Academy of Political and Social Science, 1916), 154.

64. Ibid., 148–49; Mary V. Grice, "Home and School Association: The High School's Right Arm," in Johnston, ed., *The Modern High School,* 317.

65. Butterfield, "Neighborhood Cooperation in School Life," 445.

66. Steven Schlossman, "Before Home Start: Notes toward a History of Parent Education in America, 1897–1929," *Harvard Educational Review* 46 (August 1976): 443–52; National Congress of Parents and Teachers, *The Parent-Teacher Organization,* 144–45, 148; Olinger, "The School's Co-operative Agencies," 344–45; Grice, *Home and School,* 117–18; Margaret Strong, ed., *History of the California Congress of Parents and Teachers, 1900–1944* (Los Angeles: California Congress of Parents and Teachers, 1945), 36.

67. Owen, "Co-operation between Home and School," 1108.

68. Grice, *Home and School,* 83. See also Mary V. Grice, "Home and School As-

sociations," in *The Tenth Yearbook of the National Society for the Study of Education*, pt. 1, *The City School as a Community Center* (Chicago: University of Chicago Press, 1911), 59–60.

69. Wayne E. Fuller, *The Old Country School: The Story of Rural Education in the Middle West* (Chicago: University of Chicago Press, 1982), 113–30, 219–45; Tyack, *The One Best System,* 177–216; William A. Bullough, *Cities and Schools in the Gilded Age* (Port Washington, N.Y.: Kennikat Press, 1974), 64–77.

70. Mary S. Boone, "The Kindergarten from a Mother's Point of View," *Education* 25 (November 1904): 142–45; Charles L. Spain, Arthur B. Moehlman, and Fred W. Frostic, *The Public Elementary School Plant* (New York: Rand McNally, 1930), 178–92, 197–206; N. L. Engelhardt, "Trends in Classroom Design and Equipment," in *American School and University,* 7th annual ed. (New York: American School Publishing Corp., 1935), 214; *Twenty-Eighth Annual Report of the Board of Education of School District No. One, Arapahoe County, Colorado* (Denver, 1902), 35.

71. Aaron Gove, "The Proper Use of Schoolhouses," *Journal of Proceedings and Addresses of the Thirty-Sixth Annual Meeting* [of the National Education Association], vol. 36 (Chicago: University of Chicago Press, 1897), 255; William W. Cutler III, "Cathedral of Culture: The Schoolhouse in American Educational Thought and Practice since 1820," *History of Education Quarterly* 29 (Spring 1989): 26–33.

72. "Discussion," in *Journal of Proceedings and Addresses of the Thirty-Sixth Annual Meeting* [of the National Education Association], vol. 36 (Chicago: University of Chicago Press, 1897), 257–58; Payson Smith, "The Rural School Improvement League," in *The Annals of the American Academy of Political and Social Science,* vol. 67 (Philadelphia: American Academy of Political and Social Science, 1916), 157–60.

73. Butler, "Parents' Associations," 81–82; Mrs. Charles F. Harding, "Annual Report of the Home Committee of the Parents' Association of the School of Education of the University of Chicago," *Elementary School Teacher* 5 (October 1904): 69.

74. Helen M. Hefferan, "Parents' and Teachers' Organizations," *Elementary School Teacher* 5 (December 1904): 241–43.

75. Julia Grant, *Raising Baby by the Book: The Education of American Mothers* (New Haven, Conn.: Yale University Press, 1998), 29–32; Andrews, "Parents' Associations and the Public Schools," 341; Boston Public Schools, "School Document No. 13," in *Annual Report of the Superintendent, July 1909* (Boston, 1909), 123–24, 127. For an analysis of Roxbury's development as a middle-class district in Boston, see Sam Bass Warner Jr., *Streetcar Suburbs: The Process of Growth in Boston, 1870–1900* (Cambridge: Harvard University Press, 1962), 52–64.

76. Boston Public Schools, "School Document No. 13," 128.

77. Boston Public Schools, "School Document No. 10," in *Annual Report of the Superintendent, December 1913* (Boston, 1913), 71, 196–203; Boston Public

Schools, *Annual Report of the Superintendent, December 1914* (Boston, 1914), 96; Boston Public Schools, *Annual Report of the Superintendent, December 1915* (Boston, 1916), 61; Boston Public Schools, *Annual Report of the Superintendent, December 1917* (Boston, 1918), 144–50.

78. Margaret Lighty and Leroy E. Bowman, *Parenthood in a Democracy* (New York: Parents' Institute, 1939), 24–25.

79. Jeanette B. Gutman, "The Parent-Teacher Association in the Philadelphia Public Schools" (master's thesis, Temple University, 1936), 12–14, 22, 41–42; "The Home and the School: How the Two Can Come Together," *Ladies Home Journal* 29 (April 1912): 91; "Will Reveal Work of School League," *Philadelphia Evening Bulletin,* April 17, 1911, Bulletin Clippings Collection, Urban Archives, Samuel Paley Library, Temple University, Philadelphia (hereafter cited as BCC).

80. "Reorganize School League," *Evening Bulletin,* September 6, 1913, BCC.

81. *Annual Report of the Philadelphia League of Home and School Associations,* vol. 3 (Philadelphia, 1908), 5–6, 19–20; *Annual Report of the Home and School League of Philadelphia, 1911–1912,* vol. 7 (Philadelphia, 1912), 6–7, 16–34. Formed in 1899, the home and school association at the Heston School in West Philadelphia was the first of its kind in the city. *Annual Report of the League of Home and School Associations of Philadelphia,* vol. 4 (Philadelphia, 1909), 17, 26.

82. "Will Reveal Work of School League"; Grice, "Home and School Associations," 61; *Ninety-Seventh Annual Report of the Board of Education, School District of Philadelphia* (Philadelphia, 1915), 46.

83. Grice, "Home and School Associations," 62.

84. "The Frankford High School Fathers' Association," *High School Teacher* 1 (June 1925): 188, 200; Charles F. Troxell, *Twenty-Year History of Frankford High School, Philadelphia, Pa.* (Philadelphia: Frankford High School, 1931), 42–45; Historical Society of Frankford, Scrapbooks, vol. 14, pp. 8, 10, Philadelphia.

85. Strong, ed., *History of the California Congress of Parents and Teachers,* 80–81; Leroy E. Bowman, "Fathers in the P.T.A.," *Child Welfare: The National Parent-Teacher Magazine* 28 (September 1933): 32–35; idem, "Making a Parent of Father," *Parents' Magazine* 10 (November 1935): 12; Sara E. Baldwin and Edward G. Osborne, *Home-School Relations: Philosophy and Practice* (New York: Progressive Education Association, 1935), 132; Martha Sprague Mason, ed., *Parents and Teachers: A Survey of Organized Cooperation of Home, School, and Community* (New York: Ginn, 1928), 160, 204.

86. Andrews, "Parents' Associations and the Public Schools," 343; Butler, "Parents' Associations," 87.

Chapter Two

1. *New York Times,* September 14, 1965, p. 39, col. 1.

2. Angelo Patri, *A Schoolmaster of a Great City* (1917; reprint, New York:

Macmillan, 1928), 96-100, 107-14; Angelo Patri, "The Things I Wish Parents Would Remember," *Parents' Magazine* 7 (April 1932): 16-17, 57.

3. Julian E. Butterworth, *The Parent-Teacher Association and Its Work* (New York: Macmillan, 1929), 7; Ellen C. Lombard, *Recent Development of Parent-Teacher Associations*, Bulletin 5, 1923 (Washington, D.C.: U.S. Bureau of Education, 1923), 6; Margaretta W. Reeve and Ellen C. Lombard, *The Parent-Teacher Associations, 1924-1926*, [U.S.] Bureau of Education, Bulletin 11 (Washington, D.C.: U.S. Government Printing Office, 1927), 2-3.

4. Lombard, *Recent Development of Parent-Teacher Associations*, 4; William A. Yeager, *Home-School-Community Relations: A Textbook in the Theory and Practice of Public School Relations* (Pittsburgh: University of Pittsburgh Press, 1939), 363.

5. *Annual Report of the Philadelphia League of Home and School Associations*, vol. 4 (Philadelphia, 1909), 26; Elmer S. Holbeck, *An Analysis of the Activities and Potentialities for Achievement of the Parent-Teacher Association with Recommendations*, Teachers College Contributions to Education, no. 601 (New York: Teachers College, Columbia University, 1934), 4; Butterworth, *Parent-Teacher Association*, 3-7.

6. Martha Sprague Mason, ed., *Parents and Teachers: A Survey of Organized Cooperation of Home, School, and Community* (New York: Ginn, 1928), 152-62.

7. Butterworth, *Parent-Teacher Association*, 98-100.

8. Ibid., 102.

9. Mrs. A. H. Reeve, "First Steps in Parent-Teacher Cooperation—Abridged," in *Proceedings of the Sixty-Fourth Annual Meeting* [of the National Education Association], vol. 64 (Washington, D.C.: National Education Association, 1926), 40.

10. James Newell Emery, "The School and the Parent-Teacher Association," *Child Welfare: The National Parent-Teacher Magazine* 23 (June 1929): 523-24; Arthur B. Moehlman, *Social Interpretation: Principles and Practices of Community and Public School Interpretation* (New York: Appleton-Century Co., 1938), 323-27.

11. Holbeck, *Analysis of the Activities*, 13-14; Butterworth, *Parent-Teacher Association*, 14-23.

12. Sara E. Baldwin and Ernest G. Osborne, *Home-School Relations: Philosophy and Practice* (New York: Progressive Education Association, 1935), 23, 58-59.

13. Steven L. Schlossman, "The Formative Era in American Parent Education: Overview and Interpretation," in *Parent Education and Public Policy*, ed. Ron Haskins and Diane Adams (Norwood, N.J.: Ablex, 1983), 10-26. See also Ellen C. Lombard, *Parent Education, 1926-1928*, [U.S.] Bureau of Education, Bulletin 15, 1929 (Washington, D.C.: U.S. Government Printing Office, 1929), 1-21.

14. Holbeck, *Analysis of the Activities*, 15; Lombard, *Parent Education, 1926-1928*, 10-18; Reeve and Lombard, *The Parent-Teacher Associations, 1924-1926*, 17; Margaretta Willis Reeve, "The Best Is Yet to Be," *Child Welfare Magazine* 21 (August 1927): 555.

15. Bird T. Baldwin et al., *The Twenty-Eighth Yearbook of the National Society for the Study of Education: Preschool and Parental Education* (Bloomington, Ill.:

Public School Publishing Co., 1929), 61–63, 68–69, 311–12, 341–42. The director of the Institute for Child Development at Teachers College, Lois Hayden Meek, would not have disagreed. "Parents," she said, "are realizing that in order to do best for children they must keep in touch with the new knowledge of psychology, nutrition, and education. . . . Some parents . . . can do this for themselves, but many parents today are finding that they need help in interpreting family experiences, in evaluating new knowledge, in integrating and synthesizing all into a guiding philosophy of family life." Lois Hayden Meek, "A Bird's-Eye View of Parent Education," *Parents' Magazine* 6 (June 1931): 19.

16. Margaretta Willis Reeve, "The Meaning of the Movement," *Child Welfare Magazine* 21 (November 1926): 107; Mason, ed., *Parents and Teachers,* 189–201.

17. Baldwin et al., *Twenty-Eighth Yearbook of the National Society for the Study of Education,* 312, 341; Sheldon E. Davis, *The Teacher's Relationships* (New York: Macmillan, 1930), 228–29; Margaretta Willis Reeve, "The Power of the Program," *Child Welfare Magazine* 21 (January 1927): 212; C. E. Marston, "How a Parent-Teacher Association Can Help a School," *School and Society* 25 (May 21, 1927): 607–9; Mason, ed., *Parents and Teachers,* 217.

18. David B. Tyack and Elizabeth Hansot, *Managers of Virtue: Public School Leadership in America, 1820–1980* (New York: Basic Books, 1982), 130–67; David L. Angus, Jeffrey E. Mirel, and Maris A. Vinovskis, "Historical Development of Age Stratification in Schooling," *Teachers College Record* 90 (Winter 1988): 224–25.

19. "Parent-Teacher Associations," *American School Board Journal* 50 (June 1919): 28. As was not uncommon when *The American School Board Journal* wanted to endorse a particular point of view, the editors attributed this article only to "a superintendent's wife," whose gender, no doubt, was supposed to enhance her credibility. See also Holbeck, *Analysis of the Activities,* 16; Mason, ed., *Parents and Teachers,* 133–34.

20. Angelo Patri, *School and Home* (New York: D. Appleton, 1925), 207–8; Amos Nevin Sponseller, "Educational Contributions of Parent-Teacher Associations in Fourth-Class Districts in Pennsylvania" (M.Ed. thesis, Temple University, 1933), 33, 35–37; Margaret Strong, ed., *History of the California Congress of Parents and Teachers, 1900–1944* (Los Angeles: California Congress of Parents and Teachers, 1945), 33.

21. Reeve and Lombard, *The Parent-Teacher Associations, 1924–1926,* 6–8; Robert J. Taggart, *Private Philanthropy and Public Education: Pierre S. du Pont and the Delaware Schools, 1890–1940* (Newark: University of Delaware Press, 1988), 121.

22. "P.T.A. Projects," *Parents' Magazine* 9 (October 1934): 97. In Bronxville, New York, the PTA involved fathers by organizing evening smokers to discuss school plans. Worth Tuttle, "Your Child's School Needs You," ibid. 9 (October 1934): 15.

23. LeRoy E. Bowman, "Fathers in the P.T.A.," *Child Welfare: The National*

Parent-Teacher Magazine 28 (September 1933): 32–35. See also idem, "Making a Parent of Father," *Parents' Magazine* 10 (November 1935): 13.

24. Reeve, "First Steps in Parent-Teacher Cooperation," 40; Helen R. Wentworth, "The P.T.A. at Work," *Child Welfare: The National Parent-Teacher Magazine* 28 (April 1934): 432–34; ibid. 28 (May 1934): 488–89.

25. Hazel Hillis, *The First Fifty Years: Iowa Congress of Parents and Teachers, 1900–1950* (Des Moines, Iowa: Iowa Congress of Parents and Teachers, 1951), 46–47; Strong, ed., *History of the California Congress of Parents and Teachers,* 83; Elizabeth Harrison, "Report of Congress of Mothers' and Parent-Teachers' Associations," in *Addresses and Proceedings of the Fifty-Seventh Annual Meeting* [of the National Education Association], vol. 57 (Washington, D.C.: National Education Association, 1919), 429; Helen R. Wentworth, "The P.T.A. at Work," *Child Welfare: The National Parent-Teacher Magazine* 28 (September 1933): 40; ibid. 28 (February 1934): 327; ibid. 28 (June–July 1934): 541–42; Helen R. Wentworth, "The P.T.A. at Work," *National Parent-Teacher Magazine* 29 (November 1934): 32; ibid. 29 (April 1935): 39; ibid. 29 (August 1935): 45; Reeve and Lombard, *The Parent-Teacher Associations, 1924–1926,* 25; "What a PTA Can Do," *Parents' Magazine* 6 (November 1931): 51; Mason, ed., *Parents and Teachers,* 260–61.

26. Sponseller, "Educational Contributions of Parent-Teacher Associations," 61–62; Butterworth, *Parent-Teacher Association,* 45–46. According to Holbeck, 100 PTA presidents thought that both passive and active parent education outranked community work in the priorities of their organizations. Hence, they placed "study groups," parent education programs, the study of child psychology, and the study of educational methods at the top of their list of PTA activities. Holbeck, *Analysis of the Activities,* 52. See also Reeve, "First Steps in Parent-Teacher Cooperation," 39; Mason, ed., *Parents and Teachers,* 19.

27. Willard Waller, *The Sociology of Teaching* (1932; reprint, New York: Wiley, 1965), 68–69, 74.

28. Carleton Washburne, "The Public School and the Parent," *Child Study* 5 (March 1928): 9–10; Baldwin and Osborne, *Home-School Relations,* 93–95.

29. *White House Conference on Child Health and Protection: Home and School, Partners in a Common Venture,* no. 2, Series on Personality prepared by Marion L. Faegre (Washington, D.C.: n.p., n.d.), 3–6.

30. Baldwin and Osborne, *Home-School Relations,* 84; Gerald H. J. Pearson, "What the Preschool Child Needs," *Parents' Magazine* 6 (January 1931): 13, 32.

31. Margaretta Willis Reeve, "The Parent," in *Addresses and Proceedings of the Sixty-Second Annual Meeting* [of the National Education Association], vol. 62 (Washington, D.C.: National Education Association, 1924), 193; Helen Bott, "What Home Should Mean," *Parents' Magazine* 8 (May 1933): 16.

32. Angelo Patri, *Child Training* (New York: D. Appleton, 1923), 168; Patri, *School and Home,* 106–8.

33. Janet Sligh, "The Home-Work Bugbear," *Child Welfare: The National Parent-Teacher Magazine* 28 (December 1933): 200–202; Brian Gill and Steven

Schlossman, "A Sin against Childhood: Progressive Education and the Crusade to Abolish Homework, 1897–1941," *American Journal of Education* 105 (November 1996): 27–66.

34. A. E. Winship, "The School's Growing Service to the Home: A Rapid Survey of the Progressive Tendencies in Our American Public Schools," *Good Housekeeping* 55 (October 1912): 517; *White House Conference on Child Health and Protection,* no. 7, p. 10.

35. "Home Preparation for School," *Massachusetts Teacher* 3 (October 1850): 315–19; "Do You Believe in Homework?" *Parents' Magazine* 11 (January 1936): 58; Gill and Schlossman, "A Sin against Childhood," 39–40, 43.

36. Minutes of the Parent Teacher Association of Haddonfield, N.J., September 20, 1922, Historical Society of Haddonfield, Haddonfield, N.J.

37. Henrietta Sperry Ripperger, "Getting Them Off to School," *Children: The Magazine for Parents* 3 (September 1928): 11; Elsie S. Conners, "How Can I Help My Child with His Homework?" ibid. 3 (October 1928): 62; Gladys Bleiman, "Help Your Child to Study," *Parents' Magazine* 6 (February 1931): 13; Davis, *The Teacher's Relationships,* 239–40; Baldwin and Osborne, *Home-School Relations,* 84; Gladys Bleiman, "Home Study Helps," *Parents' Magazine* 6 (March 1931): 67.

38. "Do You Believe in Homework?" 14–15, 58.

39. "Home Influences," *Massachusetts Teacher* 3 (July 1850): 202. See also "Some Hints to Parents," ibid. 3 (May 1850): 139.

40. Mason, ed., *Parents and Teachers,* 25; Alfred E. Stearns et al., *The Education of the Modern Boy* (Boston: Small, Maynard, 1925), 4–5. See also Mary Alden Hopkins, "Youth Shapes Its Social Code," *Parents' Magazine* 9 (August 1934): 21, 61.

41. Benjamin C. Gruenberg and Sidonie M. Gruenberg, "The Challenge of Parenthood," *Parents' Magazine* 7 (June 1932): 18–19; idem, "The Parent Faces a New World," *Parents' Magazine* 6 (October 1931): 56–57; Ada H. Arlitt, "The P.T.A.—A Unique Home Influence," in *The Parent-Teacher Organization: Its Origins and Development* (Chicago: National Congress of Parents and Teachers, 1944), 74; George A. Hastings, "Every Child Has Three Parents," *Parents' Magazine* 7 (May 1932): 5; M. E. Moore, *Parent, Teacher, and School* (New York: Macmillan, 1923), 211–12.

42. Baldwin and Osborne, *Home-School Relations,* 95, 103, 129–30; Butterworth, *Parent-Teacher Association,* 40; Margaretta Willis Reeve, "New Order in Educational Cooperation," *School Life* 9 (October 1923): 46; Isabel Damman, "The Parents Association of the North Shore Country Day School," *Progressive Education* 6 (December 1929): 340–45.

43. Fred Charles, "My Boy's Grades Give Me the Collywobbles," *Children: The Magazine for Parents* 4 (January 1929): 42; Alice Fox Pitts, "Make It the Best Year Ever," *Parents' Magazine* 4 (September 1929): 44.

44. Stanwood Cobb, "The Modern School Needs Co-operative Parents," *Children: The Parents' Magazine* 4 (March 1929): 5.

45. Benjamin C. Gruenberg and Sidonie M. Gruenberg, "The Challenge of Parenthood," *Parents' Magazine* 7 (June 1932): 17 (italics theirs); Martha Ray Reynolds, "Parents and Teachers Need Each Other," *Parents' Magazine* 10 (October 1935): 66.

46. Elizabeth Cleveland, "If Parents Only Knew: Letters from a School Teacher," part 2, *Children: The Magazine for Parents* 2 (December 1927): 12, 38; ibid. 3 (January 1928): 13, 52; Elizabeth Cleveland, "If Parents Only Knew—Home and School Together Can Build Character," *Children: The Magazine for Parents* 3 (May 1928): 40.

47. Butterworth, *Parent-Teacher Association*, 61–62.

48. Patri, *Child Training*, 140; Patri, *School and Home*, 7, 22, 199, 204.

49. Patri, *Child Training*, 158, 173–74; Patri, *School and Home*, 109–10.

50. Angus, Mirel, and Vinovskis, "Historical Development of Age Stratification," 228–29; David Tyack, Robert Lowe, and Elizabeth Hansot, *Public Schools in Hard Times: The Great Depression and Recent Years* (Cambridge: Harvard University Press, 1984), 38.

51. Alan P. Raucher, *Public Relations and Business, 1900–1929*, Johns Hopkins University Studies in Historical and Political Science, Series 86, no. 2 (Baltimore: Johns Hopkins University Press, 1968), 7–11, 39–40, 52–57, 151–52; Marvin N. Olasky, *Corporate Public Relations: A New Historical Perspective* (Hillsdale, N.J.: Erlbaum, 1987), 25–43, 67–77; Scott M. Cutlip, *Public Relations History: From the 17th to the 20th Century, The Antecedents* (Hillsdale, N.J.: Erlbaum, 1995), 148–53, 197–204.

52. Raucher, *Public Relations and Business*, 78, 87.

53. Cutlip, *Public Relations History*, 231–32; Raucher, *Public Relations and Business*, 70, 146; Olasky, *Corporate Public Relations*, 83, 93.

54. Raymond E. Callahan, *Education and the Cult of Efficiency: A Study of the Social Forces That Have Shaped the Administration of the Public Schools* (Chicago: University of Chicago Press, 1962), 198, 223–26; Ellwood P. Cubberley, *Public School Administration: A Statement of the Fundamental Principles Underlying the Organization and Administration of Public Education*, rev. ed. (Boston: Houghton Mifflin, 1922), 428–29; Arthur B. Moehlman, *Public School Relations: A Discussion of the Principles Underlying Informational Service in the Public Schools and a Technique for Practical Use* (Chicago: Rand McNally, 1927), 1, 4.

55. Moehlman, *Public School Relations*, 11, 14 (italics his).

56. Ibid., 77–148, 187–92, 197–210. See also Yeager, *Home-School-Community Relations*, 125–32.

57. Strong, ed., *History of the California Congress of Parents and Teachers*, 93–96; Moehlman, *Public School Relations*, 149–58.

58. Jessie Gray, "Parents to the Rescue!" *Parents' Magazine* 8 (October 1933): 9. See also Carleton Washburne, "Wanted: A Parents' Bloc," *Parents' Magazine* 9 (February 1934): 43–44.

59. Tyack, Lowe, and Hansot, *Public Schools in Hard Times*, 47–48, 72–79, 193–94.

60. Arthur B. Moehlman, *Social Interpretation: Principles and Practices of Community and Public-School Interpretation* (New York: Appleton-Century, 1938), vii–viii, 22.

61. Moehlman, *Public School Relations*, 158–60; "Vitalized Commencements and the Home," *Journal of the National Education Association* 18 (December 1929): 298; Lyle W. Ashby, "New Commencements for Old," *Nation's Schools* 5 (May 1930): 70–73. See also Robert C. Shaw, "Commencement Programs," *Pennsylvania School Journal* 78 (April 1930): 473–76; Harrison Lyseth, "The New Commencement," *High School Teacher* 9 (May 1933): 177–79. On the introduction of the Seven Cardinal Principles of Secondary Education, see Edward A. Krug, *The Shaping of the American High School* (New York: Harper & Row, 1964), 382–93.

62. Shaw, "Commencement Programs," 475; Lyle W. Ashby, "Interpreting the Schools through the Graduation Program," *Nation's Schools* 9 (April 1932): 37.

63. "A Commencement in Harmony with the Times," *American School Board Journal* 96 (February 1935): 53–54.

64. C. Richard Snyder, "An Evolution in Graduation Exercises," *School Activities* 9 (January 1938): 205, 245; F. R. Powers and F. J. Herda, "Conflicting Ideas of Commencement," *Nation's Schools* 19 (April 1937): 28–29; "Commencements Break with Tradition," *Secondary Education* 4 (1935): 91–95. Historical pageants designed to make the high school commencement an exercise in good public relations were held in many communities such as Gettysburg and Sellersville-Perkasie, Pennsylvania; Danville, Illinois; Council Bluffs, Iowa; Wakeman, Ohio; and Flint, Michigan. See "Commencements Break with Tradition," 92–93; Lyle W. Ashby, "Your Commencement Program," *Secondary Education* 6 (January 1937): 35–37; G. W. Kirn, "Pupils and Parents Liked This Commencement," *Nation's Schools* 13 (May 1934): 37–39.

65. Moehlman, *Public School Relations*, 185.

66. Mason, ed., *Parents and Teachers*, 272, 276–77; Holbeck, *Analysis of the Activities*, 35–37, 43, 99; Jeanette B. Gutman, "The Parent-Teacher Association in the Philadelphia Public Schools" (M.Ed. thesis, Temple University, 1936), 98–102; Ellwood P. Cubberley, *The Principal and His School: The Organization, Administration, and Supervision of Instruction in an Elementary School* (New York: Houghton Mifflin, 1923), 554; Ward G. Reeder, *An Introduction to Public-School Relations* (New York: Macmillan, 1937), 137.

67. Moehlman, *Social Interpretation*, 338–39, 347, 354.

68. Yeager, *Home-School-Community Relations*, 403–20, 425–38, 444, 449–58.

69. Cubberley, *The Principal and His School*, 551–52; The principal, said James Newell Emery, "should try, with all the tact at his command, to lead the association along the lines of really worth while [sic] accomplishment, without antagonizing it." Emery, "The School and the Parent-Teacher Association," 525; Holbeck, *Analysis of the Activities*, 34–38.

70. E. J. Moffitt, "Public Relations to the Rescue," *Nation's Schools* 14 (September 1934): 31–32; Moehlman, *Public School Relations*, 180; Moore, *Parent, Teacher, and School*, 67.

71. Butterworth, *Parent-Teacher Association,* 49; Mason, ed., *Parents and Teachers,* 167.

72. Arthur Zilversmit, *Changing Schools: Progressive Education Theory and Practice, 1930–1960* (Chicago: University of Chicago Press, 1993), 88–89.

73. Baldwin et al., *Twentieth-Eighth Yearbook of the National Society for the Study of Education,* 312; Katharine Taylor, oral history interview with William W. Cutler III, July 1967, 294, Cornell University Regional History Collection, Ithaca, N.Y.

74. Flora K. Houston, "An Experiment in Parent Participation in the Activities of a First Grade," *Educational Method* 13 (January 1934): 199–200; Flora Houston, "Enlisting the Parents," ibid. 14 (February 1935): 273–76; Louise R. Hughes, "Parental Cooperation," *Childhood Education* 10 (March 1934): 307–13; Larry Cuban, *How Teachers Taught: Constancy and Change in American Classrooms, 1880–1990,* 2nd ed. (New York: Teachers College Press, 1993), 94–95.

75. Burton P. Fowler, "Father Goes to School," *Parents' Magazine* 5 (March 1930): 22; "Home-School Relationships," *Child Study* 5 (March 1928): 4; LeRoy E. Bowman, "Putting the Parent in Parent Education," *Progressive Education* 11 (April–May 1934): 297.

76. Taylor, oral history interview, 263–65; Elmer S. Holbeck, "New Work for the Parent-Teacher Association," *Educational Method* 14 (November 1934): 98; Cleveland, "If Parents Only Knew," part 2, p. 12; Ernest G. Osborne, "New Duties of Parents and Schools," *Progressive Education* 12 (April 1935): 274.

77. Baldwin and Osborne, *Home-School Relations,* 79–80, 90–91; Osborne, "New Duties of Parents," 272; Kathyrn McHale, "Special Education for Parents and Teachers," *Childhood Education* 7 (January 1931): 246–48; Winifred E. Bain, *Parents Look at Modern Education: A Book to Help an Older Generation Understand the Schools of the New* (New York: D. Appleton-Century, 1935), 270–73. For a good example from this era of a more limited and conservative conception of parental involvement in school, see Jessie Chase Fenton, "Help Your Child Succeed at School," *Parents' Magazine* 6 (October 1931): 24–25, 58–59. As a psychologist with the California Bureau of Juvenile Research, Fenton was perhaps less inclined to favor an enlarged role for parents in school than McHale, who was both executive and education secretary of the American Association of University Women. For a discussion of the increasingly unequal balance of power between the family and the helping professions, see Christopher Lasch, *Haven in a Heartless World: The Family Besieged* (New York: Basic Books, 1977), 111–25, 167–74.

78. Osborne, "New Duties of Parents," 272; Bain, *Parents Look at Modern Education,* 132; Baldwin and Osborne, *Home-School Relations,* 46.

79. Lois Hayden Meek, "Parents and Progressive Schools," *Childhood Education* 8 (February 1932): 284–85; Lois Hayden Meek, "Parents and Teachers Together," *Parents' Magazine* 7 (September 1932): 7.

80. Bain, *Parents Look at Modern Education,* 76.

81. Ibid., 140, 170–72, 189, 229–31; Baldwin and Osborne, *Home-School Relations,* 111.

Chapter Three

1. Children, preferably girls dressed in white, were to recite the poem, displaying cardboard letters at the appropriate moments.

2. Emma Middleton, Vertical Clippings File, Haddonfield Public Library, Haddonfield, N.J.; Obituary of Emma Middleton, Scrapbook 39-35, vol. 2, Historical Society of Haddonfield, Haddonfield, N.J.

3. Middleton, Vertical Clippings File, Haddonfield Public Library; Minutes of the Haddonfield Board of Public Education, March 19, 1918, September 18, 1919, April 17, 1934, Haddonfield School District, Haddonfield, N.J. (hereafter cited as MHBE); Minutes of the Haddonfield Mothers' and Teachers' Club, May 17, 1905, May 4, 1910, Historical Society of Haddonfield, Haddonfield, N.J. (hereafter cited as HMTC). On careerism among teachers, see, for example, David F. Labaree, "Career Ladders and the Early Public High School Teacher: A Study of Inequality and Opportunity," in *American Teachers: Histories of a Profession at Work,* ed. Donald Warren (New York: Macmillan, 1989), 164–85; James W. Fraser, "Agents of Democracy: Urban Elementary-School Teachers and the Conditions of Teaching," in Warren, ed., *American Teachers,* 118–26.

4. David B. Tyack, *The One Best System: A History of American Urban Education* (Cambridge: Harvard University Press, 1974); Jonathan Zimmerman, "The Dilemma of Miss Jolly: Scientific Temperance and Teacher Professionalism, 1882–1904," *History of Education Quarterly* 34 (Winter 1994): 413–31; Wayne Fuller, "The Teacher in the Country School," in Warren, ed., *American Teachers,* 104–14; Marjorie Murphy, *Blackboard Unions: The AFT and the NEA, 1900–1980* (Ithaca, N.Y.: Cornell University Press, 1990), 14–23, 35–45; Paul E. Peterson, *The Politics of School Reform, 1870–1940* (Chicago: University of Chicago Press, 1985).

5. Nancy F. Cott, *The Grounding of Modern Feminism* (New Haven, Conn.: Yale University Press, 1987), 87, 108–9; Ann Firor Scott, *Natural Allies: Women's Associations in American History* (Urbana: University of Illinois Press, 1987), 83–85, 100.

6. William L. Pieplow, "Cooperation between Boards of Education and the Public," *School and Society* 10 (September 13, 1919): 329–30; Alice Fox Pitts, "A Challenge to Parent-Teacher Associations," *Parents' Magazine* 4 (November 1929): 15.

7. Scott, *Natural Allies,* 124–25; William J. Reese, *Power and the Promise of School Reform: Grassroots Movements during the Progressive Era* (Boston: Routledge & Kegan Paul, 1986), 181–85.

8. Introduced at the annual carnival of the Philadelphia Home and School League, "For Home and School" celebrated the idea of the school as a neighborhood social center. Mary Van Meter Grice, *Home and School: United in Widening Circles of Inspiration and Service* (Philadelphia: Christopher Sower Co., 1909), 131–32. Two members of the Middlesex County Council of Parent-Teacher Associations in New Jersey wrote words and music for the "Marching Song" of their organization. Returning from the convention of the Delaware State PTA, Mrs.

Dallas C. Moore copied a similar song into the minute book of her local PTA. To be sung to the tune of "Marching through Georgia," its chorus was:

Hurrah! Hurrah! We'll sing a glad new song!
Hurrah! Hurrah. We'll shout it loud and long!
PTA stands out today for service true and strong
For home and school and nation.

Middlesex County Council of Parent-Teacher Associations, Special Collections and Archives, Acquisition 1436, Box BI 26, Alexander Library, Rutgers University, New Brunswick, N.J.; Delaware Entry by Mrs. Dallas C. Moore, n.d. (ca. 1920), Middletown [Delaware] PTA Minute Books, 1915–34, 2 vols., Papers of the Delaware Department of Public Instruction, Box 2962, Delaware State Archives, Dover (hereafter cited as MMPTA).

9. Joy Elmer Morgan, Plan of Work for the Bureau of Publications of the National Congress of Parents and Teachers, 1930–1931, Elizabeth Hewes Tilton Papers, Box 8, Folder 230, Schlesinger Library, Radcliffe College, Cambridge, Mass.

10. Minutes of the Executive Committee of the Public Education and Child Labor Association (PEA), April 27, 1908; and Minutes of the Board of Directors of the PEA, April 24, 1916, November 17, 1916, January 19, 1917, March 28, 1919, May 26, 1919, January 31, 1929, all in Accession 177B, Box labeled Child Labor, and Accession 177C, Box 1 in the Papers of the Citizens Committee on Public Education/Public Education and Child Labor Association, Urban Archives, Samuel Paley Library, Temple University, Philadelphia (hereafter cited as PEA Papers); "School Board Called Senile," *Philadelphia Evening Bulletin,* January 11, 1917; and "Board Objects to Discard at 65," ibid., April 19, 1919, all in the Bulletin Clippings Collection, Urban Archives, Samuel Paley Library, Temple University, Philadelphia (hereafter cited as BCC); "New Blood for School Board," *Philadelphia Public Ledger,* October 2, 1919; "Young Democracy Will Wage War on Education Board," ibid., October 7, 1919.

11. William H. Issel, "Modernization in Philadelphia School Reform, 1882–1905," *Pennsylvania Magazine of History and Biography* 94 (July 1970): 358–83; David John Hogan, *Class and Reform: School and Society in Chicago, 1880–1930* (Philadelphia: University of Pennsylvania Press, 1985), 210–11; Peterson, *The Politics of School Reform, 1870–1940,* 138–53; Jeffrey Mirel, *The Rise and Fall of an Urban School System: Detroit, 1907–1981* (Ann Arbor: University of Michigan Press, 1993), 24–27.

12. *Annual Report of the Home and School League of Philadelphia, 1911–1912,* vol. 7 (Philadelphia, 1912), 16–34; *Annual Report of the Philadelphia League of Home and School Associations,* vol. 4 (Philadelphia, 1909), 14–23; *Ninety-Third Annual Report of the Board of Public Education, School District of Philadelphia* (Philadelphia, 1912), 74–85, 254–66. The segregated schools affiliated with the league in 1909 were Catto and Ramsey, both near the historically black neighborhood whose center was at Seventh and Lombard Streets, while in 1912 the league's

black affiliates were at Joseph Hill and Thomas Meehan in Germantown and Wil-
mot, just above the downtown. For an analysis of the black community's overall relationship with the school district, see Vincent P. Franklin, *The Education of Black
Philadelphia: The Social and Educational History of a Minority Community, 1900–
1950* (Philadelphia: University of Pennsylvania Press, 1979), 50–51.

13. Minutes of the Executive Committee of the PEA, November 25, 1907,
May 25, 1908, September 28, 1908, January 25, 1909; Minutes of the Board of Directors of the PEA, April 22, 1912, March 24, 1913, December 28, 1914; and Minutes of the Thirty-First Annual Meeting of the PEA, May 31, 1912, all in Accession
177B, PEA Papers; *Ninety-Ninth Annual Report of the Board of Public Education, School District of Philadelphia* (Philadelphia, 1917), 18; Jeanette B. Gutman,
"The Parent-Teacher Association in the Philadelphia Public Schools" (M.Ed. thesis, Temple University, 1936), 43–44, 47. See also Mirel, *The Rise and Fall of an
Urban School System,* 59–66; Ronald D. Cohen, *Children of the Mill: Schooling
and Society in Gary, Indiana, 1906–1960* (Bloomington: Indiana University Press,
1990), 17–18, 29, 72–74.

14. "The League," said Grice in 1912, "is gradually forming itself into the thing
it was meant to be, a channel through which the many forms of social activity, as
approved by those in authority, shall flow into the larger life of the community, as
it touches upon the life of the school." *Annual Report of the Home and School
League of Philadelphia, 1911–1912,* 8; Gutman, "Parent-Teacher Association," 126.

15. "Asks for Probe of School Board," *Evening Bulletin,* January 3, 1919;
"Mrs. Grice Arraigns School Management," ibid., January 9, 1919; "Plan Housing
Reform," ibid., March 6, 1919; and "Deplore Housing Item Cut," ibid., June 17,
1919, all in BCC.

16. Minutes of the Thirtieth Annual Meeting of the PEA, April 24, 1911, Accession 177B, PEA Papers; *Jenkintown (Pa.) Times Chronicle,* July 8, 1916.

17. "More Money Urged for Teachers," *Public Ledger,* January 13, 1919; Harlan Updegraff, "Teachers' Salaries and the Increased Cost of Living," *American
School Board Journal* 57 (November 1918): 22; A. S. Martin, "Teachers' Salary Increase in Pennsylvania Paramount to the Welfare of the Children of the State,"
ibid. 58 (January 1919): 78.

18. "Raise for Teachers Urged by Governor," *Public Ledger,* February 5, 1915;
"Teachers Favor School-Tax Rise," ibid., February 11, 1919; "Good Schooling
Urged as Bolshevism Cure," ibid., February 21, 1919.

19. "Gratz Hits School Critics," *Evening Bulletin,* December 3, 1919, BCC;
"Mrs. Grice Resigns [as] Head of Home and School League," ibid., March 28,
1919, BCC.

20. "Mrs. Grice Quits League," *Evening Bulletin,* late ed., March 28, 1919, BCC.
Although the state legislature and the school board collaborated to give Philadelphia's teachers a raise in 1919, the salary issue continued to plague school officials
in the city for the next several years. *Journal of the Board of Public Education,
School District of Philadelphia for the Year 1919* (Philadelphia, 1920), 114; "Teachers' Salary Raise Approved," *Public Ledger,* September 9, 1919; *One Hundred and*

First Annual Report of the Board of Public Education, School District of Philadelphia (Philadelphia, 1919), 10; "The Philadelphia Schools," *School and Society* 11 (February 28, 1920): 252–53.

21. *The Golden Rung, Golden Jubilee History of the New Jersey Congress of Parents and Teachers, 1900–1950* (Trenton, N.J.: New Jersey Congress of Parents and Teachers, 1950), 17–18.

22. Lois B. Merk, "Boston's Historic Public School Crisis," *New England Quarterly* 31 (June 1958): 172, 176; Polly Welts Kaufman, *Boston Women and City School Politics, 1872–1905* (New York: Garland, 1994), 96–98; Neale McGoldrick and Margaret Crocco, *Reclaiming Lost Ground: The Struggle for Woman Suffrage in New Jersey* (New Jersey: sine nomine, 1993), 20; Alice Hyneman Rhine, "The Work of Women's Clubs," *Forum* 12 (December 1891): 527; Reese, *Power and the Promise of School Reform,* 58–60.

23. Scott, *Natural Allies,* 75–76; Merk, "Boston's Historic Public School Crisis," 181–97; Kaufman, *Boston Women and City School Politics,* 24, 27–28, 30–35, 150, 156–58. In 1875, there were 116 members of the Boston School Committee, representing the city's wards. One year later bureaucratic reformers reduced that number to twenty-four, elected at large.

24. Minutes of the Board of Directors of the PEA, April 24, 1916, January 19, 1917, Accession 177B, PEA Papers; "Mrs. E. C. Grice Indorsed for School Director," *Public Ledger,* September 9, 1915.

25. Violet M. (Mrs. William W.) Birdsall to Simon Gratz, Philadelphia, April 19, 1918 (1919?), File Marked Correspondence, 1916–1920, Simon Gratz Papers, Historical Society of Pennsylvania, Philadelphia. In 1917, Margaret Haley, the head of the Chicago Teachers Federation, and Ella Flagg Young, the school superintendent, openly opposed the Loeb Rule, adopted by the Chicago school board, which challenged the right of teachers to remain employed if they were unionized. Meanwhile, Denver was perhaps the only major city in the United States to have a woman preside over its school board before World War I. Mrs. Myron Jones held the post for a year, beginning in May 1913. PTAs were very active in the city at that time. Murphy, *Blackboard Unions,* 80–90; Hogan, *Class and Reform,* 211; *Tenth Annual Report—School District Number One in the City and County of Denver, Colorado* (Denver, 1913), 3, 12.

26. Theda Skocpol, *Protecting Mothers and Soldiers: The Political Origins of Social Policy in the United States* (Cambridge: Harvard University Press, 1992), 317–20, 329–31; Margaret Gibbons Wilson, *The American Woman in Transition: The Urban Influence, 1879–1920* (Westport, Conn.: Greenwood Press, 1979), 98; "Women on Public Boards," *Public Ledger,* January 2, 1915; MMPTA, May 4, 1917, June 1, 1917, September 28, 1917; "Woman Leader in School Fight," *Public Ledger,* September 11, 1919.

27. William L. O'Neill, *Everyone Was Brave: A History of Feminism in America,* rev. ed. (Chicago: Quadrangle, 1971), 50–51, 176; Cott, *Grounding of Modern Feminism,* 29–30; Edith V. Alvord, "Why Is a School Board?" *American School*

Board Journal 60 (June 1920): 33; "Women on School Boards," *American School Board Journal* 58 (February 1918): 33.

28. William Estabrook Chancellor, *Our Schools: Their Administration and Supervision* (Boston: Heath, 1909), 15; James Newell Emery, "The School and the Parent-Teacher Association," *Child Welfare: The National Parent-Teacher Magazine* 23 (June 1929): 526; David Tyack and Elizabeth Hansot, *Managers of Virtue: Public School Leadership in America, 1820–1980* (New York: Basic Books, 1982), 108–9, 180, 190–93.

29. Isabel Underwood Blake, "An Invitation to Parents," *American School Board Journal* 55 (October 1917): 22; Harold O. Rugg, "Cooperation between Boards of Education and the Public," *National Education Association: Addresses and Proceedings* (Washington, D.C.: National Education Association, 1919), 433–34.

30. George S. Counts, *The Social Composition of Boards of Education: A Study in the Social Control of Public Education* (Chicago: University of Chicago Press, 1927), 42–44; Scott Nearing, "Who's Who on Our Boards of Education," *School and Society* 5 (January 20, 1917): 89–90. Nearing confined his study to cities of 40,000 or more, discovering that in cities of 40,000 to 100,000 people, women represented 5 percent of board members; in cities of 100,000 to 500,000, 8 percent; and in cities over 500,000, 12 percent. Counts reported finding a similar pattern in 1926.

31. Mirel, *Rise and Fall of an Urban School System*, 28; Cohen, *Children of the Mill*, 48; "Mrs. Clarke Sullivan: President, Board of Education, Dayton, Ohio," *American School Board Journal* 68 (March 1924): 45; "Mrs. Frederick C. Murray: President, Board of Education, Independent School District, Cedar Rapids, Iowa," ibid. 69 (July 1924): 48.

32. Bruce M. Watson, "Tendencies in City School Board Organization," *National Municipal Review* 7 (January 1918): 60–61.

33. "Fling at Old Men on School Boards," *Evening Bulletin*, May 26, 1917, BCC. In Philadelphia, the ward or neighborhood school boards were not eliminated altogether until 1931. Marilyn Gittell and Edward T. Hollander, "The Process of Change: Case Study of Philadelphia," in *The Politics of Urban Education*, ed. Marilyn Gittell and Alan G. Hevesi (New York: Praeger, 1969), 217–35.

34. "Woman Is Named on School Board," *Evening Bulletin*, February 21, 1920, BCC; "Woman Sees Great Crisis in Schools," ibid., BCC; Minutes of the Board of Directors of the PEA, March 22, 1920, Accession 177B, PEA Papers. The other women considered for the board in 1920 were Marion Reilly, dean of Bryn Mawr College; Mrs. I. H. O'Hara, a reformer associated with the PEA, the Playground Association, and the Home and School League; and Mrs. B. F. Richardson, a prominent club woman. The Home and School League did not place anyone on the board until 1929, when its president, Anna B. Pratt, became the third woman to serve on the board. "Men and Things," *Evening Bulletin*, May 25, 1929, BCC; "Elect Miss Pratt to School Board," ibid., June 7, 1929, BCC.

35. Cott, *Grounding of Modern Feminism*, 99–114, 318–19.

36. Gutman, "Parent-Teacher Association," 23–25, 38–39, 63; *One Hundred and Tenth Annual Report of the Board of Public Education, School District of Philadelphia* (Philadelphia, 1928), 306; "Principals Like Home-School Idea," *Evening Bulletin,* May 1, 1929, BCC.

37. Gutman, "Parent-Teacher Association," 63–65, 98, 111–12, 116–17, 127.

38. Ibid., 54–55; Franklin, *The Education of Black Philadelphia,* 71–82, 134–36. For example, black teachers were squeezed in 1931 when the district proposed to enroll all seventh and eighth graders in existing junior highs. The black teachers who would have taught them in segregated schools with pupils in grades one through eight now had no one to teach.

39. Gutman, "Parent-Teacher Association," 65–68, 134–35; "Drastic School Economy Fought," *Evening Bulletin,* November 23, 1933, BCC; Franklin, *The Education of Black Philadelphia,* 135–36.

40. For a comparison of Chicago suburbs on the matter of progressive education, see Arthur Zilversmit, *Changing Schools: Progressive Education Theory and Practice, 1930–1960* (Chicago: University of Chicago Press, 1993); John Modell, "An Ecology of Family Decisions: Suburbanization, Schooling, and Fertility in Philadelphia, 1880–1920," *Journal of Urban History* 4 (August 1980), 409–12.

41. PTAs were active in the middle-class suburbs of other cities. For their role in school politics in Somerville, Massachusetts, a suburb of Boston, see Reed Ueda, *Avenues to Adulthood: The Origins of the High School and Social Mobility in an American Suburb* (New York: Cambridge University Press, 1987), 206. The desire to be politically involved at school was not exclusive to the middle class, but historians of education disagree about the extent to which labor's involvement in school politics was based on class. See Ira Katznelson and Margaret Weir, *Schooling for All: Class, Race and the Decline of the Democratic Ideal* (New York: Basic Books, 1985), 121–41; Mirel, *The Rise and Fall of an Urban School System,* 136, 151–52; Cohen, *Children of the Mill,* 157–209.

42. Edward S. Ling, "Home and School Associations," *American School Board Journal* 60 (January 1920): 52; *Annual Report of the Home and School League of Philadelphia, 1911–1912,* 33.

43. Ling, "Home and School Associations," 52–53; *Times Chronicle,* June 26, 1915, February 5, 1916, March 18, 1916.

44. Ling, "Home and School Associations," 53.

45. *Times Chronicle,* May 20, 1916, July 8, 1916, January 13, 1917, September 22, 1917, November 17, 1917.

46. Ling, "Home and School Associations," 53.

47. Margaret Marsh, *Suburban Lives* (New Brunswick, N.J.: Rutgers University Press, 1990), 103–7.

48. Marsh, *Suburban Lives,* 109–11; Minutes of the Haddonfield Mothers' and Teachers' Club, April 26, 1905, Historical Society of Haddonfield, Haddonfield, N.J. (hereafter cited as HMTC).

49. MHBE, April 21, 1904; Minutes of the HMTC, April 26, 1905, May 17, 1905,

January 17, 1906, March 9, 1910, April 12, 1910; "Borough P.T.A. Founded 30 Years," Haddonfield PTA Scrapbook, Historical Society of Haddonfield, Haddonfield, N.J.; Emma G. Gibson, *Pioneer Women of Historic Haddonfield* (West Collingswood, N.J.: n.p., 1973), 126–28.

50. Gibson, *Pioneer Women,* 126; Minutes of the HMTC, April 3, 1906, May 2, 1906, March 5, 1907, November 6, 1907, May 13, 1908.

51. Minutes of the HMTC, May 1, 1907.

52. Marsh, *Suburban Lives,* 74–83. Marsh calls the participation by men in family life "male domesticity" and points out that in order to have such relationships with their husbands women had "to agree to share only partially in the world of men." Ibid., 82.

53. MHBE, 1901–31, *passim.* All subsequent information regarding membership on the Haddonfield school board comes from this source.

54. Obituary of Anna Eastburn Willits, Scrapbook, MS 39-35, Historical Society of Haddonfield, Haddonfield, N.J.; Glover/Banister Collection, File Box 91-1104-1190, Folder 1149-1169, Historical Society of Haddonfield, Haddonfield, N.J. Willits lost when she ran for a second term on the board in 1911. MHBE, March 21, 1911. "William J. Boning," in *Biographical Review: Camden and Burlington Counties, N.J.* (Boston: Biographical Review Publishing Co., 1897), 19:115–17.

55. Obituary of William W. Hodgson, Scrapbook, MS 39-35, Historical Society of Haddonfield, Haddonfield, N.J.; *Haddon (N.J.) Gazette,* April 4, 1929, Haddonfield Parent-Teacher Association Scrapbook, Historical Society of Haddonfield, Haddonfield, N.J.

56. Minutes of the HMTC, November 1, 1905, May 1, 1907, May 13, 1908; MHBE, May 15, 1919; "Henry S. Scovel," in *Biographical Review of Camden and Burlington Counties, N.J.,* 19:472–73.

57. MHBE, March 16, 1915; Minutes of the Haddonfield Parent-Teacher Association, June 16, 1920, Historical Society of Haddonfield, Haddonfield, N.J. (hereafter cited as HPTA).

58. Minutes of the Executive Committee of the HPTA, October 19, 1919, November 11, 1919, September 11, 1922, April 8, 1926, May 9, 1927, December 1, 1927. In the 1920s, there were presentations on such topics as nutrition, health, adolescent social life, and school punishment. Speakers included Mrs. A. H. Reeve, president of the NCPT; Josiah Penniman, president of the University of Pennsylvania; and John Logan, New Jersey Commissioner of Education. Minutes of the HPTA, April 19, 1922, November 15, 1922, November 20, 1923, March 18, 1924, April 20, 1926, February 18, 1928; *Camden Courier,* October 17, 1929, HPTA Scrapbook.

59. Minutes of the Executive Committee of the HPTA, November 11, 1919, November 10, 1920, October 11, 1921, September 11, 1922, November 29, 1926.

60. Minutes of the Executive Committee of the HPTA, January 12, 1921, May 18, 1921, May 31, 1921.

61. Elia W. Peattie, "Friends of the Family: The Teacher," *Good Housekeeping*

50 (1910): 187. See also Labaree, "Career Ladders and the Early Public High School Teacher," in Warren, ed., *American Teachers,* 164–85; Fraser, "Agents of Democracy: Urban Elementary-School Teachers and the Conditions of Teaching," in ibid., 118–26.

62. MHBE, April 20, 1905, September 20, 1906, December 21, 1906, November 17, 1910, December 15, 1910, February 21, 1918, February 14, 1922; Minutes of the HPTA, May 16, 1923.

63. Minutes of the Executive Committee of the HPTA, April 13, 1920; MHBE, November 17, 1910, April 15, 1920, May 20, 1920, June 17, 1920.

64. Minutes of the HMTC, October 14, 1908, January 6, 1909; Minutes of the Executive Committee of the HPTA, October 11, 1921; MHBE, October 20, 1921.

65. MHBE, October 21, 1920, November 18, 1920; Minutes of the Executive Committee of the HPTA, February 10, 1925; Minutes of the HPTA, February 18, 1925.

66. Minutes of the HPTA, December 20, 1922; Minutes of the Executive Committee of the HPTA, December 22, 1922, January n.d., 1923.

67. Minutes of the HPTA, February 16, 1920; MHBE, August 3, 1903, March 17, 1908, February 14, 1922, March 20, 1922.

68. MHBE, June 16, 1921, November 22, 1921, December 2, 1921, May 11, 1922.

69. MHBE, March 27, 1924, September 25, 1924, October 30, 1924, November 20, 1924, December 16, 1924, October 27, 1925, November 24, 1925; Minutes of the HPTA, September 17, 1924; "To Vote on New School," *Evening Bulletin,* November 18, 1924, BCC; "Dedicate School at Haddonfield," ibid., October 14, 1927, BCC; "Black School Anniversary," October 12, 1944, Scrapbook, MS 39-35, Historical Society of Haddonfield, Haddonfield, N.J.

70. Albert Starkey, "What Is the Paramount Need of Haddonfield," *The Shield* (1924), 82–83; Joseph Walto, "A Paramount Need of Haddonfield," ibid., 83–84. Appearing in the high school yearbook, these two essays jointly received the prize for merit from the Haddonfield Civic Association.

71. Minutes of the Executive Committee of the HPTA, September 8, 1920, September 13, 1921; Minutes of the HPTA, September 15, 1920; MHBE, September 21, 1921, October 20, 1921. The board responded by thanking the HPTA for its help and inviting the president and two other members to come to a meeting to discuss "the housing condition of the school children." Minutes of the Executive Committee of the HPTA, December 5, 1921.

72. MHBE, December 15, 1921, March 19, 1925; Thirteenth Census of the United States, 1910, Manuscript Schedules, Borough of Haddonfield, Camden County, N.J.; Fourteenth Census of the United States, 1920, Manuscript Schedules, Borough of Haddonfield, Camden County, N.J. That more blacks were living with their own families in 1920 is made apparent by shifts in the gender ratio. In 1910, black women outnumbered black men in Haddonfield by almost two to one, but ten years later there was virtual parity.

73. MHBE, June 29, 1922, October 26 1922, February 13, 1923; Minutes of the

HPTA, January 16, 1923. Mrs. Henry S. Pennypacker chaired the Program and Child Welfare Committees of the HPTA in the mid-1920s and served as the organization's vice president in 1924–25. Minutes of the Executive Committee of the HPTA, July 16, 1923; Minutes of the HPTA, May 21, 1924. Pennypacker's term of eleven months was also the shortest of any board member between 1900 and 1930. However, two other board members also had brief terms at this time—Charles Vaughan served slightly more than a year, beginning in February 1922, and William Standwitz slightly less—indicating the political turmoil in Haddonfield caused by the school building issue. MHBE, February 14, 1922, June 12, 1922, February 13, 1923.

74. Minutes of the HPTA, September 17, 1924, October 21, 1925; Minutes of the Haddonfield Civic Association, October 16, 1925, November 27, 1925, Historical Society of Haddonfield, Haddonfield, N.J. No relation to Henry Pennypacker, James L. Pennypacker lobbied the civic association. His wife, Grace, was president of the HPTA in 1924–25.

Chapter Four

1. Helen Grinnell Mears was the daughter of Mary Grinnell Mears, cofounder of the National Congress of Mothers and its vice president from 1905 to 1923.

2. Schoff served as president longer than anyone in the history of the NCPT before 1950; Reeve's five years rank her second. Harry Allen Overstreet and Bonaro Overstreet, *Where Children Come First: A Study of the P.T.A. Idea* (Chicago: National Congress of Parents and Teachers, 1949), 195–200.

3. The *National Congress of Mothers Magazine* became *Child Welfare Magazine* in 1909. Its name has changed several times since then. "Hannah Kent Schoff," in *Notable American Women: A Biographical Dictionary,* ed. Edward T. James (Cambridge: Harvard University Press, 1971), 3:237–39; Obituary of Mrs. Augustus H. Reeve, *New York Times,* December 26, 1954; "Founder to Address Body," *Philadelphia Evening Bulletin,* February 7, 1929, Bulletin Clippings Collection, Urban Archives, Samuel Paley Library, Temple University, Philadelphia (hereafter cited as BCC).

4. "Hannah Kent Schoff," 238; Mary H. Weeks, "Hannah Kent Schoff," in *Parents and Their Problems,* ed. Mary H. Weeks, vol. 8 of *Child Welfare in Home, School, Church, and State* (Washington, D.C.: National Congress of Mothers and Parent-Teacher Associations, 1914), 42–43, 46; "Mrs. Schoff Fights Child Labor Bill," *Evening Bulletin,* January 26, 1925, BCC.

5. *Philadelphia Public Ledger,* September 19, 1905; "Divorce Blamed for Juvenile Vice," *Evening Bulletin,* July 19, 1925; and "Scored by Woman," *Philadelphia Evening Ledger,* October 20, 1926, all in BCC.

6. Hannah Kent Schoff, "Outlook for the National Congress of Mothers and Parent-Teacher Associations," in Weeks, ed., *Parents and Their Problems,* 8:53;

Margaretta Willis Reeve, "The Power of the Program," *Child Welfare Magazine* 21 (January 1927): 212.

7. Hugh Hawkins, *Banding Together: The Rise of National Associations in American Higher Education, 1887–1950* (Baltimore: Johns Hopkins University Press, 1992), 2–23; David Tyack and Elizabeth Hansot, *Managers of Virtue: Public School Leadership in America, 1820–1980* (New York: Basic Books, 1982), 136–40.

8. Robyn Muncy, *Creating a Female Dominion in American Reform, 1890–1935* (New York: Oxford University Press, 1991), xiii–xv; Molly Ladd-Taylor, *Mother-Work: Women, Child Welfare, and the State, 1890–1930* (Urbana: University of Illinois Press, 1994), 7–9, 45–50.

9. Schoff, "Outlook for the National Congress," 51.

10. Julia Grant, *Raising Baby by the Book: The Education of American Mothers* (New Haven, Conn.: Yale University Press, 1998), 55, 59–60; Mrs. Wilbur F. Crafts, "Mothers and the Schools," in *National Congress of Mothers: The First Conventions,* ed. David J. Rothman and Sheila M. Rothman (New York: Garland, 1987), 73, 76.

11. Overstreet and Overstreet, *Where Children Come First,* 201; National Congress of Parents and Teachers, *The Parent-Teacher Organization: Its Origins and Development* (Chicago: National Congress of Parents and Teachers, 1944), 84; "Membership of the NCPT," *P.T.A. Magazine* 49 (September 1954): frontispiece. After 1954, membership growth leveled off, amounting to 9,681,209 in 1971. See "P.T.A. Roll Call by States," *P.T.A. Magazine* 65 (February 1971): frontispiece.

12. Overstreet and Overstreet, *Where Children Come First,* 10–11; Hamilton Cravens, *Before Head Start: The Iowa Station and America's Children* (Chapel Hill: University of North Carolina Press, 1993), 59–67.

13. Christine A. Woyshner, "To Reach the Rising Generation through the Raising Generation: The Origins of the National Parent-Teacher Association" (Ed.D. diss., Harvard University, 1999), 64–65, 130–31; Overstreet and Overstreet, *Where Children Come First,* 12–13; Minutes of the Executive Committee of the National Congress of Mothers and Parent-Teacher Associations (NCMPTA), October 17, 1922, Elizabeth Hewes Tilton Papers, Box 7, Folder 222, Schlesinger Library, Radcliffe College, Cambridge, Mass. (hereafter cited as Tilton Papers). The NCMPTA became the National Congress of Parents and Teachers (NCPT) in 1924.

14. Minutes of the National Board of Managers of the NCPT, April 28, 1923, Box 7, Folder 223; September 20–23, 1927, Box 8, Folder 225; Report of the Committee to Study and Recommend Changes in Standards of Excellence, September 1928, Box 8, Folder 227; and Minutes of the Executive Committee of the NCPT, September 19, 1927, Box 8, Folder 226, all in Tilton Papers. Among 14,249 PTAs reporting, the NCPT judged only 259 to be in compliance with its standards.

15. Plan of Work for the Bureau of Publications of the NCPT, 1928–29, September 1928, Box 8, Folder 227, Tilton Papers; President's Reports (Mrs. A. H. Reeve) for 1926 and 1927, Box 8, Folders 225 and 226, Tilton Papers.

16. Hazel Hillis, *The First Fifty Years: Iowa Congress of Parents and Teachers, 1900–1950* (Des Moines, Iowa: Iowa Congress of Parents and Teachers, 1951), 30,

55, 58, 79–81, 84; Nellie M. Wistrup and Emily Louise McCabe, *History of the Parent-Teacher Association of Connecticut, Inc., 1900–1945* (Hartford, Conn.: National Congress of Parents and Teachers, 1945), 6–7; Margaret Strong, ed., *History of the California Congress of Parents and Teachers, 1900–1944* (Los Angeles: California Congress of Parents and Teachers, 1945), 14–19, 26–28.

17. National Congress of Parents and Teachers, *Through the Years: From the Scrapbook of Mrs. Mears* (Washington, D.C.: National Congress of Parents and Teachers, n.d.), 33–34; Overstreet and Overstreet, *Where Children Come First,* 49–50, 55–56.

18. Overstreet and Overstreet, *Where Children Come First,* 147–48.

19. NCPT, *Through the Years,* 28; Helen H. Gardner, "The Moral Responsibility of Women in Heredity," in *Proceedings of the First National Congress of Mothers* (Washington, D.C.: National Congress of Mothers, 1897), 130–47.

20. Ladd-Taylor, *Mother-Work,* 2–5, 45–50. See also Seth Koven and Sonya Michel, "Introduction: 'Mother Worlds,'" in *Mothers of a New World: Maternalist Politics and the Origins of Welfare States,* ed. Seth Koven and Sonya Michel (New York: Routledge, 1993), 6.

21. Minutes of the 27th Annual Convention of the NCMPTA, April 23–28, 1923, Box 7, Folder 223; Legislative Report of the NCMPTA, April 23, 1923, Box 8, Folder 234; and Suggested Resolution of the Legislative Committee of the NCPT, 1926, Box 8, Folder 235, all in Tilton Papers; National Congress of Parents and Teachers, *The Parent-Teacher Organization,* 155–59.

22. Legislative Report of the NCPT, May 1927, Box 8, Folder 236, Tilton Papers; Ladd-Taylor, *Mother-Work,* 140; Sonya Michel, "The Limits of Maternalism: Policies toward American Wage-Earning Mothers during the Progressive Era," in Koven and Michel, eds., *Mothers of a New World,* 292–300; Theda Skocpol, *Protecting Mothers and Soldiers: The Political Origins of Social Policy in the United States* (Cambridge: Harvard University Press, 1992), 336, 448.

23. Hannah K. Schoff, "Next Step Forward for Juvenile Court and Probation," in Weeks, ed., *Parents and Their Problems,* 8:94; Minutes of the 27th Annual Convention of the NCPT, April 23–28, 1923, Box 7, Folder 223, Tilton Papers; Plans of Work for the Committee on Legislation of the NCPT, 1927–28, Box 7, Folder 224, Tilton Papers.

24. Mrs. A. H. Reeve and Ruth Bottomly, Report of the Summer Round-Up of the Children, Board [of Managers of the National Congress of Parents and Teachers], 1927, Box 8, Folder 226, Tilton Papers; Mary H. Weeks, "Co-operation for Child Hygiene," in Weeks, ed., *Parents and Their Problems,* 8:59–61, 8:71–72; NCPT, *The Parent-Teacher Organization,* 171; Hillis, *The First Fifty Years,* 61–62.

25. Facts about the Summer Round-Up of the Children, 1926, Box 7, Folder 224, Tilton Papers; Reeve and Bottomly, Report of the Summer Round-Up of the Children, Tilton Papers. For a discussion of the NCM's shift from social reform to family therapy, see Skocpol, *Protecting Mothers and Soldiers,* 519–21; Ladd-Taylor, *Mother-Work,* 65–66; Michel, "The Limits of Maternalism," 308.

26. Hillis, *The First Fifty Years,* 107. In Haddonfield, New Jersey, the PTA did

not hesitate to adopt the program. In 1927, it sent Summer Round-Up forms to the parents of the 137 children about to enter kindergarten and first grade, urging them to have any problems corrected before September, "at which time another examination will be made by the school doctor." The following year the Haddonfield PTA arranged a group examination day in May at Community House, giving parents plenty of time to remedy any defects over the summer. Minutes of the Haddonfield Parent-Teacher Association, Special Planning Meeting for Officers and Committee Chairs, July 1927, Historical Society of Haddonfield, Haddonfield, N.J.; *Haddon (N.J.) Gazette,* May 3, 1928, May 10, 1928, and *Birdwood Bulletin,* May 1928, Haddonfield PTA Scrapbook, Historical Society of Haddonfield, Haddonfield, N.J.

27. Margaretta Willis Reeve, "The Summer Round-Up of the Children for 1929," *Child Welfare: The National Parent-Teacher Magazine* 23 (January 1929): 269 (italics hers); *Journal of the American Medical Association,* quoted in *School and Society* 38 (November 25, 1933): 711–12; W. W. Bauer, "The Summer Round-Up of the Children: A Significant Experiment," *National Parent-Teacher* 35 (May 1941): 25. On the opposition of the AMA to Sheppard-Towner, see Sheila M. Rothman, *Woman's Proper Place: A History of Changing Ideals and Practices, 1870 to the Present* (New York: Basic Books, 1978), 139–53.

28. NCPT, National Legislative Program: Whither This Congress? December 1931, Box 8, Folder 240, Tilton Papers; Muncy, *Creating a Female Dominion,* 120–22.

29. Grace Abbott, "The Summer Round-Up," *Child Welfare: The National Parent-Teacher Magazine* 27 (January 1933): 239–40; Bauer, "The Summer Round-Up," 25; "PTA Health Milestones," *PTA Magazine* 66 (February 1972): frontispiece; Overstreet and Overstreet, *Where Children Come First,* 154.

30. Ladd-Taylor, *Mother-Work,* 46–47; Cravens, *Before Head Start,* 9–17.

31. Hillis, *The First Fifty Years,* 19–20; Strong, ed., *History of the California Congress,* 37–38, 85–86; Margaretta Willis Reeve, Report of the [NCPT] President for 1927 and Report of the Special Committee for Cooperation in Regard to Motion Pictures, March 1927, Box 8, Folder 225, Tilton Papers.

32. Minutes of the Thirty-Fourth Annual Meeting of the NCPT, July 1930, Box 8, Folder 229, Tilton Papers. Many NCPT committees recommended such a policy, including the Home Economics and School Education Committees. Tentative Program of the Committee on Home Economics and Plan of Work: Committee on School Education, July 1930, Box 8, Folder 230, Tilton Papers.

33. Edna N. White to Beardsley Ruml, New York, October 28, 1929; Revell McCallum to Edna N. White, New York, April 3, 1930; Minutes of the Joint Committee of the National Congress of Parents and Teachers and the National Council of Parent Education, Denver, May 20, 1930; and Minnie B. Bradford to Theresa Ide, Washington, D.C., April 5, 1932, all in Series 3.5, Box 35, Folder 375, Laura Spelman Rockefeller Memorial Archives, North Tarrytown, N.Y.

34. Bird T. Baldwin et al., *The Twenty-Eighth Yearbook of the National Society*

for the Study of Education: Preschool and Parental Education (Bloomington, Ill.: Public School Publishing Co., 1929), 386–88; Steven L. Schlossman, "The Formative Era in American Parent Education: Overview and Interpretation," in *Parent Education and Public Policy,* ed. Ron Haskins and Diana Adams (Norwood, N.J.: Ablex, 1983), 12–16; Ada Hart Arlitt, Report of Work Done under the Spelman Grant to the Joint Committee of the NCPT and the NCPE, September 1930– August 31, 1931, Series 3.5, Box 35, Folder 375, Laura Spelman Rockefeller Memorial Archives, North Tarrytown, N.Y.

35. Elizabeth Tilton, Report of the Legislative Committee [of the NCPT]: Suggested Resolutions, 1926, Box 8, Folder 235; idem, Report of National Committee on Legislation, 1926, Box 7, Folder 224; idem, Legislative Report, May 1927, Box 8, Folder 236; idem, Report of the Committee on Legislation, 1927, Box 8, Folder 226; idem, Busy Bees in Legislation, n.d. (1928?), Box 8, Folder 237; idem, Legislation, 1928, Box 8, Folder 237; Charl Williams, Report of the Committee on School Education, September 1928, Box 8, Folder 227; P. H. Crane, Report of Work Done by Citizenship and Legislation Chairman, for Missouri, 1931–1932, Box 8, Folder 240; and Mrs. B. C. Hopkins, Report of Legislative Committee: Iowa Congress of Parents and Teachers, March 15, 1932, Box 8, Folder 240, all in Tilton Papers.

36. "The Department of Parent-Teacher Associations," in Weeks, ed., *Parents and Their Problems,* 8:112; Minutes of the Middlesex County Council of Parent Teacher Associations, October 13, 1927, Special Collections and Archives, Acquisition 1436, Box BI 26, Alexander Library, Rutgers University, New Brunswick, N.J.; Hillis, *The First Fifty Years,* 12–13; Overstreet and Overstreet, *Where Children Come First,* 127.

37. Elizabeth Tilton, Legislative [Committee] Report, January 27, 1927, Box 8, Folder 236, Tilton Papers; idem, Legislative [Committee] Report, September 9, 1930, Box 8, Folder 238, Tilton Papers. At the end of her tenure as chair of the Legislative Committee, Tilton concluded that the national program for "Federal Legislation was acceptable to the States and that on the whole, the States that take up Legislation have done well by it. We have States that do not feel themselves equipped to take up Federal Legislation. This, of course, is their own affair and probably, in some instances, is a wise course for them to pursue." Elizabeth Tilton, Legislative Report, 1930–1931, Box 8, Folder 238, Tilton Papers.

38. *Proceedings of the National Congress of Parents and Teachers, 1942* (Chicago: National Congress of Parents and Teachers, 1942), 198, quoted in Overstreet and Overstreet, *Where Children Come First,* 124. Thirty state congresses now had to approve a recommended measure for it to become a part of the national program. See also Mary T. Bannerman, "Public Opinion and the P.T.A.," in NCPT, *The Parent-Teacher Organization,* 115–16.

39. Strong, ed., *History of the California Congress,* 128–30; NCPT, *The Parent-Teacher Organization,* 70–71; Reeve, Report of [NCPT] President for 1927, Box 8, Folder 225, Tilton Papers.

40. Strong, ed., *History of the California Congress,* 42–46, 50–56, 105, 123–24.

41. Ibid., 65–67, 108; Rowayne C. Martin, Report of [California] Chairman of Legislation, 1927, Box 8, Folder 236, Tilton Papers.

42. Sharon Harley and Roslyn Torberg-Penn, *The Afro American Woman: Struggles and Images* (Port Washington, N.Y.: Kennikat Press, 1978), 17–27; Eileen Boris, "The Power of Motherhood: Black and White Activist Women Redefine the 'Political,'" in Koven and Michel, eds., *Mothers of a New World,* 224–26; Overstreet and Overstreet, *Where Children Come First,* 268.

43. Brochure of the National Congress of Colored Parents and Teachers (NCCPT), Papers of the Delaware Department of Public Instruction, Box 4391, PTA File, Delaware State Archives, Dover (hereafter cited as DDPI/DSA); Mrs. Fred Wessels, Report of the National Chairman on Extension of Work among Colored People, 1926, Box 7, Folder 224, Tilton Papers.

44. Linda Gordon, "Black and White Visions of Welfare: Women's Welfare Activism, 1890–1940," *Journal of American History* 78 (September 1991): 560–61, 577–78; Ladd-Taylor, *Mother-Work,* 58–63.

45. Service Citizens of Delaware, *Delaware State Parent-Teacher Association Year Book, 1922–1923, Bulletin,* vol. 4, no. 2 (1922), 35; Delaware Citizens Association, *Delaware State Parent-Teacher Association Year Book, 1931–1932, Bulletin,* vol. 13, no. 1 (1931), 70; Woyshner, "To Reach the Rising Generation," 79; Minutes of the Board of Managers [of the NCPT], September 21–24, 1926, Box 7, Folder 224, Tilton Papers; Mrs. Fred Wessels, Report of the Committee on Extension among Colored Peoples, 1927, Box 8, Folder 226, Tilton Papers; Suggested Plan of Work: Committee on Extension among Colored People, July 1930, Box 8, Folder 230, Tilton Papers. The NCPT Executive Committee accepted this plan in July 1930.

46. Report of the National Chairman on Extension of Work among Colored People, 1927, Box 7, Folder 224; Report of the Committee on Extension among Colored Peoples, 1927, Box 8, Folder 226; and Minutes of the Board of Managers [of the NCPT], Postconvention Meeting, April 28, 1923, Box 7, Folder 223, all in Tilton Papers.

47. Brochure of the NCCPT, PTA File, Box 4391, DDPI/DSA; Overstreet and Overstreet, *Where Children Come First,* 272–74.

48. Overstreet and Overstreet, *Where Children Come First,* 269–71.

49. Wayne E. Fuller, *The Old Country School: The Story of Rural Education in the Middle West* (Chicago: University of Chicago Press, 1982), 113, 150–51, 226–30, 238–39; William A. Link, *A Hard Country and a Lonely Place: Schooling, Society and Reform in Rural Virginia, 1870–1920* (Chapel Hill: University of North Carolina Press, 1986), 25–39, 45–46, 74–76, 116, 127–29, 139–42.

50. John Shilling, "An Adventure in Financing a State School System," *Educational Administration and Supervision* 9 (February 1923): 81–86; Robert J. Taggart, *Private Philanthropy and Public Education: Pierre S. du Pont and the Delaware Schools, 1890–1940* (Newark: University of Delaware Press, 1988), 78–81, 87–89.

51. Taggart, *Private Philanthropy and Public Education,* 123–40; Harry Vance Holloway (hereafter cited as HVH) to the Dover Board of Education, Dover,

Delaware, May 17, 1928 (italics his), Box 4381, DDPI/DSA. For insights into Holloway's philosophy of education, see his correspondence with Etta Wilson, the executive director of the Delaware Citizens' Association, especially HVH to Etta Wilson, Dover, Delaware, January 4, 1938, in which he said that "interest is the tool, so to speak, with which we build the temple of knowledge." Box 4391, DDPI/DSA.

52. See, for example, Mrs. Annie E. Allen to HVH, Nassau, Delaware, March 15, 1937; HVH to Annie E. Allen, Dover, Delaware, March 18, 1937; and Petitions from Nassau Residents to HVH Dated May 3, 1940, and May 29, 1940, all in Box 4251, File 198-C, DDPI/DSA. In the black schools of Middletown, some parents complained that "the trustees of our School have framed one of our good teachers to put in a teacher who is not fit to teach in any School." Two trustees responded by telling Holloway that if their decision was overturned, "the community will always be rising up against the school board." But "if the trustees win out it will be history for us . . . and teachers will carry out instructions laid down by our State Superintendent." From an anonymous parent and taxpayer to HVH, Middletown, Delaware, n.d. (received June 21, 1940), and George Pierce and Leroy Draper to HVH, Middletown, Delaware, June 19, 1940, both in Box 4343, DDPI/DSA.

53. Ruth W. Lewis to HVH, Ross Point, Delaware, February 26, 1934, and HVH to Ruth W. Lewis, Dover, Delaware, March 7, 1934, both in Box 4251, File 215-C, DDPI/DSA. In asking Holloway to help her retain her teaching position, Lewis attributed her dismissal to her unwillingness to give preferential treatment to the children of a powerful group in her community.

54. Robert J. Taggart, "Etta J. Wilson (1883–1971): A Delaware Reformer," *Delaware History* 24 (Spring–Summer 1990): 43–44; Mrs. Clara Dennis to HVH, Farmington, Delaware, October 13, 1945, and Albert Early to HVH, Georgetown, Delaware, October 17, 1945, Box 4251, File 39, DDPI/DSA.

55. S. M. Stouffer to HVH, Wilmington, Delaware, August 24, 1934; HVH to S. M. Stouffer, Dover, Delaware, August 29, 1934; M. Channing Wagner to John Shilling, Wilmington, Delaware, August 23, 1934; Madeline Dixon to HVH, Wilmington, Delaware, August 23, 1943; HVH to Madeline Dixon, Dover, Delaware, August 26, 1943; and Madeline Dixon to HVH, Wilmington, Delaware, May 13, 1946, all in Box 4281, DDPI/DSA; H. E. Stahl to HVH, Claymont, Delaware, December 2, 1941, Box 4381, DDPI/DSA. Taggart, *Private Philanthropy and Public Education*, 162–64.

56. Mrs. Annie West to HVH, Georgetown, Delaware, n.d. (received September 9, 1937), Box 4381, DDPI/DSA; Petition Signed by 29 Parents, June 9, 1931, Magnolia, District #50, Box 4343, DDPI/DSA. These parents wanted the Magnolia District to consolidate with the Dover Special District, not the Logan District, so "that some reasonable provision shall be made for our children who have completed the grades at Magnolia to attend high school." In the 1920s, opposition to rural school consolidation slowly diminished as parents and taxpayers weighed the respective merits of local control and state appropriations. Taggart, *Private Philanthropy and Public Education*, 91–94.

57. Petition to the State Board of Education from Frederica, Delaware, August 20, 1923, Box 4343, File 7; Mrs. Lotie T. Stanley to HVH, Bridgeville, Delaware, August 1, 1945, Box 4251, File 206-C; Anonymous Parent to HVH, Middletown, Delaware, February 1943, and HVH to Alfred G. Waters, Dover, Delaware, n.d., Box 4343, Middletown File; and Petition from 19 Residents (who were also most likely parents of children attending the Mt. Olive Colored School), n.d. (ca. 1940), Box 4343, File 155-C, all in DDPI/DSA.

58. Julian F. Smith to HVH, Wilmington, Delaware, April 19, 1939, and HVH to Julian F. Smith, Dover, Delaware, April 20, 1939, both in Box 4381, DDPI/DSA.

59. Ethel B. Gibson to HVH, Greenwood, Delaware, September 22, 1942; HVH to Ethel Gibson, Dover, Delaware, September 27, 1942; Ethel B. Gibson to HVH, Greenwood, Delaware, January 14, 1943; HVH to Ethel Gibson, Dover, Delaware, January 18, 1943; Ethel B. Gibson to HVH, Greenwood, Delaware, February 26, 1944; and HVH to Ethel Gibson, Dover, Delaware, February 28, 1944, all in Box 4251, Folder 91, DDPI/DSA; Virgil B. Wiley to HVH, Bridgeville, Delaware, January 20, 1943; HVH to Virgil Wiley, Dover, Delaware, January 28, 1943; Virgil B. Wiley to HVH, Bridgeville, Delaware, November 29, 1943; and HVH to Virgil Wiley, Dover, Delaware, December 22, 1943, all in Box 4251, Folder 90, DDPI/DSA.

60. Valerie Grim, "History Shared through Memory: The Establishment and Implementation of Education in the Brooks Farm Community, 1920–1957," *Oral History Review* 23 (Summer 1996): 1–17; Mrs. Howard Griffith to HVH, Blades, Delaware, December 9, 1935, and HVH to Mrs. Howard Griffith, Dover, Delaware, December 13, 1935, Box 4251, Folder 172, DDPI/DSA; Ollie Drew to HVH, Millville, Delaware, October 12, 1936, and HVH to Ollie Drew, Dover, Delaware, October 15, 1936, Box 4343, Folder 207-C, DDPI/DSA; Virgil B. Wiley to HVH, Bridgeville, Delaware, March 8, 1944, and HVH to Virgil Wiley, Dover, Delaware, March 9, 1944, Box 4251, Folder 90, DDPI/DSA.

61. Alice Fox Pitts, "A Challenge to Parent-Teacher Associations," *Parents Magazine* 4 (December 1929): 22–23.

62. Service Citizens of Delaware, *Delaware State Parent-Teacher Association Year Book, 1924–1925, Bulletin,* vol. 6, no. 4 (1924), 8 (hereafter cited as *DSPTA Year Book*); Service Citizens of Delaware/Delaware Citizens Association, "A Record of Twenty Years of Service," Typescript, February 1940, Box 4391, Delaware Citizens Association File, DDPI/DSA.

63. Taggart, *Private Philanthropy and Public Education,* p. 200, n. 68; Irene Earll, Announcement, May 26, 1914, Box 18, Ephemera File, PTA, Delaware Historical Society, Wilmington.

64. Taggart, *Private Philanthropy and Public Education,* 115–16; Taggart, "Etta J. Wilson," 39–40, 42–44; Service Citizens of Delaware, *DSPTA Year Book, 1925–1926, Bulletin,* vol. 7, no. 2 (1926), 150; Delaware Citizens Association, *DSPTA Year Book, 1930–1931, Bulletin,* vol. 12, no. 1 (1930), 9; Ellen C. Lombard, *Recent Development of Parent-Teacher Associations,* Bulletin 5, 1923 (Washington, D.C.: U.S. Department of the Interior, Bureau of Education, 1923), 8.

65. Taggart, *Private Philanthropy and Public Education*, 116–18, 120; Taggart, "Etta J. Wilson," 42–43, 45; Link, *A Hard Country and a Lonely Place*, 186–87.

66. *DSPTA Year Book, 1924–1925*, 17; *DSPTA Year Book, 1925–1926*, 18; *DSPTA Year Book, 1926–1927*, Bulletin, vol. 8, no. 2. (1927), 15; *DSPTA Year Book, 1927–1928*, Bulletin, vol. 9, no. 3 (1928), 13; *DSPTA Year Book, 1930–1931*, 3–80; Seth Harmon, ed., *Who's Who in Delaware: A Biographical Dictionary of Delaware's Leading Men and Women* (Philadelphia: National Biography Society, 1932), 19, 89, 122, 158.

67. Taggart, *Private Philanthropy and Public Education*, 121; Taggart, "Etta J. Wilson," 46; *DSPTA Year Book, 1922–1923*, 10, 110; *DSPTA Year Book, 1925–1926*, 14–17; Service Citizens, "A Record of Twenty Years of Service," 10–11, DDPI/DSA.

68. *DSPTA Year Book, 1930–1931*, 11.

69. Minutes of the Middletown [Delaware] Parent-Teachers Association, January 29, 1915, January 14, 1916, March 17, 1916, Middletown [Delaware] PTA Minute Books, 1915–34, 2 vols., Papers of the Delaware Department of Public Instruction, Box 2962, Delaware State Archives, Dover (hereafter cited as DDPI/MMPTA).

70. DDPI/MMPTA, October 28, 1921, November 2, 1922, December 7, 1922.

71. DDPI/MMPTA, October 29, 1920, September 6, 1923, September 14, 1923, October 4, 1923, April 3, 1924, February 10, 1925, January 19, 1926, March n.d., 1926.

72. For meetings devoted to student presentations and teacher demonstrations, see DDPI/MMPTA, February 25, 1921, April 4, 1921, March 6, 1924, February 18, 1926; for meetings at which funds were appropriated to purchase equipment, see DDPI/MMPTA, June 1, 1917, September 28, 1917, April 25, 1919, January 20, 1920, February 24, 1922, March n.d., 1930.

73. DDPI/MMPTA, January 18, 1927, April 20, 1927; Taggart, *Private Philanthropy and Public Education*, 157.

74. DDPI/MMPTA, October 24, 1929, December 1, 1927; Taggart, "Etta J. Wilson," 47; *DSPTA Year Book, 1930–1931*, 8; Service Citizens, "A Record of Twenty Years of Service," 12, 15, 17–18, DDPI/DSA.

75. Minutes of the Annual Meeting of the Delaware Citizens Association, June 16, 1932, and Minutes of the Board of Directors of the Delaware Citizens Association, May 19, 1933 (including the Proposed Working Program for the DCA, 1933–34), both in DPI Library Box 1, DDPI/DSA (hereafter cited as DCAM/DDPI); Delaware Citizens Association, *DSPTA Year Book, 1928–1929*, Bulletin, vol. 10, no. 1 (1928), 7; DDPI/MMPTA, January 15, 1934.

76. Delaware Citizens Association, *DSPTA Year Book, 1929–1930*, Bulletin, vol. 11, no. 1 (1929), 9; Minutes of the DCA Executive Committee and Educational Council, January 9, 1930, March 13, 1930; Report of the DCA Board of Directors for the year ending June 1, 1930; Report of the Director of the Demonstration

School, June 1930; and Minutes of the Trustees Meeting, Georgetown Demonstration School, November 5, 1930, all in DCAM/DDPI. For a full account of the history of the Georgetown Demonstration School, see Robert J. Taggart, "Elite Educational Reform in a Traditional Community: The Georgetown Demonstration School, 1929–1933," *Delaware History* 21 (Winter 1987): 233–55.

77. Minutes of the DCA Educational Council, January 27, 1932, DCAM/DDPI; Minutes of the DCA Executive Committee, January 27, 1932, May 8, 1932, DCAM/DDPI. That Georgetown was unprepared for the teaching methods of the demonstration school was apparent to the school's board of trustees by 1931. Defending a $6,000 appropriation for staff development and adult education, it said: "There is a much more intensive job in parental education than in a community which has grown into the idea, just as life insurance for the project if for no other reason." Advance Notes for a Meeting of the Trustees of the Demonstration School, January 11, 1931, DCAM/DDPI.

78. Minutes of the DCA Annual Meeting, June 23, 1936, DCAM/DDPI; Minutes of the DCA Board of Directors, January 12, 1938, DCAM/DDPI.

79. Hugh Morris to the Members of the Delaware Citizens Association, December 29, 1942, Box 4391, DDPI/DSA. Morris reported that the Executive Committee of the DCA took action on November 25, 1942. In 1946, Holloway congratulated the president of the DSPTA, Mrs. John W. Reynolds, for encouraging PTAs to work with the school. "The change in its program from an organization to be entertained by the school to one to bring help . . . is most appreciated." HVH to Helen C. Reynolds, Dover, Delaware, April 4, 1946, DDPI/DSA.

Chapter Five

1. "Liberty Belles," *Philadelphia Record,* February 28, 1931; "Miss Anna B. Pratt Dies in 65th Year," *Philadelphia Evening Bulletin,* January 4, 1932; and "Anna Pratt Dies; Noted as Educator," *Philadelphia Record,* January 4, 1932, all in the Bulletin Clippings Collection, Urban Archives, Samuel Paley Library, Temple University, Philadelphia (hereafter cited as BCC).

2. Anna B. Pratt, "Should the Visiting Teacher Be a New Official," *Journal of Social Forces* 1 (March 1923): 300–304; Anna B. Pratt and Edith M. Everett, "Vocational, Educational and Social Guidance," *School and Society* 22 (August 1, 1925): 145–46; Anna B. Pratt, "Shall It Be an Ounce of Prevention before Six Years or a Pound of Cure at Sixteen?" Typescript of a Radio Address, October 13, 1924, Magdalen Society/White-Williams Foundation Papers, Box Marked Miscellaneous Correspondence and Papers of Anna B. Pratt, Historical Society of Pennsylvania, Philadelphia (hereafter cited as Pratt Papers, WWF).

3. William H. Maxwell, "The Attitude of the American Parent toward Education," *Educational Review* 45 (February 1913): 173–77; James S. Hiatt, *The Truant Problem and the Parental School,* United States Bureau of Education Bulletin 29 (Washington, D.C.: U.S. Government Printing Office, 1915), 17.

4. Leonard Covello, *The Social Background of the Italo-American School Child,* ed. Francesco Cordasco (Leiden, Netherlands: E. J. Brill, 1967), 309–27; Stephen F. Brumberg, *Going to America, Going to School: The Jewish Immigrant Public School Encounter in Turn-of-the-Century New York City* (New York: Praeger, 1986), 119–24, 136–37, 201.

5. Edward J. Rowse, "The Father's Occupation as a Factor of Elimination," *School and Society* 8 (August 17, 1918): 194; Charles E. Holley, *The Fifteenth Yearbook of the National Society for the Study of Education,* pt. 2, *The Relationship between Persistence in School and Home Conditions* (Bloomington, Ill.: Public School Publishing Co., 1919), 96. See also Joseph K. Van Denburg, *Causes of the Elimination of Students in Public Secondary Schools* (New York: Teachers College, Columbia University, 1911); Charles H. Keyes, *Progress through the Grades of City Schools: A Study of Acceleration and Arrest,* Teachers College Contributions to Education, no. 42 (New York: Teachers College, Columbia University, 1911). Historians have confirmed the importance of social class to persistence in school. See, for example, David L. Angus and Jeffrey Mirel, "From Spellers to Spindles: Work-Force Entry by Children of Textile Workers, 1888–1890," *Social Science History* 9 (Spring 1985): 139.

6. Edith Abbott and Sophonisba Breckinridge, *Truancy and Non-attendance in the Chicago Schools* (1917; reprint, New York: Arno Press, 1970), 136, 147, 157, 330.

7. Ibid., 352; Frank T. Carlton, "The Home and the School," *Education* 26 (September 1905): 212–14.

8. Hiatt, *The Truant Problem and the Parental School,* 19–33; Abbott and Breckinridge, *Truancy and Non-attendance,* 86, 170.

9. Gardner B. Perry, "On Primary Education," in *The Introductory Discourse and the Lectures Delivered before the American Institute of Instruction in Boston, August, 1833* (Boston: Carter, Hendee, 1834), 111.

10. Sarah Louise Arnold, "Concerning Home and School," *New England Magazine* n.s., 35 (November 1906): 334, 337; *Eighteenth Annual Report of the Board of Education of School District No. One, Arapahoe County, Colorado, August 1, 1892* (Denver, 1892), 11.

11. Holley, *Fifteenth Yearbook of the National Society for the Study of Education,* 107; Lucy Wheelock, "Kindergartens and Parent-Teacher Associations," *School Life* 9 (October 1923): 47; Maxwell, "Attitude of the American Parent toward Education," 183.

12. Bird T. Baldwin et al., *The Twenty-Eighth Yearbook of the National Society for the Study of Education: Preschool and Parental Education,* pt. 1, *Organization and Development;* pt. 2, *Research and Method* (Bloomington, Ill.: Public School Publishing Co., 1929), 68–69, 277–83, 342.

13. Judith Rosenberg Raftery, *Land of Fair Promise: Politics and Reform in Los Angeles Schools, 1885–1941* (Stanford, Calif.: Stanford University Press, 1992), 68–84, 106; Minutes of the Board of Directors of the Public Education and Child Labor Association, June 22, 1928, Box Labeled Child Labor and Accession 177C,

Box 1 in the Records of the Citizens Committee on Public Education/Public Education and Child Labor Association, Urban Archives, Samuel Paley Library, Temple University, Philadelphia; Stanley K. Schultz, *The Culture Factory: Boston Public Schools, 1789–1860* (New York: Oxford University Press, 1973), 292.

14. Baldwin et al., *Twenty-Eighth Yearbook of the National Society for the Study of Education,* 85.

15. Barbara Beatty, "Child Gardening: The Teaching of Young Children in American Schools," in *American Teachers: Histories of a Profession at Work,* ed. Donald Warren (New York: Macmillan, 1989), 69, 82; Margaret O'Brien Steinfels, *Who's Minding the Children: The History and Politics of Day Care in America* (New York: Simon & Schuster, 1973), 36–39; Sheila M. Rothman, "Other People's Children: The Day Care Experience in America," *Public Interest* 30 (Winter 1973): 13–14; Maris Vinovskis, "Family and Schooling in Colonial and Nineteenth-Century America," *Journal of Family History* 12, no. 3 (1987): 27–28; Maris A. Vinovskis, *Education, Society, and Economic Opportunity: A Historical Perspective on Persistent Issues* (New Haven, Conn.: Yale University Press, 1995), 32–37, 41–42.

16. Beatty, "Child Gardening," 76, 84; Steinfels, *Who's Minding the Children,* 49, 52–55; Rothman, "Other People's Children," 14–15; *A Study of the Day Nurseries of Philadelphia Made for the Philadelphia Association of Day Nurseries by the Child Federation* (Philadelphia, 1916), 3, 32; Virginia Kerr, "One Step Forward—Two Steps Back: Child Care's Long American History," in *Child Care, Who Cares,* ed. Pamela Roby (New York: Basic Books, 1973), 159.

17. *Study of the Day Nurseries of Philadelphia,* 58; Barbara Beatty, *Preschool Education in America: The Culture of Young Children from the Colonial Era to the Present* (New Haven, Conn.: Yale University Press, 1995), 94–95, 99–100, 111; Nina C. Vandewalker, *The Kindergarten in American Education* (New York: Macmillan, 1908), 124–28; Beatty, "Child Gardening," 77, 84.

18. Beatty, *Preschool Education in America,* 136–42; Baldwin et al., *Twenty-Eighth Yearbook of the National Society for the Study of Education,* 28–33; Edna Noble White, "The Nursery School: A Teacher of Parents," *Child Study* 4 (October 1926): 8; Winifred Rand, "Parenthood and the Nursery School," *Child Study* 5 (March 1928): 11; Elizabeth Irwin, "Going to School," *Child Study* 10 (February 1933): 128; Jean McPherson Kitchen, "When Babies Go to School," *Parents' Magazine* 10 (March 1935): 47.

19. White, "The Nursery School," 8; Lois Hayden Meek, "Our Educational Program," *Journal of the AAUW* 18 (May 1925): 26; Arnold Gesell, *The Preschool Child from the Standpoint of Public Hygiene and Education* (Boston: Houghton Mifflin, 1923), xi; Catherine F. Magee, "Methods That Succeed with Youngsters," *Parents' Magazine* 9 (December 1934): 27; Baldwin et al., *Twenty-Eighth Yearbook of the National Society for the Study of Education,* 29–35, 155–61. In her dissertation, Sonya Michel argued that nursery educators thought middle-class parents were more likely than either their working- or upper-class counterparts to teach the right habits and values at home. Sonya A. Michel, "Children's Interests/Moth-

ers' Rights: Women, Professionals, and the American Family, 1920-1945" (Ph.D. diss., Brown University, 1986), 132-36.

20. Kerr, "One Step Forward," 161; Steinfels, *Who's Minding the Children,* 58-60; Michel, "Children's Interests/Mothers' Rights," 170-74.

21. *Study of the Day Nurseries of Philadelphia,* 7-10.

22. Bureau of Jewish Social Research, General Report of the Survey of the Jewish Child Care Situation in Philadelphia, December 1920, 4, 13-14, 88, Neighborhood Centre Collection, Philadelphia Jewish Archives Center, Balch Institute for Ethnic Studies, Philadelphia (hereafter cited as NC/PJAC); Julian L. Greifer, "Neighborhood Centre: A Study of the Adjustment of a Culture Group in America" (Ph.D. diss., New York University, 1948), 170-71, 186; Phoebe Tobin, Outline History of the First Family Day Care Association, 1863-1974, Papers of the First Family Day Care Association, Urban Archives, Samuel Paley Library, Temple University, Philadelphia.

23. Greifer, "Neighborhood Centre," 196; Annual Report of the Day Nursery and Shelter, April 10, 1912-April 10, 1913, Series 1, Box 2, Folder 13; Annual Report of the Day Nursery and Shelter, April 10, 1913-April 10, 1914, Series 1, Box 2, Folder 10; Report of the Day Nursery and Shelter, February 1915, Series 1, Box 2, Folder 12; Annual Report of the Neighborhood Centre, 1915-16, Series 1, Box 2, Folder 10; and Neighborhood Centre Annual Report for 1919, Series 1, Box 2, Folder 19, all in NC/PJAC.

24. Greifer, "Neighborhood Centre," 272, 429-30; Neighborhood Centre to Have Nursery School, Press Release, n.d. (ca. October 1925), Series 1, Box 3, Folder 1, NC/PJAC.

25. Baldwin et al., *Twenty-Eighth Yearbook of the National Society for the Study of Education,* 155-60; Michel, "Children's Interests/Mothers' Rights," 174-75; Yvonne S. Perry, The Historical Development of Day Care Service at the Wharton Centre (Philadelphia, 1963), 15-16, Manuscript, Papers of the Wharton Centre, Urban Archives, Samuel Paley Library, Temple University, Philadelphia; Summary of Work of Neighborhood Centre, October 22, 1925, Series 1, Box 2, Folder 13, NC/PJAC.

26. Rae Lewis, Report of the Executive Director—Day Nursery Committee Meeting, September 29, 1925; Carrie Younker, Nursery Report, October 1928; and Nursery Report, January 1929, all in Series 1, Box 2, Folder 11; Esther F. Siegel, Untitled Manuscript Dated November 22, 1940, and idem, Report on Talk by Dr. Nathan Schlezinger to Nursery School PTA, March 26, 1941, both in Series 1, Box 3, Folder 3, all in NC/PJAC.

27. Survey of the Federation of Jewish Charities Day Nurseries, December 13, 1935, and Forty-Eighth Annual Report of the Neighborhood Centre, 1929, both in Series 1, Box 2, Folder 19; and Thelma Day, Nursery School Report, September 1928, Series 1, Box 3, Folder 1, all in NC/PJAC. Among day nurseries for blacks in Philadelphia, the St. Nicholas Day Nursery had a mothers' club as early as 1915. Meeting every other week, it taught sewing and knitting. *Fifth Annual*

Report of the St. Nicholas Day Nursery of Philadelphia for Colored Children (Philadelphia, 1915), 5.

28. Hazel Gabbard, Nursery School Report, September 1929, Series 1, Box 3, Folder 1; E. F. Siegel, An Analysis of the Philosophy and Practices of the Neighborhood Centre Nursery School, July 18, 1940, Series 1, Box 3, Folder 3; and E. F. Siegel, Annual Report of the Director of the Nursery School, May 27, 1941, Series 1, Box 3, Folder 3, all in NC/PJAC.

29. Nursery School Committee, November 14, 1941, December 16, 1941, Series 1, Box 1, Folder 10; Cornelia F. Minsinger, Overview of Nursery School Families, 1929–1931, in Nursery School Report, February–March 1931, Series 1, Box 3, Folder 1; Meeting of the Council of Social Agencies—Day Nursery Division, December 9, 1942, Series 1, Box 2, Folder 20; and Philadelphia Committee on Day Care of Children: Plans for Day Care Center, Tasker Homes Area, June 1942, Series 1, Box 8, Folder 22, all in NC/PJAC.

30. Nursery School Committee, May 8, 1942, Series 1, Box 1, Folder 10; Typescript Describing the Nursery School Program and Services at the Neighborhood Centre, n.d. (ca. 1941), Series 1, Box 3, Folder 2; Esther F. Siegel, Nursery School Annual Report—1942, Series 1, Box 3, Folder 3; and Nursery School Committee, May 15, 1942, Series 1, Box 1, Folder 10, all in NC/PJAC.

31. Steinfels, *Who's Minding the Children,* 60–64.

32. Day Nursery Experiment in Which One Visitor Represented Both Neighborhood Centre and Jewish Welfare Society in Handling Family Situation, n.d. (ca. 1930), Series 1, Box 2, Folder 13; Esther F. Siegel, Day Nursery Report, October 1938, November 1938, Series 1, Box 2, Folder 11; and Esther F. Siegel, Report of the Nursery School Department: Summary of Summer Events, September 1939, Series 1, Box 3, Folder 2, all in NC/PJAC.

33. A Social Study of the Population of the Neighborhood Centre Nursery School, February 12, 1942, Series 1, Box 3, Folder 3; Minutes of the Meeting of the Neighborhood Centre Day Care Committee, October 19, 1943, Series 1, Box 1, Folder 1; and Joseph E. Beck, Relationship of Jewish Welfare Society to Day Nursery Program, n.d. (ca. 1943), Series 1, Box 2, Folder 13, all in NC/PJAC.

34. Luther H. Gulick and Leonard P. Ayres, *Medical Inspection of Schools,* rev. ed. (New York: Russell Sage Foundation, 1917), 11–13.

35. Ibid., viii, 13–18; National Society for the Study of Education, *The Ninth Yearbook of the National Society for the Study of Education,* pt. 1, *Health and Education,* by Thomas D. Wood (Bloomington, Ill.: Public School Publishing Co., 1910), 14.

36. Agnes Daley, "Parents' Meetings in the New York Schools," *Journal of Home Economics* 12 (November 1920): 496–98; Eva W. White, "The Home and Social Efficiency," *Journal of Home Economics* 5 (April 1913): 122–30; Carrie A. Lyford, "Home Economics in Negro Schools," *Journal of Home Economics* 15 (November 1923): 633–37; John L. Rury, *Education and Women's Work: Female Schooling and the Division of Labor in Urban America, 1870–1930* (Albany: SUNY Press, 1991), 139–47.

37. Gulick and Ayres, *Medical Inspection,* viii.

38. National Society for the Study of Education, *The Ninth Yearbook of the National Society for the Study of Education,* pt. 2, *The Nurse in Education* (Chicago: University of Chicago Press, 1911), 22, 26; Marlene H. Woodfill and Mary K. Beyrer, *The Role of the Nurse in the School Setting: A Historical Perspective* (Kent, Ohio: American School Health Association, 1991), 5–6. Although the first school nurses were often supplied by the Visiting Nurses Association, they soon became public employees, working for either the department of health or the board of education in many cities, including Boston (1907), Philadelphia (1908), Chicago (1907), and Los Angeles (1904). Lina Rogers Struthers, *The School Nurse: A Survey of the Duties and Responsibilities of the Nurse in the Maintenance of Health and Physical Perfection and the Prevention of Disease among School Children* (New York: G. P. Putnam's Sons, 1917), 31–34.

39. Gulick and Ayres, *Medical Inspection,* 1, 117, 162–63; Struthers, *The School Nurse,* 8, 17; William S. Allen, *Civics and Health* (Boston: Ginn, 1909), 36; Ruth Peck McLeod, "Is Your Child Ready for School?" *Child Welfare Magazine* 21 (September 1926): 10.

40. National Society for the Study of Education, *The Nurse in Education,* 15, 50; Struthers, *The School Nurse,* 8, 62, 92–93, 134; "How Parents May Help," *Pennsylvania School Journal* 52 (July 1903): 22; Gulick and Ayres, *Medical Inspection,* 71.

41. Allen, *Civics and Health,* 38–39; Struthers, *The School Nurse,* 22, 71, 130, 257–58; National Society for the Study of Education, *The Nurse in Education,* 34–35; Raftery, *Land of Fair Promise,* 33.

42. Gulick and Ayres, *Medical Inspection,* 5, 168–69; Struthers, *The School Nurse,* 2, 231.

43. Allen, *Civics and Health,* 173; National Society for the Study of Education, *The Nurse in Education,* 10–11, 30, 55; Struthers, *The School Nurse,* 232.

44. Allen, *Civics and Health,* 320; Elizabeth Cleveland, "If Parents Only Knew: Letters from a School Teacher," *Children: The Magazine for Parents* 2 (November 1927): 13; Barbara Beatty, *Preschool Education in America,* 155–56.

45. Woodfill and Beyrer, *The Role of the Nurse in the School Setting,* 15, 25–27, 36, 47–49.

46. Julius John Oppenheimer, *The Visiting Teacher Movement with Special Reference to Administrative Relationships* (New York: Public Education Association, 1924), iv–v, 56–57; Julia Grant, *Raising Baby by the Book: The Education of American Mothers* (New Haven, Conn.: Yale University Press, 1998), 101.

47. Oppenheimer, *Visiting Teacher Movement,* 1–4; Harriet M. Johnson, *The Visiting Teacher in New York City: A Statement of the Function and an Analysis of the Work of the Visiting Teacher Staff of the Public Education Association from 1912 to 1915 Inclusive* (New York: Public Education Association, 1916), vii; Murray Levine and Adele Levine, *A Social History of Helping Services: Clinic, Court, School and Community* (New York: Appleton Century Crofts, 1970), 129, 134.

48. Oppenheimer, *Visiting Teacher Movement,* 3, 7.

49. Ibid., 5, 7–8; Levine and Levine, *A Social History of Helping Services*, 130; Jane F. Culbert, "The Visiting Teacher," in *The Annals of the American Academy of Political and Social Science*, vol. 98 (Philadelphia: American Academy of Political and Social Science, 1921), 85; *The Visiting Teacher in the United States: A Survey by the National Association of Visiting Teachers and Home and School Visitors* (New York: Public Education Association of the City of New York, 1921), 11; Agnes Benedict, *Children at the Crossroads* (New York: Commonwealth Fund, 1930), 8–9.

50. Oppenheimer, *Visiting Teacher Movement*, 11; Mary B. Sayles, *The Problem Child in School: Narratives from Case Records of Visiting Teachers with a Description of the Purpose and Scope of Visiting Teacher Work by Howard W. Nudd* (New York: Commonwealth Fund, 1927), 278–80.

51. Oppenheimer, *Visiting Teacher Movement*, 3, 10, 23; Culbert, "The Visiting Teacher," 82; Margo Horn, *Before It's Too Late: The Child Guidance Movement in the United States, 1922–1945* (Philadelphia: Temple University Press, 1989), 22–34, 44–45, 50.

52. *The Visiting Teacher in the United States*, 28–29, 34–39, 43–45; Johnson, *The Visiting Teacher in New York City*, xv; Jane F. Culbert, *The Visiting Teacher at Work* (New York: Commonwealth Fund, 1930), 55–58.

53. Sayles, *The Problem Child in School*, 255–57; *The Visiting Teacher in the United States*, 9–10; Johnson, *The Visiting Teacher in New York City*, x–xi.

54. Oppenheimer, *Visiting Teacher Movement*, 93–94, 104; Culbert, "The Visiting Teacher," 86–87; National Society for the Study of Education, *The Nurse in Education*, 59; Sophia C. Gleim, *The Visiting Teacher*, U.S. Bureau of Education, Bulletin 10 (Washington, D.C.: U.S. Government Printing Office, 1921), 8–9; Abbott and Breckinridge, *Truancy and Non-attendance*, 233–38, 242–44; Allen, *Civics and Health*, 188–89; Johnson, *The Visiting Teacher in New York City*, xi, xv, 3–4, 58–59.

55. Oppenheimer, *Visiting Teacher Movement*, 22–23, 63, 96.

56. Benedict, *Children at the Crossroads*, 15–16; William A. White, "The Origin, Growth, and Significance of the Mental-Hygiene Movement," *Mental Hygiene* 14 (July 1930): 555–64; C. E. A. Winslow, "The Mental Hygiene Movement and Its Founder," ibid. 17 (October 1933): 533–42.

57. Oppenheimer, *Visiting Teacher Movement*, 27, 72, 109–13; Sayles, *The Problem Child in School*, 272–75. In 1927, Howard Nudd chaired the National Committee on Visiting Teachers. Exemplifying the therapeutic mindset of the mental hygiene movement, the committee's secretary, Jane F. Culbert, wrote in 1930 that "the causes of bad behavior, of truancy, or of the underlying physical and mental maladjustment, are linked up so closely with the totality of the child's experience that the school must share, along with the home and the neighborhood, the responsibility for the cause of these maladjustments." Culbert, *The Visiting Teacher at Work*, xiii.

58. Hamilton Cravens, *Before Head Start: The Iowa Station and America's Children* (Chapel Hill: University of North Carolina Press, 1993), 90–105; Kate Rouse-

maniere, *City Teachers: Teaching and School Reform in Historical Perspective* (New York: Teachers College Press, 1997), 122–26.

59. Edith Everett, "Helping Fathers and Mothers to Be Better Parents," *Family* 4 (July 1923): 124–26; Sayles, *The Problem Child in School,* 40, 55–56; Culbert, *The Visiting Teacher at Work,* 20, 30; Horn, *Before It's Too Late,* 139, 152.

60. James H. Ryan, "The Visiting Teacher," *Catholic Educational Review* 23 (April 1925): 203–5; Sara E. Laughlin, "The Visiting Teacher in the Parish Schools of Philadelphia," *Catholic Educational Review* 23 (May 1925): 275–86.

61. Johnson, *The Visiting Teacher in New York City,* 8.

62. Ibid., 66–67; Culbert, *The Visiting Teacher at Work,* 21–22, 25, 36–37, 53–54; Anna B. Pratt, "Social Work in the First Grade of a Public School," *American Journal of Sociology* 28 (January 1923): 442.

63. Anna Beach Pratt, "The Relation of the Teacher and the Social Worker," in *The Annals of the American Academy of Political and Social Science,* vol. 98 (Philadelphia: American Academy of Political and Social Science, 1921), 90–96.

64. Minutes of the Board of Managers, February 19, 1916, April 18, 1916, September 20, 1916, Reports of the White-Williams Foundation, 1916–19, Papers of the Magdalen Society/White-Williams Foundation, Historical Society of Pennsylvania, Philadelphia (hereafter cited as Reports of the WWF); Minutes of the Annual Meeting, February 13, 1917, Annual Reports of the White-Williams Foundation, 1917–23, Papers of the Magdalen Society/White-Williams Foundation, Historical Society of Pennsylvania, Philadelphia (hereafter cited as Annual Reports of the WWF).

65. The White-Williams Foundation took its name from the Magdalen Society's first president, Episcopal Bishop William White, and the chairman of its board of managers in 1849, George Williams, who was the first to recommend preventive work for the organization. The directors hoped to advance their organization's new mission by disconnecting it from the "stigma" associated with fallen women. Minutes of the Board of Managers, January 15, 1918, Reports of the WWF, 1916–19; One Hundred Eighteenth Annual Report, February 1918, Annual Reports of the WWF, 1917–23. For a brief treatment of the foundation's history, see Carolyn J. Friedman, "White-Williams Foundation," in *Invisible Philadelphia: Community through Voluntary Organizations,* ed. Jean Barth Toll and Mildred Gillam (Philadelphia: Atwater Kent Museum, 1995), 349–50.

66. Director's Report, April 17 to May 15, 1917, and Minutes of the Board of Managers, March 20, 1917, April 17, 1917, Reports of the WWF, 1916–19; Oppenheimer, *Visiting Teacher Movement,* 89; Pratt, "Should the Visiting Teacher Be a New Official," 301; Anna B. Pratt, Report for Schoolmen's Week, April 11, 1919, Pratt Folders, Pratt Papers, WWF.

67. Minutes of the Board of Managers, March 20, 1917, and Director's Report, December 1, 1916, to April 1, 1917, Reports of the WWF, 1916–19; Director's Report, February 1918, Annual Reports of the WWF, 1917–23.

68. Director's Report, December 1918, and Minutes of the Board of Managers,

October 8, 1919, Reports of the WWF, 1916–19; One Hundred Twentieth Annual Report of the WWF, August 1920, Annual Reports of the WWF, 1917–23; Director's Report, February 1920, April 1920, and Minutes of the Executive Committee, February 14, 1921, Reports of the WWF, 1920–21; Minutes of the Board of Managers, March 17, 1925, Reports of the WWF, 1923–25; School Children as Social Workers See Them, June 1917–June 1929, 11–12, Pratt Papers, WWF.

69. One Hundred Eighteenth Annual Report, February 1918; One Hundred Nineteenth Annual Report, December 1919; and The White-Williams Foundation: Five Year's Review for the Period Ending December 31, 1921, all in Annual Reports of the WWF, 1917–23; Anna B. Pratt, The New Work of the Magdalen Society, December 1917, and Director's Report, April 1919, Reports of the WWF, 1916–19.

70. Pratt, "Should the Visiting Teacher Be a New Official," 302; Director's Reports, October 1917, October 1918, April 1919, February 1920, Reports of the WWF, 1916–19; One Hundred Nineteenth Annual Report, Annual Reports of the WWF, 1917–23.

71. Director's Report, September–October 1920, Reports of the WWF, 1920–21; One Hundred Twentieth Annual Report for the Period Ending August 31, 1920, Annual Reports of the WWF, 1917–23, 7–8, 22–23, 35–36, 41–42; Anna B. Pratt, The Correlation of Home and School, Pratt Papers, WWF.

72. Director's Report, September 1918, Reports of the WWF, 1916–18; Director's Report, May 1924, Reports of the WWF, 1923–25.

73. Matilda Montanye, Scholarship Work, and Marian L. Bach, Trade School for Girls, Reports of the WWF, 1923–25; Minutes of the Scholarship Committee, October 16, 1928, Reports of the WWF, 1926–30; School Children as Social Workers See Them, 6.

74. Director's Report, May–August 1937, Reports of the WWF, 1937–42; Director's Report, November–December 1930, September–October 1935, Reports of the WWF, 1931–36.

75. Anna B. Pratt, Untitled Manuscript of a Talk Delivered to the Dayton PTA, December 17, 1925, Pratt Papers, WWF; Emilie C. Bradbury, "Scholarship Work," *Vocational Guidance Magazine* 4 (January 1926): 173–76; Scholarship Committee Minutes, February 27, 1929, Reports of the WWF, 1926–30.

76. Pratt, "Social Work in the First Grade of a Public School," 440–41; Director's Report, Annual Meeting of the WWF, September 29, 1920, Annual Reports of the WWF, 1917–23; School Children as Social Workers See Them, 8; Director's Report, November 1917, Reports of the WWF, 1916–19.

77. Sayles, *The Problem Child in School,* 242–43.

78. Pratt, Report for Schoolmen's Week; Director's Report, January 1920, Reports of the WWF, 1920–21; Director's Report, March–April 1931, Reports of the WWF, 1931–36; School Children as Social Workers See Them, 8.

79. Muriel Brown, The Mathematics of School Counseling: A Statistical Study of Certain Aspects of the Work of the White Williams Foundation, 22–32, Re-

ports of the WWF, 1923–25; Director's Report, April 1920, Reports of the WWF, 1920–21.

80. One Hundred Twentieth Annual Report, 11; Board of Managers, 1921, Reports of the WWF, 1920–21. See also Board of Managers, 1919, Reports of the WWF, 1916–19; Board of Managers, 1924, Reports of the WWF, 1923–25; Board of Managers, February 1930, Reports of the WWF, 1926–30. In 1925, Margaretta Willis Reeve joined the WWF board, in whose records she was listed as the editor of *Child Welfare Magazine*. Minutes of the Board of Managers, November 15, 1922, Reports of the WWF, 1922; ibid., March 24, 1924, Reports of the WWF, 1923–25. The Commonwealth Fund temporarily renewed this award in 1923. Minutes of the Board of Managers, January 29, 1924, Reports of the WWF, 1923–25.

81. Anna B. Pratt, "Training for Educational and Vocational Counselors from the Standpoint of the Field Worker," *Vocational Guidance Magazine* 5 (April 1927): 321; Charles W. Palmer, Statement of Summer Work, Reports of the WWF, 1923–25; School Children as Social Workers See Them, 4.

82. Anna B. Pratt, "The Home, the School and the Community—for the Average Intelligent Woman," *Philadelphia Public Ledger*, May 11, 1927, Pratt Papers, WWF; Executive Committee Minutes, April 21, 1925, and Director's Report, September 17, 1925, Reports of the WWF, 1923–25; Minutes of the Board of Managers, January 21, 1926, Reports of the WWF, 1926–30.

83. Minutes of the Board of Managers, May 21, 1925, and Director's Report, November 1925, Reports of the WWF, 1923–25; Anna B. Pratt, Address at Belmont School, November 6, 1925, Pratt Papers, WWF.

84. Anna B. Pratt, "What Parent-Teacher Associations Can Do for Social Workers," *Family* 10 (March 1929): 11–14; Director's Report, May 3, 1929, and Minutes of a Special Meeting of the Board of Managers, June 3, 1929, Reports of the WWF, 1926–30.

85. Anna B. Pratt, Parents and the School, Radio Talk, Home and School League Series, no. 1, June 17, 1925, Pratt Papers, WWF; Director's Report, March 1927 and May 3, 1929, Reports of the WWF, 1926–30; Emilie Rannells, The Conwell School of Practice, August 1929, Reports of the WWF, 1926–30; Anna B. Pratt, The Visiting Teacher in the United States, May 25, 1929, Pratt Papers, WWF.

86. Rannells, Conwell School, and Director's Report, March–April 1930, Reports of the WWF, 1926–30.

87. Director's Report for the Year 1930, February 1931; Director's Report, September–October 1932; Director's Report, March–April 1933; Director's Report, September 25, 1933; and WWF Pamphlet Bound with the Director's Report, November–December 1934, all in Reports of the WWF, 1931–36.

88. William John Cooper, "Mental Hygiene in the School," *Mental Hygiene* 17 (October 1933): 551; Charles L. Worth, "A Home-School Co-ordinator," *American School Board Journal* 105 (December 1942): 22.

89. Burton P. Fowler, "The Child as Affected by the Family," *Mental Hygiene* 18 (July 1934): 431–41; Carleton Washburne, "The Educator's Response," *Mental*

Hygiene 19 (January 1935): 58. See also Arthur Zilversmit, *Changing Schools: Progressive Education Theory and Practice, 1930–1960* (Chicago: University of Chicago Press, 1993), 49; Ira S. Wile, "The Visiting Teacher: Interpreting the School to the Home and the Home to the School," *Mental Hygiene* 18 (July 1934): 380–92; Henry C. Patey, "The Teacher as a General Practitioner in Mental Hygiene," *Mental Hygiene* 24 (October 1940): 600–613.

90. Director's Report, January–February 1933, March–April 1933, Reports of the WWF, 1931–36; Michael W. Sedlak, "Attitudes, Choices, and Behavior: School Delivery of Health and Social Services," in *Learning from the Past,* ed. Diane Ravitch and Maris A. Vinovskis (Baltimore: Johns Hopkins University Press, 1995), 69–70, 77; Edwin A. Juckett, "Meaningful Relationships between Home and School," *School Review* 52 (February 1944): 97. In 1942, Englewood, Colorado, a suburb of Denver, counted among its school employees a "Director of Personal Relationships," who tried "to unite the child, the home and the school for the good of all concerned." Edna Dorothy Baxter, "Personality Guidance Promotes Home-School Relations," *Nation's Schools* 30 (October 1942): 37.

91. Director's Report, November–December 1933, January–February 1934, Reports of the WWF, 1931–36; Edith M. Everett, "Trends in School Counseling in Public Elementary Schools," Reports of the WWF, 1931–36; *One Hundred Sixteenth Annual Report of the Board of Public Education, School District of Philadelphia* (Philadelphia, 1934), 232–33.

92. Minutes of the Board of Managers, March 16, 1942, April 20, 1942, Reports of the WWF, 1937–42; Resolution #10, May 12, 1942, *Journal of the Board of Public Education for the Year 1942* (Philadelphia: School District of Philadelphia, 1942), 125.

93. Director's Report, September 1940, Reports of the WWF, 1937–42.

94. At least one educator understood the problem. Commenting on the school's role in sugar rationing during World War II, H. C. Whiteside, the superintendent in New Castle, Delaware, cautioned against getting involved. "No matter who does the rationing, there will be those who object," he pointed out. "Schools depend in a very real way on public approval and . . . we don't want to be faced by people who have petty grudges . . . when we need popular support and understanding from them." H. C. Whiteside to H. E. Stahl, Claymont, Delaware, February 24, 1942, Papers of the Delaware Department of Public Instruction, Box 4343, Delaware State Archives, Dover.

Chapter Six

1. "We Can't Let the Children Down," *Ladies Home Journal* 69 (March 1952): 104–7.

2. National Congress of Parents and Teachers, *The Parent-Teacher Organization: Its Origins and Development* (Chicago: National Congress of Parents and Teachers, 1944), 19, 22, 91–92, 130.

3. Anna H. Hayes, "What Kind of Home-School Partnership," *National Parent-Teacher* 42 (November 1947): 31–32; Ivan A. Booker, "When Home and School Disagree," *National Parent-Teacher* 42 (November 1947): 4–7.

4. Angelo Patri, *How to Help Your Child Grow Up* (New York: Rand McNally, 1948), 266; Paul J. Misner and Robert Lacosse, "Parents Are Partners," *Educational Leadership* 3 (February 1946): 224.

5. Myron Lieberman, *Education as a Profession* (Englewood Cliffs, N.J.: Prentice-Hall, 1956), 428–29.

6. Sidonie M. Gruenberg, *We the Parents: Our Relationship to Our Children and the World Today*, rev. ed. (New York: Harper Bros., 1948), 240, 289; Mary Frank and Lawrence K. Frank, *How to Help Your Child in School* (New York: Viking Press, 1950), 183; Sonya A. Michel, "Children's Interests/Mothers' Rights: Women, Professionals, and the American Family, 1920–1945" (Ph.D. diss. Brown University, 1986), 188–89; Julia Grant, *Raising Baby by the Book: The Education of American Mothers* (New Haven, Conn.: Yale University Press, 1998), 47, 51–53. See also Salvatore G. Di Michael, "The Public School vs. the Home," *Education* 66 (October 1945): 87–88.

7. Patri, *How to Help Your Child Grow Up*, 262; Gruenberg, *We the Parents*, 242. See also Grace Langdon and Irving W. Stout, *Helping Parents Understand Their Child's School: A Handbook for Teachers* (Englewood Cliffs, N.J.: Prentice-Hall, 1957), 335–36.

8. Frank and Frank, *How to Help Your Child in School*, 116, 128, 137, 233–34, 273–80, 312–17, 322; Gruenberg, *We the Parents*, 253–54.

9. Bernard Iddings Bell, "The School Can't Take the Place of the Home," *New York Times Magazine*, May 9, 1948, 11, 57–58, 60; Martha Shull, "Parents Are Teachers, Too," *Education* 77 (February 1957): 358–60.

10. James L. Hymes Jr., *Effective Home-School Relations* (Englewood Cliffs, N.J.: Prentice-Hall, 1953), 8, 35–36, 47, 52–53, 63.

11. Alice Sowers, "Projects Express the P.T.A.," in National Congress of Parents and Teachers, *The Parent-Teacher Organization*, 55; Langdon and Stout, *Helping Parents Understand Their Child's School*, 4.

12. National Society for the Study of Education, *Citizen Co-operation for Better Public Schools: The Fifty-Third Yearbook of the National Society for the Study of Education* (Chicago: University of Chicago Press, 1954), 82–83, 101, 123–31; Marie Williams Myers, "Parents Come to School," *Grade Teacher* 70 (February 1953): 44; Frank Himmelman, "Give Parents a Real Place in School," *Childhood Education* 32 (November 1955): 118; Hymes, *Effective Home-School Relations*, 175.

13. Bess Goodykoontz, "Parents Know What They Want for Their Children," *Educational Leadership* 7 (February 1950): 287–91; Adolph Unruh, "Life Adjustment Education—A Definition," *Progressive Education* 29 (February 1952): 138.

14. Michael Imber, "The Analysis of a Curriculum Reform Movement: The American Social Hygiene Association's Campaign for Sex Education, 1900–1930" (Ph.D. diss., Stanford University, 1980), 32, 55–56, 67–68; Maurice A. Bigelow,

Sex Education, rev. ed. (New York: American Social Hygiene Association, 1936), 77-85.

15. Barry M. Franklin, *Building the American Community: The School Curriculum and the Search for Social Control* (Philadelphia: Falmer Press, 1986), 157-63; Helen Creasy Hunter, "Education for Better Living," *Educational Leadership* 7 (February 1950): 303-7; Mary Beauchamp and Maren Fulton, "A Program of Parent-School Cooperation," ibid. 7 (February 1950): 325-27. Long after life adjustment education had lost its luster, the president of the NCPT was still touting the virtues of education for "home and family living." See Arthur H. Rice, "How to Improve the Home-School Partnership: An Interview with Mrs. James C. Parker," *Nation's Schools* 66 (July 1960): 50.

16. Brother Henry C. Ringkamp, S.M., "Home-School Relationships," *Catholic School Journal* 54 (September 1954): 222; Miriam Theresa Rooney, "The Right to Educate—The Role of the Parent," *National Catholic Educational Association Bulletin* 55 (August 1958): 307-11; William H. Conley, "Home-School Cooperation," *Catholic School Journal* 61 (December 1961): 4; Sister M. Beatrice, C.S.S.F., "School *versus* Home," *Education* 73 (December 1952): 245-47; "Organizing the Home-School Council," *Catholic School Journal* 59 (April 1959): 23-24, 42.

17. Alice V. Keliher, "You Are a Good Teacher if . . . ," *Grade Teacher* 72 (March 1955): 113; Langdon and Stout, *Helping Parents Understand Their Child's School,* 339, 350-51, 361.

18. In 1953, Dorothy Barclay, the education reporter for *The New York Times Magazine,* characterized the parent-teacher conference as "a thoroughly promising development in home-school communication," even though it had been an accepted practice in Inglewood, California, for nearly twenty years. Dorothy Barclay, "Two Aspects of Home-School Relations," *New York Times Magazine,* November 8, 1953, 51; Chester A. Taft, "Fostering Home-School Relations," *Educational Leadership* 7 (February 1950): 315.

19. Hymes, *Effective Home-School Relations,* 147; William H. Johnson, "Interpreting the Schools to the Public," *School Review* 51 (February 1943): 88; Esther Rupright, "Let's Talk It Over," *Educational Leadership* 7 (February 1950): 314.

20. Mary Harden, "Teacher and Parent Talk It Over," *National Parent-Teacher* 51 (September 1956): 17; Gertrude H. Fitzwater, "Cooperation Helps Individual Classrooms," in National Society for the Study of Education, *Citizen Co-operation for Better Public Schools,* 76-79.

21. Diane Ravitch, *The Troubled Crusade: American Education, 1945-1980* (New York: Basic Books, 1983), 93-113; Joel Spring, *The Sorting Machine: National Educational Policy since 1945* (New York: David McKay, 1976), 7-12; James Gilbert, *A Cycle of Outrage: America's Reaction to the Juvenile Delinquent in the 1950s* (New York: Oxford University Press, 1986), 17-18.

22. On the social history of Christmas in the United States, see William B. Waits, *The Modern Christmas in America: A Cultural History of Gift Giving* (New York: New York University Press, 1993), 1-6.

23. Zinnetta A. Hastings, "The President's Message—Let Us Keep Christmas," *National Parent-Teacher* 39 (December 1944): 3; Mabel W. Hughes, "The President's Message—Alight with Faith," ibid. 42 (December 1947): 3.

24. "Opinion Poll: How Should the Public Schools Celebrate the Holidays—or Should They?" *Nation's Schools* 59 (February 1957): 92, 94. As late as 1964, Arthur H. Rice, an editorial advisor to *The Nation's Schools*, expressed the "special wish" that the spirit of Christmas not only continue throughout the year but also permeate the life of schools, colleges, and universities. Arthur H. Rice, "Where Christmas Fits in the Public Schools," *Nation's Schools* 74 (December 1964): 24.

25. Karla V. Parker, "The President's Message: The Festival of the Child," *National Parent-Teacher* 55 (December 1960): 3; "Christmas in the Schools," *NEA Journal* 56 (December 1967): 57. Polled again in 1968, school administrators still believed in observing Christmas but in a nonsectarian way. "Opinion Poll: Educators Favor Religion in Yule School Programs," *Nation's Schools* 82 (December 1968): 49.

26. Jonathan Kozol, "School-Community Relations: Alienation or Interaction?" *NEA Journal* 57 (May 1968): 48–49, 67. Kozol was fired eight days before the end of the 1964–65 school year for reading a poem by Langston Hughes. Two years later he was working as a fifth grade teacher in Newton, Massachusetts, an affluent Boston suburb, whose schools he praised in print for their receptivity to child-centered instruction. See his *Death at an Early Age: The Destruction of the Hearts and Minds of Negro Children in the Boston Public Schools* (Boston: Houghton Mifflin, 1967), 196–98, and "A Junior High School That's Like a College," *New York Times Magazine*, October 29, 1967, 32 ff.; Ernest Osborne, *You and Your Child's School*, Public Affairs Pamphlet 321 (New York: Public Affairs Committee, 1961), 2, 5–9.

27. James B. Conant, *Slums and Suburbs* (New York: McGraw-Hill, 1961), 23–27.

28. Peter Schrag, *Village School Downtown: Politics and Education—A Boston Report* (Boston: Beacon Press, 1967), 163–64; Fred M. Hechinger, "Education: Suburb Schools Mirror Urban Problems," *New York Times*, September 12, 1965, sec. 4, p. 11; David B. Tyack, "Governance and Goals: Historical Perspectives on Public Education," in *Communities and Their Schools*, ed. Don Davies (New York: McGraw-Hill, 1981), 19–28.

29. Stanley M. Elam, ed., *The Phi Delta Kappa Gallup Polls of Attitudes toward Education, 1969–1984* (Bloomington, Ind.: Phi Delta Kappa, 1984), 17, 67.

30. Herbert Kohl, *36 Children* (New York: New American Library, 1967), 187–89; James Herndon, *The Way It Spozed to Be* (New York: Simon & Schuster, 1968); Richard De Lone, *Small Futures: Children, Inequality, and the Limits of Liberal Reform* (New York: Harcourt Brace Jovanovich, 1979), 74–77; Kenneth Keniston, *All Our Children: The American Family under Pressure* (New York: Harcourt Brace Jovanovich, 1977), 202–6; James Comer, *School Power: Implications of an Intervention Project* (New York: Free Press, 1980), 5–6, 9–14.

31. Daniel Levine, "Prerequisites for Success in Working with Parents of Dis-

advantaged Youth," *Journal of Negro Education* 35 (Spring 1966): 180–83; "Editorial Comment: Home-School Relationships," ibid. 36 (Fall 1967): 349–52; Dwight Roper, "Parents as the Natural Enemy of the School System," *Phi Delta Kappan* 59 (December 1977): 239–42; Joseph M. Cronin, "Parents and Educators: Natural Allies," ibid. 59 (December 1977): 242–43.

32. Schrag, *Village School Downtown*, 138–41; Marilyn Gittell with Bruce Hoffacker, Eleanor Rollins, and Samuel Foster, *Citizen Organizations: Citizen Participation in Educational Decisionmaking: Final Research Report* (New York: Institute for Responsive Education, 1979), 177; Mario Fantini, Marilyn Gittell, and Richard Magat, *Community Control and the Urban School* (New York: Praeger, 1970), 74–77.

33. "The Value of the PTA," *Today's Education* 58 (May 1969): 31–33.

34. Gene C. Fusco, "Preparing the City Child for His School," *School Life* 46 (May 1964): 5–8; Leon Hymovitz, "Our Man in the Field: The School-Home Coordinator," *Clearing House* 41 (November 1966): 158–60.

35. Don Davies with Miriam Clasby, Ross Zerchykov, and Brian Powers, *Patterns of Citizen Participation in Educational Decisionmaking*, vol. 1, *Overview of the Status of Citizen Participation* (Boston: Institute for Responsive Education, 1978), 39–53; Julie Roy Jeffrey, *Education for Children of the Poor: A Study of the Origins and Implementation of the Elementary and Secondary Education Act* (Columbus: Ohio State University Press, 1978), 132–33; Don Davies, "Citizen Participation in Decision Making in the Schools," in Davies, ed., *Communities and Their Schools*, 98–99.

36. Lloyd T. Ueker, "The Women's Advisory Board of the Mitchell Public Schools," *American School Board Journal* 115 (October 1947): 33–34.

37. Don Davies et al., *Patterns of Citizen Participation in Educational Decisionmaking*, vol. 2, *Grassroots Perspectives* (Boston: Institute for Responsive Education, 1979), 37–39, 50; J. Anthony Lukas, *Common Ground: A Turbulent Decade in the Lives of Three American Families* (New York: Random House, 1985), 337–38.

38. Annie Stein, "Strategies for Failure," *Harvard Educational Review* 41 (May 1971): 160, 163, 165–67, 170; Diane Ravitch, *The Great School Wars: New York City, 1805–1973* (New York: Basic Books, 1974), 261–62, 271–79; Kenneth B. Clark, "Introduction," in Fantini, Gittell, and Magat, *Community Control and the Urban School*, x, xviii; Fantini, Gittell, and Magat, *Community Control and the Urban School*, 93, 142, 185, 240.

39. Davies et al., *Patterns of Citizen Participation in Educational Decisionmaking*, 2:37–38; Davies, "Citizen Participation in Decision Making in the Schools," 109; Jeanette Valentine and Evan Stark, "The Social Context of Parent Involvement in Head Start," in *Project Head Start: A Legacy of the War on Poverty*, ed. Edward Zigler and Jeanette Valentine (New York: Free Press, 1979), 307.

40. Preston Wilcox, "Changing Conceptions of Community," *Educational Leadership* 29 (May 1972): 683–84.

41. Jeffrey, *Education for Children of the Poor*, 133–35; Dale Mann, "Political

Representation and Urban School Advisory Councils," *Teachers College Record* 75 (February 1974): 300–301; C. C. Carpenter, "Principal Leadership and Parent Advisory Groups," *Phi Delta Kappan* 56 (February 1975): 426; Gittell et al., *Citizen Organizations*, 43, 62–63, 170–71.

42. Paul Lauter, "The Short, Happy Life of the Adams-Morgan Community School Project," *Harvard Educational Review* 38 (Spring 1968): 245–57, Gittell et al., *Citizen Organizations*, 62, 63, 66–67, 221–22.

43. Allan C. Ornstein, *Race and Politics in School/Community Organizations* (Pacific Palisades, Calif.: Goodyear, 1974), 123–27; Jeffrey Mirel, *The Rise and Fall of an Urban School System* (Ann Arbor: University of Michigan Press, 1993), 298–306, 326–37.

44. Marilyn Gittell with Maurice R. Berube, Boulton H. Demas, Daniel Flavin, Mark Rosentraub, Adele Spier, and David Tatage, *School Boards and School Policy: An Evaluation of Decentralization in New York City* (New York: Praeger, 1973), 64, 86–87, 90–97, 103–5, 122–41.

45. "Teacher Strikes, 1960–61 to 1969–70," *NEA Research Bulletin* 48 (October 1970): 69–72; Andrew R. Weintraub and Robert J. Thornton, "Why Teachers Strike: The Economic and Legal Determinants," *Journal of Collective Negotiations in the Public Sector* 5 (1976): 194; Marshall O. Donley Jr., "The American School Teacher: From Obedient Servant to Militant Professional," *Phi Delta Kappan* 58 (September 1976): 114–15.

46. Elizabeth S. Hendryson, "Parent Reaction to Teacher Power," *National Elementary Principal* 48 (January 1969): 14–16.

47. Ibid., 17–18.

48. Ibid., 19; Mario D. Fantini, *What's Best for the Children: Resolving the Power Struggle between Parents and Teachers* (New York: Anchor Press, 1974), 55.

49. Kenneth W. Haskins and Charles W. Cheng, "Community Participation and Teacher Bargaining: A Clash of Interests," *Boston University Journal of Education* 158 (August 1976): 49–56; Joseph M. Conforti, "The Equity Package: Cities, Families, and Schools," *Society* 12 (November/December 1974): 22–33; Mirel, *Rise and Fall of an Urban School System*, 359–60.

50. Myron Lieberman, "Negotiations: Past, Present, and Future," *School Management* 17 (May 1973): 14, 18; John Ryor, "Teachers' Changing Image: 'Good-Bye Mr. Peepers, Hello Lucas Tanner,'" *Pennsylvania School Journal* 124 (March 1976): 108–10, 132; Shirley Riemer, "Teachers Are Strike-Happy!" *Pennsylvania School Journal* 124 (December 1975): 60–62, 84.

51. Ken Arnold, "Attitudes toward Teacher Strikes," *Thrust for Educational Leadership* 12 (September 1982): 29–31; Annette Lareau, *Home Advantage: Social Class and Parental Intervention in Elementary Education* (Philadelphia: Farmer Press, 1989).

52. Maria Lambin Rogers, *A Contribution to the Theory and Practice of Parents Associations* (New York: United Parents Associations, 1931), 25–27, 39–40; Margaret Lighty and Leroy E. Bowman, *Parenthood in a Democracy* (New York: Parents' Institute, 1939), 111–12.

53. Pat Gilbert, History of the UPA, Papers of the United Parents Associations, Series 2, Box 1, Folder 3, Special Collections Department, Milbank Memorial Library, Teachers College, Columbia University, New York (hereafter cited as UPA Papers); Sixty Years of Parent Involvement, Series 2.1, Box 1, Folder 6, 13, UPA Papers; Rogers, *Contribution to the Theory and Practice of Parents Associations*, 16–18, 29–30, 36–37, 42–44, 52; Lighty and Bowman, *Parenthood in a Democracy*, 149–54, 160–61.

54. Rogers, *Contribution to the Theory and Practice of Parents Associations*, 60–61; Sixty Years of Parent Involvement, 11; Report of the Joint Committee on Home-School Relations, United Parents Associations and the Board of Education of New York, 1939, Series 2, Box 2, Folder 2, UPA Papers.

55. "Parents Associations' Rights in Schools Upheld by State Education Commissioner," *School Parent* 4 (October 1947): 3; Brief Submitted by Mrs. Esther Henry Asking the Board of Education to Issue a Directive Setting Forth a Basic Constitution for the Guidance of Parent Associations and PTAs, March 24, 1948, Series 2, Box 4, Folder 16, UPA Papers; Blanche Funk(?) to David I. Ashe, New York, November 12, 1948, Series 2, Box 4, Folder 16, UPA Papers; Sixty Years of Parent Involvement, 5.

56. Rose B. Shapiro, "The First Twenty-Five Years of the U.P.A.," *Journal of Educational Sociology* 20 (March 1947): 391; Newspaper Clipping from the *New York Sun*, January 5, 1949, Series 2, Box 2, Folder 3, UPA Papers; Parents Associations or Parent-Teacher Associations, n.d. (ca. 1950), Series 2, Box 4, Folder 17, UPA Papers.

57. Sixty Years of Parent Involvement, 5, 14; William Jansen, Parent Associations and the Schools, Series 2, Box 3, Folder 7, UPA Papers; Ruth Farbman, Parents—Guardians of Democracy, 1951, Series 3.1, Box 1, Folder 2, UPA Papers.

58. Sixty Years of Parent Involvement, 15; David Rogers, *110 Livingston Street: Politics and Bureaucracy in the New York City School System* (New York: Vintage Books, 1969), 168–69, 174–75; Remarks by Mrs. Adele B. Tunick, President of the United Parents Associations at Board of Education Public Hearing on Local School Boards, December 14, 1961; Adele B. Tunick to Lloyd Garrison, New York, April 19, 1962; and Statement of East Harlem Schools Committee on Proposals for Revitalizing the Local School Boards, all in Series 8, Box 12, Folder 119, UPA Papers.

59. Report of the Joint Committee on Home-School Relations, 1939, and Remarks Delivered by Florence Flast, President, United Parents Associations at the NYC Elementary School Principals Association Conference, February 27, 1965, both in Series 3, Box 1, Folder 4, UPA Papers.

60. United Parents Associations' Self-Help Program in Parent Education, August 1967, ii, iv, v, Series 2.1, Box 1, Folder 16, UPA Papers.

61. "UPA Presents Parents' Demands in UFT-Board Negotiations," *School Parent* (August 1967), Series 2.3, Box 4, Folder 18, UPA Papers; Ravitch, *The Great School Wars*, 279, 281, 286, 352–57, 366–76; Maurice R. Berube and Marilyn Git-

tell, eds., *Confrontation at Ocean Hill–Brownsville* (New York: Praeger, 1969), 15, 79–81.

62. Berube and Gittell, eds. *Confrontation at Ocean Hill–Brownsville*, 82; Ravitch, *The Great School Wars*, 381.

63. "Teachers' Union Ends Relations with United Parents Association," *New York Times*, October 31, 1967, 40; Statement of Mrs. Blanche Lewis, President, United Parents Associations at Elementary School Principals Conference, Saturday, February 7, 1970, Series 3.1, Box 2, Folder 12, UPA Papers. See also Transcript of Television Program "Direct Line," Series 3.1, Box 2, Folder 12, UPA Papers.

64. Statement of Mrs. Blanche Lewis, February 7, 1970.

65. "Parents Associations Rights Upheld by Court," *School Parent* (August 1967), Series 2.3, Box 4, Folder 18, UPA Papers.

66. Parent Associations and the Schools, Series 2, Box 3, Folder 11; UPA Newsletter, October 1970, Series 20.1, Box 3, Folder 41; and Lilian Ashe to Blanche Lewis, La Crosse, Wis., December 12, 1970, Series 3.1, Box 2, Folder 13, all in UPA Papers.

67. "Parent Legal Education and Assistance," UPA Newsletter, December 1973, and Report on Project PLEA, September 1973–June 30, 1974, both in Series 16, Folder 4; and Sources of Information re: Consultation Rights of Parents Associations, Series 16, Folder 5, all in UPA Papers; Sixty Years of Parent Involvement, 20.

68. "Student Records," *Congressional Quarterly Almanac* 30 (1974): 483–84; "Federal Law on Open School-Records: Accountability and Privacy in Conflict," *New York Times*, November 27, 1974, 19.

69. Peter Binzen, *Whitetown, USA* (New York: Vintage Books, 1970), 222–34, 295–96; Jon S. Birger, "Race, Reaction, and Reform: The Three R's of Philadelphia School Reform Politics, 1965–1971," *Pennsylvania Magazine of History and Biography* 120 (July 1996): 192–96, 208–9. For a general discussion of race in American school politics, see Ira Katznelson and Margaret Weir, *Schooling for All: Class, Race, and the Decline of the Democratic Ideal* (New York: Basic Books, 1985), chap. 7.

70. Daniel J. McGinley and Bernard F. Rafferty, "The Principal and the Teachers' Strike," *Urban Education* 10 (April 1975): 49–53. The winter walkout lasted from January 5 to March 1, 1973. The PFT also struck the Philadelphia schools in September 1970, when three days of instruction were lost. Mary Bishop et al., "The Shame of the Schools: How Philadelphia's Children Are Neglected by the System," *Philadelphia Inquirer*, August 30–September 6, 1981, reprint, 18–24. See also James Sanzare, "A Study of Teacher Unionism in Philadelphia, 1941–1973: The Case of Local 3, Philadelphia Federation of Teachers" (Ed.D. diss., Temple University, 1976), chap. 6.

71. Philadelphia Home and School Council, etc. vs. the Board of Education of the School District of Philadelphia and the School District of Philadelphia, January 1973, Papers of the [Philadelphia] Home and School Council, Series 6, Box 5,

Folder 98, Urban Archives, Samuel Paley Library, Temple University, Philadelphia (hereafter cited as Home & School Council Papers); Happy (Gladys) Fernandez, oral history interview with William W. Cutler III, July 14, 1997, 2–3, Urban Archives, Samuel Paley Library, Temple University, Philadelphia.

72. Statement of Purpose: Parents Union for Public Schools in Philadelphia, and Why a Parents Union? n.d. (ca. November 1973), Series 6, Box 6, Folder 130, Home & School Council Papers (italics theirs).

73. E. Babette Edwards, "Why a Harlem Parents Union?" in James S. Coleman et al., *Parents, Teachers and Children: Prospects for Choice in American Education* (San Francisco: Institute for Contemporary Education, 1977), 60, 65.

74. Happy (Gladys) Craven Fernandez, "Parents' Influence on School Policy and Practice: A History of the Parents Union for Public Schools in Philadelphia, 1980–1982" (Ed.D. diss., Temple University, 1984), 54; "Year-Old Parents' Union Takes Off the Gloves," *Philadelphia Evening Bulletin,* January 13, 1974, Bulletin Clippings Collection, Urban Archives, Samuel Paley Library, Temple University, Philadelphia (hereafter cited as BCC). According to Peter Binzen, Dilworth and Shedd avoided working with the Home and School Council because they considered it to be too white and too conservative. Binzen, *Whitetown, USA,* 295–96.

75. Fernandez Interview, 3, 6; Minutes of the Home and School Council Officers Meeting with Dr. Matthew Costanzo, Philadelphia Superintendent of Schools, June 12, 1974, Series 6, Box 1, Loose-Leaf Binder, Home & School Council Papers.

76. Parents Union for Public Schools in Philadelphia, etc., et al. vs. Board of Education of the School District of Philadelphia, etc., Papers of the Philadelphia Federation of Teachers, Box 67, Parents Union Folder, Urban Archives, Samuel Paley Library, Temple University, Philadelphia; "Emergency Schools Brace for Classes," *Evening Bulletin,* September 6, 1978, BCC; Kathe Zepernick, oral history interview with William W. Cutler III, October 3, 1997, 7, Urban Archives, Samuel Paley Library, Temple University, Philadelphia.

77. Zepernick Interview, 8; Helen Williams, Attitudes of Staff, Parents Union for Public Schools: Newsletter Supplement, November 1973, Series 6, Box 6, Folder 130, Home & School Council Papers.

78. Fernandez Interview, 11; Zepernick Interview, 3–5; Parents' Bill of Rights and Responsibilities Presented by Mrs. William Schobert to the Philadelphia Board of Education, May 6, 1974, Series 6, Box 6, Folder 129, Home & School Council Papers.

79. Happy Fernandez to Mrs. Nancy Westerfield, Philadelphia, December 30, 1974; Parents Union, Revised Draft: Parents' Bill of Rights, December 1974; and Memorandum from Charles Highsmith to Matthew Costanzo, RE: Parents' Bill of Rights and Responsibilities, February 7, 1975, all in Series 6, Box 6, Folder 129, Home & School Council Papers; Home and School Council, Executive Board Minutes, May 27, 1975, Series 6, Box 1, Home & School Council Papers.

80. "Aid to Education of Handicapped Approved," *Congressional Quarterly Almanac* 31 (1975): 652; *Hearings before the Subcommittee on the Handicapped of the Committee on Labor and Public Welfare, United States Senate,* 93rd Congress,

1st sess. (1973–74), pt. 1, 25–33, 394–411; pt. 2, 789–811; Marvin Lazerson, "The Origins of Special Education," in Jay G. Chambers and William T. Hartman, eds., *Special Education Policies: Their History, Implementation, and Finance* (Philadelphia: Temple University Press, 1983), 38–40.

81. Fernandez, "Parents' Influence on School Policy and Practice," 95, 219–24, 229–40; Fernandez Interview, 15; Zepernick Interview, 9, 20; Karen Bojar and Sandra Featherman, "Parents Union: Parent Advocacy and Education," in Jean Barth Toll and Mildred S. Gillam, eds., *Invisible Philadelphia: Community through Voluntary Organizations* (Philadelphia: Atwater Kent Museum, 1995), 702–5.

82. Fernandez, "Parents' Influence on School Policy and Practice," 131, 150, 174–77, 294, 309; Zepernick Interview, 9–10; Bojar and Featherman, "Parents Union," 703; "Parents Disrupt School Board Session," *Evening Bulletin,* December 4, 1978, BCC; "Fight Brewing as Marcase Vote Nears," *Evening Bulletin,* August 15, 1980, BCC.

83. Gittell et al., *Citizen Organizations,* 8–12; Fernandez, "Parents' Influence on School Policy and Practice," 184–97; Zepernick Interview, 12–14. In keeping with its grassroots origins, the PUPS called its chief executive a "coordinator" rather than a "director." Fernandez Interview, 9.

84. Bojar and Featherman, "Parents Union," 704. It did not prove easy to overcome PUPS' reputation for conflict and criticism. The Philadelphia Association of School Administrators refused to cooperate with the PUPS on the Year of the Good Principal because it did not want its members to be evaluated by parents, especially those associated with the PUPS. Zepernick Interview, 15–16.

85. For examples of this kind of analysis, see Christopher Lasch, *Haven in a Heartless World: The Family Besieged* (New York: Basic Books, 1977); Gerald Grant, *The World We Created at Hamilton High* (Cambridge: Harvard University Press, 1988).

86. Thomas Bender, *Community and Social Change in America* (Baltimore: Johns Hopkins University Press, 1978); David S. Seeley, *Education through Partnership: Mediating Structures and Education* (New York: Ballinger/American Enterprise Institute, 1981), 46, 54–56, 59, 71–74, 79, 87, 159.

87. Seeley, *Education through Partnership,* 216–19; Comer, *School Power,* 9–14, 57–60, 69, 132–33, 144–45, 232–33.

88. James S. Coleman and Thomas Hoffer, *Private and Public High Schools: The Impact of Communities* (New York: Basic Books, 1987), 12–13, 93, 135, 147–48, 224–25; James S. Coleman, "Families and Schools," *Educational Researcher* 16 (August–September 1987): 32–33, 36–38.

89. Coleman and Hoffer, *Public and Private High Schools,* 236–40.

Epilogue

1. Romesh Rafnesar, "Class-Size Warfare," *Time,* October 6, 1997, 85.

2. Scott Thompson, "Moving from Publicity to Engagement," *Educational*

Leadership 55 (May 1998): 54-57; Ron Brandt, "Listen First," *Educational Leadership* 55 (May 1998): 25-30.

3. For a discussion of the relationship between social class and parental involvement at school, see Annette Lareau, *Home Advantage: Social Class and Parental Intervention in Elementary Education* (New York: Falmer Press, 1989); Kathleen V. Hoover-Dempsey and Howard M. Sandler, "Why Do Parents Become Involved in Their Children's Education?" *Review of Educational Research* 67 (Spring 1997): 3-42.

4. Susan Black, "Parent Support," *American School Board Journal* 185 (April 1998): 52. For a long list of research centers and advocacy organizations concerned with the home-school relationship in the United States, consult the World Wide Web site of the North Central Regional Educational Laboratory at <http://www.ncrel.org>.

5. *Common Ground: Beyond the Politics of Education* (Philadelphia: Philadelphia Education Summit, 1998), 86-87; Concha Delgado-Gaitan, "Research and Policy in Reconceptualizing Family-School Relationships," in *Renegotiating Cultural Diversity in American Schools,* ed. Patricia Phelan and Ann Locke Davidson (New York: Teachers College Press, 1993), 145.

6. See, for example, Richard L. Weinberg and Lynn Goetsch Weinberg, *Parent Prerogatives: How to Handle Teacher Misbehaviors and Other School Disorders* (Chicago: Nelson Hall, 1979), ix-x, 209-10.

7. General Assembly of Pennsylvania, House Bill 1010 (draft), Session of 1997; Ursula Casanova, "Parent Involvement: A Call for Prudence," *Educational Researcher* 25 (November 1996): 30-32, 46.

8. Roger S. Glass, "The Parent Connection: Our Best Allies for Improving Schools," *American Teacher* 83 (April 1999): 6-7, 15.

9. "Ridge's School Plan Signals Unraveling of 'Outcomes Concept,'" *Philadelphia Inquirer,* May 14, 1995, E5; "When [the] Christian Right Tries to Rule," *Philadelphia Inquirer,* September 10, 1995, A9; Melitta J. Cutright, *The National PTA Talks to Parents: How to Get the Best Education for Your Child* (New York: Doubleday, 1989), 8, 13, 54-59, 69-72, 99.

10. Patricia Sullivan, "The PTA National Standards," *Educational Leadership* 55 (May 1998): 43-44.

11. Joyce L. Epstein, "School/Family Partnerships: Caring for the Children We Share," *Phi Delta Kappan* 76 (May 1995): 701-12. See also Joyce L. Epstein, *School and Family Partnerships,* Report 6 (Baltimore: Johns Hopkins University Center on Families, Communities, Schools, and Children's Learning, 1992). When her *Phi Delta Kappan* article appeared in 1995, Epstein was codirector of what was then known as the Center on Families, Communities, Schools, and Children's Learning. That she now directs something called the Center on School, Family, and Community Partnerships may be evidence of a more collaborative approach to the home-school relationship.

12. James P. Comer, *Waiting for a Miracle: Why Schools Can't Solve Our Prob-*

lems—and How We Can (New York: Dutton, 1997), 48–58, 177–78, 192–93, 212, 219, 226; idem, *Maggie's American Dream: The Life and Times of a Black Family* (New York: New American Library, 1988), 48, 64–68, 93–101, 110–14, 128–30, 147, 168. See also by James P. Comer, "Educating Poor Minority Children," *Scientific American* 259 (November 1988): 42–48; Amy R. Hanson, Thomas D. Cook, Farah Habib, Michael Grady, Norris Haynes, and James P. Comer, "The Comer School Development Program: A Theoretical Analysis," *Urban Education* 26 (April 1991): 56–82.

13. Dorothy Rich, *Schools and Families: Issues and Actions* (Washington, D.C.: National Education Association, 1987), 60, 64–67; Dorothy Rich, *MegaSkills: How Families Can Help Children Succeed in School and Beyond* (Boston: Houghton Mifflin, 1988), 248.

14. Rich, *Schools and Families*, 11, 17, 21–22, 44–45, 57; Dorothy Rich, *The Forgotten Factor in School Success: The Family* (Washington, D.C.: Home and School Institute, 1985), 12–14, 51; Dorothy Rich, *Teachers and Parents: An Adult-to-Adult Approach* (Washington, D.C.: National Education Association, 1987), 8, 15, 23–24, 90–94; Barbara Schneider, "Parents, Their Children and Schools: An Introduction," in *Parents, Their Children and Schools,* ed. Barbara Schneider and James S. Coleman (Boulder, Colo.: Westview Press, 1993), 11–12.

15. Rich, *MegaSkills,* 4, 9, 146–48, 167, 274; Dorothy Rich, *What Do We Say? What Do We Do?* (New York: Tom Doherty Associates, 1997), 17–21.

16. J. Gary Knowles, Stacey E. Marlow, and James A. Muchmore, "From Pedagogy to Ideology: Origins and Phases of Home Education in the United States, 1970–1990," *American Journal of Education* 100 (February 1992): 195–235.

17. June Cavarretta, "Parents Are a School's Best Friend," *Educational Leadership* 55 (May 1998): 12–15; "Parents for Public Schools," *American Teacher* 83 (April 1999): 7.

18. Myron Lieberman, *The Teacher Unions: How the NEA and AFT Sabotage Reform and Hold Students, Parents, Teachers, and Taxpayers Hostage to Bureaucracy* (New York: Free Press, 1997), 225–28.

19. G. Alfred Hess Jr., *School Restructuring, Chicago Style* (Newbury Park, Calif.: Corwin Press, Sage Publications, 1991), 97; John F. Witte and Christopher A. Thorn, "Who Chooses? Voucher and Interdistrict Choice Programs in Milwaukee," *American Journal of Education* 104 (May 1996): 186–94.

20. John E. Chubb and Terry L. Moe, *Politics, Markets, and America's Schools* (Washington, D.C.: Brookings Institution, 1990), 35, 183.

21. Chubb and Moe, *Politics, Markets, and America's Schools,* 35, 41, 44–45, 164.

22. Hess, *School Restructuring, Chicago Style,* 109–10, 146–55; Michael B. Katz, *Improving Poor People: The Welfare State, the "Underclass," and Urban Schools as History* (Princeton, N.J.: Princeton University Press, 1995), 119–20, 126.

23. Mike Rose, "Charter Schools: Can They Meet the Challenge," *American Teacher* 83 (May/June 1999): 12–13; William Windler, "Colorado's Charter Schools:

A Spark for Change and a Catalyst for Reform," *Phi Delta Kappan* 78 (September 1996): 67; James N. Goenner, "Charter Schools: The Revitalization of Public Education," *Phi Delta Kappan* 78 (September 1996): 34; John O'Neil, "New Options, Old Concerns," *Educational Leadership* 54 (October 1996): 7; Doug Thomas, "The Choice to Charter," *American School Board Journal* 183 (July 1996): 20–21; Claudia Wallis, "A Class of Their Own," *Time* 144 (October 31, 1994): 53–58, 61.

24. Witte and Thorn, "Who Chooses? Voucher and Interdistrict Choice Programs in Milwaukee," 196–210.

Bibliographic Note

The primary and secondary sources on which this book is based are as diverse and multifaceted as the topic itself. The former include both published and unpublished material; the latter draw from several topics in American social and cultural history. I used many different kinds of primary sources. Prescriptive literature, personal correspondence, oral histories, institutional minutes, and educational policy reports all figured into the final product. My secondary sources came primarily from the historiography of American education, but I also built on the interesting and provocative work now being done by scholars in women's history, family history, social welfare history, regional history, and educational policy studies. The topic required no less because public pronouncements and private thoughts on the subject of parent-teacher relations have always been multidimensional and not infrequently at odds.

Primary Sources

Manuscript Collections

Twenty manuscript collections contributed to the research for this book. No single collection provided a framework for the work as a whole, but some collections proved to be more useful than others. The Elizabeth Tilton Papers at the Arthur and Elizabeth Schlesinger Library on the History of Women in America, located at Radcliffe College, were invaluable for the material on the National Congress of Parents and Teachers, especially annual meeting minutes, committee reports, and policy statements from the 1920s and 1930s. Housed at the Historical Society of Pennsylvania, the Magdalen Society/White-Williams Foundation Papers shed considerable light on the origins and development of school outreach to the home and the career of Anna Beach Pratt, a pioneer in the field of school counseling. The Papers of the Delaware Department of Public Instruction, which can be found at the Delaware State Archives in Dover, document the work of Harry Vance Holloway, Delaware's first superintendent of public instruction, and the relationship among

bureaucrats, reformers, and parents in this small but complex state. The Special
Collections Department of the Milbank Memorial Library at Teachers College,
Columbia University maintains the records of the United Parents Associations of
New York City. This enormous collection, which dates to the organization's founding 1921, enhanced my knowledge of parents rights' and my understanding of how
they evolved between 1950 and 1975. The UPA Papers remain an underutilized
resource for many topics in the history of urban education in America. Finally, the
minutes of the Haddonfield Mothers' and Teachers' Club and the Haddonfield
Parent-Teacher Association, preserved at the Historical Society of Haddonfield,
opened the door on suburbia, but these records would have been far less useful had
not the minutes of the Haddonfield Board of Public Education been made available to me by this district's central administration.

Published Primary Sources

At the beginning of the twentieth century, many urban school districts began to
publish data on the growth of parent-teacher organizations. Those compiled by
superintendents in Boston, New York, Philadelphia, and Denver were most useful. However, I found periodicals to be a better source of insight into the professionals' perspective on the home-school relationship. For the mid-nineteenth century, I relied on *The Massachusetts Teacher,* the *Pennsylvania School Journal,* and
Henry Barnard's *American Journal of Education.* The proliferation of such materials over the next fifty years meant that by 1900 school administrators and teachers could choose among many national journals; those that had the most to say
about the parent-teacher relationship included *Education, The Elementary School
Teacher,* and *The School Review.* But important articles on this subject intended
for a more general audience appeared in *The Atlantic Monthly, Charities and the
Commons,* and *Good Housekeeping,* among others. After World War I, the periodical literature on the home-school relationship became truly enormous. Most
journals spoke primarily to the professionals, including *The American School
Board Journal, Child Study, Educational Method,* the *Journal of Home Economics,
Mental Hygiene, The Nation's Schools,* and *School and Society.* After 1950, *Educa-
tional Leadership* and *Phi Delta Kappan* joined the professionals' preferred list.
Catholic educators took their cues from the *Catholic School Journal, The Catholic
Educational Review,* and the *National Catholic Educational Association Bulletin.*
But parents had many options, too; the best prescriptive literature for them ap-
peared in *Children: The Magazine for Parents,* which became *Parents' Magazine* in
1929, and in *Child Welfare Magazine,* which started life in 1906 as *The National
Congress of Mothers Magazine* and was subsequently known by such names as *The
National Parent-Teacher* (1934–1961) and *The PTA Magazine* (1961–1985). When
family life issues took center stage in the 1950s, popular outlets like *The Ladies
Home Journal* and *The New York Times Magazine* displayed a strong interest in the
home-school relationship.

Books about this topic were rare in the nineteenth century and concentrated on giving parents and teachers practical advice. Perhaps the most important was *The Teacher and the Parent: A Treatise upon Common-School Education Containing Practical Suggestions to Teachers and Parents* (New York: A. S. Barnes, 1853) by Charles Northend, which went through many editions. By the beginning of the twentieth century, academic and trade publishers alike saw a market for books dealing with both the theory and the practice of the parent-teacher relationship. They responded with a spate of volumes, including *Home and School: United in Widening Circles of Inspiration and Service* (Philadelphia: Christopher Sower Co., 1909) by Mary Van Meter Grice; *School and Home* (New York: Appleton, 1925) by Angelo Patri; *Parents and Teachers: A Survey of Organized Cooperation of Home, School, and Community* (New York: Ginn, 1928) edited by Martha Sprague Mason; *The Parent-Teacher Association and Its Work* (New York: Macmillan, 1929) by Julian Butterworth; *An Analysis of the Activities and Potentialities for Achievement of the Parent-Teacher Association with Recommendations* (New York: Teachers College, 1934) by Elmer S. Holbeck; and *Home-School Relations: Philosophy and Practice* (New York: Progressive Education Association, 1935) by Sara E. Baldwin and Edward G. Osborne. Books designed to help educators explain changing educational theory and practice to parents appeared with some frequency in the 1930s. Two good examples are *Home-School-Community Relations: A Textbook in the Theory and Practice of Public School Relations* (Pittsburgh: University of Pittsburgh Press, 1939) by William A. Yeager and *Parents Look at Modern Education: A Book to Help an Older Generation Understand the Schools of the New* (New York: D. Appleton-Century, 1935) by Winifred E. Bain.

Experts in psychology, sociology, medicine, and education responded to heavy demand from parents for advice on the home-school relationship in the late 1940s and early 1950s. Interested readers could choose from among *We the Parents: Our Relationship to Our Children and the World Today*, rev. ed. (New York: Harper Bros., 1948) by Sidonie Matsner Gruenberg; *How to Help Your Child in School* (New York: Viking Press, 1950) by Mary Frank and Lawrence K. Frank; and *Effective Home-School Relations* (Englewood Cliffs, N.J.: Prentice-Hall, 1953) by James L. Hymes Jr. More recently, Dorothy Rich has built on this tradition with *Schools and Families: Issues and Actions* (Washington, D.C.: National Education Association, 1987) and *MegaSkills: How Families Can Help Children Succeed in School and Beyond* (Boston: Houghton Mifflin, 1988). I have treated the important work of James Comer as a primary source, especially *Maggie's American Dream: The Life and Times of a Black Family* (New York: New American Library, 1988) and *Waiting for a Miracle: Why Schools Can't Solve Our Problems—and How We Can* (New York: Dutton, 1997).

The institutional history of the movement to facilitate and improve parent-teacher relations features many in-house histories of national, state, and local organizations. For the National Congress of Parents and Teachers, there are several, including *Through the Years: From the Scrapbook of Mrs. Mears* (Washington,

D.C.: National Congress of Parents and Teachers, 1932); *The Parent-Teacher Organization: Its Origins and Development* (Chicago: National Congress of Parents and Teachers, 1944); and *Where Children Come First: A Study of the P.T.A. Idea* (Chicago: National Congress of Parents and Teachers, 1949) by Harry and Bonaro Overstreet. Representative of the many state histories are *History of the California Congress of Parents and Teachers, 1900–1944* (Los Angeles: California Congress of Parents and Teachers, 1945) edited by Margaret Strong; *The First Fifty Years: Iowa Congress of Parents and Teachers, 1900–1950* (Des Moines, Iowa: Iowa Congress of Parents and Teachers, 1951) by Hazel Hillis; and *The Golden Rung, Golden Jubilee History of the New Jersey Congress of Parents and Teachers, 1900–1950* (Trenton, N.J.: New Jersey Congress of Parents and Teachers, 1950). New York's United Parents Associations has been the subject of two private histories: *A Contribution to the Theory and Practice of Parents Associations* (New York: United Parents Associations, 1931) by Maria Lambin Rogers and *Parenthood in a Democracy* (New York: Parents' Institute, 1939) by Margaret Lighty and Leroy E. Bowman. The UPA pamphlet *Sixty Years of Parent Involvement*, published privately in 1981, highlights the organization's accomplishments.

Specialized topics that impinge on the home-school relationship have been the subject of many full-length treatments by educators and policy makers since the beginning of the twentieth century. For school nursing, see Lina Rogers Struthers, *The School Nurse: A Survey of the Duties and Responsibilities of the Nurse in the Maintenance of Health and Physical Perfection and the Prevention of Disease Among School Children* (New York: G. P. Putnam's Sons, 1917). For visiting teachers, see Julius John Oppenheimer, *The Visiting Teacher Movement with Special Reference to Administrative Relationships* (New York: Public Education Association, 1924); Mary B. Sayles, *The Problem Child in School: Narratives from Case Records of Visiting Teachers with a Description of the Purpose and Scope of Visiting Teacher Work by Howard W. Nudd* (New York: Commonwealth Fund, 1927); and Jane F. Culbert, *The Visiting Teacher at Work* (New York: Commonwealth Fund, 1930).

School decentralization generated an outpouring of comment and criticism in the 1970s, when this reform was just beginning. The Institute for Responsive Education (IRE) published several useful research reports, including Don Davies et al., *Patterns of Citizen Participation in Educational Decisionmaking*. Vol. 1, *Overview of the Status of Citizen Participation* (Boston: IRE, 1978) and Vol. 2, *Grassroots Perspectives* (Boston: IRE, 1979) as well as Marilyn Gittell et al., *Citizen Organizations: Citizen Participation in Educational Decisionmaking: Final Research Report* (New York: IRE, 1979). More qualitative accounts can be found in Mario Fantini, Marilyn Gittell, and Richard Magat, *Community Control and the Urban School* (New York: Praeger, 1970), and Mario D. Fantini, *What's Best for the Children: Resolving the Power Struggle between Parents and Teachers* (New York: Anchor Press, 1974).

Secondary Sources

Many historians have touched on the history of the home-school relationship in works dealing primarily with other topics. Conflict between private families and public institutions like schools received path-breaking attention in Christopher Lasch, *Haven in a Heartless World: The Family Besieged* (New York: Basic Books, 1977), and W. Norton Grubb and Marvin Lazerson, *Broken Promises: How Americans Fail Their Children* (New York: Basic Books, 1982). For an early work focusing mainly on schools, see Carl F. Kaestle, "Social Change, Discipline, and the Common School in Early Nineteenth-Century America," *Journal of Interdisciplinary History* 9 (Summer 1978): 1–17. Maris Vinovskis has brought together several of his articles on families and schools in *Education, Society, and Economic Opportunity: A Historical Perspective on Persistent Issues* (New Haven, Conn.: Yale University Press, 1995), Part One especially. Parents and teachers have appeared together as supporting cast in many books and articles about urban school bureaucratization. The best of these include *The One Best System: A History of American Urban Education* (Cambridge: Harvard University Press, 1974) by David B. Tyack; *Class, Bureaucracy, and Schools: The Illusion of Educational Change in America* (New York: Praeger, 1971) by Michael B. Katz; and its sequel, *Reconstructing American Education* (Cambridge: Harvard University Press, 1987). Treatments of the same theme for rural schools appear in *A Hard Country and a Lonely Place: Schooling, Society, and Reform in Rural Virginia, 1870–1920* (Chapel Hill: University of North Carolina Press, 1986) by William L. Link and *The Old Country School: The Story of Rural Education in the Middle West* (Chicago: University of Chicago Press, 1982) by Wayne E. Fuller.

Several historians of elementary and early childhood education have considered the role of parents at school. The pioneering work in this field was *Worlds Apart: Relationships between Families and Schools* (New York: Basic Books, 1978) by Sarah Lawrence Lightfoot. For a recent and more thorough overview, see Barbara Beatty, *Preschool Education in America: The Culture of Young Children from the Colonial Era to the Present* (New Haven, Conn.: Yale University Press, 1995). Still useful is Barbara Finkelstein, "In Fear of Childhood: Relationships between Parents and Teachers in Popular Primary Schools in the Nineteenth Century," *History of Childhood Quarterly* 3 (Winter 1976): 321–37. Day care parents have their day in Margaret O'Brien Steinfels, *Who's Minding the Children: The History and Politics of Day Care in America* (New York: Simon & Schuster, 1973), and Sonya Michel, *Children's Interests/Mothers' Rights: The Shaping of American Child Care Policy* (New Haven, Conn.: Yale University Press, 1999). Families with young children have been the primary audience for parent education. It has been the subject of one book and several articles, beginning with Steven L. Schlossman, "Before Home Start: Notes toward a History of Parent Education in America, 1897–1929," *Harvard Educational Review* 46 (August 1976): 436–67. His "The Formative Era in American Parent Education: Overview and Interpretation" appeared in Ron

Haskins and Diane Adams, eds., *Parent Education and Public Policy* (Norwood, N.J.: Ablex, 1983), 7–39. The subject has received its fullest treatment in *Raising Baby by the Book: The Education of American Mothers* (New Haven, Conn.: Yale University Press, 1998) by Julia Grant.

Parents turn up in some historical studies of educational and social reform. There is no published professional history of the National Congress of Parents and Teachers, but its leaders receive thoughtful attention in Molly Ladd-Taylor, *Mother-Work: Women, Child Welfare, and the State, 1890–1930* (Urbana: University of Illinois Press, 1994). For a recent dissertation on the early years of the NCPT, see Christine A. Woyshner, "To Reach the Rising Generation through the Raising Generation: The Origins of the National Parent-Teacher Association" (Ed.D. diss., Harvard University, 1999). Representative works on parents and school reform include Michael B. Katz, *Improving Poor People: The Welfare State, the "Underclass," and Urban Schools as History* (Princeton, N.J.: Princeton University Press, 1995); Polly Welts Kaufman, *Boston Women and City School Politics, 1872–1905* (New York: Garland, 1994); Julia Rosenberg Raftery, *Land of Fair Promise: Politics and Reform in Los Angeles Schools, 1885–1941* (Stanford, Calif.: Stanford University Press, 1992); and William J. Reese, *Power and the Promise of School Reform: Grassroots Movements during the Progressive Era* (Boston: Routledge & Keegan Paul, 1986). Robert Taggart's work on the history of school reform in Delaware does not neglect the parents' role. See, for example, his "Elite Educational Reform in a Traditional Community: The Georgetown Demonstration School, 1929–1933," *Delaware History* 21 (Winter 1987): 233–55; and *Private Philanthropy and Public Education: Pierre S. du Pont and the Delaware Schools, 1890–1940* (Newark: University of Delaware Press, 1988). For a study of contemporary reform that includes parents as players, see G. Alfred Hess Jr., *School Restructuring, Chicago Style* (Newbury Park, Calif.: Corwin Press, Sage Publications, 1991).

Parental attitudes about the value of schooling have been explored by many historians interested in the impact of race, ethnicity, and social class on equal opportunity in American education. A sample of recent works concerned with the variable of ethnicity include Stephen F. Brumberg, *Going to America, Going to School: The Jewish Immigrant Public School Encounter in Turn-of-the-Century New York* (New York: Praeger, 1986); Thomas Kessner, *The Golden Door: Italian and Jewish Immigrant Mobility in New York City, 1880–1915* (New York: Oxford University Press, 1977); Joel Perlmann, "Who Stayed in School? Social Structure and Academic Achievement in the Determination of Enrollment Patterns, Providence, Rhode Island, 1880–1925," *Journal of American History* 72 (December 1985): 588–614; and David Galenson, "Ethnic Differences in Neighborhood Effects on the School Attendance of Boys in Early Chicago," *History of Education Quarterly* 38 (Spring 1998): 17–35. A shortage of primary sources perhaps explains the dearth of secondary works on the history of the relationship between black parents and schools, but the topic deserves more attention if suitable records can be retrieved.

Index